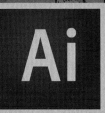

Adobe
Illustrator CC
2015 release

Diego L. Rodríguez

CLASSROOM IN A BOOK®
The official training workbook from Adobe

Brian Wood

WHERE ARE THE LESSON FILES?

Purchasing this Classroom in a Book gives you access to the lesson files you'll need to complete the exercises in the book.

You'll find the files you need on your **Account** page at peachpit.com on the **Lesson & Update Files** tab.

For complete instructions, see "Accessing the Classroom in a Book files" in the Getting Started section of this book.

The example below shows how the files appear on your **Account** page. The files are packaged as ZIP archives, which you will need to expand after downloading. You can download the lessons individually or as a single large ZIP file if your network connection is fast enough.

CONTENTS

Where are the Lesson Files   iii

Getting Started   1
About Classroom in a Book. 1
Prerequisites. 1
Installing the program 2
Fonts used in this book. 2
Accessing the Classroom in a Book files 2
Web Edition 3
Restoring default preferences 3
To delete or save the current Illustrator preferences file. 4
To restore saved preferences after completing the lessons. . . . 5
Additional resources 5
Adobe Authorized Training Centers. 5

What's New in Adobe Illustrator CC (2015 Release)   6
CC Libraries enhancements 6
Shaper tool 6
Dynamic Symbols. 7
New SVG Export 7
Live Shapes. 8
Smarter Guides and Spacing 8
Other enhancements 8

A Quick Tour of Adobe Illustrator CC (2015 release)   10
Getting started 12
Creating a new document. 12
Drawing a shape. 13
Rounding the corners of a shape 13
Applying color. 14

Editing color 14

Editing strokes 15

Working with layers 15

Drawing with the Pencil tool 16

Creating shapes using the Shape Builder tool 17

Creating a blend 18

Transforming artwork 19

Drawing with the Shaper tool 19

Sampling formatting with the Eyedropper tool 21

Placing an image in Illustrator 21

Using Image Trace 22

Creating and editing gradients 22

Working with type 23

Aligning artwork 25

Working with brushes 26

Working with symbols 27

Creating a clipping mask 29

Working with effects 29

1   GETTING TO KNOW THE WORK AREA   30

Introducing Adobe Illustrator 32

Starting Illustrator and opening a file 32

Exploring the workspace 34

Getting to know the Tools panel 35

Working with the Control panel 38

Working with panels 40

Working with panel groups 42

Resetting and saving your workspace 44

Using panel menus 45

Changing the view of artwork 46

Using view commands 46

Using the Zoom tool 47

Scrolling through a document 49

Viewing artwork 50

Navigating artboards 51
    Using the Artboards panel 53
Arranging multiple documents. 53
    Finding resources for using Illustrator. 55

2   TECHNIQUES FOR SELECTING ARTWORK   58

Getting started 60
Selecting objects 60
    Using the Selection tool. 60
    Using the Direct Selection tool 62
    Creating selections with a marquee 63
    Selecting artwork with the Magic Wand tool 64
    Selecting similar objects 65
    Selecting in Outline mode. 66
Aligning objects 67
    Aligning objects to each other 67
    Aligning to a key object. 67
    Aligning anchor points. 68
    Distributing objects. 68
    Aligning to the artboard 69
Working with groups. 70
    Grouping items 70
    Working in Isolation mode 70
    Creating a nested group 71
    Selecting using the Group Selection tool 72
Exploring object arrangement. 72
    Arranging objects. 72
    Selecting objects behind. 73
Hiding and locking objects. 74

3   USING SHAPES TO CREATE ARTWORK FOR A POSTCARD   76

Getting started 78
Creating a new document. 78
Working with basic shapes 80
    Creating and editing rectangles 80
    Rounding corners. 82
    Creating a rounded rectangle 83
    Creating and editing an ellipse 86

Creating and editing a circle. 87

Creating and editing a polygon. 88

Changing stroke width and alignment. 90

Drawing lines. 91

Creating a star 92

Working with the Shaper tool 94

Drawing shapes. 94

Editing shapes with the Shaper tool 95

Combining shapes with the Shaper tool 96

Working with drawing modes 98

Working with Draw Behind mode 98

Using the Draw Inside mode 99

Editing content drawn inside. 100

Using Image Trace 101

4   EDITING AND COMBINING SHAPES AND PATHS   104

Getting started 106

Editing paths and shapes. 107

Cutting with the Scissors tool 107

Joining paths 108

Cutting with the Knife tool 109

Using the Eraser tool 111

Combining shapes. 113

Working with the Shape Builder tool. 113

Working with the Pathfinder panel 115

Creating a compound path. 117

Using the Width tool 119

Outlining strokes 121

Finishing up the illustration 122

5   TRANSFORMING ARTWORK   124

Getting started 126

Working with artboards. 127

Adding artboards to the document. 127

Editing artboards 128

Renaming artboards 129

Reordering artboards 130

Transforming content. 132

Working with rulers and guides 132

Positioning objects precisely 135

Scaling objects 137

Reflecting objects.................................... 138

Distorting objects with effects........................ 139

Rotating objects 141

Shearing objects..................................... 143

Transforming with the Free Transform tool............... 145

Creating a PDF... 148

6   CREATING AN ILLUSTRATION WITH THE DRAWING TOOLS   150

Getting started 152

An intro to drawing with the Pen tool..................... 153

Selecting paths 154

Drawing straight lines with the Pen tool 156

Introducing curved paths 157

Drawing a curve with the Pen tool..................... 159

Drawing a series of curves with the Pen tool 160

Converting smooth points to corner points 161

Combining curves and straight lines................... 163

Creating artwork with the Pen tool 165

Drawing a coffee cup 166

Drawing with the Curvature tool 170

Editing curves 172

Reflecting the spoon shape 172

Rounding corner points.............................. 173

Editing paths and points 173

Deleting and adding anchor points..................... 175

Converting between smooth points and corner points 176

Working with the Anchor Point tool 177

Creating a dashed line 178

Adding arrowheads to a path............................ 179

Working with the Pencil tool 180

Drawing freeform paths with the Pencil tool 180

Drawing straight segments with the Pencil tool........... 181

Joining with the Join tool 183

7   USING COLOR TO ENHANCE SIGNAGE   186

Getting started 188

Exploring color modes 189

Working with color. 190

Applying an existing color. 190

Creating a custom color using the Color panel 191

Saving a color as a swatch. 192

Creating a copy of a swatch 193

Editing a swatch 194

Creating and editing a global swatch 194

Using the Color Picker to create color 196

Using Illustrator swatch libraries. 197

Adding a spot color 198

Creating and saving a tint of a color 199

Adjusting colors 200

Copying appearance attributes. 200

Creating a color group 201

Creative inspiration with the Color Guide panel 202

Editing a color group in the Edit Colors dialog box 204

Editing colors in artwork 207

Assigning colors to your artwork 209

Working with Live Paint 212

Creating a Live Paint group. 212

Painting with the Live Paint Bucket tool. 213

Modifying a Live Paint group 214

8   ADDING TYPE TO A POSTER   216

Getting started 218

Adding type to the poster. 219

Adding text at a point. 219

Adding area type 220

Working with Auto Sizing 221

Converting between area and point type 222

Importing a plain-text file 223

Threading text. 224

Formatting type 226

Changing font family and font style 226

Changing font size 230

Changing font color. 231

Changing additional character formatting 232

Changing paragraph formatting. 234

Resizing and reshaping type objects. 235

Creating columns of text 236

Modifying text with the Touch Type tool 237

Creating and applying text styles. 239

Creating and applying a paragraph style. 239

Editing a paragraph style. 240

Creating and applying a character style. 241

Editing a character style. 242

Sampling text formatting 242

Wrapping text 242

Warping text. 243

Reshaping text with a preset envelope warp 243

Editing the envelope warp 244

Working with type on a path 245

Creating type on a path 245

Creating type on a closed path 246

Creating text outlines 248

9   ORGANIZING YOUR ARTWORK WITH LAYERS   250

Getting started 252

Understanding layers 252

Creating layers and sublayers. 254

Editing layers and objects 257

Locating layers. 257

Moving layers and content between layers 258

Duplicating layer content 261

Merging layers. 262

Pasting layers 264

Changing layer order. 266

Viewing layers 267

Applying appearance attributes to layers 268

Creating a clipping mask. 270

10 GRADIENTS, BLENDS, AND PATTERNS   274

Getting started 276

Working with gradients 277

    Applying a linear gradient to a fill. 277

    Editing a gradient. 278

    Saving a gradient 279

    Adjusting a linear gradient fill 280

    Applying a linear gradient to a stroke. 282

    Edit a gradient on a stroke. 283

    Applying a radial gradient to artwork. 285

    Editing the colors in the radial gradient. 285

    Adjusting the radial gradient 288

    Applying gradients to multiple objects 290

    Adding transparency to gradients 291

Working with blended objects 294

    Creating a blend with specified steps 294

    Modifying a blend 296

    Creating and editing a smooth color blend 298

Painting with patterns 300

    Applying an existing pattern 300

    Creating your own pattern 301

    Applying your pattern 303

    Editing your pattern 304

11 USING BRUSHES TO CREATE A POSTER   306

Getting started 308

Working with brushes. 309

Using Calligraphic brushes 309

    Applying a Calligraphic brush to artwork 309

    Drawing with the Paintbrush tool 310

    Editing paths with the Paintbrush tool. 312

    Editing a brush 313

    Removing a brush stroke. 314

Using Art brushes. 315

    Applying an existing Art brush 315

    Creating an Art brush using a raster image. 316

    Editing an Art brush. 318

Using Bristle brushes. 319

   Changing Bristle brush options. 319

   Painting with a Bristle brush. 320

Using Pattern brushes. 322

   Creating a Pattern brush 324

   Applying a Pattern brush. 326

   Editing the Pattern brush. 326

Working with the Blob Brush tool. 328

   Drawing with the Blob Brush tool. 328

   Merging paths with the Blob Brush tool. 330

   Editing with the Eraser tool. 331

12   EXPLORING CREATIVE USES OF EFFECTS AND GRAPHIC STYLES   334

Getting started 336

Using the Appearance panel 338

   Editing appearance attributes 339

   Adding another stroke and fill. 341

   Reordering appearance attributes 344

Using live effects. 345

   Applying an effect 346

   Editing an effect 347

   Styling text with a Warp effect. 348

   Applying the Offset Path effect 349

Applying a Photoshop Effect 350

   Working with 3D effects. 352

   Applying a 3D Rotate effect 352

Using graphic styles. 354

   Applying an existing graphic style. 354

   Creating and applying a graphic style 355

   Updating a graphic style 358

   Applying a graphic style to a layer 360

   Scaling strokes and effects 362

13 CREATING ARTWORK FOR A T-SHIRT 364

Getting started 366
Working with symbols 367
    Using existing Illustrator symbol libraries 367
    Editing a symbol 369
    Working with dynamic symbols 370
    Creating a symbol 372
    Duplicating symbols 373
    Replacing symbols................................... 374
    Breaking a link to a symbol 376
Working with Creative Cloud Libraries 378
    Adding assets to CC Libraries......................... 378
    Using Library assets................................. 381
    Updating a Library asset 382
Working with the perspective grid......................... 384
    Using a preset grid.................................. 385
    Adjusting the perspective grid 385
    Drawing artwork in perspective 388
    Selecting and transforming objects in perspective 390
    Moving planes and objects together 391
    Drawing artwork with no active grid................... 392
    Adding and editing text in perspective 392
    Moving objects in a perpendicular direction 393
    Moving a plane to match an object..................... 395
    Bringing content into perspective 395
    Editing symbols in perspective 396
    Finishing Up 397

14 USING ILLUSTRATOR CC WITH OTHER ADOBE APPLICATIONS 400

Getting started 402
Combining artwork 403
Placing image files 404
    Placing an image 404
    Scaling a placed image............................... 405
    Placing a Photoshop image with Show Import Options..... 406
    Placing multiple images.............................. 409
    Applying color edits to an image 410

Masking images 412

    Applying a simple mask to an image. 412

    Editing a clipping path (mask) 413

    Masking an object with text 414

    Creating an opacity mask 415

    Editing an opacity mask. 417

Sampling colors in placed images 419

Working with image links 419

    Finding link information. 420

    Embedding and unembedding images 421

    Replacing a linked image. 421

Packaging a file 424

15 PREPARING CONTENT FOR THE WEB   426

Getting started 428

Saving content for the web. 429

    Aligning content to the pixel grid. 429

    Slicing content. 432

    Selecting and editing slices 433

    Using the Save For Web command 434

Creating CSS code 437

    Setting up your design for generating CSS 437

    Working with character styles and CSS code 440

    Working with graphic styles and CSS code 442

    Copying CSS. 443

    Exporting CSS 445

Saving artwork as SVG 446

Index   452

GETTING STARTED

Adobe® Illustrator® CC is the industry-standard illustration application for print, multimedia, and online graphics. Whether you are a designer or a technical illustrator producing artwork for print publishing, an artist producing multimedia graphics, or a creator of web pages or online content, Adobe Illustrator offers you the tools you need to get professional-quality results.

About Classroom in a Book

Adobe Illustrator CC Classroom in a Book® (2015 release) is part of the official training series for Adobe graphics and publishing software developed with the support of Adobe product experts. The features and exercises in this book are based on Illustrator CC (2015.1 release).

The lessons are designed so that you can learn at your own pace. If you're new to Adobe Illustrator, you'll learn the fundamentals you need to master to put the application to work. If you are an experienced user, you'll find that *Classroom in a Book* teaches many advanced features, including tips and techniques for using the latest version of Adobe Illustrator.

Although each lesson provides step-by-step instructions for creating a specific project, there's room for exploration and experimentation. You can follow the book from start to finish or do only the lessons that correspond to your interests and needs. Each lesson concludes with a review section summarizing what you've covered.

Prerequisites

Before beginning to use *Adobe Illustrator CC Classroom in a Book (2015 release)*, you should have working knowledge of your computer and its operating system. Make sure that you know how to use the mouse and standard menus and commands and also how to open, save, and close files. If you need to review these techniques, see the printed or online documentation for your Windows or Mac OS.

Installing the program

Before you begin using *Adobe Illustrator CC Classroom in a Book (2015 release)*, make sure that your system is set up correctly and that you've installed the required software and hardware.

You must purchase the Adobe Illustrator CC software separately. For complete instructions on installing the software, visit http://helpx.adobe.com/illustrator.html. You must install Illustrator from Adobe Creative Cloud onto your hard disk. Follow the onscreen instructions.

Fonts used in this book

The *Classroom in a Book* lesson files use fonts that are part of the Typekit Portfolio plan included with your Creative Cloud subscription, and trial Creative Cloud members have access to a selection of fonts from Typekit for web and desktop use.

For more information about fonts and installation, see the Adobe Illustrator CC Read Me file on the Web at http://helpx.adobe.com/illustrator.html.

Accessing the Classroom in a Book files

In order to work through the projects in this book, you will need to download the lesson files from your Account page at peachpit.com. You can download the files for individual lessons or download them all in a single file. Although each lesson stands alone, some lessons use files from other lessons, so you'll need to keep the entire collection of lesson assets on your computer as you work through the book.

If you purchased an eBook from peachpit.com or adobepress.com, the files will automatically appear on your Account page, under the Lesson & Update Files tab.

If you purchased an eBook from a different vendor or a print book, use the unique code in the back of this book to gain access to the lesson files.

To access the *Classroom in a Book* files, follow these steps:

1 On a Mac or PC, go to www.peachpit.com/redeem and enter the code found at the back of your book. **This code is not the same as the book's ISBN.**

2 Click Redeem Code and sign in or create an account. You will be taken to your Account page.

You only need to enter the code once. After you redeem the code, you'll be able to access your lesson files on peachpit.com anytime you want without entering the code again.

3 Click the Lesson & Update Files tab of your Account page to see a list of downloadable files.

4 Click the lesson file links to download them to your computer.

The files are compressed into ZIP archives to speed up download time and to protect the contents from damage during transfer. You must uncompress (or "unzip") the files to restore them to their original size and format before you use them with the book. Modern Mac and Windows systems are set up to open ZIP archives by simply double-clicking.

5 On your hard drive, create a new folder in a convenient location and give it the name "Lessons," following the standard procedure for your operating system:

- If you're running Windows, right-click and choose New > Folder. Then enter the new name for your folder.

- If you're using Mac OS, in the Finder, choose File > New Folder. Type the new name and drag the folder to the location you want to use.

6 Drag the unzipped Lessons folder (which contains folders named Lesson01, Lesson02, and so on) that you downloaded onto your hard drive to your new Lessons folder. When you begin each lesson, navigate to the folder with that lesson number to access all the assets you need to complete the lesson.

● **Note:** If for any reason you need to download fresh copies of the lesson files, you can download them from your account again at any time.

Web Edition

This book comes with a free Web Edition that provides many benefits and can be accessed from any device with a connection to the Internet.

Your Web Edition contains the complete text of the book, plus hours of instructional video keyed to the text and interactive quizzes. In addition, the Web Edition will be updated when Adobe adds significant feature updates between major Creative Cloud releases.

● **Note:** Registering to access the Web Edition does not automatically provide access to your lesson files, and vice versa. You must follow the instructions for each to claim the full benefits of your purchase.

Accessing the Free Web Edition

You must register your book purchase on peachpit.com in order to access the free Web Edition:

1 Go to www.peachpit.com/register, and then sign in or create a new account.

2 Enter the book's ISBN: 9780134308111.

3 Answer the questions as proof of purchase. The Web Edition will appear under the Digital Purchases tab on your Account page.

4 Click the Launch link to access the product.

Restoring default preferences

Note: If finding the preferences file proves difficult, please contact me at brian@ brianwoodtraining.com for assistance.

The preferences file controls how command settings appear on your screen when you open the Adobe Illustrator program. Each time you quit Adobe Illustrator, the position of the panels and certain command settings are recorded in different preference files. If you want to restore the tools and settings to their original default settings, you can delete the current Adobe Illustrator CC preferences file. Adobe Illustrator creates a new preferences file, if one doesn't already exist, the next time you start the program and save a file.

You must restore the default preferences for Illustrator before you begin each lesson. This ensures that the tools and panels function as described in this book. When you have finished the book, you can restore your saved settings, if you like.

To delete or save the current Illustrator preferences file

1 Exit Adobe Illustrator CC.

Note: In Windows 7 or later, the AppData folder is hidden by default. You will most likely need to enable Windows to show hidden files and folders. For instructions, refer to your Windows documentation.

2 Locate the Adobe Illustrator Prefs file for Mac OS 10.7 and later* as follows:

   • The Adobe Illustrator Prefs file is located in the folder [startup drive]/Users/ [username]/Library/Preferences/Adobe Illustrator 19 Settings/en_US**.

3 Locate the Adobe Illustrator Prefs file for Windows 7 [Service Pack 1], Windows 8, or Windows 10 as follows:

   • The AIPrefs file is located in the folder [startup drive]\Users\[username]\ AppData\Roaming\Adobe\Adobe Illustrator 19 Settings\en_US**\x86 or x64.

*On Mac OS 10.7 (Lion) and later, the Library folder is hidden by default. To access this folder, in the Finder, hold down the Option key, and choose Library from the Go menu in the Finder.

**Folder name may be different depending on the language version you have installed.

Tip: To quickly locate and delete the Adobe Illustrator preferences file each time you begin a new lesson, create a shortcut (Windows) or an alias (Mac OS) to the Adobe Illustrator 19 Settings folder.

For more information, refer to Illustrator help: https://helpx.adobe.com/illustrator/kb/preference-file-location-illustrator.html

If you can't find the file, either you haven't started Adobe Illustrator CC yet or you have moved the preferences file. The preferences file is created after you quit the program the first time and is updated thereafter.

4 Copy the file and save it to another folder on your hard disk (if you want to restore those preferences) or delete it.

5 Start Adobe Illustrator CC.

To restore saved preferences after completing the lessons

1 Exit Adobe Illustrator CC.

2 Delete the current preferences file. Find the original preferences file that you saved and move it to the Adobe Illustrator 19 Settings folder.

● **Note:** You can move the original preferences file rather than renaming it.

Additional resources

Adobe Illustrator CC Classroom in a Book (2015 release) is not meant to replace documentation that comes with the program or to be a comprehensive reference for every feature. Only the commands and options used in the lessons are explained in this book. For comprehensive information about program features and tutorials, please refer to these resources:

Adobe Illustrator Learn & Support: helpx.adobe.com/illustrator.html (accessible in Illustrator by choosing Help > Illustrator Support Center) is where you can find and browse tutorials, help, and support on Adobe.com.

Adobe Forums: forums.adobe.com lets you tap into peer-to-peer discussions, questions, and answers on Adobe products.

Adobe Create Magazine: create.adobe.com offers thoughtful articles on design and design issues, a gallery showcasing the work of top-notch designers, tutorials, and more.

Resources for educators: www.adobe.com/education and edex.adobe.com offer valuable information for instructors who teach classes on Adobe software. Find solutions for education at all levels, including free curricula that can be used to prepare for the Adobe Certified Associate exams.

Also check out these useful links:

Adobe Illustrator CC product home page: See www.adobe.com/products/illustrator.

Adobe Add-ons: creative.adobe.com/addons is a central resource for finding tools, services, extensions, code samples, and more to supplement and extend your Adobe products.

Adobe Authorized Training Centers

Adobe Authorized Training Centers offer instructor-led courses and training on Adobe products. A directory of AATCs is available at training.adobe.com/trainingpartners.

WHAT'S NEW IN ADOBE ILLUSTRATOR CC (2015 RELEASE)

Adobe Illustrator CC (2015 release) is packed with new and innovative features to help you produce artwork more efficiently for print, web, and digital video publication. The features and exercises in this book are based on Illustrator CC (2015.1 release). In this section, you'll learn about many of these new features—how they function and how you can use them in your work.

CC Libraries enhancements

In Illustrator CC (2015 release), there have been many improvements and enhancements to Creative Cloud Libraries, including the following:

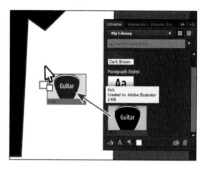

- Graphics are now linked so that when they're changed, you and your team members have the option of updating them across any Illustrator CC, Photoshop® CC, or InDesign® CC projects where they're used.

- Add swatches to libraries with the enhanced New Swatch dialog box.

- Add color groups or color themes to libraries from the Swatches panel.

- Add color themes from color libraries to the Swatches panel.

- Add character styles or paragraph styles to libraries.

- Use character styles or paragraph styles from libraries in a document.

- Add character styles or paragraph styles from libraries to the Character Styles or Paragraph Styles panel.

Shaper tool

There is a new way to draw and edit shapes in Illustrator. The Shaper tool (🖊) recognizes natural gestures and produces Live Shapes from those gestures. After the shapes have been created, you can use the same tool to select, scale, and move the shape.

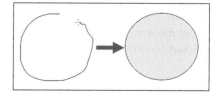

When shapes overlap, you can scribble within the overlapping area or shape edge to perform functions such as punching or combining. The individual shapes can still be edited after having performed operations such as a punch, or merge, between shapes.

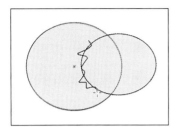 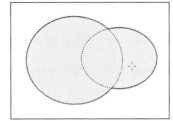

Scribble across an overlapping edge.   The shapes are now combined.

Dynamic Symbols

Symbols can now be saved as Dynamic when creating them. After placing an instance of a dynamic symbol in the document, you can select elements within the symbol using the Direct Selection tool and make appearance overrides such as color, gradient, or patterns. The symbol instance is still linked to the original symbol, and any change in the symbol reflects in the instance too, keeping appearance overrides intact.

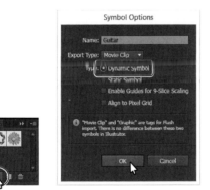

New SVG Export

The new SVG export improves the general quality of SVG exported from Illustrator. By using the new export, the user will be able to output modern, standard SVG code that is minified as well as responsive.

Live Shapes

In the latest release of Illustrator, ellipse and polygon shapes are now also Live Shapes. You can change the appearance properties of these Live Shapes through widgets or other methods. And you don't have to change to selection tools to edit the shape (widget); this can done from the shape tools.

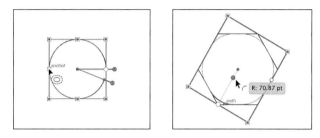

Examples of an ellipse (left) and polygon (right)

Smarter Guides and Spacing

The Smart Guides now include functionality such as a preview of the extension of a line in its own angle and feedback when rectangles become squares and/or when ellipses become circles. For adjoining shapes, there are also now gap hints.

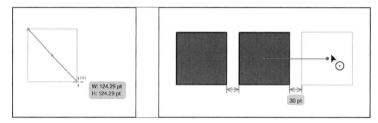

Other enhancements

- **10x faster zoom, pan, and scroll**—Zoom, pan, and scroll up to 10 times faster, thanks to Mercury Performance System enhancements that bring GPU acceleration to both Mac and Windows. Zoom is also now animated, so you can quickly zoom in and out of your document by scrubbing left and right.

- **10x greater zoom magnification**—Work with greater precision and make accurate and exact edits with the new 64,000 percent zoom level. Previously, the maximum zoom achievable was 6,400 percent.

- **Recover data in your files**—When an improper shutdown such as Illustrator crashing, an operating system error, or a power outage occurs, simply relaunch Illustrator to restore your work.

- **Safe Mode**—Safe Mode is a new feature that enables Illustrator to launch even if there are fatal, crash-inducing files (for example, corrupt fonts, out-of-date plug-ins, or incorrect drivers) in the system. You can choose to diagnose the cause of the error. When the application starts after isolating and disabling crash-causing files, Illustrator is in Safe Mode.

- **Adobe Stock**—With Adobe Stock, you can purchase, access, and manage high-quality, high-resolution, royalty-free images directly from Illustrator CC, Photoshop CC, InDesign CC, and other Adobe desktop apps. You can save images directly to Creative Cloud Libraries. You can license an image immediately or save a watermarked preview to use in a comp. Thanks to Adobe CreativeSync, you can immediately access your images across your desktop and mobile devices and even share them with your team. When you're ready to use the nonwatermarked version, you can license the image for use directly in Illustrator.

Although this list touches on just a few of the new and enhanced features of Illustrator CC (2015 release), it exemplifies Adobe's commitment to providing the best tools possible for your publishing needs. We hope you enjoy working with Illustrator CC (2015 release) as much as we do.

—The *Adobe Illustrator CC Classroom in a Book (2015 release)* team

A QUICK TOUR OF ADOBE ILLUSTRATOR CC (2015 RELEASE)

Lesson overview

In this interactive demonstration of Adobe Illustrator CC (2015 release), you'll get an overview of the main features of the application.

 This lesson takes approximately 45 minutes to complete.

Download the project files for this lesson from the Lesson & Update Files tab on your Account page at www.peachpit.com and store them on your computer in a convenient location, as described in the "Getting Started" section of this book.

Your Account page is also where you'll find any updates to the chapters or to the lesson files. Look on the Lesson & Update Files tab to access the most current content.

In this demonstration of Adobe Illustrator CC, you will be introduced to some key fundamentals for working in the application.

Getting started

For the first lesson of this book, you will get a quick tour of the tools and features in Adobe Illustrator CC, offering a sense of the many possibilities. Along the way, you will create artwork for a bakery.

● **Note:** If you have not already downloaded the project files for this lesson to your computer from your Account page, make sure to do so now. See "Getting Started" at the beginning of the book.

1 To ensure that the tools and panels function exactly as described in this lesson, delete or deactivate (by renaming) the Adobe Illustrator CC preferences file. See "Restoring default preferences" in the "Getting Started" section at the beginning of the book.

2 Start Adobe Illustrator CC.

Creating a new document

● **Note:** Learn more about creating and editing artboards in Lesson 5, "Transforming Artwork."

An Illustrator document can contain up to 100 artboards (*artboards* are similar to *pages* in a program like Adobe InDesign®). Next, you will create a document with only one artboard.

1 Choose Window > Workspace > Reset Essentials.

● **Note:** If you don't see Reset Essentials in the Workspace menu, choose Window > Workspace > Essentials before choosing Window > Workspace > Reset Essentials.

2 Choose File > New.

3 In the New Document dialog box, change only the following options (leaving the rest at their default settings):

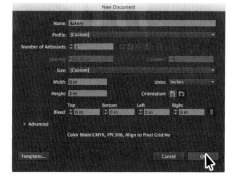

- Name: **Bakery**

- Units: **Inches**

- Width: **6 in**

- Height: **3 in**

4 Click OK. A new, blank document appears.

5 Choose File > Save As. In the Save As dialog box, leave the name as **Bakery.ai**, and navigate to the Lessons > Lesson00 folder. Leave the Format option set to Adobe Illustrator (ai) (Mac OS) or Save As Type option set to Adobe Illustrator (*.AI) (Windows), and click Save. In the Illustrator Options dialog box, leave the Illustrator options at their default settings, and then click OK.

6 Choose View > Rulers > Show Rulers to show rulers in the Document window.

7 Choose View > Fit Artboard In Window.

8 Choose View > Zoom Out.

The white area is the artboard, and it's where your printable artwork will go.

9 Click the Libraries panel tab to collapse the panel on the right.

Drawing a shape

Drawing shapes is the cornerstone of Illustrator, and you will create many of them in the coming lessons. Next, you will create a rectangle.

Note: Learn more about creating and editing shapes in Lesson 3, "Using Shapes to Create Artwork for a Postcard."

1 Select the Rectangle tool (■) in the Tools panel on the left.

2 Position the pointer in the upper-left part of the artboard (see the red X in the figure). Click and drag down and to the right edge of the white artboard. When the gray measurement label shows a width of 5.5 in and a height of 2.2 in, release the mouse button. The shape will remain selected.

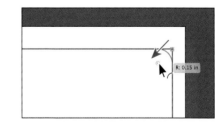

Shapes can be created by drawing them or clicking the artboard with a shape tool and modifying shape properties before it is created.

Rounding the corners of a shape

Shapes such as rectangles, rounded rectangles, ellipses, and polygons are called Live Shapes because properties such as width, height, rounded corners, corner types, and radii (individually or collectively) can continue to be modified. Next, you will round the corners of the rectangle you created.

Note: Learn more about creating and editing Live shapes in Lesson 3, "Using Shapes to Create Artwork for a Postcard."

1 Select the Selection tool (▶) in the Tools panel on the left, and with the rectangle still selected on the artboard, click and drag the upper-right-corner widget toward the center of the rectangle. When the gray measurement label shows a value of approximately 0.15 in, release the mouse button.

R: 0.15 in

Applying color

● **Note:** Learn more about creating and applying color in Lesson 7, "Using Color to Enhance Signage."

Applying colors to artwork is a common Illustrator task. You can either create your own color using a variety of methods or use colors that come with each document by default called *swatches*.

1   With the Selection tool (▶) selected and the rectangle still selected, click the Fill color in the Control panel (circled in the figure) to reveal the Swatches panel. Position the pointer over an orange swatch (in the second row of colors). When the tooltip appears that shows "C=0, M=35, Y=85, K=0," click to apply the orange swatch to the fill of the shape.

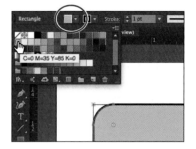

2   Press the Escape key to hide the Swatches panel and leave the shape selected.

Editing color

● **Note:** Learn more about editing color in Lesson 7, "Using Color to Enhance Signage."

There are many ways in Illustrator to both create your own colors and edit colors that appear in each document by default. In this section, you will edit the color values for the orange swatch you just applied.

1   With the rectangle still selected, click the Fill color in the Control panel (circled in the figure), and double-click the orange swatch you applied in the previous steps to edit it.

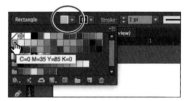

2   In the Swatch Options dialog box, change the values to C=**8**, M=**18**, Y=**63**, K=**0**. Click OK to edit the color for the rectangle and change the swatch color values.

3   Press the Escape key to hide the Swatches panel.

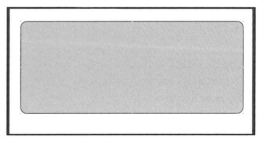

4   Choose File > Save.

Editing strokes

You can also apply a stroke (border) to artwork. A stroke can be the visible outline of artwork like shapes and paths. There are a lot of appearance properties you can change for a stroke including width, color, dashes, and more. In this section, you'll adjust the stroke of the rectangle.

Note: Learn more about working with strokes in Lesson 3, "Using Shapes to Create Artwork for a Postcard."

1   With the rectangle still selected, click the Stroke color in the Control panel (circled in the figure) to reveal the Swatches panel. Click the same orange-colored swatch you used for the fill.

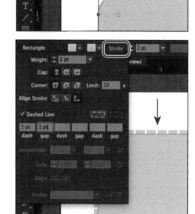

2   With the rectangle shape still selected, click the word "Stroke" in the Control panel above the document to open the Stroke panel. Change the following options:

   • Stroke Weight: **2 pt**

   • Align Stroke:
     Align Stroke to Outside ( )

   • Dashed Line: **Selected**

   • Dash: **5 pt**

   • Gap: **1 pt**

3   Press the Escape key to hide the Stroke panel.

4   Choose Object > Lock > Selection to lock the rectangle so that it can't be selected until you unlock it later.

Working with layers

Layers allow you to organize and more easily select artwork. Next, using the Layers panel, you will organize your artwork.

Note: Learn more about working with layers and the Layers panel in Lesson 9, "Organizing Your Artwork with Layers."

1   Choose Window > Layers to show the Layers panel in the workspace.

2   Double-click the text "Layer 1" (the layer name) in the Layers panel. Type **Background**, and press Enter or Return to change the layer name.

   Naming layers can be helpful when organizing content. Currently, the rectangle you created is on this layer.

3 Click the Create New Layer button () at the bottom of the Layers panel. Double-click Layer 2 (the new layer name), and type **Content**. Press Enter or Return.

Drawing with the Pencil tool

Note: Learn more about working with the Pencil tool and other drawing tools in Lesson 6, "Creating an Illustration with the Drawing Tools."

The Pencil tool (✐) lets you draw free-form open and closed paths that contain curves and straight lines. As you draw with the Pencil tool, anchor points are created on the path where necessary and according to the Pencil tool options you set.

1 Click and hold down on the Shaper tool (✐) in the Tools panel on the left. In the tools menu that appears, select the Pencil tool (✐). If a window appears that discusses the Shaper tool, close it.

2 Double-click the Pencil tool (✐) in the Tools panel on the left to open the Pencil Tool Options dialog box. Select Fill New Pencil Strokes and Close Paths When Ends Are Within. Click OK.

3 Press the letter D to set the default fill (White) and stroke (Black) for the artwork you are about to create.

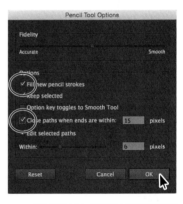

4 Choose Window > Swatches to show the Swatches panel. Click the Stroke box (circled in the figure) and select a Dark Gray swatch to change the stroke.

You'll probably need to scroll down in the Swatches panel.

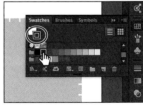

5 On the artboard, starting where you see the red X in the figure, click and drag to create the top of a chef's hat that's roughly an inch in width (look at the rulers). Come back to where you started drawing. When a circle appears next to the Pencil tool (✐), indicating that the path will be closed, release the mouse button to close the path. Leave the path selected.

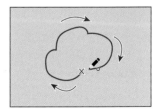

Creating shapes using the Shape Builder tool

The Shape Builder tool (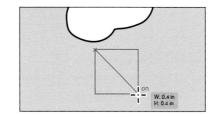) is an interactive tool for creating complex shapes by merging and erasing simpler shapes. Next, you will finish the chef hat you started drawing in the previous section, using the Shape Builder tool.

Note: Learn more about working with the Shape Builder tool in Lesson 4, "Editing and Combining Shapes and Paths."

1 Select the Rectangle tool (▪) in the Tools panel on the left. Shift-drag below the shape you just drew to draw a square with a height and width of 0.4 in. When the gray measurement label next to the pointer shows the correct size, release the mouse button and then the Shift key.

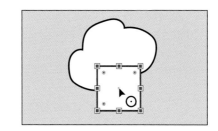

2 Select the Selection tool (▸) in the Tools panel on the left. Position the pointer over the center of the rectangle. When the pointer changes (▸ₒ), drag the rectangle from its center roughly into position like you see in the figure.

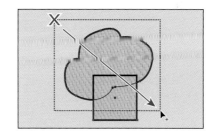

3 Shift-click the shape you drew with the Pencil tool to select both objects.

4 Select the Shape Builder tool (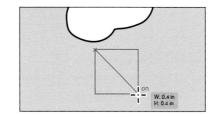) in the Tools panel on the left. Position the pointer to the left and above all of the selected shapes (see the red X in the figure). Press the Shift key and drag to the right and down. Make sure you drag across all the selected shapes. Release the mouse button and then the Shift key to combine the shapes.

5 Select the Selection tool and position the pointer just off one of the corners. When the pointer changes (↱), drag counterclockwise to rotate roughly 7°.

6 Choose Object > Hide > Selection to temporarily hide the hat.

7 Choose File > Save.

Creating a blend

● **Note:** Learn more about working with blends in Lesson 10, "Gradients, Blends, and Patterns."

You can blend two distinct objects to create and distribute shapes evenly between two objects. For instance, to create a fence, you could blend two rectangles together and Illustrator will create all the copies between the two original rectangles.

Next, you will create the bottom part of a muffin using a blend.

1 Choose View > Zoom In to zoom into the artboard a bit.

2 Select the Rectangle tool (■) in the Tools panel on the left. Draw a rectangle with a width of 0.1 in and a height of 0.4 in.

3 With the rectangle still selected, click the Fill color in the Control panel (circled in the figure), and select the brown swatch in the third row of colors with the tooltip "C=25, M=40, Y=65, K=0."

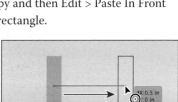
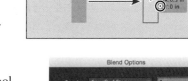

4 Change the Stroke weight to **0** in the Control panel.

5 With the rectangle selected, choose Edit > Copy and then Edit > Paste In Front to paste a copy directly on top of the original rectangle.

6 Position the pointer over the center of the rectangle. When the pointer changes (▸○), drag to the right. Drag straight to the right until the gray measurement label shows a distance (dX) of about .5 in. Release the mouse button.

7 Double-click the Blend tool (🞂) in the Tools panel to set a few settings for the tool. In the Blend Options dialog box, choose Specified Steps from the Spacing menu, and change the value to the right to **3**. Click OK.

● **Note:** A Blend object acts like a group that consists of the original two objects and a path that the copies follow called a *spine*.

8 Click within the rectangle on the left when you see the cursor look like 🞂* and then click within the rectangle to the right when the cursor looks like 🞂+ to create a blend of the two objects. You just created a Blend object.

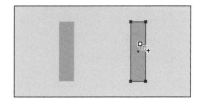

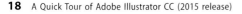

9 Choose Object > Blend > Expand
to convert it from a Blend object to
a group of shapes. Leave the
group selected.

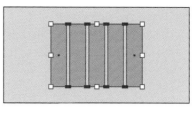

Transforming artwork

In Illustrator, there are a number of ways to move, rotate, skew, scale, distort, and
shear (and more) artwork so you can get it just the way you want. This is called
transforming artwork and something you'll do a bit of next.

● **Note:** Learn more
about transforming
artwork in Lesson 5,
"Transforming Artwork."

1 With the group still selected, select the Free Transform tool (⊞) in the
Tools panel. After selecting the Free Transform tool, the Free Transform widget
appears in the Document window. This widget contains options to change how
the Free Transform tool works.

2 In the Free Transform widget, select
Perspective Distort (circled in the
figure). Click and drag the bottom-left
corner of the group to the right a little.

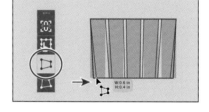

3 Choose Select > Deselect.

Drawing with the Shaper tool

Another way to draw and edit shapes in Illustrator involves the Shaper tool (🖌).
The Shaper tool recognizes drawn gestures and transforms them into shapes. Next,
you will use the Shaper tool to create the top of the muffin.

● **Note:** Learn more
about working with the
Shaper tool in Lesson 3,
"Using Shapes to Create
Artwork for a Postcard."

1 Click and hold down the Pencil tool (✏) in the Tools panel to reveal a tools
menu. Select the Shaper tool (🖌).

2 Press the letter D to set the default fill (White) and stroke (Black) for the artwork
you are about to create.

3 Above (or below) the brown group of objects, draw a small circle. You can always
choose Edit > Undo if you make a mistake.

Initially the drawing looks rough, but Illustrator takes your gesture and converts
it to a shape like a circle or an oval when you release the mouse button.

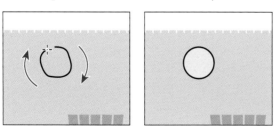

4 Draw another larger circle to the right of the first, making sure they overlap.

5 Position the pointer over the line between the two circles. Draw a scribble over the line between the circles so that they appear to combine.

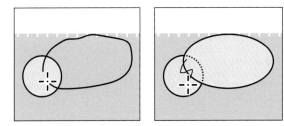

6 Choose Select > Deselect. Draw a few more circles, overlapping the originals. Use the following figure as a guide.

7 Position the pointer over the lines between each of the circles. Draw a scribble over them so that they appear to combine the shapes.

8 With the Shaper tool, click one of the circle shapes once to select the entire object. Click the small down arrow on the right side of the bounding box to temporarily access the individual shapes.

9 Click the larger shape to first select it. Drag it *a little* to move it.

After shapes have been created with the Shaper tool, you can use it to select by tapping over the shape. Selected shapes have control widgets that can be used for scaling, moving, and more.

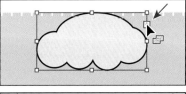

10 Select the Selection tool (➤) in the Tools panel on the left and drag the shape you just created down on top of the group to create the muffin. Leave the new artwork selected.

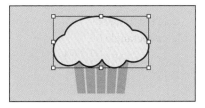

Sampling formatting with the Eyedropper tool

At times you may want to simply copy appearance attributes, like character or paragraph formatting, fill, and stroke, from one object to another. This can be done with the Eyedropper tool (🖋) and can really speed up your creative process.

Note: Learn more about the Eyedropper tool in Lesson 7, "Using Color to Enhance Signage."

1   With the shape still selected, select the Eyedropper tool (🖋) in the Tools panel.

2   Click the group of objects that started as a blend to copy the appearance properties to the selected artwork.

3   Select the Selection tool (▶) in the Tools panel on the left. Shift-click the group of muffin bottom shapes and choose Object > Group to group them together.

4   Choose Object > Hide > Selection to temporarily hide the muffin.

Placing an image in Illustrator

In Illustrator, you can place raster images, like JPEG (jpg, jpeg, jpe) and Adobe Photoshop® (psd, pdd) files, and either link to them or embed them. Next, you will place an image of hand-drawn text.

Note: Learn more about placing images in Lesson 14, "Using Illustrator CC with Other Adobe Applications."

1   Choose File > Place. In the Place dialog box, navigate to the Lesson00 folder in the Lessons folder, and select the Lettering.psd file. Make sure that the Link option in the dialog box is selected, and click Place.

2   Choose View > Fit Artboard In Window.

3   With the loaded graphics cursor, click in the upper-left corner of the rectangle to place the image.

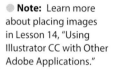

4   With the Selection tool (▶) selected, drag the image over the center of the large rectangle in the background so that it's roughly in the center of the artboard.

Note: The hand lettering for this project was created by Danielle Fritz (www.behance.net/danielle_fritz).

Using Image Trace

● **Note:** Learn more about Image Trace in Lesson 3, "Using Shapes to Create Artwork for a Postcard."

You can use Image Trace to convert photographs (raster images) into vector artwork. Next, you will trace the Photoshop file.

1 With the image selected, click the Image Trace button in the Control panel.

2 Choose Window > Image Trace. In the Image Trace panel, click the Black And White button at the top of the panel. The image is converted to vector paths, but it is not yet editable.

▶ **Tip:** Another method for converting the hand-drawn lettering is by using the Adobe Capture CC app. To learn more about Adobe Capture, visit www.adobe.com/ creativecloud/catalog/ mobile.html.

3 In the Image Trace panel, click the toggle arrow to the left of Advanced. Select Ignore White near the bottom of the panel. Close the Image Trace panel by clicking the small X in the corner.

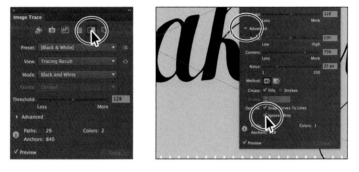

4 With the lettering still selected, click the Expand button in the Control panel to make the object a series of vector shapes that are grouped together.

Creating and editing gradients

● **Note:** Learn more about working with gradients in Lesson 10, "Gradients, Blends, and Patterns."

Gradients are color blends of two or more colors that you can apply to the fill or stroke of artwork. Next, you will apply a gradient to the lettering.

1 With the lettering still selected, choose Window > Gradient to show the Gradient panel on the right side of the workspace. In the Gradient panel, change the following options:

- Click the black Fill box (an arrow is pointing to it in the figure), if it's not already selected, so that you can apply the gradient to the fill of the lettering.

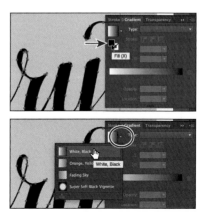

- Click the Gradient menu button (■—the little arrow) to the left of the word "Type," and choose White, Black from the menu.

2 Double-click the white color stop on the left side of the gradient slider in the Gradient panel (circled in the figure). In the panel that appears, click the Swatches button (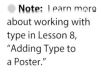) (if it's not already selected), and select the brown swatch with the tooltip "C=50, M=70, Y=80, K=70."

3 Press the Escape key to hide the Swatches panel.

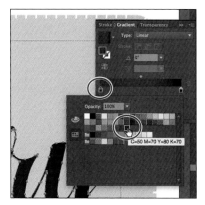

4 Select the Gradient tool (■) in the Tools panel on the left. While pressing the Shift key, click and drag down, across the lettering on the artboard, starting at the red X in the figure, to reposition and resize the gradient. Release the mouse button and then the key.

Working with type

Next, you will add some text to the project and apply formatting. You will choose a Typekit font that requires an Internet connection. If you don't have an Internet connection, you can choose another font.

● **Note:** Learn more about working with type in Lesson 8, "Adding Type to a Poster."

1 Select the Type tool (**T**) in the Tools panel on the left, and click in a blank area of the artboard, below the "The Bakery" lettering. Type **San Francisco**.

2 With the cursor still in the text, choose Select > All to select it.

3 In the Control panel above the artwork, choose **14 pt** from the Font Size menu (to the right of the Font Family).

Next, you will apply a Typekit font. You will need an Internet connection. If you don't have an Internet connection or access to the Typekit fonts, you can choose any other font from the font menu.

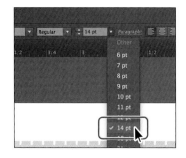

● **Note:** If you don't see the character options like Font Size in the Control panel, click the word "Character" to see the Character panel.

4 Click the arrow to the right of the Font field. Click the Add Fonts From Typekit button to sync a font from Typekit.

This opens a browser, launches the Typekit.com website, and signs you in to the site.

● **Note:** If you are taken to the Typekit.com home page, you can simply click the Browse Fonts button. It may also ask you to log in with your Creative Cloud (Adobe) ID.

5 Type **Proxima Nova** in the Search Typekit field (or another font, if you can't find that one). Choose Proxima Nova from the menu that appears.

6 Click Use Fonts on the next page.

7 Click Sync Selected Fonts in the window that appears.

8 After it is synced, click the Launch The Creative Cloud Application button to open the Creative Cloud Desktop application.

In the Creative Cloud desktop application, you will be able to see any messages indicating that font syncing is turned off (turn it on in that case) or any other issues.

9 Return to Illustrator. With the text still selected, begin typing **Prox** in the Font field in the Control panel.

10 Click Proxima Nova in the menu that appears to apply the font.

Note: It may take a few minutes for the font to sync with your computer.

11 Choose File > Save.

Aligning artwork

Illustrator makes it easy to align or distribute multiple objects relative to each other, the artboard, or a key object. In this section, you'll align several objects to the center of the artboard.

Note: Learn more about aligning artwork in Lesson 2, "Techniques for Selecting Artwork."

1 Choose Object > Unlock All to unlock the rectangle in the background and select it.

2 Select the Selection tool (▶) in the Tools panel and choose Select > All.

3 Click the Align To Selection button (▦▾) in the Control panel above the document, and choose Align To Artboard in the menu that appears, if it isn't already. The selected content will now align to the artboard.

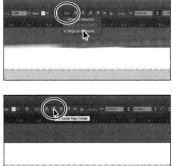

Note: The Align options may not appear in the Control panel. If you don't see the Align To Selection button (▦▾), click the word "Align" in the Control panel to open the Align panel. The number of options displayed in the Control panel depends on your screen resolution.

4 Click the Horizontal Align Center button (▤) to align the selected artwork to the horizontal center of the artboard.

5 Choose Object > Show All, and then choose Select > Deselect.

6 Click the chef hat and drag it into position like you see in the figure. You may need to move the muffin group out of the way as well.

7 Choose Select > Deselect.

Working with brushes

● **Note:** Learn more about working with brushes in Lesson 11, "Using Brushes to Create a Poster."

Brushes let you stylize the appearance of paths. You can apply brush strokes to existing paths, or you can use the Paintbrush tool () to draw a path and apply a brush stroke simultaneously.

1 Open the Layers panel by choosing Window > Layers. Click the Content layer to make sure that it is selected. You want to make sure that the rest of the artwork goes on this layer.

2 Select the Line Segment tool (╱) in the Tools panel on the left. Pressing the Shift key, click and drag from the left side of the text to the left (see the red X in the figure for where to start). When the gray measurement label shows a width of *roughly* 1.6 in, release the mouse button and then the key.

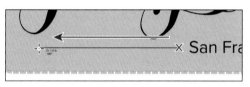

3 Choose Window > Brush Libraries > Borders > Borders_Novelty to open the Borders_Novelty collection of brushes as a panel.

4 Select the Selection tool (▶) and click the Laurel brush in the panel to apply it to the path you just drew. Click the X in the corner of the Borders_Novelty panel to close it.

● **Note:** The brush is a pattern brush, which means that it repeats artwork (in this case) along the path. The brush artwork is scaled on the path based on the stroke weight.

5 Change the Stroke weight to **0.5 pt** in the Control panel above the artwork.

6 With the path still selected, choose Object > Transform > Reflect. In the Reflect dialog box, select Vertical, and click **Copy**.

A reflected copy of the line is placed directly on top of the original.

7 With the Selection tool (▶) selected, drag both into position like you see in the following figure. As you drag the lines, alignment guides will appear, showing you when artwork is aligned with the text.

▶ **Tip:** You can also press the Arrow keys to move selected artwork.

8 Choose Select > Deselect.

Working with symbols

A *symbol* is a reusable art object stored in the Symbols panel. They're useful because they can help you save time and can save on file size as well. You will now create a symbol from artwork.

● **Note:** Learn more about working with symbols in Lesson 13, "Creating Artwork for a T-Shirt."

1 With the Selection tool (▶) selected, click the brown muffin group to select it.

2 Choose Window > Symbols to open the Symbols panel. Click the New Symbol button (▭) at the bottom of the Symbols panel.

3 In the Symbol Options dialog box that appears, name the symbol **Muffin**, and click OK. If a warning dialog box appears, click OK as well.

The artwork now appears as a saved symbol in the Symbols panel, and the muffin artwork on the artboard you used to create the symbol is now a symbol *instance*.

4 With the Selection tool (▶) selected, drag the muffin that's already on the artboard to the approximate center of the artboard.

5 Choose Object > Arrange > Send To Back to send the muffin behind all of the artwork on the Content layer.

Note: Your Muffin symbol instances may be in different locations than those in the figure. That's okay.

6 From the Symbols panel, drag the Muffin symbol thumbnail onto the artboard *twice* and arrange them on either side of the "San Francisco" text, like you see in the figure. Make sure that the muffin instances to the left and right of the original muffin instance hang off the larger rectangle in the background.

7 Select the muffin instance in the center of the artboard. Option+Shift-drag (Mac OS) or Alt+Shift-drag (Windows) any corner of the artwork away from its center to make it larger. After you resize it, drag it into position. Use the figure as a guide. Leave it selected.

8 Click the Edit Symbol button in the Control panel above the artwork to edit the symbol artwork in Isolation mode without affecting the other artwork. In the dialog box that appears, click OK.

9 Choose Select > All.

10 *Shift-click* the Fill color in the Control panel (circled in the following figure) and change the CMYK color values to C=**6**, M=**13**, Y=**49**, K=**0** to change the fill color of the muffin. Press the Escape key to close the panel.

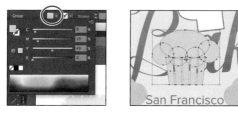

▶ **Tip:** You can also double-click away from the selected artwork to exit Isolation mode.

11 Press the Escape key to exit the editing (Isolation) mode and notice that the other muffins have changed.

12 Shift-click all three of the muffin instances and choose Object > Group.

13 Choose Object > Arrange > Send To Back.

Creating a clipping mask

A *clipping mask* is an object that masks other artwork so that only areas that lie within its shape are visible—in effect, clipping the artwork to the shape of the mask. Next, you will copy the background rectangle and use the copy to mask the artwork.

Note: Learn more about working with clipping masks in Lesson 14, "Using Illustrator CC with Other Adobe Applications."

1 With the Selection tool (▶) selected, click the large rectangle in the background.

2 Choose Edit > Copy.

3 Click the muffin group to select the layer that the muffins are on. Choose Edit > Paste In Front to paste a copy of the rectangle in the same position as the original but on top of the muffins.

4 With the rectangle still selected, press the Shift key, and click the muffin group just showing at the bottom of the artboard to select it as well.

5 Choose Object > Clipping Mask > Make.

Working with effects

Effects alter the appearance of an object without changing the base object. Next, you will apply a subtle Drop Shadow effect to the lettering you traced earlier.

Note: Learn more about effects in Lesson 12, "Exploring Creative Uses of Effects and Graphic Styles."

1 With the Selection tool (▶), click the "The Bakery" lettering.

2 Choose Effect > Stylize > Drop Shadow. In the Drop Shadow dialog box, set the following options (if necessary):

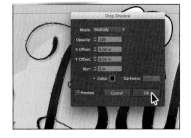

- Mode: **Multiply** (the default setting)
- Opacity: **10%**
- X Offset and Y Offset: **0.02 in**
- Blur: **0**

3 Select Preview to see it applied to the artwork, and then click OK.

4 Choose Select > Deselect, and then choose File > Save.

5 Choose File > Close.

1 GETTING TO KNOW THE WORK AREA

Lesson overview

In this lesson, you'll explore the workspace and learn how to do the following:

- Open an Adobe Illustrator CC file.

- Work with the Tools panel.

- Work with panels.

- Reset and save your workspace.

- Use viewing options to change the display magnification.

- Navigate multiple artboards and documents.

- Explore document groups.

- Find resources for using Illustrator.

 This lesson takes approximately 45 minutes to complete.

Download the project files for this lesson from the Lesson & Update Files tab on your Account page at www.peachpit.com and store them on your computer in a convenient location, as described in the "Getting Started" section of this book.

Your Account page is also where you'll find any updates to the chapters or to the lesson files. Look on the Lesson & Update Files tab to access the most current content.

ResortCompany.com

Porro ipsus idelit mosaperum a cone eum sit esequi te dolo ventur assi doluptati cum sit et omnissunt. Um qui delignihil ipsaecabor sumque pel maximin cipicaborum, seque corit eum unt.

Hillamus adigeni hilisciandae volest ommos moditae pelest, sita nat ate quatqui stiaeped ma pe volorerit quatatus accust, quuntis seresent.

occaboruptis explab inci aut min ent ut voluptatus illania quam ius aut adis

doluptatur asit et maximus ex estemperia nemperspis aut a tiam debitibus eaque delias a con periori re nobit, sum com dolupta tatiunt ionserunt.

Ugitaqu atusdanimducia cus cumenem rendit voluptatur? B rerum raes porum asperiori d porpore, qui asin cullaut offica andaectem inci voloreius mos cone omnis conse sint inci alimin volenih ilasper natusa pele

GRAND OPENING
CELEBRATION

brian@resortcompany.com   resortcompany.com

ResortCompany.com

Brian Wood
General Manager

brian@resortcompany.com

To make the most of the extensive drawing, painting, and editing capabilities of Adobe Illustrator CC, it's important to learn how to navigate the workspace. The workspace consists of the Application bar, menus, Tools panel, Control panel, Document window, and the default set of panels.

Introducing Adobe Illustrator

▶ **Tip:** To learn more about bitmap graphics, search for "Importing bitmap images" in Illustrator Help (Help > Illustrator Help).

In Illustrator, you primarily create and work with vector graphics (sometimes called vector shapes or vector objects). *Vector graphics* are made up of lines and curves defined by mathematical objects called *vectors*. You can freely move or modify vector graphics without losing detail or clarity because they are resolution-independent. In other words, vector graphics maintain crisp edges when resized, printed to a PostScript printer, saved in a PDF file, or imported into a vector-based graphics application. As a result, vector graphics are the best choice for artwork, such as logos, that will be used at various sizes and in various output media.

Illustrator also allows you to incorporate *bitmap images*—technically called *raster images*—that use a rectangular grid of picture elements (pixels) to represent the visual. Each pixel is assigned a specific location and color value. Raster images can be created in a program like Adobe Photoshop®.

A logo drawn as vector art

A logo as a raster image

Starting Illustrator and opening a file

● **Note:** Resetting the preferences is not something that you'll need to do when working on your own projects, but it ensures that what you see onscreen matches the descriptions in the lessons.

You'll be working with multiple art files during this lesson, but before you begin, you'll restore the default preferences for Adobe Illustrator CC.

● **Note:** If you have not already downloaded the project files for this lesson to your computer from your Account page, make sure to do so now. See the "Getting Started" section at the beginning of the book.

1   To ensure that the tools and panels function exactly as described in this lesson, delete or deactivate (by renaming) the Adobe Illustrator CC preferences file. See "Restoring default preferences" in the "Getting Started" section at the beginning of the book.

2   Double-click the Adobe Illustrator CC icon to start Adobe Illustrator.

With Illustrator open, you will most likely see a "welcome" screen with resources for Illustrator, that can be closed.

3 Choose File > Open. In the Lessons > Lesson01 folder on your hard disk, select the L1_start1.ai file, and click Open.

This lesson contains a fictitious business name, address, and website address made up for the purposes of the project.

4 Choose Window > Workspace > Reset Essentials to ensure that the workspace is set to the default settings.

⬤ **Note:** If you don't see Reset Essentials in the Workspace menu, choose Window > Workspace > Essentials before choosing Window > Workspace > Reset Essentials.

5 Choose View > Fit Artboard In Window.

This fits the active artboard into the Document window so that you can see the entire artboard. As you'll soon learn, an artboard is the area that contains your printable artwork and is similar to a page in Adobe InDesign.

6 Click the word "Libraries" in the panel tab on the right to collapse it, if the Libraries panel is showing (see the following figure). The Libraries panel you see may look different from the figure, and that's okay.

When the file is open and Illustrator is fully launched, the Application bar, menus, Tools panel, Control panel, and panel groups appear on the screen. Docked on the right side of the screen, you will see that default panels appear as icons by default. Illustrator also consolidates many of your most frequently accessed options in the Control panel below the menu bar. This lets you work with fewer visible panels and gives you a larger area in which to work.

You will use the L1_start1.ai file to practice navigating, zooming, and investigating an Illustrator document and the workspace.

Exploring the workspace

Note: The figures in this lesson are taken using the Windows operating system and may look slightly different from what you see, especially if you are using the Mac OS.

You create and manipulate your documents and files using various elements, such as panels, bars, and windows. Any arrangement of these elements is called a *workspace*. When you first start Illustrator, you see the default workspace, which you can customize for the tasks you perform. You can create and save multiple workspaces—one for editing and another for viewing, for example—and switch among them as you work.

Below, the areas of the default workspace are described:

A. Application bar
B. Control panel
C. Panels
D. Tools panel
E. Document window
F. Status bar

A. The **Application bar** across the top by default contains a workspace switcher, the menu bar (on Mac OS, the menu items appear *above* the Application bar—see the following figure), and application controls.

B. The **Control panel** displays options for the currently selected object.

C. **Panels** help you monitor and modify your work. Certain panels are displayed by default, and you can display any panel by choosing it from the Window menu.

D. The **Tools panel** contains tools for creating and editing images, artwork, page elements, and more. Related tools are grouped together.

E. The **Document window** displays the file you're working on.

F. The **Status bar** appears at the lower-left edge of the Document window. It displays information, zooming, and navigation controls.

Getting to know the Tools panel

The Tools panel on the left side of the workspace contains selection tools, drawing and painting tools, editing tools, viewing tools, the Fill and Stroke boxes, drawing modes, and screen modes. As you work through the lessons, you'll learn about the specific function of many of these tools.

● **Note:** The Tools panel shown here and throughout this lesson has two columns. You may see a one-column Tools panel, depending on your screen resolution and workspace.

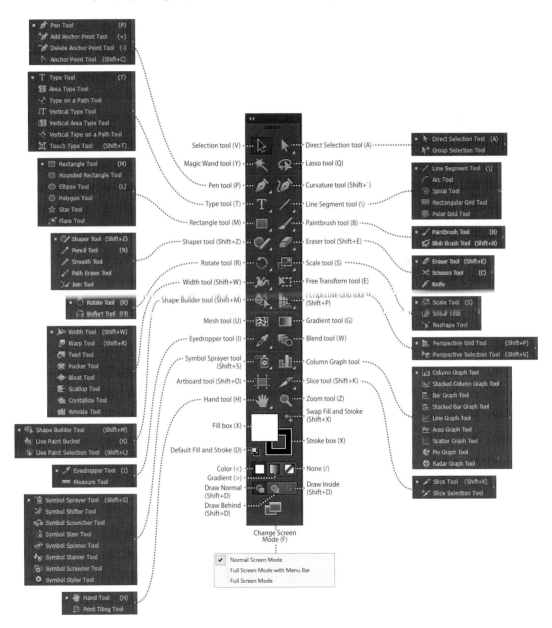

1   Position the pointer over the Selection tool ( ) in the Tools panel. Notice that the name (Selection Tool) and keyboard shortcut (V) are displayed in a tooltip.

 Tip: You can turn the tooltips on or off by choosing Illustrator CC > Preferences > General (Mac OS) or Edit > Preferences > General (Windows) and deselecting Show Tool Tips.

2   Position the pointer over the Direct Selection tool ( ), and click and hold down the mouse button until a tools menu appears. Release the mouse button, and then click the Group Selection tool to select it.

Any tool in the Tools panel that displays a small triangle contains additional tools that can be selected in this way.

3   Click and hold down the mouse button on the Rectangle tool ( ) to reveal more tools. Click the arrow at the right edge of the hidden tools panel to separate the tools from the Tools panel so that you can access them at all times.

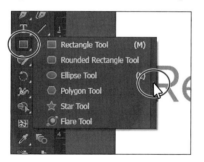

4   Click the Close button (X) in the upper-left corner (Mac OS) or upper-right corner (Windows) on the floating tool panel's title bar to close it. The tools return to the Tools panel.

 Tip: You can also collapse the floating tool panels or dock them to the workspace or each other.

Next, you'll learn how to resize and float the Tools panel. In the figures in this lesson, the Tools panel is a double column by default. As I said before, you may see a single-column Tools panel to start with, depending on your screen resolution and workspace, and that's okay.

5 Click the double arrow in the upper-left corner of the Tools panel to either expand the one column into two columns or collapse the two columns into one (depending on your screen resolution).

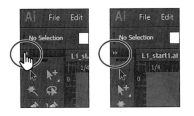

6 Click the same double arrow again to expand (or collapse) the Tools panel.

7 Click the dark gray title bar at the top of the Tools panel or the dashed line beneath the title bar, and drag the panel into the workspace. The Tools panel is now floating in the workspace.

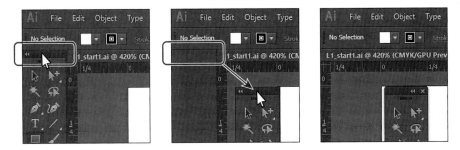

▶ **Tip:** You can click the double arrow at the top of the Tools panel or double-click the title bar at the top of the Tools panel to switch between two-column and one-column. Just be careful not to click the X!

8 To dock the Tools panel again, drag its title bar or the dashed line below it to the left side of the Application window. When the pointer reaches the left edge, a translucent blue border, called the *drop zone*, appears. Release the mouse button to dock the Tools panel neatly into the side of the workspace.

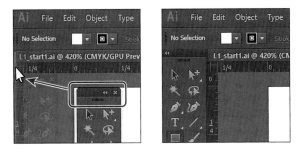

Custom Tools panels

You may find yourself using a specific set of tools most of the time. In Illustrator, you can create custom tools panels that contain the tools you use most often.

By choosing Window > Tools > New Tools Panel, you can create a custom tools panel. They are saved with Illustrator and can be closed and opened, regardless of which document is open. They are free-floating and can also be docked and saved in a custom workspace you create. Each new custom tools panel has stroke and fill controls at the bottom and a plus sign (+) where you can drag copies of tools from the main Tools panel onto the custom panel you are creating.

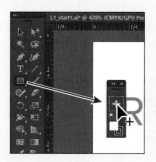

Working with the Control panel

The Control panel is the panel that's docked at the top of the workspace, just above the docked Tools panel. It offers quick access to options, commands, and other panels relevant to the currently selected content. You can click text like "Stroke" or "Opacity" to display a related panel. For example, clicking the word "Stroke" will display the Stroke panel.

1   Select the Selection tool (▶) in the Tools panel, and click the letter "s" in the word "Resort" in the artwork on the artboard.

Notice that options for that object appear in the Control panel, including the word "Group," color options, Stroke, and more.

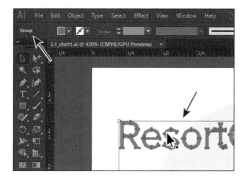

2 With any tool, drag the gripper bar (the dashed line along the left edge) of the Control panel into the workspace.

Once the Control panel is free-floating, you can drag the dark gray gripper bar that appears on the left edge of the Control panel to move it to the top or bottom of the workspace.

▶ **Tip:** You can also dock the Control panel by choosing Dock To Top or Dock To Bottom from the Control panel menu (▾▤) on the right side of the Control panel.

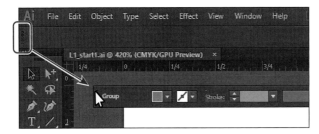

▶ **Tip:** In the default workspace, the Control panel can be dragged by the dark gray gripper bar on the left edge to the bottom of the Application window. When the pointer (not the panel) reaches the bottom of the Application window, a blue line appears, indicating the drop zone in which it will be docked. You can then release the mouse button to dock it.

3 Drag the Control panel by the gripper bar on the left edge of the panel. When the pointer reaches the bottom of the Application bar, to the right of the Tools panel, a blue line appears indicating the drop zone. When you release the mouse button, the panel is docked.

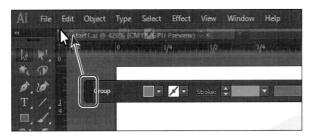

4 Choose Select > Deselect so that the content on the artboard is no longer selected.

Working with panels

Panels, which are listed alphabetically in the Window menu, give you quick access to many tools that make modifying artwork easier. By default, some panels are docked and appear as icons on the right side of the workspace.

Next, you'll experiment with hiding, closing, and opening panels.

▶ **Tip:** You can also choose Window > Workspace > Reset Essentials to reset the panels.

1 First, choose Reset Essentials from the workspace switcher in the upper-right corner of the Application bar to reset the panels to their original locations.

2 Click the Swatches panel icon (▦) on the right side of the workspace to expand the panel, or choose Window > Swatches.

Notice that the Swatches panel appears with two other panels—the Brushes panel and the Symbols panel. They are all part of the same panel group.

▶ **Tip:** To find a hidden panel, choose the panel name from the Window menu. A check mark to the left of the panel name indicates that the panel is already open and in front of other panels in its panel group. If you choose a panel name that is already selected in the Window menu, the panel and its group collapse.

3 Click the Symbols panel tab to view the Symbols panel.

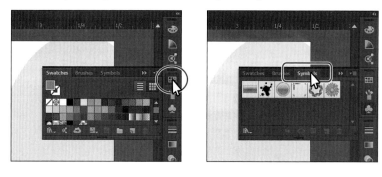

4 Now, click the Color panel icon (▦) in the dock. Notice that a new panel group appears and that the panel group that contained the Swatches panel collapses.

5 Click and drag the gripper bar at the bottom of the Color panel down to resize the panel, showing more of the color spectrum.

● **Note:** The Color panel you see may look different, and that's okay.

6 Click the Color panel icon to collapse the panel group.

7 Click the double arrow at the top of the dock to expand the panels. Click the double arrow again to collapse the panels.

Use this method to show more than one panel group at a time. Your panels may look different when expanded, and that's okay.

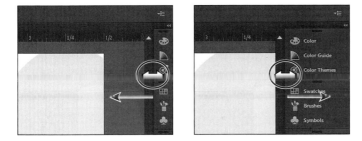

> **Tip:** To expand or collapse the panel dock, you can also double-click the panel dock title bar at the top.

8 To increase the width of all the panels in the dock, drag the left edge of the docked panels to the left until text appears. To decrease the width, click and drag the left edge of the docked panels to the right until the text disappears.

9 Choose Window > Workspace > Reset Essentials to reset the workspace.

> **Tip:** To collapse a panel back to an icon, you can click its tab, its icon, or the double arrow in the panel title bar.

Working with panel groups

You can also move panels from one panel group to another. In this way, you can create custom panel groups that contain the panels you use most often. Next, you will resize and reorganize panel groups, which can make it easier to see more important panels.

▶ **Tip:** To close a panel, drag the panel away from the dock, and click the X in the panel title bar. You can also right-click a docked panel tab or panel icon and choose Close from the menu.

1 Drag the Swatches panel icon (⊞) away from the dock to remove the panel from the dock and make it a free-floating panel. Notice that the panel stays collapsed as an icon when it is free-floating.

2 Click the double arrow in the Swatches panel title bar to expand the panel so you can see its contents.

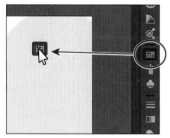

Drag the Swatches panel.   Expand the panel.   The result.

▶ **Tip:** Press Tab to toggle between hide and show for all panels. You can hide or show all panels except for the Tools and Control panels by pressing Shift+Tab to toggle between hide and show.

3 Drag the Swatches panel by the panel tab, the panel title bar, or the area behind the panel tab onto the Brushes (🖌) and Symbols (♣) panel icons. Release the mouse button when you see a blue line between the panel icons and an outline around the Brushes panel group.

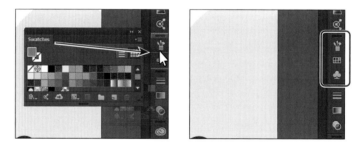

Next, you'll organize the panels to create more room in your workspace.

4 Choose Reset Essentials from the workspace switcher in the Application bar to make sure that the panels are reset to their default state.

5 Click the double arrow at the top of the dock to expand the panels.

● **Note:** Many panels only require that you double-click the panel tab twice to return to the full-size view of the panel. If you double-click one more time, the panel fully expands.

6 Click the Color Guide panel tab to make sure it's selected. Double-click the panel tab to reduce the size of the panel. Double-click the tab again to minimize the panel. This can also be done when a panel is free-floating (not docked).

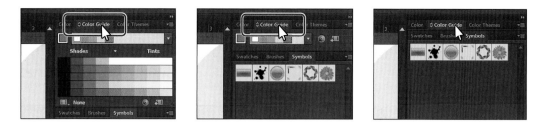

▶ **Tip:** To reduce and expand the panel size, instead of double-clicking the panel tab, you can click the small arrow icon to the left of the panel name in the panel tab, if present.

7 Click the Symbols panel tab if not already selected. Drag the dividing line between the Symbols panel group and the Stroke panel group below it, up to resize the group.

● **Note:** You may not be able to drag the divider very far, depending on your screen size, screen resolution, and number of panels expanded.

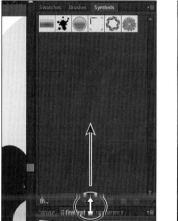 

8 Choose Reset Essentials from the workspace switcher on the far right side of the Application bar above the Control panel.

9 Choose Window > Align to open the Align panel group. Drag the title bar of the Align panel group (the bar above the Align tab) to the docked panels on the right side of the workspace. Position the pointer below the group that the Symbols panel icon () is in until a single blue line appears below the group. Release the mouse button to create a new group in the dock.

● **Note:** If you drag a group into the dock and drop it into an existing group, the two groups merge. Reset the workspace and open the panel group to try again.

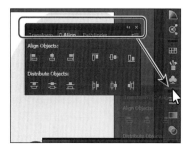 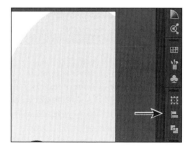

Next, you will drag a panel from one group to another in the docked panels.

▶ **Tip:** You can also dock panels next to each other on the right or left side of the workspace. This is a great way to conserve space.

10 Drag the Transform panel icon (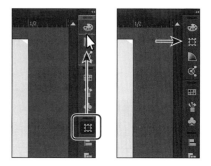) up so that the pointer is just below the Color panel icon (). A blue line appears between the Color panel icon and the Color Guide panel icon (), outlining the Color panel group in blue. Release the mouse button.

Arranging the panels in groups can help you work faster.

▶ **Tip:** You can also reorder entire panel groups in the dock by dragging the double gray line at the top of each panel group up or down.

Resetting and saving your workspace

You can reset your Tools panel and other panels to their default positions, which you've been doing throughout this lesson. You can also save the position of panels so that you can easily access them at any time by creating a workspace.

Next, you will create a workspace where the Libraries panel is collapsed.

1 Choose Reset Essentials from the workspace switcher in the Application bar.

2 Click the Libraries panel tab to hide the panel group.

● **Note:** To delete saved workspaces, choose Window > Workspace > Manage Workspaces. Select the workspace name, and click the Delete Workspace button.

3 Choose Window > Workspace > New Workspace. Change Name to **LibrariesHidden** in the New Workspace dialog box, and click OK.

The name of the workspace could be anything, as long as it makes sense to you. The workspace named "LibrariesHidden" is now saved with Illustrator until you remove it.

4 Choose Window > Workspace > Essentials.

5 Choose Window > Workspace > Reset Essentials.

Notice that the panels return to their default positions.

6 Choose Window > Workspace > LibrariesHidden. Toggle between the two workspaces using the Window > Workspace command, and return to the Essentials workspace before starting the next exercise.

▶ **Tip:** To change a saved workspace, reset the panels as you'd like them to appear, and then choose Window > Workspace > New Workspace. In the New Workspace dialog box, name the workspace with the original name. A message appears in the dialog box warning that you will overwrite an existing workspace with the same name if you click OK.

Using panel menus

Most panels have more options that are available in a panel menu. Clicking the panel menu icon (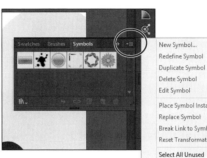) in the upper-right corner gives you access to additional options for the selected panel, including changing the panel display in some cases.

Next, you will change the display of the Symbols panel using its panel menu.

1 Click the Symbols panel icon (⬚) on the right side of the workspace. You can also choose Window > Symbols to display this panel.

2 Click the panel menu icon (⬚) in the upper-right corner of the Symbols panel.

3 Choose Small List View from the panel menu.

   This displays the symbol names, together with thumbnails. Because the options in the panel menu apply only to the active panel, only the Symbols panel view is affected.

4 Click the Symbols panel menu icon (⬚), and choose Thumbnail View to return the symbols to their original view.

5 Click the Symbols panel tab to hide the panel again.

   In addition to the panel menus, context-sensitive menus display commands relevant to the active tool, selection, or panel. Usually the commands in a context menu are available in another part of the workspace, but using a context menu can save you time.

6 Position the pointer over the Document window or the contents of a panel. Then, right-click to show a context menu with specific options.

   The context-sensitive menu shown here is displayed when you right-click the artboard with nothing selected.

● **Note:** If you position the pointer over the tab or title bar for a panel, and right-click, you can close a panel or a panel group in the context menu that appears.

Adjusting the user-interface brightness

Similar to Adobe InDesign or Adobe Photoshop, Illustrator supports a brightness adjustment for the application user interface. This is a program preference setting that allows you to choose a brightness setting from four preset levels or to specify a custom value.

To edit the user-interface brightness, you can choose Illustrator CC > Preferences > User Interface (Mac OS) or Edit > Preferences > User Interface (Windows).

Changing the view of artwork

When working in files, it's likely that you'll need to change the magnification level and navigate among artboards. The magnification level, which can range from 3.13% to 64000% (yes, 64 *thousand* percent), is displayed in the title bar (or document tab) next to the filename and in the lower-left corner of the Document window.

There are a lot of ways to change the zoom level in Illustrator, and in this section you'll explore several of the most widely used methods.

Using view commands

To enlarge or reduce the view of artwork using the View menu, do one of the following:

- Choose View > Zoom In to enlarge the display of the artwork.

- Choose View > Zoom Out to reduce the view of the artwork.

▶ **Tip:** You can also zoom in using the keyboard shortcut Command++ (Mac OS) or Ctrl++ (Windows). That's Command *and* + (Mac OS) or Ctrl *and* + (Windows). You can also zoom out using the keyboard shortcut Command+– (Mac OS) or Ctrl+– (Windows). That's Command *and* – (Mac OS) or Ctrl *and* – (Windows).

● **Note:** Using any of the viewing tools and commands affects only the display of the artwork, not the actual size of the artwork.

Each time you choose a Zoom option, the view of the artwork is resized to the closest preset zoom level. The preset zoom levels appear in a menu in the lower-left corner of the Document window, identified by a down arrow next to a percentage.

You can also use the View menu to fit the artwork for the active artboard to your screen to fit all artboards into the view area or to view artwork at actual size.

1 Choose View > Fit Artboard In Window.

Because the canvas (the area outside the artboards) extends to 227", you can easily lose sight of your illustration. By choosing View > Fit Artboard In Window or by using the keyboard shortcut Command+0 (Mac OS) or Ctrl+0 (Windows), artwork is centered in the viewing area.

2 Choose View > Actual Size to display the artwork at actual size.

The artwork is displayed at 100%. The actual size of your artwork determines how much of it can be viewed onscreen at 100%.

3 Choose View > Fit Artboard In Window before continuing to the next section.

Tip: You can also double-click the Hand tool (✋) in the Tools panel to fit the active artboard in the Document window.

Tip: You can also double-click the Zoom tool (🔍) in the Tools panel to display artwork at 100%.

Using the Zoom tool

In addition to the View menu options, you can use the Zoom tool (🔍) to magnify and reduce the view of artwork to predefined magnification levels.

1 Select the Zoom tool (🔍) in the Tools panel, and then move the pointer into the Document window.

Notice that a plus sign (+) appears at the center of the Zoom tool pointer.

2 Position the Zoom tool over the text "ResortCompany.com," and click once. The artwork is displayed at a higher magnification.

Notice that where you clicked is now in the center of the Document window.

3 Click two more times on the "ResortCompany.com" text. The view is increased again, and you'll notice that the area you clicked is magnified.

4 With the Zoom tool still selected, position the pointer over the text "ResortCompany.com" and hold down the Option (Mac OS) or Alt (Windows) key. A minus sign (–) appears at the center of the Zoom tool pointer. With the Option or Alt key pressed, click the artwork twice to reduce the view of the artwork.

Using the Zoom tool, you can also drag in the document to zoom in and out. By default, if your computer meets the system requirements for GPU Performance and it's enabled, zooming is animated.

5 Choose View > Fit Artboard In Window.

Note: If your
computer does *not*
meet the system
requirements for GPU
Performance, you
will instead select the
Zoom tool and drag a
dotted rectangle, called
a *marquee*, around
the area you want
to magnify.

Tip: If you click and
hold down with the
Zoom tool for a few
seconds, you can zoom
in using the animated
zoom if your computer
meets the system
requirements for
GPU Performance and
it's enabled.

6 With the Zoom tool still selected, from roughly in the center of the artwork, click and drag to the right to zoom in. Drag to the left to zoom out.

7 Double-click the Hand tool (🖐) in the Tools panel to fit the artboard in the Document window.

The Zoom tool is used frequently during the editing process to enlarge and reduce the view of artwork. Because of this, Illustrator allows you to select it using the keyboard at any time without first deselecting any other tool you may be using.

- To access the Zoom tool using your keyboard, press Command+spacebar (Mac OS) or Ctrl+spacebar (Windows).

- To access the Zoom out tool using your keyboard, press Command+Option+spacebar (Mac OS) or Ctrl+Alt+spacebar (Windows).

Note: In certain versions of Mac OS, the keyboard shortcuts for the Zoom tool (🔍) open Spotlight or the Finder. If you decide to use these shortcuts in Illustrator, you may want to turn off or change those keyboard shortcuts in the Mac OS System Preferences.

GPU Performance

The Graphics Processing Unit (GPU), found on video cards and as part of display systems, is a specialized processor that can rapidly execute commands for manipulating and displaying images. GPU-accelerated computing offers faster performance across a broad range of design, animation, and video applications.

The GPU Performance in Illustrator feature has a preview mode called GPU Preview, which enables rendering of Illustrator artwork on the graphics processor.

This feature is available on Windows computers that have an NVIDIA GPU installed and compatible Mac OS computers. This feature is turned on by default for RGB and CMYK documents, and options can be accessed in Preferences by clicking the GPU Performance icon in the Application bar.

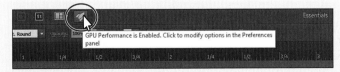

To learn more about GPU performance, visit:
https://helpx.adobe.com/illustrator/kb/gpu-performance-preview-improvements.html

Scrolling through a document

In Illustrator, you can use the Hand tool (✋) to pan to different areas of a document. Using the Hand tool allows you to push the document around much like you would a piece of paper on your desk. In this section, you'll access the Hand tool using a few methods.

1   With the Hand tool (✋) selected in the Tools panel, drag down in the Document window. As you drag, the artwork moves with the hand.

    As with the Zoom tool ($\mathbf{Q}$), you can select the Hand tool with a keyboard shortcut without first deselecting the active tool.

2   Click any other tool except the Type tool ($\mathbf{T}$) in the Tools panel, and move the pointer into the Document window. Hold down the spacebar on the keyboard to temporarily select the Hand tool, and then drag to bring the artwork back into the center of your view.

● **Note:** The spacebar shortcut for the Hand tool (✋) does not work when the Type tool ($\mathbf{T}$) is active *and* the cursor is in text. To access the Hand tool when the cursor is in text, press the Option (Mac OS) or Alt (Windows) key.

Touch workspace

In Adobe Illustrator CC, the Touch workspace is designed for Windows 8– and Windows 10–powered touch-enabled devices. The touch layout has a cleaner interface that allows you to comfortably use a stylus or your fingertip to access the tools and controls of the Touch workspace.

You can create logos, create icons, explore custom lettering and typography, create UI wireframes, and more. The Touch workspace brings traditional drawing templates and French curves to the Illustrator workspace. These shapes project a scalable, movable outline that can be traced against to quickly create refined curves.

At any time (on a supported device), you can immediately switch between the Touch and traditional workspaces to access the full range of Illustrator tools and controls. For more information on working with touch devices and Illustrator, visit Help (Help > Illustrator Help).

On touch devices (a Direct touch device [a touchscreen device], or an Indirect touch device [the Trackpad on a Mac computer], touchpads, or the Wacom Intuos5 device), you can also use standard touch gestures (pinch and swipe) to do the following:

* Pinch in or out, using two fingers (like the thumb and forefinger) to zoom
* Place two fingers on the document, and move the fingers together to pan within the document
* Swipe or flick to navigate artboards
* In artboard editing mode, use two fingers to rotate the artboard by 90°

Viewing artwork

When you open a file, it is automatically displayed in Preview mode, which shows how the artwork will print. Illustrator offers other ways of viewing your artwork, such as outlines and rasterized.

Next, you'll take a look at the different methods for viewing artwork and understand why you might view artwork that way.

1   Choose View > Fit Artboard In Window.

When you're working with large or complex illustrations, you may want to view only the outlines, or *wireframes*, of objects in your artwork so that the screen doesn't have to redraw the artwork each time you make a change. This is called Outline mode. Outline mode can also be helpful when selecting objects, as you will see in Lesson 2, "Techniques for Selecting Artwork."

2   Choose View > Outline.

Only the outlines of the objects are displayed. You can use this view to find and easily select objects that might not be visible in Preview mode.

> **Tip:** You can press Command+Y (Mac OS) or Ctrl+Y (Windows) to toggle between Preview and Outline modes.

3   Choose View > GPU Preview (or View > Preview On CPU if GPU Preview is not supported) to see all the attributes of the artwork.

Note: When switching between viewing modes, visual changes may not be readily apparent. Zooming in and out (View > Zoom In and View > Zoom Out) may help you see the differences more easily.

4   Choose View > Overprint Preview to view any lines or shapes that are set to overprint.

This view is helpful for those in the print industry who need to see how inks interact when set to overprint.

5   Choose View > Pixel Preview.

Pixel preview can be used to see how the artwork will look when it is rasterized and viewed onscreen in a web browser.

 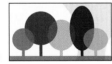 

Preview mode   Outline mode   Overprint mode   Pixel Preview mode

6   Choose View > Pixel Preview to turn off pixel preview.

7   Choose View > Fit Artboard In Window to make sure that the entire active artboard is fit in the Document window and leave the document open.

Zooming and panning with the Navigator panel

The Navigator panel is another way to navigate a document with a single artboard or multiple artboards. This is useful when you need to see all artboards in the document in one window and to edit content in any of those artboards in a zoomed-in view. You can open the Navigator panel by choosing Window > Navigator. It is in a free-floating group in the workspace.

The Navigator panel can be used in several ways, including the following:

- The red box in the Navigator panel, called the *proxy view area*, indicates the area of the document that is being shown.

- Type in a zoom value or click the mountain icons to change the magnification of your artwork.

- Position the pointer inside the proxy view area of the Navigator panel. When the pointer becomes a hand (🖑), drag to pan to different parts of the artwork.

Navigating artboards

Artboards represent the regions that can contain printable artwork (similar to pages in a program like Adobe InDesign). You can use artboards to crop areas for printing or placement purposes. Multiple artboards are useful for creating a variety of things, such as multiple-page PDFs, printed pages with different sizes or different elements, independent elements for websites, video storyboards, or individual items for animation in Adobe Flash® or Adobe After Effects. You can easily share content among designs, create multi-page PDFs, and print multiple pages by creating more than one artboard.

Illustrator allows for up to 100 artboards within a single file (depending on their size). Multiple artboards can be added when you initially create an Illustrator document or you can add, remove, and edit artboards after the document is created. Next, you will learn how to efficiently navigate a document that contains multiple artboards.

1 Choose File > Open. If a panel appears, click Open in the panel. You could also choose File > Open again. In the Open dialog box, navigate to the Lessons > Lesson01 folder and select the L1_start2.ai file on your hard disk. Click Open to open the file.

Note: At the time that this book was going to press, the panel named "Recent Files" was added to Illustrator, introducing a new way to open files.

2 Choose View > Fit All In Window to fit all artboards in the Document window. Notice that there are two artboards in the document that contain the designs for a business flyer and the front of a postcard.

The artboards in a document can be arranged in any order, orientation, or artboard size—they can even overlap. Suppose that you want to create a four-page brochure. You can create different artboards for every page of the brochure, all with the same size and orientation. They can be arranged horizontally or vertically or in whatever way you like.

3 Select the Selection tool (▶) in the Tools panel, and click to select the "GRAND OPENING CELEBRATION" text on the smaller artboard on the right.

4 Choose View > Fit Artboard In Window.

When you select artwork, it makes the artboard that the artwork is on the active artboard. By choosing the Fit Artboard In Window command, the currently active artboard is fit in the window. The active artboard is identified in the Artboard Navigation menu in the lower-left corner of the Document window.

● **Note:** Learn how to work more with artboards in Lesson 5, "Transforming Artwork."

5 Choose 1 Artboard 1 from the Artboard Navigation menu in the lower-left corner. The larger flyer appears in the Document window.

6 Choose View > Zoom Out.

Notice the arrows to the right and left of the Artboard Navigation menu. You can use these to navigate to the first (◀|), previous (◀), next (▶), and last (|▶) artboards.

7 Click the Next navigation button (▶) to view the next artboard (Artboard 2) in the Document window.

8 Choose Select > Deselect to deselect the text.

Using the Artboards panel

Another method for navigating multiple artboards is to use the Artboards panel. Next, you will open the Artboards panel and navigate the document.

1 Choose Window > Artboards to show the Artboards panel that is docked on the right side of the workspace.

The Artboards panel lists all artboards in the document. This panel allows you to navigate between artboards, rename artboards, add or delete artboards, edit artboard settings, and more.

2 Double-click the number 1 that appears to the left of the name "Artboard 1" in the Artboards panel. This fits Artboard 1 in the Document window.

3 Double-click the number 2 to the left of the name "Artboard 2" in the Artboards panel to show the smaller artboard in the Document window again.

Note: Double-clicking the artboard name in the Artboards panel allows you to change the name of the artboard. Clicking the artboard icon (▣) or (▢) to the right of the artboard name in the panel allows you to edit artboard options.

Notice that when you double-click to navigate to an artboard, that artboard is fit in the Document window.

4 Click the Artboards panel icon (▦) in the dock to collapse the panel.

Arranging multiple documents

There will be times where you open more than one Illustrator document at a time When you open more than one document, the Document windows are tabbed. You can arrange the open documents in other ways, such as side by side, so that you can easily compare or drag items from one document to another. You can also use the Arrange Documents window to quickly display your open documents in a variety of configurations.

You should currently have two Illustrator files open: L1_start1.ai and L1_start2.ai. Each file has its own tab at the top of the Document window. These documents are considered a group of Document windows. You can create document groups to loosely associate files while they are open.

1 Click the L1_start1.ai document tab to show L1_start1.ai in the Document window.

2 Click and drag the L1_start1.ai document tab to the right of the L1_start2.ai document tab. Release the mouse button to see the new tab order.

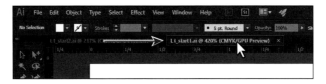

Note: Be careful to drag directly to the right. Otherwise, you could undock the Document window and create a new group. If that happens, choose Window > Arrange > Consolidate All Windows.

Dragging the document tabs allows you to change the order of the documents. This can be very useful if you use the document shortcuts to navigate to the next or previous document. These two documents are marketing pieces for the same company. To see both of them at one time, perhaps to copy a logo between them, you can arrange the Document windows by cascading the windows or tiling them. *Cascading* allows you to cascade (stack) different document groups. *Tiling* shows multiple Document windows at one time, in various arrangements.

Tip: You can cycle between open documents by pressing Command+~ (next document), Command+Shift+~ (previous document) (Mac OS) or Ctrl+F6 (next document), Ctrl+Shift+F6 (previous document) (Windows).

Next, you will tile the open documents so that you can see them both at one time. In Illustrator, all the workspace elements are grouped in a single, integrated window that lets you treat the application as a single unit. When you move or resize the Application frame or any of its elements, all the elements within it respond to each other so none overlap.

If you are using a Mac and prefer the traditional, free-form user interface, you can turn off the Application frame by choosing Window > Application Frame to toggle it on or off.

3 Choose Window > Arrange > Tile.

This shows both Document windows arranged in a pattern.

Note: Your documents may be tiled in a different order. That's okay.

4 Click in each of the Document windows to activate the documents and choose View > Fit Artboard In Window for each of the documents. Also, make sure that Artboard 1 is showing for each document in the Document window.

With documents tiled, you can drag the dividing line between each of the Document windows to reveal more or less of a particular document. You can also drag artwork between documents, which copies them from one document to another.

To change the arrangement of the tiled windows, it's possible to drag document tabs to new positions. However, it's easier to use the Arrange Documents window to quickly arrange open documents in a variety of configurations.

5 Click the Arrange Documents button (⬛▾) in the Application bar to display the Arrange Documents window. Click the Consolidate All button (⬛) to bring the documents back together.

Note: On the Mac OS, the menu bar is above the Application bar. Also, depending on the resolution of your screen, the Windows menus may appear in the Application bar.

6 Click the Arrange Documents button (⬛▾) in the Application bar to display the Arrange Documents window again. Click the 2-Up vertical button (⬚) in the Arrange Documents window.

7 Click to select the L1_start1.ai tab, if it is not already selected. Then, click the Close button (X) on the L1_start1.ai document tab to close the document. If a dialog box appears asking you to save the document, click Don't Save (Mac OS) or No (Windows).

8 Choose File > Close to close the L1_start2.ai document without saving.

▶ **Tip:** You can also choose Window > Arrange > Consolidate All Windows to return the two documents to tabs in the same group.

Finding resources for using Illustrator

For complete and up-to-date information about using Illustrator panels, tools, and other application features, visit the Adobe website. By choosing Help > Illustrator Help, you'll be connected to the Illustrator Help website, where you can search Illustrator Help and support documents, as well as other websites relevant to Illustrator users. Community Help brings together active Adobe product users, Adobe product team members, authors, and experts to give you the most useful, relevant, and up-to-date information about Adobe products.

If you choose Help > Illustrator Help, you can also download a PDF of the Illustrator Help content by clicking the download link for your version.

Data Recovery

If Illustrator crashes, you no longer have to lose work. When Illustrator restarts after a crash, you have the option of recovering work-in-progress files so that your hours of work are not wasted. The recovered files are opened with the "[Recovered]" in the filename.

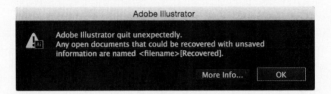

You can turn data recovery on and off as well as set options such as how often to save recovery data in the program preferences (Illustrator CC > Preferences > File Handling & Clipboard [Mac OS] or Edit > Preferences > File Handling & Clipboard [Windows]).

Review questions

1 Describe two ways to change the view of a document.

2 How do you select a tool in Illustrator?

3 How do you save panel locations and visibility preferences?

4 Describe three ways to navigate among artboards in Illustrator.

5 Describe how arranging Document windows can be helpful.

Review answers

1 You can choose commands from the View menu to zoom in or out of a document or to fit it to your screen; you can also use the Zoom tool (🔍) in the Tools panel and click or drag over a document to enlarge or reduce the view. In addition, you can use keyboard shortcuts to magnify or reduce the display of artwork. You can also use the Navigator panel to scroll artwork or to change its magnification without using the Document window.

2 To select a tool, you can either click the tool in the Tools panel or press the keyboard shortcut for that tool. For example, you can press V to select the Selection tool (▶) from the keyboard. Selected tools remain active until you click a different tool.

3 You can save panel locations and visibility preferences by choosing Window > Workspace > New Workspace to create custom work areas and to make it easier to find the controls that you need.

4 To navigate among artboards in Illustrator, you can choose the artboard number from the Artboard Navigation menu at the lower-left of the Document window; you can use the Artboard Navigation arrows in the lower-left of the Document window to go to the first, previous, next, and last artboards; you can use the Artboards panel to navigate to an artboard; or you can use the Navigator panel to drag the proxy view area to navigate between artboards.

5 Arranging Document windows allows you to tile windows or to cascade document groups. This can be useful if you are working on multiple Illustrator files and you need to compare or share content among them.

2 TECHNIQUES FOR SELECTING ARTWORK

Lesson overview

In this lesson, you'll learn how to do the following:

- Differentiate between the various selection tools and use different selection techniques.

- Recognize Smart Guides.

- Save selections for future use.

- Use tools and commands to align shapes and points to each other and the artboard.

- Group and ungroup items.

- Work in Isolation mode.

- Arrange content.

- Select objects that are behind other objects.

- Hide and lock items for organizational purposes.

This lesson takes approximately 45 minutes to complete.

Download the project files for this lesson from the Lesson & Update Files tab on your Account page at www.peachpit.com and store them on your computer in a convenient location, as described in the "Getting Started" section of this book.

Your Account page is also where you'll find any updates to the chapters or to the lesson files. Look on the Lesson & Update Files tab to access the most current content.

Selecting content in Adobe Illustrator is one of the more important things you'll do. In this lesson, you learn how to locate and select objects using the Selection tools; protect other objects by grouping, hiding, and locking them; align objects to each other and the artboard; and much more.

Getting started

When changing colors or size and adding effects or attributes, you must first select the object to which you are applying the changes. In this lesson, you will learn the fundamentals of using the selection tools. More advanced selection techniques using layers are discussed in Lesson 9, "Organizing Your Artwork with Layers."

● **Note:** If you have not already downloaded the project files for this lesson to your computer from your Account page, make sure to do so now. See "Getting Started" at the beginning of the book.

1   To ensure that the tools and panels function exactly as described in this lesson, delete or deactivate (by renaming) the Adobe Illustrator CC preferences file. See "Restoring default preferences" in the "Getting Started" section at the beginning of the book.

2   Start Adobe Illustrator CC.

3   Choose File > Open, and open the L2_start.ai file in the Lesson02 folder, located in the Lessons folder on your hard disk.

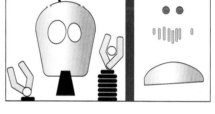

4   Choose View > Fit All In Window.

5   Choose Window > Workspace > Essentials, make sure it's selected, and then choose Window > Workspace > Reset Essentials to reset the workspace.

Selecting objects

Whether you are creating artwork from scratch or editing existing artwork in Illustrator, you will need to become familiar with selecting objects. There are many methods and tools for doing this, and in this section, you'll explore the most widely used, which includes the Selection (▶) and Direct Selection (▷) tools.

Using the Selection tool

The Selection tool (▶) in the Tools panel lets you select, move, and resize entire objects. In this first section, you'll become familiar with the tool.

1   Select the Selection tool (▶) in the Tools panel, if it's not already selected. Move the pointer over different shapes on the artboards, without clicking.

The icon that appears as you pass over objects (▶.) indicates that there is artwork that can be selected under the pointer. When you hover over an object, that object is also outlined in a color like blue (in this instance).

2   Select the Zoom tool (🔍) in the Tools panel, and click several times slowly on the two red circles on the artboard on the right to zoom in.

3 Select the Selection tool in the Tools panel, and then position the pointer over the black edge of the red circle on the left. A word such as "path" or "anchor" may appear, because Smart Guides are turned on by default.

Smart Guides are temporary snap-to guides that help you align, edit, and transform objects or artboards.

▶ **Tip:** You'll learn more about Smart Guides in Lesson 3, "Using Shapes to Create Artwork for a Postcard."

4 Click anywhere inside the red circle on the left to select it. A bounding box with eight handles appears.

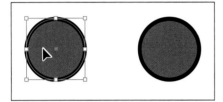

The *bounding box* is used when making changes to artwork (vector or raster), such as resizing or rotating. The bounding box also indicates that an item is selected and ready to be modified, and the color of the bounding box indicates which layer the object is on. Layers are discussed more in Lesson 9.

5 Using the Selection tool, click in the red circle on the right. Notice that the left red circle is now deselected and only the right circle is selected.

6 Holding down the Shift key, click the left red circle to add it to the selection, and then release the key. Both red circles are now selected, and a larger bounding box surrounds them.

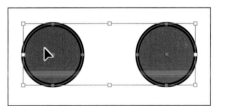

● **Note:** To select an item without a fill, you can click the stroke (the edge) or drag a selection marquee across the object.

7 Move the circles anywhere in the document by clicking inside either selected circle (in the red area) and dragging. Because both circles are selected, they move together.

As you drag, you may notice the magenta lines that appear. These are called *alignment guides* and are visible because Smart Guides are turned on (View > Smart Guides). As you drag, the objects are aligned to other objects on the artboard. Also notice the measurement label (gray box) next to the pointer that shows the object's distance from its original position. Measurement labels also appear because Smart Guides are turned on.

8 Deselect the circles by clicking a blank area of the artboard or by choosing Select > Deselect.

9 Revert to the last saved version of the document by choosing File > Revert. In the dialog box that appears, click Revert.

Using the Direct Selection tool

In Illustrator, as you draw, you create vector paths that are made up of anchor points and paths. Anchor points are used to control the shape of the path and work like pins holding a wire in place. A shape you create, like a square, is composed of at least four anchor points on the corners with paths in between the anchor points. You change the shape of a path or shape by dragging its anchor points (among other things). The Direct Selection (➤) tool selects anchor points or path segments within an object so that it can be reshaped. Next, you will become familiar with selecting anchor points using the Direct Selection tool and reshaping a path.

1 Choose View > Fit All In Window.

2 Select the Zoom tool (🔍) in the Tools panel, and click several times on the series of orange shapes below the red circles you selected previously to zoom in.

Tip: You can also click in the middle of a shape to select it and to see the anchor points around its edge. This can be an easy way to see where the points are, and then you can click a point to select it.

3 Select the Direct Selection tool (➤) in the Tools panel. Without clicking, position the pointer over the top edge of one of the orange shapes. Move the pointer along the top edge of the shape until the word "anchor" appears by the pointer.

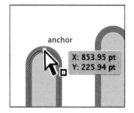

When the Direct Selection tool is over an anchor point of a path or object, the word "anchor" appears. The "anchor" label is showing because Smart Guides are turned on (View > Smart Guides). Also notice the little white box to the right of the pointer. The small dot that appears in the center of the white box indicates that the cursor is positioned over an anchor point.

4 Click to select that anchor point.

Notice that only the anchor point you selected is solid (filled), indicating that it is selected, and the other anchor points in the shape are hollow, indicating that they are not selected. Also notice the small blue lines extending from the selected anchor point. These are called *direction lines*. The angle and length of the direction lines determine the shape and size of the curved segments. Moving the direction points (at the end of the direction lines) can reshape the path.

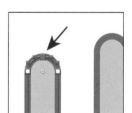

Note: The gray measurement label that appears as you drag the anchor point has the values dX and dY. *dX* indicates the distance that the pointer has moved along the x-axis (horizontal), and *dY* indicates the distance that the pointer has moved along the y-axis (vertical).

5 With the Direct Selection tool still selected, drag the selected anchor point up to edit the shape of the object.

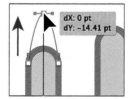

6 Try clicking another point on the edge of the shape, and notice that the previous point is deselected.

7 Revert to the last saved version of the file by choosing File > Revert. In the dialog box that appears, click Revert.

Exploring selection and anchor point preferences

To display selection and anchor point preferences, choose

- Illustrator CC > Preferences > Selection & Anchor Display (Mac OS)
- Edit > Preferences > Selection & Anchor Display (Windows)

You can change the size of anchor points (called *anchors* in the dialog box) or the display of the direction handles (called *handles* in the dialog box), among other settings related to paths.

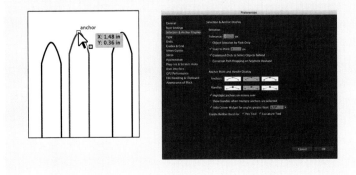

Creating selections with a marquee

Another way to select content is by dragging a marquee around the objects that you want to select, which is what you'll do next.

1 Choose View > Fit All In Window.

2 Select the Zoom tool (🔍) in the Tools panel, and click three times, slowly, on the red circles.

3 Select the Selection tool (▶) in the Tools panel. Position the pointer above and to the left of the leftmost red circle, and then drag downward and to the right to create a marquee that overlaps just the tops of the circles.

> **Tip:** When dragging with the Selection tool (▶), you need to encompass only a small part of an object to select it.

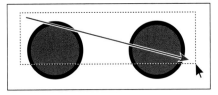
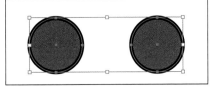

4 Choose Select > Deselect, or click where there are no objects.

Now you'll use the Direct Selection tool to select multiple anchor points in the red circles by dragging a marquee around anchor points.

5 Select the Direct Selection tool (⬚) in the Tools panel. Starting off the top-left of the leftmost red circle (see the figure), drag across the top edges of the two circles. Only the top anchor points become selected.

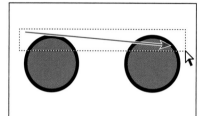 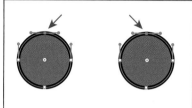

● **Note:** Selecting points using this method might take some practice. You'll need to drag across only the points you want selected; otherwise, more points will be selected. You can always click away from the objects to deselect them and then try again.

6 Click and drag one of the selected anchor points to see how the anchor points reposition together.

You can use this method when selecting points so that you don't have to click exactly on the anchor point that you want to select.

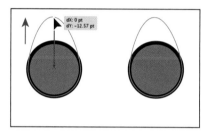

7 Revert to the last saved version of the file by choosing File > Revert. In the dialog box that appears, click Revert.

Selecting artwork with the Magic Wand tool

You can use the Magic Wand tool (🪄) to select all objects in a document that have the same attributes, like a color fill. The fill is a color applied to the inside of an object. You can customize the Magic Wand tool to select objects based on options, like stroke weight, stroke color, and more, by double-clicking the Magic Wand tool in the Tools panel.

Next, you'll select artwork with the Magic Wand tool.

1 Select the Selection tool (▶), and click in a blank area of the smaller artboard on the right. This makes that artboard the active artboard.

2 Choose View > Fit Artboard In Window.

3 Select the Magic Wand tool (🪄) in the Tools panel. Click one of the red circles on the right artboard, and notice that the other red circle becomes selected as well.

No bounding box (a box surrounding the two shapes) appears because the Magic Wand tool is still selected.

4 Holding down the Shift key, notice that the pointer has a plus sign (+) next to it. Click one of the orange shapes (below the red shapes) with the Magic Wand tool, and then release the key.

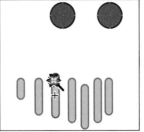

This adds all of the shapes filled with that same orange color to the selection.

5 With the Magic Wand tool still selected, hold down the Option key (Mac OS) or Alt key (Windows) and notice that a minus sign (−) appears next to the pointer. Click one of the orange shapes to deselect all of the shapes with that same fill, and then release the key. The red circles should still be selected.

6 Choose Select > Deselect, or click where there are no objects.

Selecting similar objects

You can also select objects based on similar fill color, stroke color, stroke weight, and more, using the Select Similar Objects button or the Select > Same command. The stroke of an object is the outline (border), and the stroke weight is the width of the stroke. Next, you will select several objects with the same fill and stroke applied.

1 Select the Selection tool ( ), and click to select one of the red circles.

2 Click the arrow to the right of the Select Similar Objects button ( ) in the Control panel to show a menu. Choose Fill Color to select all objects on any artboard with the same fill color (red) as the selected object.

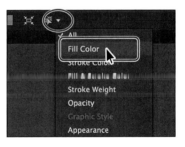

Notice that the circles with the same red-colored fill are selected.

3 Click to select one of the orange shapes, and then choose Select > Same > Fill & Stroke.

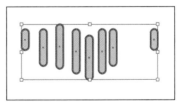

All of the orange-filled shapes with the same stroke and fill and are now selected.

If you know that you may need to reselect a series of objects again, like the orange objects, you can save the selection you make so that you can easily recall it later. Saved selections are saved only with that document. That's what you'll do next.

4 With the orange shapes still selected, choose Select > Save Selection. Name the selection **RobotMouth** in the Save Selection dialog box, and click OK so that you'll be able to choose this selection at a later time.

5 Choose Select > Deselect.

> **Tip:** It is helpful to name selections according to use or function. If you name the selection "1 pt stroke," for instance, the name may be misleading if you later change the stroke weight of the artwork.

Selecting in Outline mode

By default, Adobe Illustrator displays all artwork with their paint attributes, like fill and stroke, showing. However, you can choose to display artwork so that only outlines (or paths) are visible. The next method for selecting involves viewing artwork in Outline mode and can be very useful if you want to select objects within a series of stacked objects.

1 Choose View > Fit Artboard In Window to fit the artboard with the orange shapes into the Document window, if necessary.

2 With the Selection tool (▶), click within the gray half-circle shape at the bottom of the artboard to select it. This will become the body of the robot.

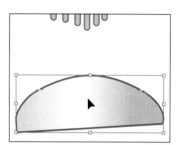

Since the shape has a fill (a color, pattern, or gradient filling the inside of an object), you can click anywhere within the bounds of the object to select it.

3 Choose Select > Deselect to deselect the shape.

4 Choose View > Outline to view the artwork as outlines.

5 With the Selection tool, click inside that same half-circle shape.

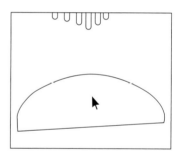

Notice that you cannot select the object using this method. Outline mode displays artwork as outlines with no fill. To select in Outline mode, you can click the edge of the object or drag a marquee across the shape to select it.

6 Click the Previous artboard button (◀) in the lower-left corner of the Document window to fit the first artboard in the window.

7 On the left artboard, with the Selection tool selected, drag a marquee across the right (smaller) ellipse that makes the robot's eye. Press the Left Arrow key several times to move the ellipse so that it almost touches the ellipse to the left.

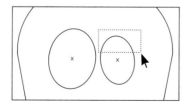 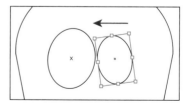

8 Choose View > GPU Preview or View > Preview On CPU, if not available, to see the painted artwork.

Aligning objects

Illustrator makes it easy to align or distribute multiple objects relative to each other, the artboard, or a key object. In this section, you'll explore the different options for aligning objects.

Aligning objects to each other

One type of alignment is aligning objects to each other, and that's what you'll do next.

1   Choose Select > RobotMouth to reselect the orange shapes.

2   Click the Next artboard button (▶) in the lower-left corner of the Document window to fit the artboard with the orange and red shapes in the window.

3   Select the Zoom tool (Q) in the Tools panel, and click several times on the orange-filled shapes to zoom in.

4   Choose Align To Selection from the Align To button (▦▾) in the Control panel, if it's not already selected, to ensure that the selected objects are aligned to each other.

● **Note:** The Align options may not appear in the Control panel. If you don't see the Align options, click the word "Align" in the Control panel to open the Align panel. The number of options displayed in the Control panel depends on your screen resolution.

5   Click the Vertical Align Bottom button (▥) in the Control panel.

Notice that the bottom edges of all the orange objects move to align with the lowest orange object.

6   Choose Edit > Undo Align to return the objects to their original positions. Leave the objects selected for the next section.

Aligning to a key object

A *key object* is an object that you want other objects to align to. You specify a key object by selecting all the objects you want to align, including the key object, and then clicking the key object again. When selected, the key object has a thick outline, and the Align To Key Object icon (▦▾) appears in the Control panel and the Align panel. Next, you will align the orange shapes.

● **Note:** The key object outline color is determined by the layer color that the object is on.

▶ **Tip:** In the Align panel, you can choose Show Options from the panel menu (▤) and then choose Align To Key Object from the Align To option. The object that is in front becomes the key object.

1   With the orange shapes still selected, click the leftmost shape with the Selection tool (▶).

The thick blue outline indicates that the leftmost shape is the key object that other objects will align to.

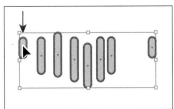

Note: To stop aligning and distributing relative to an object, click the object again to remove the blue outline, or choose Cancel Key Object from the Align panel menu (■).

2 Click the Vertical Align Top button (■) in the Align options in the Control panel. Notice that all of the orange shapes move to align to the top edge of the key object.

3 Choose Select > Deselect.

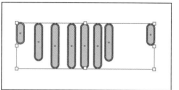

Aligning anchor points

Next, you'll align two anchor points to each other using the Align options. Like setting a key object in the previous section, you can also set a key anchor point that other anchor points will align to.

1 Choose View > Fit Artboard In Window.

2 Select the Direct Selection tool (�)), and click the lower-left corner point of the gray half-circle at the bottom of the artboard. Shift-click to select the lower-right point of the same gray half-circle (see the following figure).

You select the points in a specific order because the last selected anchor point is the key anchor point. Other points align to this point.

3 Click the Vertical Align Top button (■) in the Control panel. The first anchor point selected aligns to the second anchor point selected.

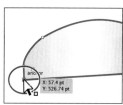
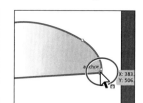
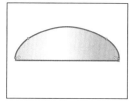

Select the first point.   Select the second point.   After aligning the points.

4 Choose Select > Deselect.

Distributing objects

Distributing objects using the Align panel enables you to select multiple objects and distribute the spacing between the centers or edges of those objects equally. Next, you will make the spacing between the orange shapes even.

Note: Using the Horizontal Distribute Center or Vertical Distribute Center button distributes the spacing equally between the *centers* of the objects. If the selected objects are not the same size, unexpected results may occur.

1 Select the Selection tool (▶) in the Tools panel. Choose Select > RobotMouth to reselect all the orange shapes.

2 Click the Horizontal Distribute Center button (■) in the Control panel.

Distributing moves all the orange shapes so that the spacing between the *center* of each of them is equal.

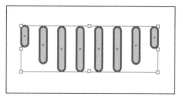

3 Choose Edit > Undo Align.

4 Choose Select > Deselect.

5 Choose View > Zoom In, twice, to zoom in to the orange shapes.

6 With the Selection tool selected, hold down the Shift key and drag the rightmost orange shape slightly to the left. Stop dragging just before the shape touches the orange shape to its left. Release the mouse button and then the key.

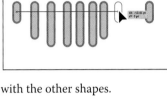

The Shift key keeps the shape aligned vertically with the other shapes.

7 Choose Select > RobotMouth to select all of the orange shapes again, and then click the Horizontal Distribute Center button (▨) again. Notice that, with the rightmost shape repositioned, the objects move to redistribute the spacing between the centers.

8 Choose Select > Deselect.

● **Note:** When distributing objects horizontally, make sure that the leftmost and rightmost objects are where you want them, and then distribute the objects between them. For vertical distribution, position the topmost and bottommost objects, and then distribute the objects between them.

Aligning to the artboard

You can also align content to the artboard rather than to a selection or a key object. Aligning to the artboard aligns each selected object separately to the artboard. Next, you'll get the gray half-circle shape on the artboard with the rest of the robot and align it to the bottom center of the artboard.

1 With the Selection tool (▶) selected, click the gray half-circle shape at the bottom of the artboard to select it. Choose Edit > Cut.

2 Click the Previous artboard button (◀) in the lower-left corner of the Document window to navigate to the first (left) artboard in the document, which contains the robot head.

3 Choose Edit > Paste to paste the gray half-circle.

4 Click the Align To Selection button (▨▾) in the Control panel, and choose Align To Artboard in the menu that appears. Selected content will now align to the artboard.

▶ **Tip:** If you need a refresher on the Align To Selection button, refer to the "Aligning objects to each other" section.

5 Click the Horizontal Align Center button (▨) (just in case), and then click the Vertical Align Bottom button (▨) to align the selection to the horizontal center and vertical bottom of the artboard.

6 Choose Select > Deselect.

Working with groups

You can combine objects into a group so that the objects are treated as a single unit. This way, you can move or transform a number of objects without affecting their individual attributes or positions relative to each other.

Grouping items

Next, you will select multiple objects and create a group from them.

1   Choose View > Fit All In Window to see both artboards.

2   Choose Select > RobotMouth to reselect the series of orange shapes.

3   Choose Object > Group, and notice that the word "Group" appears in the Selection Indicator on the left side of the Control panel with the shapes still selected.

4   Choose Select > Deselect.

> **Tip:** One way to select the objects in a group individually is to select the group and then choose Object > Ungroup. This ungroups them permanently.

5   With the Selection tool (➤) selected, click one of the orange shapes in the group. Because they are grouped together, all are now selected.

6   Drag the group of orange shapes onto the robot head (below the eyes).

7   Choose Select > Deselect.

Working in Isolation mode

Isolation mode isolates groups (or sublayers) so that you can easily select and edit specific objects or parts of objects without having to ungroup the objects. When in Isolation mode, all objects outside of the isolated group are locked and dimmed so that they aren't affected by the edits you make.

Next, you will edit a group using Isolation mode.

1   With the Selection tool (➤), click the robot's hand at the end of the longer arm. You will see that it selects a group of shapes that make up the hand.

> **Tip:** To enter Isolation mode, you can also select a group with the Selection tool and then click the Isolate Selected Object button (▣) in the Control panel.

2   Double-click a shape in that hand to enter Isolation mode.

3   Choose View > Fit Artboard In Window, and notice that the rest of the content in the document appears dimmed (you can't select it).

At the top of the Document window, a gray bar appears with the words "Layer 1" and "<Group>." This indicates that you have isolated a group of objects that is on Layer 1. You will learn more about layers in Lesson 9.

4 Choose View > Smart Guides to turn them off. Smart guides make it so that content snap-aligns to other content, and right now you don't want that.

5 Drag the light-gray circle down to approximately match the position of the circle shape in the other hand.

When you enter Isolation mode, groups are temporarily ungrouped. This enables you to edit objects in the group or to add new content without having to ungroup.

6 Double-click outside of the shapes within the group to exit Isolation mode.

▶ **Tip:** To exit Isolation mode, you can also click the gray arrow in the upper-left corner of the Document window or deselect all content and click the Exit Isolation Mode button (◀) in the Control panel. You can also press the Escape key when in Isolation mode or double-click a blank area of the Document window to exit Isolation mode.

7 Click to select the same circle shape. Notice that it is once again grouped with the rest of the shapes in the hand, and you can also select other objects.

8 Choose Select > Deselect.

Creating a nested group

Groups can also be *nested*—grouped within other objects or grouped to form larger groups. Nesting is a common technique used when designing artwork. It's a great way to keep associated content together.

In this section, you will explore how to create a nested group

1 With the Selection tool (▶), drag a marquee across the series of black shapes below the hand that make up the longer arm of the robot.

2 Choose Object > Group.

3 With the Selection tool, Shift-click the hand above the arm to select that group as well. Choose Object > Group.

You have created a *nested group*—a group that is combined with other objects or groups to form a larger group.

4 Choose Select > Deselect.

5 With the Selection tool, click one of the grouped objects in that same arm. All objects in the nested group become selected.

6 Click a blank area on the artboard to deselect the objects.

Selecting using the Group Selection tool

Instead of ungrouping a group to select the content within, the Group Selection tool (⯈⁺) lets you select an object within a group, a single group within multiple groups, or a set of groups within the artwork. Next, you will explore the Group Selection (⯈⁺) tool.

1   Hold down on the Direct Selection tool (⯈) in the Tools panel to reveal more tools. Click the Group Selection tool (⯈⁺) to select it. The Group Selection tool adds the object's parent group(s) to the current selection.

2   Click one of the shapes in the same robot hand to select it. Click again, on the same shape, to select the object's parent group (the group of hand shapes). Click once more, on that same shape, to select the group composed of the hand and arm. The Group Selection tool adds each group to the selection in the order in which it was grouped.

 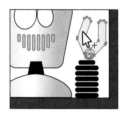 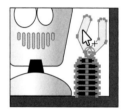

Click once.   Click twice to select   Click a third time to select all
                  the parent group.   artwork in the nested group.

3   Choose Select > Deselect.

● **Note:** To ungroup *all* of the selected objects, even the hand and arm shapes, you would choose Object > Ungroup twice.

4   With the Selection tool (⯈), click any of the objects in the nested group to select the group. Choose Object > Ungroup to ungroup the objects.

5   Choose Select > Deselect.

6   Click to select the hand. Notice that it is still a group of objects.

Exploring object arrangement

▶ **Tip:** To learn more about objects and stacking order, see the PDF "Stack_order.pdf" in the Lessons > Lesson_extras folder.

As you create objects, Illustrator stacks them in order on the artboards, beginning with the first object created. The order in which objects are stacked (called *stacking order*) determines how they display when they overlap. You can change the stacking order of objects in your artwork at any time, using either the Layers panel or Object > Arrange commands.

Arranging objects

Next, you will work with the Arrange commands to change how objects are stacked.

1   Choose View > Fit All In Window to see both artboards in the document.

2 With the Selection tool (▶) selected, click to select the black shape below the robot's head (the robot's "neck").

3 Choose Object > Arrange > Send To Back to send the shape behind the robot's head.

4 Click to select either of the red circles on the right artboard.

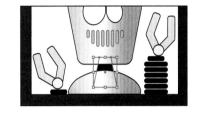

5 Drag the selected circle on top of the smaller eye for the robot. Release the mouse, and notice that the red circle disappears, but it's still selected.

It went behind the ellipse (the eye) because it was probably created before the eye shape, which means it is lower in the stacking order.

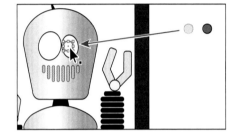

6 With the red circle still selected, choose Object > Arrange > Bring To Front. This brings the red circle to the front of the stack, making it the topmost object.

Selecting objects behind

When you stack objects on top of each other, sometimes it becomes difficult to select objects that are underneath other objects. Next, you will learn how to select an object through a stack of objects.

1 With the Selection tool (▶), select the other red circle on the right artboard, drag it onto the larger robot eye shape on the left artboard, and then release the mouse.

Notice that this circle disappears like the other but is still selected.
This time, you will deselect the circle and then reselect it using another method.

2 Choose Select > Deselect, and the red circle is no longer selected.

3 With the pointer positioned over the location of the second red circle you just deselected, the one behind the eye shape, hold down the Command (Mac OS) or Ctrl (Windows) key, and click until the circle is selected again (this may take several clicks).

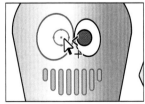

● **Note:** You may see an angle bracket displayed with the pointer (▶<).

● **Note:** To select the hidden red circle, make sure that you click where the circle and the eye overlap. Otherwise, you won't be able to select the red circle.

4 Choose Object > Arrange > Bring To Front to bring the circle on top of the eye.

5 Choose Select > Deselect.

Hiding and locking objects

▶ **Tip:** To learn more selection techniques, see the PDF named "Selections.pdf" in the Lesson_extras folder in the Lessons folder.

When working on complex artwork, it may become more difficult to make selections. In this section, you'll learn how to lock and hide content to make selecting objects easier.

1 Choose View > Fit Artboard In Window.

2 Choose Object > Show All to reveal a mask over the robot's eyes. Choose Object > Arrange > Bring To Front to bring the mask to the front.

3 With the Selection tool (▶), click to attempt to select one of the eyes.

Notice that you can't, since the mask is on top of them. In order to access the eyes, you could use one of the methods we previously discussed or use one of two other methods: hide or lock.

4 With the mask still selected, choose Object > Hide > Selection, or press Command+3 (Mac OS) or Ctrl+3 (Windows). The mask is hidden so that you can more easily select other objects. (This is how I hid the mask when I set up the file.)

5 Click to select one of the red circles in the eyes, and move it.

6 Choose Object > Show All to show the mask again.

7 With the mask selected, choose Object > Lock > Selection, or press Command+2 (Mac OS) or Ctrl+2 (Windows).

The mask is still visible, but you cannot select it.

8 With the Selection tool, click to select one of the eye shapes.

9 Choose Object > Unlock All, and then choose Object > Hide > Selection to hide the mask again.

10 Choose View > Smart Guides to turn them on.

11 Choose File > Save to save the file, and then choose File > Close.

Review questions

1 How can you select an object that has no fill?

2 Explain two ways you can select an item in a group without choosing Object > Ungroup.

3 Of the two Selection tools (Selection [▸] and Direct Selection [▹]), which allows you to edit the individual anchor points of an object?

4 What should you do after creating a selection that you are going to use repeatedly?

5 Sometimes you are unable to select an object because it is underneath another object. Explain two ways to get around this issue.

6 To align objects to the artboard, what do you need to first select in the Align panel or Control panel before you choose an alignment option?

Review answers

1 You can select an object that has no fill by clicking the stroke or by dragging a marquee across any part of the object.

2 Using the Group Selection tool (▹+), you can click once to select an individual item within a group. Click again to add the next grouped items to the selection. Read Lesson 9, "Organizing Your Artwork with Layers," to see how you can use layers to make complex selections. You can also double-click the group to enter Isolation mode, edit the shapes as needed, and then exit Isolation mode by pressing the Escape key or by double-clicking outside of the group.

3 Using the Direct Selection tool (▹), you can select one or more individual anchor points and make changes to the shape of an object.

4 For any selection that you anticipate using again, choose Select > Save Selection. Name the selection so that you can reselect it at any time from the Select menu.

5 If your access to an object is blocked, you can choose Object > Hide > Selection to hide the blocking object. The object is not deleted. It is just hidden in the same position until you choose Object > Show All. You can also use the Selection tool (▸) to select an object that's behind other objects by pressing the Command (Mac OS) or Ctrl (Windows) key and then clicking the overlapping objects until the object you want to select is selected.

6 To align objects to an artboard, first select the Align To Artboard option.

3 USING SHAPES TO CREATE ARTWORK FOR A POSTCARD

Lesson overview

In this lesson, you'll learn how to do the following:

- Create a document with multiple artboards.
- Use tools and commands to create a variety of shapes.
- Understand Live Shapes.
- Round corners.
- Work with the Shaper tool.
- Work with drawing modes.
- Use Image Trace to create shapes.

 This lesson takes approximately 60 minutes to complete.

Download the project files for this lesson from the Lesson & Update Files tab on your Account page at www.peachpit.com and store them on your computer in a convenient location, as described in the "Getting Started" section of this book.

Your Account page is also where you'll find any updates to the chapters or to the lesson files. Look on the Lesson & Update Files tab to access the most current content.

Basic shapes are at the foundation of creating Illustrator artwork. In this lesson, you'll create a new document and then create and edit a series of shapes using the shape tools for a postcard.

Getting started

In this lesson, you'll explore the different methods for creating artwork using the shape tools and various creation methods to create artwork for a postcard.

1 To ensure that the tools and panels function exactly as described in this lesson, delete or deactivate (by renaming) the Adobe Illustrator CC preferences file. See "Restoring default preferences" in the "Getting Started" section at the beginning of the book.

2 Start Adobe Illustrator CC.

● **Note:** If you have not already downloaded the project files for this lesson to your computer from your Account page, make sure to do so now. See the "Getting Started" section at the beginning of the book.

3 Choose File > Open. Locate the file named L3_end.ai, which is in the Lesson03 folder in the Lessons folder that you copied onto your hard disk. These are the finished illustrations that you will create in this lesson.

4 Choose View > Fit All In Window; leave the file open for reference, or choose File > Close.

Creating a new document

You will now create a document for the postcard that will have two artboards, each with content that you will later combine.

1 Choose File > New to open a new, untitled document. In the New Document dialog box, change the following options:

- Name: Enter **Postcard**.
- Profile: Choose Print (the default setting).
- Number Of Artboards: Enter **2** (to create two artboards). (When you change the number of artboards, Profile changes to [Custom].)
- Arrange By Row (⭢): **Selected**.
- Make sure that the Left To Right Layout arrow (⭢) is showing.

Next, you'll jump to the units so that the rest of the changes are in inches.

- Units: **Inches**
- Spacing: **1 in** (The spacing value is the distance between each artboard.)
- Width: **6 in** (You don't need to type the **in** for inches, since the units are set to inches.)
- Height: **4.25 in**

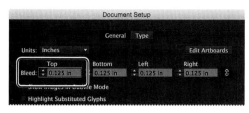

Note: You can set up a document for different kinds of output, such as print, web, video, and more, by choosing a profile. For example, if you are designing a web-page mock-up, you can use a web document profile, which automatically displays the page size and units in pixels, changes the color mode to RGB, and changes the raster effects to Screen (72 ppi).

2 Click OK in the New Document dialog box.

Tip: To learn more about the New Document dialog options, search for "New document dialog" in Illustrator Help (Help > Illustrator Help).

3 Choose File > Save As. In the Save As dialog box, ensure that the name of the file is Postcard.ai (Mac OS) or Postcard (Windows), and choose the Lesson03 folder. Leave the Format option set to Adobe Illustrator (ai) (Mac OS) or the Save As Type option set to Adobe Illustrator (*.AI) (Windows), and click Save. In the Illustrator Options dialog box, leave the Illustrator options at their default settings, and click OK.

4 Click the Document Setup button in the Control panel.

The Document Setup dialog box is where you can change the artboard size (by clicking the Edit Artboards button), units, bleeds, and more, after a document is created.

Note: If the Document Setup button does not appear in the Control panel, it may mean that content in the document is selected. You can also choose File > Document Setup.

5 In the Bleed section of the Document Setup dialog box, change the value in the Top field to **0.125 in**, either by clicking the Up Arrow to the left of the field once or by typing the value, and all four fields change. Click OK.

Notice the red line that appears around both artboards. The red line indicates the bleed area. Typical bleeds for printing are about 1/8 of an inch, but it can depend on the printing vendor.

Note: You could have set up the bleeds when you first set up the document in the New Document dialog box by choosing File > New.

Working with basic shapes

In the first part of this lesson, you'll create a series of basic shapes, such as rectangles, ellipses, rounded rectangles, polygons, and more. A shape you create is composed of *anchor points* with paths connecting the anchor points. A basic square, for instance, is composed of four anchor points on the corners with paths connecting the anchor points (see the figure at right). A shape is referred to as a *closed path*.

A path can be closed, or it can be open with distinct anchor points on each end (called *endpoints*). Both open and closed paths can have fills applied to them.

You'll begin this exercise by setting up the workspace.

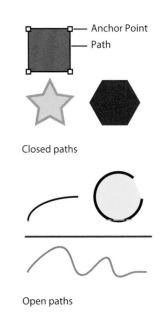

Anchor Point
Path

Closed paths

Open paths

1 Choose Window > Workspace > Essentials (if it's not already selected), and then choose Window > Workspace > Reset Essentials.

2 Choose 2 from the Artboard Navigation menu in the lower-left corner of the Document window.

3 Choose View > Fit Artboard In Window, if necessary.

Creating and editing rectangles

● **Note:** As you go through this section, know that you don't have to match the sizes of the drawn shapes exactly. They are just there as a guide.

First, you'll create a series of rectangles that will be the start of a satellite on the postcard. All of the shape tools, except for the Star tool and Flare tool, create what are called Live Shapes. This means that attributes such as width, height, rotation, corner radius, and corner style are still editable later and are retained even if you scale or rotate the shape.

1 Select the Rectangle tool (■) in the Tools panel. Position the pointer near the center of the artboard, and click and drag down and to the right. As you drag, notice the gray tooltip that appears indicating width and height. Drag until the rectangle is approximately 1.25 in wide and has a height of 1.5 in, as shown in the tooltip next to the cursor.

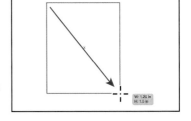

W: 1.25 in
H: 1.5 in

▶ **Tip:** Holding down Option (Mac OS) or Alt (Windows) as you drag with the Rectangle, Rounded Rectangle, or Ellipse tool draws a shape from its center point.

As you drag to create shapes, the tooltip that appears next to the pointer is called the *measurement label* and is a part of the Smart Guides (View > Smart Guides), which will be discussed throughout this lesson. When you release the mouse button, the rectangle is selected. Also, by default, shapes are filled with a white color and have a black stroke (border).

Next, you'll create another rectangle by entering values (such as width and height) rather than by drawing it. Using any of the shape tools, you can either draw a shape or click the artboard with a shape tool selected to enter values in a dialog box.

2 With the Rectangle tool still selected, position the pointer below the rectangle you drew, and click. In the Rectangle dialog box, you will see the same values as the previous shape you drew. Click OK. Leave the rectangle selected for the next step.

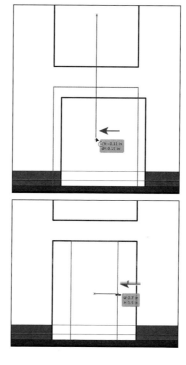

● **Note:** The values may not be *exactly* 1.25 in for width and 1.5 in for height, and that's okay.

3 With the rectangle still selected, position the pointer over the center of the rectangle. When the pointer changes (▶○), drag the shape to center it horizontally with the rectangle above it. A magenta guide will appear when the shapes are aligned. It should still be below the rectangle above it.

4 Option-drag (Mac OS) or Alt-drag (Windows) the center-right bounding point of the selected rectangle to the left to resize from the center. When you see a width of 0.7 in, release the mouse button and then the key.

You can also change the size, position, and more of a selected shape by entering specific values for width, height, position, and more, which you need at times.

▶ **Tip:** Depending on the resolution of your screen, you may also see the Transform options such as Width and Height in the Control panel. The Transform panel contains most of the transformation properties for Live Shapes.

5 Choose Window > Transform. In the Transform panel, make sure Constrain Width And Height Proportions (⬚) to the right of Width (W:) and Height (H:) is off. Change Height (H:) to **0.1 in**. Typing the **in** for inches isn't necessary; it is added automatically. Close the Transform panel.

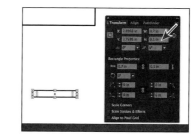

From the Transform panel, you can change the appearance of your Live Shape, including its dimensions, rotation, and corner properties. The center point of the rectangle lets you drag to align the object with other elements in your artwork.

▶ **Tip:** You'll learn a lot more about the Transform panel and transformations in general in Lesson 5, "Transforming Artwork."

Working with the document grid

The grid allows you to work more precisely by creating a series of nonprinting horizontal and vertical guides behind your artwork in the Document window that objects can snap to. To turn the grid on and use its features, do the following:

- To show the grid, choose View > Show Grid. To hide the grid, choose View > Hide Grid.

- To snap objects to the gridlines, choose View > Snap To Grid, select the object you want to move, and drag it to the desired location. When the object's boundaries come within 2 pixels of a gridline, it snaps to the point.

- To specify grid properties such as the spacing between gridlines, grid style (lines or dots), grid color, or whether grids appear in the front or back of artwork, choose Illustrator CC > Preferences > Guides & Grid (Mac OS) or Edit > Preferences > Guides & Grid (Windows).

—From Illustrator Help

Rounding corners

Rounding corners on rectangles and rounded rectangles is easy since the shapes you create are Live Shapes. In this section, you'll learn a few ways to be able to round corners of the rectangles you created.

1 Choose Select > Deselect.

2 Select the Selection tool (▸) in the Tools panel, and click the top (larger) rectangle. A corner widget appears next to each corner point of the rectangle. Drag any of the corner widgets toward the center of the rectangle to change the corner radius without worrying about how much right now.

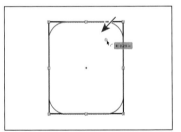

▶ **Tip:** You can Option-click (Mac OS) or Alt-click (Windows) a corner widget in a shape to cycle through the different corner types.

3 Double-click any corner widget to open the Transform panel. In the panel, ensure that the Link Corner Radius Values (▤) is on, and change any of the Radius values to **0.15 in** to change them all.

4 Close the Transform panel.

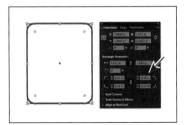

5 Select the Direct Selection tool (⟨k⟩) and double-click the upper-left corner widget (first part of the following figure). In the Corners dialog box, change the radius to **0** (zero) and click OK. Notice that only that corner changed.

6 Double-click the upper-right corner widget (last part of the following figure) and change the value to **0** in the Corners dialog box. Click OK.

▶ **Tip:** In the Transform panel, with a Live Shape selected, you will see the Scale Corners option. With this option selected, if you were to scale the Live Shape larger or smaller, the corner radius would scale as well. Otherwise, without the option selected, the corner radius would stay the same.

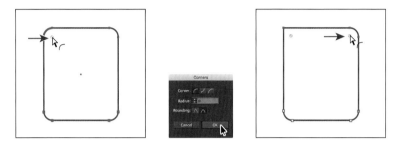

The Corners dialog box allows you to edit the corner type and radius, but it also has an extra option called Rounding for setting absolute versus relative rounding. Absolute means the rounded corner is exactly the radius value. Relative makes the radius value based on the angle of the corner point.

▶ **Tip:** You can also drag a corner widget away from the rectangle center to remove the corner radius. The measurement label will show as 0 in (in this case).

7 Select the Selection tool in the Tools panel. Click in a blank area to deselect. Shift-click both rectangles to select them.

8 Click the Fill color (▢▾) in the Control panel. Click the black color to apply it.

9 Choose Select > Deselect.

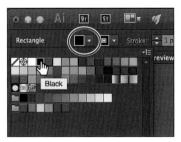

Creating a rounded rectangle

Next, you'll create a rectangle with rounded corners using the Rounded Rectangle tool. Similar to rectangles, rounded rectangles are Live Shapes, which means you can edit properties such as the corner radius after the fact.

1 Click and hold down the mouse button on the Rectangle tool (▉), and select the Rounded Rectangle tool (▉) in the Tools panel.

▶ **Tip:** You can also
press and hold the
Down Arrow or Up
Arrow key to change
the corner radius faster.

● **Note:** The values
you see in the
measurement label may
not be the same as you
see in the figure, and
that's okay.

2 Position the pointer to the right of the larger
rectangle. Click and drag down and to the
right until the rectangle has an approximate
width of 1.1 inches and a height of 2 inches,
but *do not release the mouse button yet.*
With the mouse button still held down, press
the Down Arrow key a few times to see the
corner radius become less rounded (the R
value in the tool tip). Press the Up Arrow
key to see the corner become more rounded.
Don't worry about the R (radius) value in the
tooltip since you can edit it later, and release
the mouse button. Leave the shape selected.

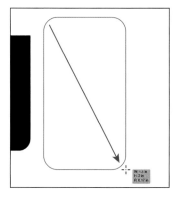

3 With the rounded rectangle selected and
the Rounded Rectangle tool still selected,
drag any of the corner widgets until the
measurement label shows a value of 0.05 in.

It may be difficult to see the corner widgets
because the shape is filled with black. You may want to zoom in or you can
choose View > Outline to temporarily remove the fill of the shape.

▶ **Tip:** You can also edit the corner radius and type for all corners at once in the Control panel if the
resolution of your screen supports it.

● **Note:** If you don't
see the Corner Type
button, you can either
select the Selection tool
or access the corner
types by clicking Shape
in the Control panel and
editing the corner type
for each corner.

4 Click the Corner Type button in the Control panel and select Chamfer to change
all four corners of the rectangle.

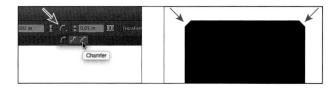

5 Choose Edit > Undo Corner Type as many times as necessary to return the
corners to round or Click the Corner Type button in the Control panel and
select Round.

6 Choose Window > Swatch Libraries > Patterns > Basic Graphics > Basic
Graphics_Lines. In the Basic Graphics_Lines panel, choose the 10 lpi 90% swatch
to apply to the fill.

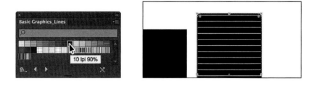

7 Close the Basic Graphics_Lines panel.

8 Select the Selection tool (⭠) in the Tools panel. Drag the rounded rectangle so that it's centered horizontally with the rectangle to the left, as shown in the figure. When a horizontal magenta line appears (Smart Guides), release the mouse button.

Make sure the horizontal distance between the original rectangle and the rounded rectangle is roughly like you see in the figure.

▶ **Tip:** The color of the Smart Guides can be changed to another color by choosing Illustrator CC > Preferences > Smart Guides (Mac OS) or Edit > Preferences > Smart Guides (Windows).

9 Option-drag (Mac OS) or Alt-drag (Windows) the rounded rectangle to the left to copy it. Drag it to the left of the original rectangle filled with black. When you see a magenta horizontal Smart Guide appear (indicating that all three shapes are aligned horizontally) and you see the equivalent gap hint appear, indicating that the distance between the three shapes is the same, release the mouse button and then the key.

● **Note:** You may need to move all the shapes onto the artboard if they currently aren't. You can select all 3 and move them at one time.

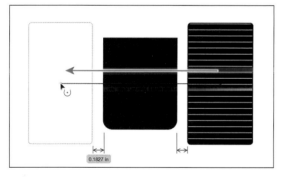

Smart Guides (View > Smart Guides) are on by default and can be really useful when trying to align shapes and other artwork to each other.

10 Choose Select > Deselect and then choose File > Save.

Creating and editing an ellipse

Next, you'll draw and edit an ellipse with the Ellipse tool (⬤).

1 Click and hold down the mouse button on the Rounded Rectangle tool (▣)
   in the Tools panel, and select the Ellipse tool (⬤).

2 Position the pointer above the center black rectangle and aligned with its left
   edge. A magenta Smart Guide will appear when the pointer is aligned. See the
   first part of the following figure.

3 Click and drag to make a circle that has a width of 1.25 in and a height of 0.3 in.

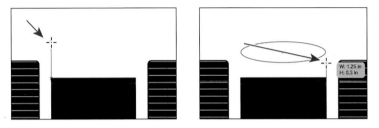

The pointer will most likely "snap" to the right edge of the black rectangle, and a
magenta alignment guide will appear.

4 Press the letter D to apply the default fill of white and stroke of black.

5 Drag the Pie Angle widget off the right side of the circle clockwise around
   the ellipse a bit.

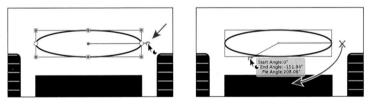

Dragging this widget allows you to control the pie angle of an ellipse. After
dragging the widget initially, you will then see a second widget. The widget you
dragged initially controls the end angle. The widget that now appears on the
right side of the circle controls the start angle.

6 Click the word "Shape" in the Control panel, and change Pie End Angle to **180°**.
   Press Escape to hide the Shape panel.

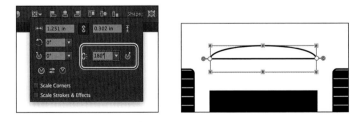

7 Drag the circle from what was the center down until the center snaps to the top edge of the black rectangle.

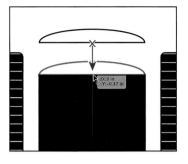

Make sure that the magenta alignment guide is showing in the center of the black rectangle to ensure that it is center-aligned horizontally with the rectangle.

8 Click the Fill color in the Control panel, and select a gray color. I chose a gray with the tooltip that shows "C=0 M=0 Y=0 K=50."

9 Choose Select > Deselect, and then choose File > Save.

Creating and editing a circle

Next, you'll draw and edit a perfect circle with the Ellipse tool (⬤).

1 Choose 1 from the Artboard Navigation menu in the lower-left corner of the Document window.

2 Choose View > Fit Artboard In Window, if necessary, to see the whole artboard.

3 With the Ellipse tool still selected, position the pointer over a blank area of the artboard. Begin dragging down and to the right to begin drawing an ellipse. As you drag, press the Shift key to create a perfect circle. When the width and height are both roughly 2 in, release the mouse button and then the Shift key.

Without switching to the Selection tool, you can reposition and modify an ellipse with the Ellipse tool, which is what you'll do next.

> **Tip:** If you draw an ellipse so that the width and height are close to the same (a circle), a magenta "crosshair" will appear in the circle. This makes it possible to draw a circle without holding down the Shift key (Smart Guides need to be turned on).

4 Press the letter D to apply the default fill of white and stroke of black.

5 With the Ellipse tool selected, position the pointer over the left-middle bounding point of the circle. When the pointer changes (🖱️), click and drag away from the center of the circle to make it larger. Drag until the measurement label shows a width and height of approximately 5.5 in.

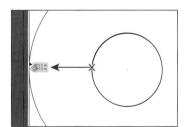

> **Note:** An ellipse is also a Live Shape like a rectangle or rounded rectangle.

6 Choose View > Zoom Out a few times until you see the whole circle.

7 Option-drag (Mac OS) or Alt-drag (Windows) the top middle bounding point down until you see a height of approximately 3.9 in. Release the mouse button and then the key.

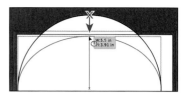

8 With the circle selected, change Fill color to a blue with the tooltip "C=85 M= 50 Y=0 K=0."

9 Choose Align To Artboard from the Align To Selection menu in the Control panel. Click Horizontal Align Center (⊟) and Vertical Align Center (⊞) to align the ellipse to the center of the artboard.

10 Choose Object > Hide > Selection to temporarily hide it.

Creating and editing a polygon

Polygons are drawn from the center by default, which is different from the other tools you've worked with so far. Now you'll create a triangle to add to the satellite artwork using the Polygon tool (⬡).

1 Click the Next Artboard button (▶) in the lower-left corner of the Document window.

2 Select the Zoom tool (🔍), and click a few times near the bottom of the artboard.

3 Click and hold down the mouse button on the Ellipse tool (⬤) in the Tools panel, and select the Polygon tool (⬡).

4 Choose View > Smart Guides to turn them off.

So far, you've been working in the default Preview mode, which lets you see how objects are painted with fill and stroke colors. If paint attributes seem distracting, you can also work in Outline mode, which you'll do next.

Note: Outline mode temporarily removes all paint attributes, such as colored fills and strokes, to speed up selecting and redrawing artwork. You can't select or drag shapes by clicking in the middle of a shape, because the fill temporarily disappears.

5 Press the letter D to apply the default fill of white and stroke of black.

6 Choose View > Outline to switch to Outline mode.

7 Position the pointer in a blank area of the artboard. Drag to the right to begin drawing a polygon, but *don't release the mouse button yet.* Press the Down Arrow key three times to reduce the number of sides on the polygon to three, and don't release the mouse yet. Hold down the Shift key to straighten the shape. Release the mouse button and then the key.

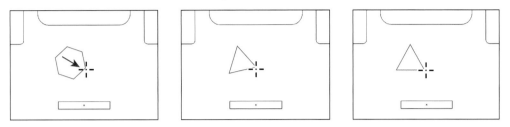

Notice that you cannot see the size of the shape in the gray measurement label (the tooltip), since the tooltip is part of the Smart Guides that you turned off. The magenta alignment guides are also not showing since the shape is not snapping to other content on the artboard. Smart Guides can be useful in certain situations, such as when more precision is necessary, and can be toggled on and off when needed.

8 Choose View > Smart Guides to turn them back on.

9 Drag the Radius widget either away from the center or toward the center of the shape until you see a radius of approximately 32.

> **Note:** As of the writing of this book, the measurement label does not show a unit. This may be different than what you see. Look at the figure for relative sizing.

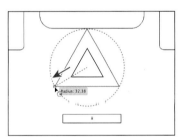

> **Tip:** In one corner of the triangle (in this case), you'll see a corner widget. You can drag the corner widget away from the center or toward the center of the shape to change the corner radius.

10 With the Polygon tool still selected, drag the small white square on the bounding box to change the number of sides. Make sure you wind up with three sides again.

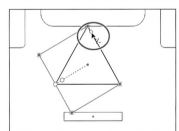

11 Drag the triangle from its center into position below the first rectangle you created. Drag until the vertical magenta guide appears, indicating that the triangle is aligned horizontally with the rectangle. Use the figure as a guide.

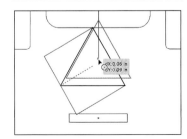

12 Choose Select > Deselect.

Changing stroke width and alignment

So far in this lesson, you've mostly edited the fill of shapes but haven't done too much with the strokes (a visible outline or border of an object or path). Every shape and path, by default, is created with a 1-point black stroke. You can easily change the color of a stroke or the weight of a stroke to make it thinner or thicker, which is what you'll do next.

● **Note:** Your rectangle may be under the triangle and that's okay since you will drag it into position next.

1   Select the Zoom tool (Q) in the Tools panel, and click the small rectangle beneath the triangle a few times to zoom in more closely. Make sure you can still see the triangle above it.

2   With the Selection tool selected (▶), click the border of the bottom rectangle beneath the triangle to select it. Press Command (Mac OS) or Control (Windows) to switch temporarily to the Direct Selection tool. Drag the upper-left point to the lower-left point of the triangle. When the anchor point appears (gets larger), release the mouse button and then the key.

▶ **Tip:** You can also turn off the bounding box by choosing View > Hide Bounding Box so that you can drag a shape by the anchor points with the Selection tool without reshaping it.

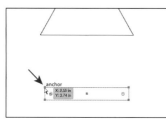   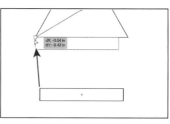

3   Drag the upper-right bounding point of the rectangle to the right until the right edge is aligned with the right edge of the triangle. The word "anchor" will appear when it's aligned.

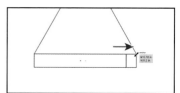

4   Choose View > GPU Preview or View > Preview On CPU if GPU Preview is not available.

5   Change the stroke weight to **0** in the Control panel, and change the Fill color to Black, if necessary.

6   Choose Select > Deselect.

● **Note:** You can also open the Stroke panel by choosing Window > Stroke, but you may need to choose Show Options from the panel menu (▼≡).

7   Click to select the triangle, and then click the word "Stroke" in the Control panel to open the Stroke panel. In the Stroke panel, change the Stroke weight to **5 pt**, and click the Align Stroke To Inside button (▣). This aligns the stroke to the inside edge of the triangle.

● **Note:** Going forward, you will find that by opening a panel in the Control panel (such as the Stroke panel in this step), you will need to hide it before moving on. You can do this by pressing the Escape key.

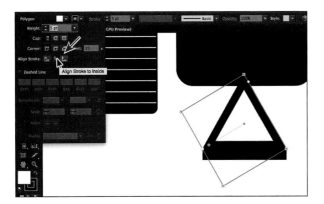

Note: The fill you see on the selected shape may not be the same as the figure and that's okay right now.

Strokes are aligned to the center of a path edge by default, but you can change the alignment as well using the Stroke panel.

8   With the triangle still selected, click the Stroke color in the Control panel (to the left of the word "Stroke"), and change the stroke color to a gray with the tooltip "C=0 M=0 Y=0 K=80." Change the fill color to Black in the Control panel.

9   Choose Object > Arrange > Send To Back.

10 Choose Select > Deselect.

Drawing lines

Next, you'll work with straight lines and line segments, known as *open paths*, to create the last part of the satellite. Shapes can be created in many ways in Illustrator, and the simpler way is usually better.

1   Choose View > Fit Artboard In Window.

2   Choose View > Outline to switch to Outline mode.

3   Select the Line Segment tool (╱) in the Tools panel. Position the pointer on the left edge of the rounded rectangle (see the red arrow in the first part of the following figure). When a magenta alignment guide appears indicating that the pointer is aligned with the center of the rounded rectangle, Shift-drag to the right edge of the rounded rectangle on the right (see the figure). Release the mouse button and then the key.

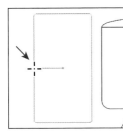
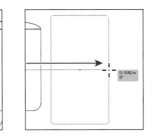

4 Choose View > GPU Preview if available or View > Preview On CPU if GPU Preview is not available.

5 With the line selected, change the Stroke weight to **10 pt** and change the Stroke color to Black in the Control panel, if necessary.

6 Choose Select > All On Active Artboard, and then choose Object > Group.

● **Note:** You'll notice that the pattern in the satellite rounded rectangles was not rotated with the artwork after you click OK. I didn't want to, but if you want to rotate the pattern along with the artwork, you could also have selected Transform Patterns in the Transform Each dialog box before clicking OK.

7 Choose Object > Transform > Transform Each. In the Transform Each dialog box, Transform Objects is selected by default, but change the following:

- Scale Strokes & Effects: Select
- Scale Corners: Select
- Scale Horizontal: **50%**
- Scale Vertical: **50%**
- Angle: **-30%**

8 Select Preview, and then click OK.

9 Choose View > Fit All In Window.

10 Select the Selection tool, and drag the group to the left, onto the first artboard. Don't worry about positioning right now.

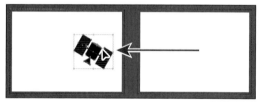

11 Choose Object > Hide > Selection.

Creating a star

Next, you'll use the Star tool (★) to create a few stars. The Star tool does not create Live Shapes, which means editing the star after the fact can be more difficult. When drawing with the Star tool, you'll use a few keyboard modifiers to get the number of points you want and to change the radius of the arms of the star (the length of the arms). Here are the keyboard modifiers you'll use in this section when drawing the star and what each does:

- **Arrow keys:** Pressing the Up Arrow and Down Arrow keys adds and removes arms from the star as you draw it.

- **Shift:** This straightens the star (constrains it).
- **Command (Mac OS) or Ctrl (Windows):** Pressing the key and dragging while creating a star allows you to change the radius of the arms of the star (make the arms longer or shorter).

Next, you'll create a star. This will take a few keyboard commands, so *don't release the mouse button* until you are told.

1 Choose 1 from the Artboard Navigation menu in the lower-left corner of the Document window. Choose View > Fit Artboard In Window, if necessary, to see the whole artboard.

2 Choose View > Zoom In a few times to zoom in closer.

3 Click and hold down the mouse button on the Polygon tool (⬢) in the Tools panel, and select the Star tool (★). Position the pointer somewhere on the artboard.

4 Click and drag slowly to the right to create a small star shape. Drag until the measurement label shows a width of about 0.2 in. Notice that as you move the pointer, the star changes size and rotates freely.

> **Tip:** You can also click in the Document window with the Star tool (★) and edit the options in the Star dialog box instead of drawing it.

- *Without releasing the mouse button*, stop dragging and press the Up Arrow key twice (to increase the number of points on the star to six). See the second part of the following figure.
- Press Command (Mac OS) or Ctrl (Windows), and continue dragging to the right a little. This keeps the inner radius constant, making the arms longer. Drag until you see a width of approximately 0.3 in, and stop dragging, without releasing the mouse button. Release Command or Ctrl, *but not the mouse*. See the third part of the following figure.
- Hold down the Shift key, and drag until the measurement label shows a width of about 0.4 in. Finally, release the mouse button, and then release the Shift key, and you should see a star. See the fourth part of the following figure.

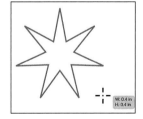

The next time you draw a star, it will have the same settings. If you want to practice creating another star, try using the keyboard modifiers you've explored. Remember, do not release the mouse button until you are sure you are finished drawing the star. If you do try a few more, delete them, and then select the star you made in this step before moving on. Your star doesn't have to exactly match the stars in the figures.

5 Change the Stroke weight of the selected star, to the right of the word "Stroke" in the Control panel, to **0**.

6 Change the Fill color in the Control panel to the color with the tooltip that shows "CMYK Yellow." Press the Escape key to hide the Swatches panel.

● **Note:** You may want to zoom out a bit by choosing View > Zoom Out.

7 With the Selection tool selected, Option-drag (Mac OS) or Alt-drag (Windows) the star from its center to a blank area of the artboard. Release the mouse button and then the key.

Do this a few times so that you have five or so stars out there.

8 Choose Select > All On Active Artboard, and then choose Object > Hide > Selection.

Working with the Shaper tool

● **Note:** The Shaper tool is present in the Tools panel of the classical workspace. In the Touch Workspace, it is a top-level tool in the toolbar. This tool works best with a stylus on touch surfaces, such as Surface Pro 3 or Wacom Cintiq, or through indirect inputs such as the Wacom Intuos.

Another way to draw and edit shapes in Illustrator involves the Shaper tool (●). The Shaper tool recognizes natural gestures and produces Live Shapes from those gestures. Without switching tools, you can transform individual shapes you create and even perform operations such as punch and combine. In this section, you'll get a feeling for how the tool works by exploring the most widely used features.

Drawing shapes

To get started with the Shaper tool, you'll draw a few simple shapes that will eventually become an asteroid.

1 Choose View > Fit Artboard In Window.

2 Select the Shaper tool (●) in the Tools panel.

You may see a window appear the first time you select the Shaper tool, which gives a brief description of the capabilities of the tool. Click to close it.

3 Draw an ellipse anywhere on the artboard. Use the following figure as a guide.

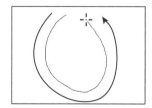 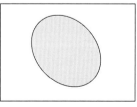

When you finish drawing the shape, the gesture will be converted to a Live Shape such as an ellipse. If the shape you draw doesn't look exactly like what I drew, don't worry. As long as it's an ellipse of some kind.

4 Draw a rectangle, and then draw a triangle in a blank area of the artboard.

There are a variety of shapes that can be drawn with the Shaper tool including (but not limited to) rectangles, squares, ellipses (circles), triangles, hexagons, lines, and more.

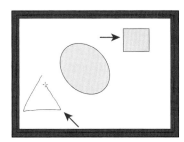

5 Draw a scribble over the rectangle, and then draw another over the triangle to delete them.

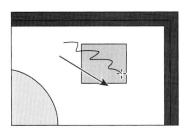 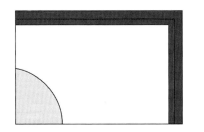

Note: If you try to draw a scribble and draw more of a straight line, a line will be created instead. Simply scribble across all the shapes to remove them.

This simple gesture is an easy way to delete shapes. Note that you can scribble across more than one object to remove it, and you simply need to scribble over part of the artwork, not the whole thing to delete it.

6 Choose File > Save.

Editing shapes with the Shaper tool

Once shapes are created, you can also use the Shaper tool to edit those shapes without having to switch tools. Next, you'll edit the ellipse you created previously.

1 Click the ellipse with the Shaper tool to select it. Drag any corner of the ellipse until you see a magenta crosshair in the center.

The magenta crosshair is a part of Smart Guides and indicates that the ellipse becomes a circle (an ellipse with equal width and height).

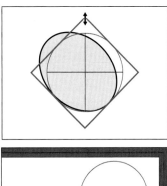

Note: Your shape most likely doesn't look like mine and may or may not be rotated (like mine). Don't worry about that.

2 Drag the shape from its center toward the upper-right corner of the artboard. Use the figure as a guide.

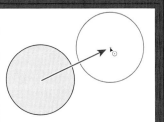

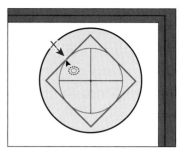

Note: As of the writing of this book, measurement labels don't show for most transformation operations on live shapes using the Shaper tool.

3 Drag either widget that looks like a hollow circle away from the center or toward it until it looks something like the figure. You can look in the Transform panel (Window > Transform) to see the width and height. My circle is roughly 1.2 inches in width and height.

Shapes drawn with the Shaper tool are live and dynamically adjustable, so you can draw and edit intuitively without the extra hassle of switching between tools.

Combining shapes with the Shaper tool

Not only does the Shaper tool let you draw shapes, but you can then combine, subtract, and continuously edit them, all with a single tool. Next, you'll draw a few more shapes and use the Shaper tool to add and subtract them from the original circle.

1 Select the Zoom tool, and click several times on the circle in the upper-right corner to zoom in closely.

Note: It's important to deselect in this step, or you may wind up editing the existing circle.

2 With the Shaper tool selected, click in a blank area to deselect the circle. Draw a series of small ellipses around the edge of the circle. It doesn't matter if they are perfect circles.

If need be, you can always click within one of the circles you created to select it, and then press Backspace or Delete to remove it.

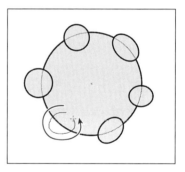

3 Position the pointer in a blank area, close to one of the little circles. Scribble across the circle shape, stopping before the pointer reaches the edge of small the circle that is closest to the center of the larger circle.. When you release, it will appear to be removed from the larger circle.

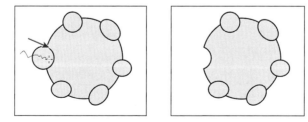

4 For the next small circle, position the pointer inside the larger circle, and scribble across the smaller circle. Stop just short of the stroke of the smaller circle (see the following figure).

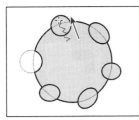 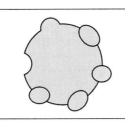

5 Scribble across the other smaller circles to either add them the larger circle or remove them. I did it in an alternating pattern.

6 Click any of the merged shapes with the Shaper tool to select the merged group (called a *Shaper Group*).

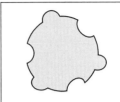

7 Click again, and you'll see crosshatching, which means you can change the color of areas of the merged group (called a *Shaper Group Select*). Change the Fill color to a gray swatch with the tooltip "C=0 M=0 Y=0 K=50" in the Control panel.

Note: Make sure that the entire shape is selected. If not, try deselecting (Select > Deselect), and then clicking twice, slowly, on the shape.

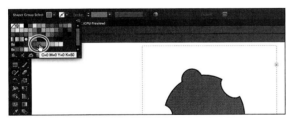

8 Click the arrow toward the upper-right corner of the dotted box surrounding the artwork to edit each shape independently (circled in the first part of the following figure).

9 With the Shaper tool selected, click one of the smaller ellipses. Drag the ellipse from within to reposition it. Notice that it is still merged with the larger shape. If after dragging, the fill color of the small ellipse changes, change it back to C=0 M=0 Y=0 K=50.

Tip: With the Shaper tool selected, you can also double-click one of the shapes within the Shaper Group to access the individual shapes.

10 Try clicking each ellipse to resize, rotate, reposition, and more. See the following figure. When finished, click in a blank area of the Document window to deselect.

 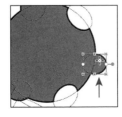  

11 Choose View > Fit All In Window.

12 Choose Object > Show All to show the ellipse, satellite, and stars.

Working with drawing modes

● **Note:** To learn more about clipping masks, see Lesson 14, "Using Illustrator CC with Other Adobe Applications."

Illustrator has three different drawing modes available that are found at the bottom of the Tools panel: Draw Normal, Draw Behind, and Draw Inside. Drawing modes allow you to draw shapes in different ways. The three drawing modes are as follows:

Draw Normal —⌐ ⌐— Draw Inside
Draw Behind —

- **Draw Normal mode:** You start every document by drawing shapes in Normal mode, which stacks shapes on top of each other.

- **Draw Behind mode:** This mode allows you to draw objects behind other objects without choosing layers or paying attention to the stacking order.

- **Draw Inside mode:** This mode lets you draw objects or place images inside other objects, including live text, automatically creating a clipping mask of the selected object.

Working with Draw Behind mode

Throughout this lesson, you've been working in the default Draw Normal mode. Next, you'll draw a rectangle that will cover the artboard and go behind the rest of the content using Draw Behind mode.

1 Choose View > Fit Artboard In Window.

● **Note:** If the Tools panel you see is displayed as a single column, you can click the Drawing Modes button (◙) at the bottom of the Tools panel and choose Draw Behind from the menu that appears.

2 Click the Draw Behind button (◙) at the bottom of the Tools panel.

As long as this drawing mode is selected, every shape you create using the different methods you've learned will be created behind the other shapes on the page. The Draw Behind mode also affects placed content (File > Place).

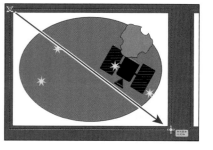

3 Select the Rectangle tool (▣) in the Tools panel. Position the pointer off the upper-left corner of the artboard in the corner of the red bleed guides. Click and drag off the lower-right side of the artboard to the corner of the red bleed guides.

● **Note:** If artwork were selected, clicking the Draw Behind button would allow you to draw artwork behind the selected artwork.

4 With the new rectangle selected, click the Fill color in the Control panel, and change the fill color to Black. Press the Escape key to hide the Swatches panel.

5 Change the Stroke weight to **0** in the Control panel.

6 Choose Object > Lock > Selection.

7 Click the Draw Normal button (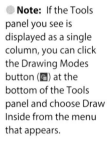) at the bottom of the Tools panel.

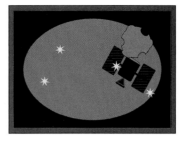

Using the Draw Inside mode

Next, you will learn how to draw a shape inside another using the Draw Inside drawing mode. This can be useful if you want to hide (*mask*) part of artwork.

1 Select the Selection tool (↖) in the Tools panel. Click to select the blue circle.

2 Click the Draw Inside button (▣), near the bottom of the Tools panel.

This button is active when a single object is selected (path, compound path, or text), and it allows you to draw within the selected object only. Every shape you create will now be drawn inside the selected shape (the circle). Notice that the ellipse has a dotted open rectangle around it, indicating that, if you draw, paste, or place content, it will be inside the circle, even if you were to choose Select > Deselect.

> **Note:** If the Tools panel you see is displayed as a single column, you can click the Drawing Modes button (▣) at the bottom of the Tools panel and choose Draw Inside from the menu that appears.

3 Select the Ellipse tool (⬭) in the Tools panel. Position the pointer off the left edge of the blue circle and draw an ellipse that has a width that is just wider than the blue circle and a height of approximately 2 in.

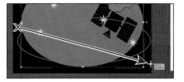

4 Change the Fill color of the new circle to a light gray with the tooltip that shows "C=0 M=0 Y=0 K=20."

5 Choose Select > Deselect.

Notice that the ellipse still has the dotted open rectangle around it, indicating that Draw Inside mode is still active.

When you are finished drawing content inside a shape, you can click the Draw Normal button (▣) so that any new content you create will be drawn normally (stacked rather than drawn inside).

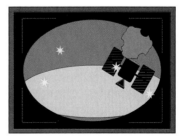

> **Note:** If you draw a shape outside of the original blue circle, it will seem to disappear. That is because the blue circle is masking all shapes drawn inside of it; so, only shapes positioned inside of the ellipse bounds will appear.

6 Click the Draw Normal button at the bottom of the Tools panel.

This ensures that any new content you create will not be drawn inside the blue circle.

> **Tip:** You can also toggle between the available Drawing Modes by pressing Shift+D.

Editing content drawn inside

Next, you will edit the ellipse inside of the blue circle to see how you can later edit content drawn inside.

1   Select the Selection tool (▶), and click to select the light gray ellipse (that is inside of the blue circle). Notice that it selects the blue circle instead.

The blue circle is now a mask, also called a *clipping path*. The ellipse and the circle together make a clip group and are now treated as a single object. If you look on the left end of the Control panel, you will see two buttons that allow you to edit either the clipping path (the blue circle) or the contents (the gray ellipse).

Tip: You can separate the shapes by right-clicking the shapes and choosing Release Clipping Mask. This would make two shapes, stacked one on another.

2   Click the Edit Contents button (⬚) on the left end of the Control panel to select the light gray ellipse.

Tip: You can also double-click the blue circle to enter Isolation mode and press the Escape key to exit.

3   Drag the light gray ellipse from within the light gray fill color down to match the figure as best you can.

Tip: Sometimes it can be helpful to choose View > Outline to more easily see and select shapes when in Isolation mode.

4   Click the Edit Clipping Path button (⬚) on the left end of the Control panel to select the blue circle.

5   Change the Stroke weight to **0** in the Control panel.

If you find it difficult to change the Stroke weight to **0** (zero), try changing it to another value first and then **0**.

6   Choose Select > Deselect, and then choose File > Save.

7   Choose View > Fit Artboard In Window, if necessary.

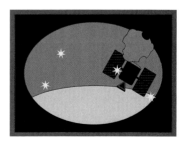

Using Image Trace

In this part of the lesson, you'll learn how to work with the Image Trace command. Image Trace traces existing artwork, like a raster picture from Adobe Photoshop. You can then convert the drawing to vector paths or a Live Paint object. This can be useful for turning a drawing into vector art, tracing raster logos, tracing a pattern or texture, and much more.

1   Choose File > Place. In the Place dialog box, select the rocket-ship.jpg file in the Lessons > Lesson03 folder on your hard disk, and click Place (shown in the figure). Click within the artboard to place the image.

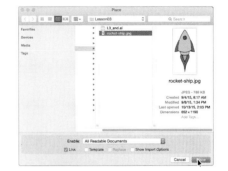

rocket-ship.jpg

> **Tip:** You will learn more about placing images in Lesson 14, "Using Illustrator CC with Other Adobe Applications."

2   Click the Image Trace button in the Control panel. The tracing results you see may differ slightly from the figure, and that's okay.

This converts the image into an image tracing object using the default tracing options. That means you can't edit the vector content yet, but you can change the tracing settings or even the original placed image and then see the updates.

3   Choose 6 Colors from the Preset menu on the left end of the Control panel.

Illustrator comes with preset tracing options that you can apply to your image tracing object. You can then make changes to the tracing settings, if need be, using the default preset as a starting point.

4   Choose Outlines With Source Image from the View menu in the Control panel, and take a look at the image. Choose Tracing Result from that same menu.

An image tracing object is made up of the original source image and the tracing result (which is the vector artwork). By default, only the tracing result is visible.

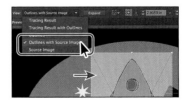

> **Tip:** Use Adobe Capture CC on your device to photograph any object, design, or shape and convert it into vector shapes in a few simple steps. Store the resulting vectors in your Creative Cloud Libraries, and access them or refine them in Illustrator or Photoshop. Adobe Capture is currently available for iOS (iPhone and iPad) and Android.

> **Tip:** Tracing a larger image or higher-resolution image will most likely result in better results.

> **Note:** You can also choose Object > Image Trace > Make, with raster content selected, or begin tracing from the Image Trace panel (Window > Image Trace).

However, you can change the display of both the original image and the tracing result to best suit your needs.

▶ **Tip:** The Image Trace panel can also be opened by choosing Window > Image Trace.

5 Click the Image Trace Panel button (▤) in the Control panel. In the panel, click the Auto-Color button (◈) at the top of the panel.

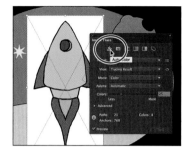

The buttons along the top of the Image Trace panel are saved settings for converting the image to grayscale, black and white, and more. Below the buttons at the top of the Image Trace panel, you will see the Preset and View options. These are the same as those in the Control panel. The Mode option allows you to change the color mode of resulting artwork (color, grayscale, or black and white). The Palette option is also useful for limiting the color palette or for assigning colors from a color group.

6 In the Image Trace panel, click the toggle arrow to the left of the Advanced options to reveal them. Change only the following options, using the values as a starting point:

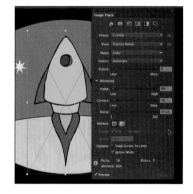

- Colors: **8**
- Paths: **4%**
- Corners: **5%**
- Noise: **13 px**
- Ignore White: **Selected**

7 Close the Image Trace panel.

8 With the rocket image tracing object still selected, click the Expand button in the Control panel. The rocket is no longer an image tracing object but is composed of shapes and paths that are grouped together.

9 With the Selection tool selected and the rocket artwork selected, choose Object > Transform > Rotate. In the Rotate dialog box, change the Angle value to **30**, select Preview, if necessary, and click OK.

10 Drag all the artwork into position like you see in the figure. I scaled some of the stars as well.

11 Choose File > Save, and choose File > Close.

Review questions

1 What are the basic tools for creating shapes?

2 What is a Live Shape?

3 How do you select a shape with no fill?

4 What is the Shaper tool?

5 How can you convert a raster image to editable vector shapes?

Review answers

1 There are six shape tools: Rectangle, Rounded Rectangle, Ellipse, Polygon, Star, and Flare. As explained in Lesson 1, "Getting to Know the Work Area," to tear off a group of tools from the Tools panel, position the pointer over the tool that appears in the Tools panel, and hold down the mouse button until the group of tools appears. Without releasing the mouse button, drag to the triangle on the right side of the group, and then release the mouse button to tear off the group.

2 After you draw a rectangle, rounded rectangle, ellipse, or polygon using the shape tool, you can continue to modify its properties such as width, height, rounded corners, corner types, and radii (individually or collectively). This is what is known as a Live Shape. The shape properties such as corner radius are editable later in the Transform panel, in the Control panel, or directly on the art.

3 Items that have no fill can be selected by clicking the stroke or by dragging a selection marquee across the item.

4 Another way to draw and edit shapes in Illustrator involves the Shaper tool. The Shaper tool recognizes natural gestures and produces Live Shapes from those gestures. Without switching tools, you can transform individual shapes you create and even perform operations such as punch and combine.

5 You can convert a raster image to editable vector shapes by tracing it. To convert the tracing to paths, click Expand in the Control panel or choose Object > Image Trace > Expand. Use this method if you want to work with the components of the traced artwork as individual objects. The resulting paths are grouped.

4 EDITING AND COMBINING SHAPES AND PATHS

Lesson overview

In this lesson, you'll learn how to do the following:

- Cut with the Scissors tool.

- Join paths.

- Work with the Knife tool.

- Work with the Eraser tool.

- Work with the Shape Builder tool.

- Work with Pathfinder commands to create shapes.

- Create a compound path.

- Edit strokes with the Width tool.

- Outline strokes.

This lesson takes approximately 45 minutes to complete.

Download the project files for this lesson from the Lesson & Update Files tab on your Account page at www.peachpit.com and store them on your computer in a convenient location, as described in the "Getting Started" section of this book.

Your Account page is also where you'll find any updates to the chapters or to the lesson files. Look on the Lesson & Update Files tab to access the most current content.

Soon after you begin creating simple paths and shapes, you will most likely want to take them further in order to create more complex artwork. In this lesson, you'll explore how to both edit and combine shapes and paths.

Getting started

● **Note:** The artwork for this project was created by Dan Stiles (www.danstiles.com).

In Lesson 3, "Using Shapes to Create Artwork for a Postcard," you learned about creating and making edits to basic shapes. In this lesson, you'll take basic shapes and paths and learn how to both edit and combine them to create new artwork.

1 To ensure that the tools and panels function exactly as described in this lesson, delete or deactivate (by renaming) the Adobe Illustrator CC preferences file. See "Restoring default preferences" in the "Getting Started" section at the beginning of the book.

2 Start Adobe Illustrator CC.

● **Note:** If you have not already downloaded the project files for this lesson to your computer from your Account page, make sure to do so now. See the "Getting Started" section at the beginning of the book.

3 Choose File > Open. Locate the file named L4_end.ai, which is in the Lessons > Lesson04 folder that you copied onto your hard disk. This file contains the finished artwork.

4 Choose View > Fit All In Window and leave the file open for reference, or choose File > Close (I closed it).

5 Choose File > Open. If a panel appears, click Open in the panel. You could also choose File > Open again. In the Open dialog box, navigate to the Lessons > Lesson04 folder and select the L4_start.ai file on your hard disk. Click Open to open the file.

▶ **Tip:** By default, the ".ai" extension shows on Mac OS, but you could add the extension on either platform in the Save As dialog box.

6 Choose File > Save As. In the Save As dialog box, change the name to **BirdInTheHand.ai** (Mac OS) or **BirdInTheHand** (Windows), and choose the Lesson04 folder. Leave the Format option set to Adobe Illustrator (ai) (Mac OS) or the Save As Type option set to Adobe Illustrator (*.AI) (Windows), and click Save.

7 In the Illustrator Options dialog box, leave the Illustrator options at their default settings, and click OK.

8 Choose View > Fit All In Window.

Editing paths and shapes

In Illustrator, you can edit and combine paths and shapes in a variety of ways to achieve the artwork you want. Sometimes, to get the artwork you desire, you start simpler and utilize different methods for achieving more complex paths. This includes working with the Scissors tool (✂), the Knife tool (✂), the Width tool (🖉), the Shape Builder tool (🔍), Pathfinder effects, the Eraser tool (🖊), outlining strokes, joining paths, and more.

Note: You'll also explore other methods for transforming artwork in Lesson 5, "Transforming Artwork."

Cutting with the Scissors tool

There are several tools that allow you to cut and divide shapes. You'll start with the Scissors tool (✂), which splits a path at an anchor point or on a line segment and makes an open path. Next, you'll cut a shape with the Scissors tool to reshape it.

1   Choose View > Smart Guides to ensure that they are on.

2   Choose "2 Bird 1" from the Artboard Navigation menu in the lower-left corner of the Document window.

3   Choose View > Fit Artboard In Window.

4   Select the Zoom tool (🔍) in the Tools panel, and click twice on the red shape in the upper-right corner of the artboard to zoom in.

5   Select the Selection tool (▶) in the Tools panel, and click the red shape to select it.

6   With the shape selected, in the Tools panel, click and hold down the Eraser tool (🖊), and select the Scissors tool (✂). Position the pointer over the blue anchor point on the path on the left side (see the figure), and when you see the word "anchor," click to cut the path at that point.

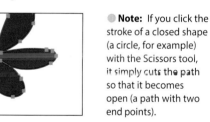

Note: If you click the stroke of a closed shape (a circle, for example) with the Scissors tool, it simply cuts the path so that it becomes open (a path with two end points).

If you don't click directly on a point or path, you will see a warning dialog box. You can simply click OK and try again. Cuts made with the Scissors tool must be on a line or a curve rather than on an end point of an open path. When you click with the Scissors tool, a new anchor point is created and is selected.

7   Choose View > Smart Guides to turn them off.

8   Select the Direct Selection tool (▷), and drag the anchor point you just clicked to the left.

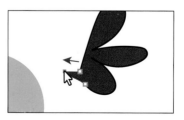

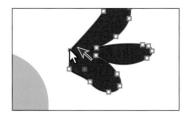

9 Drag the other anchor point, from where you originally cut the path with the scissors, up and to the left (see the figure).

Notice how the stroke (the black border) doesn't go all the way around the red shape. That's because cutting with the Scissors tool makes an open path. A circle or rectangle are examples of closed paths, and a line or "S" shape are examples of open paths (the end points are not connected). If you only want to fill the shape with a color, it is not necessary to join the path to make a closed path. An open path can have a color fill. It is, however, necessary to join a path if you want a stroke to appear around the entire fill area.

Joining paths

Suppose you draw a "U" shape and later decide you want to close the shape, essentially joining the ends of the "U" with a straight path. If you select the path, you can use the Join command to create a line segment between the end points, closing the path. When more than one open path is selected, you can join them together to create a closed path. You can also join the end points of two separate paths.

Next, you will join the ends of the red path to create a single closed shape.

1 Select the Selection tool (▶) in the Tools panel. Click away from the red path to deselect it, and then click in the red fill to reselect it.

This step is important because only one anchor point was left selected from the previous section. If you were to choose the join command, an error message would appear. By selecting the whole path, when you apply the join command, Illustrator simply finds the two ends of the path and connects them with a straight line.

Tip: If you wanted to join specific anchor points from separate paths, select the anchor points and choose Object > Join > Path or press Command+J (Mac OS) or Ctrl+J (Windows).

2 Choose Object > Path > Join.

Notice that the two anchor points on the left side of the paths are now joined with a straight path and the stroke (black border) goes all the way around now.

3 Choose Select > Deselect to see the closed path.

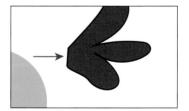

When you apply the Join command to two or more open paths, Illustrator first looks for and joins the paths that have end points stationed closest to each other. This process is repeated every time you apply the Join command until all paths are joined.

Tip: In Lesson 6, "Creating an Illustration with the Drawing Tools," you'll learn about the Join tool (✕), which allows you to join two paths at a corner, keeping the original curve intact.

4 Click the red path to select it again.

5 Select the Eyedropper tool (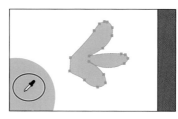) in the Tools panel, and click the blue circle in the center of the artboard.

The Eyedropper tool samples the appearance attributes like stroke and fill from what you click and applies those same appearance attributes to the selected artwork, if it can.

Tip: You'll learn more about the Eyedropper tool in Lesson 7, "Using Color to Enhance Signage."

6 Select the Selection tool, and drag the formerly red shape into position like you see in the figure.

7 Choose Select > Deselect.

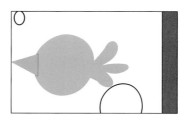

Cutting with the Knife tool

Another way to cut a shape is by using the Knife tool ( ). To cut with the Knife tool, you drag across a shape, and the result is two closed paths.

1 Choose "3 Bird 2" from the Artboard Navigation menu in the lower-left corner of the Document window.

2 Click and hold down the mouse on the Scissors tool ( ), and select the Knife tool ( ).

3 Position the Knife pointer ( ) above the green shape toward the top of the artboard. Starting above the shape (see the red X in the figure), drag down all the way across the shape to cut the shape into two.

Dragging across a shape with the Knife tool makes a very free-form cut that is not straight at all.

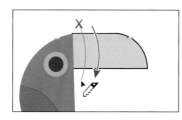

Tip: Pressing the Caps Lock key will turn the Knife tool pointer into a more precise cursor (‐¦‐). This can make it easier to see where the cut will happen.

4 Position the pointer above the green shape, to the right of where you just cut. Press and hold Option+Shift (Mac OS) or Alt+Shift (Windows) and drag down all the way across the shape to cut it into two, in a completely straight line. Release the mouse button and then the keys.

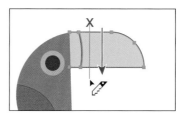

Pressing the Option key (Mac OS) or Alt key (Windows) allows you to cut in a straight line. Pressing the Shift key as well constrains the cut to 45 degrees.

5 While pressing the keys in the previous step, try making two more cuts to the right of the cut you just made.

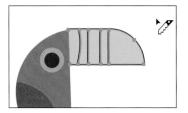

Don't worry about making the resulting shapes *exactly* the same width. See the figure for roughly where to cut.

6 Choose Select > Deselect.

7 Select the Selection tool (⬉), and click the first green shape from the left to select it. Choose the CMYK Cyan color from the Fill color in the Control panel.

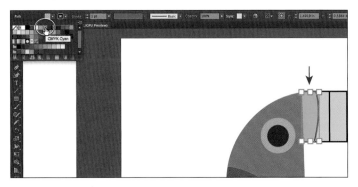

When you hover the pointer over a color in the panel that appears, you can see a yellow tooltip with the color name appear.

8 Click the green shape farthest to the right to select it. Choose a red color from the Fill color in the Control panel. I chose a color with the name "C=15 M=100 Y=90 K=10." See the following figure.

9 With three green shapes left, click the middle green shape to select it. Choose an orange color with the name "C=0 M=80 Y=95 K=0" from the Fill color in the Control panel.

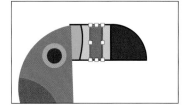

10 Drag across all of the shapes you cut to select them. Change the Stroke weight to **0** in the Control panel.

11 Choose Select > All On Active Artboard, and then choose Object > Group.

12 Choose Select > Deselect, and then choose File > Save.

Using the Eraser tool

The Eraser tool (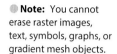) lets you erase any area of your vector artwork, regardless of the structure. You can use the Eraser tool on paths, compound paths, paths inside Live Paint groups, and clipping content.

Note: You cannot erase raster images, text, symbols, graphs, or gradient mesh objects.

Next, you'll use the Eraser tool to modify several shapes.

1 Choose 2 Bird 1 from the Artboard Navigation menu in the lower-left corner of the Document window.

2 With the Selection tool ( ), select the smaller white circle toward the upper-left corner of the artboard.

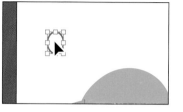

By selecting the white shape, you'll erase only that shape and nothing else. If you leave all objects deselected, you can erase any object that the tool touches, across all layers.

3 Click and hold down the mouse on the Knife tool ( ), and select the Eraser tool ( ) in the Tools panel.

4 Double-click the Eraser tool ( ) to edit the tool properties. In the Eraser Tool Options dialog box, change the Size to **20 pt**. Click OK.

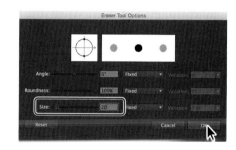

5 Position the pointer off the upper-left corner of the white circle (where you see the red X in the figure). Click and drag across the circle in a "U" shape to erase the top half of the circle.

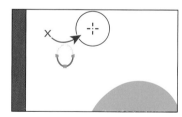

When you release the mouse button, the top half of the circle is erased, and the circle is still a closed path.

6 Change the Stroke weight to **0** in the Control panel, and choose a blue from the Fill color. I chose a blue with the color name of "C=85 M=50 Y=0 K=0" that appears in the yellow tooltip when you hover over each color swatch.

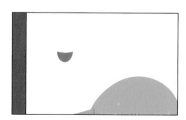

You can also erase in a straight line, which is what you'll do next.

7 Select the Selection tool, and click the white circle in the lower-right corner of the artboard.

8 Select the Eraser tool (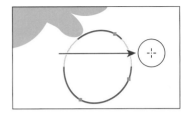) in the Tools panel. Press the Shift key and starting off the left side of the white circle, drag across the top half of the circle. Release the mouse button and then the Shift key.

The white circle is now two separate shapes, both closed paths.

Tip: If you need to erase a large part of a shape, you can always adjust the eraser size by using the Eraser Tool Options dialog box or by pressing either of the bracket keys ([or]).

9 Drag across the remaining shape at the top to erase it completely. You may need to drag across is a few times to erase it all.

It may look like you erased part of the blue shape, but since it isn't selected, it isn't erased.

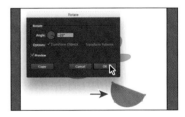

10 With the last part of the circle still selected, select the Eyedropper tool (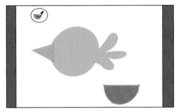) in the Tools panel, and click the small blue circle you erased part of earlier (in the upper-left corner of the artboard).

This copies the appearance attributes like fill and stroke from the small shape to the larger shape.

11 With the larger blue shape selected, choose Object > Transform > Rotate. In the Rotate dialog box, change the Angle to **-20**, and select Preview to see the change. Click OK.

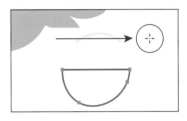

12 Select the Selection tool in the Tools panel. Drag each shape from its center onto the large blue circle in the center to create a bird (see the figure for guidance).

13 Choose Select > All On Active Artboard, and then choose Object > Group.

14 Choose File > Save.

Combining shapes

In Illustrator, you can combine vector objects in a variety of ways. A lot of the time, creating more complex shapes from simpler shapes can be easier than trying to create them with drawing tools like the Pen tool. The resulting paths or shapes differ depending on the method you use to combine the paths. In this section, you'll explore a few of the more widely used methods for combining shapes.

Working with the Shape Builder tool

The first method you will learn for combining shapes involves working with the Shape Builder tool ( ). This tool allows you to visually and intuitively merge, delete, fill, and edit overlapping shapes and paths directly in the artwork. Using the Shape Builder tool, you'll start out by creating a more complex bird shape from a series of simpler shapes like circles and squares.

1   Choose 4 Butterfly from the Artboard Navigation menu in the lower-left corner of the Document window.

2   Choose View > Fit Artboard In Window to ensure it fits in the Document window.

3   Select the Zoom tool ( ) in the Tools panel, and click a few times on the red and green shape on the left side of the artboard to zoom in.

4   Select the Selection tool ( ), and drag a marquee selection across the red/orange rectangle, white circles, and green rectangle to select the shapes on the artboard.

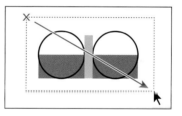

In order to edit shapes with the Shape Builder tool ( ), they need to be selected. Using the Shape Builder tool, you will now combine, delete, and paint these simple shapes to create the rest of a butterfly's wings.

5   Select the Shape Builder tool ( ) in the Tools panel. Position the pointer off the upper-left corner of the shapes, and drag from the red X in the figure down and to the right into the red/orange rectangle. Release the mouse button to combine the shapes.

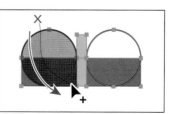

> **Tip:** You can also press the Shift key and drag a marquee across a series of shapes to combine them. Pressing Shift+Option (Mac OS) or Shift+Alt (Windows) and dragging a marquee across selected shapes with the Shape Builder tool ( ) selected allows you to delete a series of shapes within the marquee.

When you select the Shape Builder tool, the overlapping shapes are divided into separate objects temporarily. As you drag from one part to another, a red outline appears, showing you what the final shape outline will look like when it merges the shapes together after releasing the mouse button. Notice that the new combined shape is now the same blue as the bird shape you created previously.

6 Position the pointer off the upper-right corner of the shapes, and drag from the red X in the figure down and to the left into the red/orange rectangle. Release the mouse button to combine the shapes.

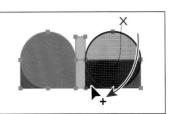

Next, you'll delete a few shapes.

7 With the shapes still selected, hold down the Option (Mac OS) or Alt (Windows) key. Notice that, with the modifier key held down, the pointer shows a minus sign (▶_). Click each red shape to delete them.

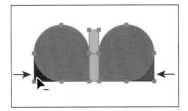

8 Double-click the Shape Builder tool in the Tools panel. In the Shape Builder Tool Options dialog box, select Straight Line from the Selection options. Click OK to close the dialog box.

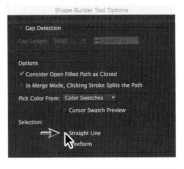

By default, the Shape Builder tool lets you drag across shapes in a freeform way.

9 With the shapes still selected, hold down the Option (Mac OS) or Alt (Windows) key and drag through the green shape in the center from top to bottom to remove it.

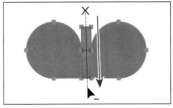

10 Select the Selection tool. With the blue shapes still selected, change the Fill color to an orange/red color with the tooltip name that shows as "C=0 M=90 Y=85 K=0."

11 Choose Object > Group to group the now orange shapes together.

12 Choose View > Fit Artboard In Window.

13 Select the Selection tool and drag one of the orange shapes in the group to the right side of the artboard, above the yellow shapes. See the following figure for how to position them.

14 Drag the orange/yellow shape (an arrow is pointing to it in the figure) into the center of the wing shapes.

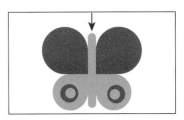

15 Choose Select > Deselect, and then choose File > Save.

Working with the Pathfinder panel

The Pathfinder panel is another place to combine shapes in different ways. When a shape mode such as Unite is applied, the original objects selected are *permanently* transformed, but you can hold down a modifier key, and the original underlying objects are preserved.

When a Pathfinder effect such as Merge is applied, the original objects selected are *permanently* transformed. If the effect results in more than one shape, they are grouped automatically.

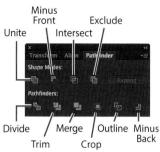

1 Choose 5 Bird 3 from the Artboard Navigation menu in the lower-left corner of the Document window.

2 Choose Window > Pathfinder to open the Pathfinder panel group.

3 With the Selection tool (↖), hold down the Shift key, and click the red oval and blue rectangle beneath it to select both objects.

You need to create a shape that looks like a bird wing. You will use the Pathfinder panel and those shapes to create the final artwork.

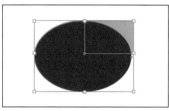

4 With the shapes selected, in the Pathfinder panel, click the Minus Front button (◻) in the Shape Modes section of the Pathfinder panel to *permanently* subtract the top shape from the bottom shape.

With the new shape selected, notice the word "Path" on the left side of the Control panel.

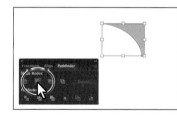

● **Note:** The Unite button in the Pathfinder panel produces a similar result as the Shape Builder tool, by combining the shapes into one.

5 Choose Edit > Undo Subtract to bring both shapes back. Leave them selected.

Shape modes in the Pathfinder panel

The buttons in the top row of the Pathfinder panel, called *shape modes*, create paths just like the Pathfinder effects, but they can also be used to create compound shapes. When several shapes are selected, clicking a shape mode while pressing the Option (Mac OS) or Alt (Windows) key creates a compound shape rather than a path. The original underlying objects of compound shapes are preserved. As a result, you can still select each original object within a compound shape. Using a shape mode to create a compound shape can be useful if you think that you may want to retrieve the original shapes at a later time.

1 With the shapes still selected, hold down the Option (Mac OS) or Alt (Windows) key, and click the Minus Front button (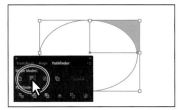) in the Shape Modes section of the Pathfinder panel.

This creates a compound shape that traces the outline of what's left after the top red shape is subtracted from the bottom blue shape. You will still be able to edit both shapes separately.

2 Choose Select > Deselect to see the final shape.

▶ **Tip:** To edit the original shapes in a compound shape like this one, you can also select them individually with the Direct Selection tool (◦).

3 With the Selection tool, double-click the blue shape to enter Isolation mode.

You could also double-click the (now) white oval, but that one is harder to see.

4 Choose View > Outline so that you can see the outlines of the two shapes, and click the edge of the oval shape or drag across the path to select it.

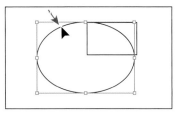

5 Choose View > GPU Preview or View > Preview On CPU if not available.

● **Note:** You can also press the Arrow keys to move the shape if you find it difficult to select.

6 Drag the white oval from the middle a little to the left.

7 Press the Escape key to exit Isolation mode.

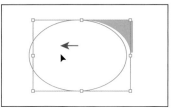

You will now expand the wing shape. Expanding a compound shape maintains the shape of the compound object, but you can no longer select or edit the original objects. You will typically expand an object when you want to modify the appearance attributes and other properties of specific elements within it.

8 Click away from the shape to deselect it, and then click to select it again.

9 Click the Expand button in the Pathfinder panel. Close the Pathfinder panel group.

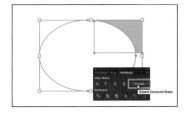
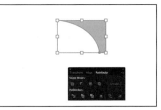

10 Drag the blue wing shape on top of the bird like you see in the figure.

11 Choose Select > All On Active Artboard, and then choose Object > Group.

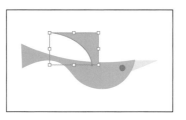

Creating a compound path

Compound paths let you use a vector object to cut a hole in another vector object. Whenever I think of a compound path, I think of a doughnut shape, which can be created from two circles. Holes appear where paths overlap. A compound path is treated like a group, and the individual objects in the compound path can still be edited or released (if you don't want them to be a compound path anymore). Next, you'll create a compound to create some art for the butterfly.

1 Choose 4 Butterfly from the Artboard menu in the lower-left corner of the Document window.

2 Choose View > Fit Artboard In Window.

3 With the Selection tool (▶) selected, select the white circle with the black stroke. Drag it onto the larger orange circle above it, a little off-center.

4 Drag across both shapes to select them.

5 Drag the shapes onto the larger orange wing of the butterfly. Notice that the white circle is on top and you can't see through it.

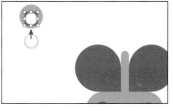

6 Choose Object > Compound Path > Make, and leave the artwork selected.

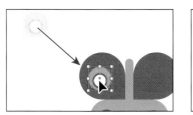

You can now see that the white circle has seemingly disappeared, and you can now see through the shape to the reddish-orange color of the butterfly wing. The white circle was used to "punch" a hole in the orange shape. With the shape still selected, you should see "Compound Path" on the left end of the Control panel above the Document window.

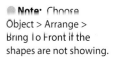

Note: Choose Object > Arrange > Bring To Front if the shapes are not showing.

Tip: You can still edit the original shapes in a compound path like this one. To edit them, select each shape individually with the Direct Selection tool (▷) or double-click the compound path with the Selection tool to enter Isolation mode and select the individual shapes.

7 Option-drag (Mac OS) or Alt-drag (Windows) the new compound path to the right side of the orange wing shape. Release the mouse button and then the key.

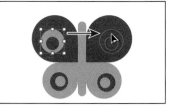

8 Select all of the shapes for the butterfly by choosing Select > All On Active Artboard.

9 Choose Object > Group.

10 Choose Object > Transform > Rotate. In the Rotate dialog box, change Angle to **-45**, select Preview, and then click OK.

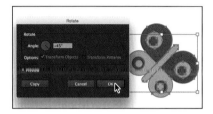

11 Choose File > Save.

Combining paths using the Shaper tool

In Lesson 3, "Using Shapes to Create Artwork for a Postcard," you learned about the Shaper tool. The Shaper tool can be used to not only create paths and shapes but also combine paths and shapes.

After combining artwork with the Shaper tool, the result is a "shaper group." The original paths are still accessible and treated like a merged group, but appearance attributes are applied to the shaper group as a whole.

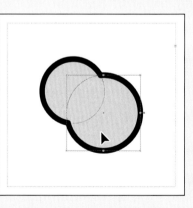

To learn more about combining paths using the Shaper tool, search for "Shaper tool" in Illustrator Help (Help > Illustrator Help).

Using the Width tool

Not only can you adjust the weight of a stroke, like you did in Lesson 3, but you can also alter regular stroke widths either by using the Width tool (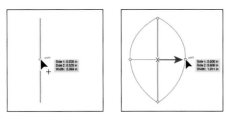) or by applying width profiles to the stroke. This allows you to create a variable width along the stroke of a path. Next, you will use the Width tool to create a bird.

1   Choose 6 Bird 4 from the Artboard menu in the lower-left corner of the Document window.

2   Choose View > Fit Artboard In Window, if necessary.

3   Choose View > Smart Guides to turn them back on.

4   Select the Width tool ( ) in the Tools panel. Position the pointer over the middle of the vertical blue line, and notice that the pointer has a plus symbol next to it ( ), indicating that if you click and drag, you will edit the stroke. Click and drag away from the line, to the right. Notice that, as you drag, you are stretching the stroke to the left and right equally. Release the mouse when the measurement label shows Side 1 and Side 2 at approximately 0.5 in.

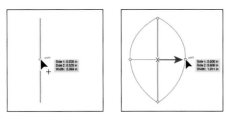

The new point on the original path that's filled with blue is called the *width point*. The lines extending from the width point are the *handles*.

5   Click in a blank area of the artboard to deselect the path. Position the pointer anywhere over the path, and the new width point you just created will appear (an arrow is pointing to it in the first part of the figure below). The width point you see inline with the pointer is where a new point would be created if you were to click. Position the pointer over the original width point, and when you see lines extending from it and the pointer changes ( ), click and drag it up a bit.

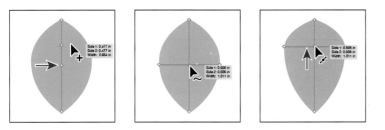

Aside from clicking and dragging to add a width point to a path, you can also double-click and enter values in a dialog box. That's what you'll do next.

> **Tip:** If you select a width point by clicking it, you can press Delete to remove it. If there was only one width point on a stroke, removing that point would remove the width completely.

> **Note:** You don't have to position the pointer over the center of the line and drag to create another width point. You can drag from anywhere in the stroke area.

6 Position the pointer over the top anchor point of the blue line, and notice that the pointer has a wavy line next to it (↖͜) and the word "anchor" appears (see the first part of the following figure). Double-click the point to create a new width point and to open the Width Point Edit dialog box.

▶ **Tip:** You can double-click anywhere along the path to add a new width point.

7 In the Width Point Edit dialog box, click the Adjust Widths Proportionately button (▨) so both Side 1 and Side 2 change together. Change the Side 1 width to **0.18 in**, and click OK.

The Width Point Edit dialog box allows you to adjust the sides together or separately, with more precision. Also, if you select the Adjust Adjoining Width Points option, any changes you make to the selected width point affect neighboring width points as well.

You can also duplicate a width point if you like, which is what you'll do next.

▶ **Tip:** You can drag one width point on top of another width point to create a discontinuous width point. If you double-click a discontinuous width point, the Width Point Edit dialog box allows you to edit both width points.

8 Position the pointer over the original anchor you created. Press the Option (Mac OS) or Alt (Windows) key, and drag down to duplicate the width point. Use the first part of the figure below to see roughly how far to drag. Release the mouse button, and then release the key.

9 Position the pointer over the right end of the width point handle and drag to the left until you see a Side 1 and Side 2 of roughly 0.3 in. You may want to select the width point you just made to see the handles.

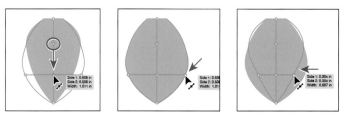

10 Click in a blank area of the artboard to deselect the path.

I'm asking you to deselect only because it's helpful to get some practice trying to select the width points. You won't need to deselect in a real-world situation.

11 Position the Width tool pointer over the blue path. The width points will appear on the path. Position the pointer over the point you just duplicated, and click when you see the width point handles appear.

To select a width point, you can click the width point, the width point handles, or the handle end points.

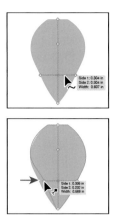

12 Option-drag (Mac OS) or Alt-drag (Windows) the left width point handle (on the left edge of the blue path area) to the right until you see a value of approximately 0.23 in for Side 2 in the measurement label. Release the mouse button and then the key.

> **Tip:** After defining the stroke width, you can save the variable width as a "profile" that you can reuse later, from the Stroke panel or the Control panel. To learn more about variable width profiles, search for "Painting with fills and strokes" in Illustrator Help (Help > Illustrator Help).

Outlining strokes

Paths, like a line, can show a stroke color but not a fill color by default. If you create a line in Illustrator and want to apply both a stroke and a fill, you can outline the stroke, which converts the line into a closed shape (or compound path).

Next, you will outline the stroke of the blue line you edited with the Width tool.

1 With the Selection tool (↖), select the blue path you edited with the Width tool and choose Object > Path > Outline Stroke. This creates a filled shape that is a closed path.

> **Tip:** After outlining the stroke, the shape you have may be composed of a lot of anchor points. You can choose Object > Path > Simplify to try and simplify the path, which usually means fewer anchor points.

> **Note:** If you outline the stroke and it shows as "Group" in the Selection Indicator on the left end of the Control panel, then there was a fill set on the line. If the artwork is a group, choose Edit > Undo Outline Stroke, apply a fill of None to the path, and then try again.

2 With the shape selected, choose Object > Transform > Rotate. In the Rotate dialog box, change the Angle to **45**, and click OK.

3 Drag the shapes into position like you see in the following figure.

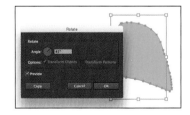

4 Choose Select > All On Active Artboard, and then choose Object > Group.

Finishing up the illustration

To finish the illustration, you will drag the artwork you grouped on each artboard into the main illustration on the left.

1 Choose View > Fit All In Window.

2 Choose View > Smart Guides to turn them off.

3 Drag each of the artwork groups into the main illustration like you see in the figure.

You may want to adjust the size of each group so they fit within the existing artwork better. With the Selection tool, you can hold down the Shift key and drag a corner point. When finished resizing, release the mouse button and then the Shift key.

4 Choose View > Smart Guides to turn them on for the next lesson.

5 Choose File > Save, and then choose File > Close.

Review questions

1 Name two ways you can combine several shapes into one.

2 What is the difference between the Scissors tool (✂) and the Knife tool (✐)?

3 How can you erase with the Eraser tool (◢) in a straight line?

4 What is the main difference between Shape Modes and Pathfinder Effects in the Pathfinder panel?

5 Why would you outline strokes?

Review answers

1 Using the Shape Builder tool (◉), you can visually and intuitively merge, delete, fill, and edit overlapping shapes and paths directly in the artwork. You can also use the Pathfinder effects, which can be found using the Effects menu or the Pathfinder panel, to create new shapes out of overlapping objects. As you saw in Lesson 3, "Using Shapes to Create Artwork for a Postcard," shapes can also be combined using the Shaper tool.

2 The Scissors tool (✂) is meant to split a path, graphics frame, or empty text frame at an anchor point or along a segment. The Knife tool (✐) cuts objects along a path you draw with the tool, dividing objects. When you cut shapes with the Knife tool, they become closed paths.

3 In order to erase in a straight line with the Eraser tool (◢), you need to press and hold the Shift key before you begin dragging with the Eraser.

4 In the Pathfinder panel, when a Shape Mode (such as Unite) is applied, the original objects selected are permanently transformed, but you can hold down a modifier key, and the original underlying objects are preserved. When a Pathfinder effect (such as Merge) is applied, the original objects selected are permanently transformed.

5 Paths, like a line, can show a stroke color but not a fill color by default. If you create a line in Illustrator and want to apply both a stroke and a fill, you can outline the stroke, which converts the line into a closed shape (or compound path).

5 TRANSFORMING ARTWORK

Lesson overview

In this lesson, you'll learn how to do the following:

- Add, edit, rename, and reorder artboards in an existing document.

- Navigate artboards.

- Work with rulers and guides.

- Move, scale, and rotate objects using a variety of methods.

- Reflect, shear, and distort objects.

- Position objects with precision.

- Position and align content with Smart Guides.

- Use the Free Transform tool to distort an object.

- Create a PDF.

 This lesson takes approximately 60 minutes to complete.

Download the project files for this lesson from the Lesson & Update Files tab on your Account page at www.peachpit.com and store them on your computer in a convenient location, as described in the "Getting Started" section of this book.

Your Account page is also where you'll find any updates to the chapters or to the lesson files. Look on the Lesson & Update Files tab to access the most current content.

You can modify objects in many ways as you create artwork, by quickly and precisely controlling their size, shape, and orientation. In this lesson, you'll explore creating and editing artboards, the various Transform commands, and specialized tools, while creating several pieces of artwork.

Getting started

In this lesson, you'll transform artwork and use it in a ticket for a sporting event. Before you begin, you'll restore the default preferences for Adobe Illustrator and then open a file containing the finished artwork to see what you'll create.

1 To ensure that the tools and panels function exactly as described in this lesson, delete or deactivate (by renaming) the Adobe Illustrator CC preferences file. See "Restoring default preferences" in the "Getting Started" section at the beginning of the book.

● **Note:** If you have not already downloaded the project files for this lesson to your computer from your Account page, make sure to do so now. See the "Getting Started" section at the beginning of the book.

2 Start Adobe Illustrator CC.

3 Choose File > Open, and open the L5_end.ai file in the Lessons > Lesson05 folder on your hard disk.

This file contains the three artboards that make up the front, back, and inside of a folding ticket for a sporting event.

4 Choose View > Fit All In Window, and leave the artwork onscreen as you work. If you don't want to leave the file open, choose File > Close (without saving).

To begin working, you'll open an existing art file.

5 Choose File > Open. If a panel appears, click Open in the panel. You could also choose File > Open again. In the Open dialog box, navigate to the Lessons > Lesson05 folder and select the L5_start.ai file on your hard disk. Click Open to open the file.

6 Choose File > Save As. In the Save As dialog box, name the file **Ticket.ai**, and navigate to the Lesson05 folder. Leave the Format option set to Adobe Illustrator (ai) (Mac OS) or the Save As Type option set to Adobe Illustrator (*.AI) (Windows), and then click Save.

● **Note:** If you don't see Reset Essentials in the Workspace menu, choose Window > Workspace > Essentials before choosing Window > Workspace > Reset Essentials.

7 In the Illustrator Options dialog box, leave the Illustrator options at their default settings, and then click OK.

8 Choose Window > Workspace > Reset Essentials.

Working with artboards

Artboards represent the regions that can contain printable artwork, similar to pages in Adobe InDesign. You can use multiple artboards for creating a variety of things, such as multiple-page PDF files, printed pages with different sizes or different elements, independent elements for websites, or video storyboards, for instance.

Adding artboards to the document

You can add and remove artboards at any time while working in a document. You can create artboards in different sizes, resize them with the Artboard tool (⌗) or Artboards panel (▦), and position them anywhere in the Document window. All artboards are numbered and can have a unique name assigned to them.

Next, you will add two more artboards to the Ticket.ai document. Since this is a ticket for a sporting event that will fold, each artboard will be a different face of the ticket (front, inside, and back).

1 Choose View > Fit Artboard In Window, and then press Command+– (Mac OS) or Ctrl+– (Windows) to zoom out.

2 Press the spacebar to temporarily access the Hand tool (✋). Drag the artboard to the left to see more of the darker canvas to the right of the artboard.

3 Select the Artboard tool (⌗) in the Tools panel. Position the Artboard tool pointer to the right of the existing artboard and in line with its top edge (a purple alignment guide appears). Drag down and to the right to create an artboard that is 3.5 in (width) by 6 in (height).

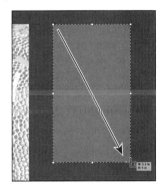

It doesn't have to be exact right now since you'll adjust the size later. The measurement label indicates the artboard size.

Tip: If you find it difficult to make the width value exactly 3.5 in, you can always change the W: (width) value in the Control panel, after you finish drawing the artboard.

4 Click the Artboards panel icon (▦) on the right side of the workspace to show it.

The Artboards panel allows you to see how many artboards the document currently contains. It also allows you to reorder, rename, add, and delete artboards and to choose many other options related to artboards. Notice that Artboard 2 is highlighted in the panel. The active (selected) artboard is always highlighted in this panel.

Next, you will create a copy of an artboard using this panel.

5 Click the New Artboard button (▣) at the bottom of the panel to create a copy of Artboard 2, called Artboard 3. The copy is placed to the right of Artboard 2 in the Document window.

6 Choose View > Fit All In Window to see all of your artboards and leave the Artboard tool selected.

Editing artboards

After creating artboards, you can edit or delete artboards at any time by using the Artboard tool (⊞), menu commands, or the Artboards panel. Next, you will reposition and change the sizes of several of the artboards using multiple methods.

1 Press Command+− (Mac OS) or Ctrl+− (Windows) *twice* to zoom out further.

2 With the Artboard tool (⊞) selected, drag Artboard 3 to the left of the original (larger) artboard. You can reposition artboards at any time and even overlap them, if necessary.

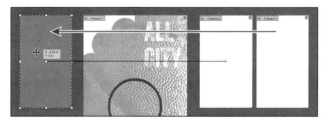

3 With the Artboard tool selected, drag the bottom-center bounding point of the artboard you moved, down until the height is 8 in, as shown in the measurement label. The bottom will snap to the bottom of the larger artboard to its right, and a magenta alignment (smart) guide will appear.

Another way to resize an artboard is to do so by entering values in the Control panel, which is what you'll do next.

4 Click in Artboard 2 to the right of the larger artboard in the middle. "Artboard 2" will be highlighted in the Artboards panel. Select the upper-middle point in the reference point locator () in the Control panel. Change the height to **8** in the Control panel and press Enter or Return to accept the value.

Tip: With the Artboard tool (⌗) selected, you can press the Shift key to resize an artboard proportionally or press the Option (Mac OS) or Alt (Windows) key and drag to resize an artboard from its center.

Selecting the upper-middle point allows you to resize an artboard from the top center of the artboard. By default, artboards are resized from their center.

In the Control panel, with the Artboard tool selected, you will see many options for editing the currently active artboard. The Preset menu lets you change a selected artboard to a set size. Notice that the sizes in the Preset menu include typical print, video, tablet, and web sizes. You can also fit the artboard to the artwork bounds or the selected art, which is a great way to fit an artboard to a logo, for instance. Other options in the Control panel include the ability to switch orientation, rename or delete the artboard, and even show other helpful guides like a center point or video-safe areas.

Note: If you don't see the Width (W) and Height (H) fields in the Control panel, click the Artboard Options button (▤) in the Control panel and enter the values in the dialog box that appears.

> **Tip:** You can see the Constrain Width and Height Proportions icon (▥) in the Control panel, between the Width and Height fields. This icon, if selected (▥), allows the width and height to change in proportion to each other.

5 Select the Selection tool (▶), and choose View > Fit All In Window.

Notice the *very* subtle black outline around Artboard 2, with "2" showing in the Artboard Navigation menu (lower-left corner of the Document window), and "Artboard 2" highlighted in the Artboards panel, all of which indicate that Artboard 2 is the currently active artboard. There can be only one active artboard at a time. Commands such as View > Fit Artboard In Window apply to the active artboard.

Renaming artboards

By default, artboards are assigned a number and a name. When you navigate the artboards in a document, it can be helpful to name them. Next, you are going to rename the artboards so that the names are more useful.

1 In the Artboards panel, double-click the name "Artboard 1." Change the name to **Inside**, and press Enter or Return.

> **Tip:** You can also change the name of an artboard by double-clicking the Artboard tool (⌗) in the Tools panel. Doing so changes the name for the currently active artboard in the Artboard Options dialog box. You can make an artboard the currently active artboard by clicking it with the Selection tool (▶).

You will now rename the rest of the artboards.

Note: You only need to single-click the icon when the artboard name is highlighted in the panel.

2 Double-click the Artboard Options icon (▣) to the right of the name "Artboard 2" in the Artboards panel. This opens the Artboard Options dialog box.

▶ **Tip:** The Artboard Options icon (▣) appears to the right of the name of each artboard in the Artboards panel. It not only allows access to the artboard options for each artboard but also indicates the orientation (vertical or horizontal) of the artboard.

3 In the Artboard Options dialog box, change Name to **Back**, and click OK.

The Artboard Options dialog box has a lot of extra options as well as a few you've already seen, like width and height.

4 Double-click the name "Artboard 3" in the panel, and change the name to **Front**. Press Enter or Return to accept the name.

5 Choose File > Save, and keep the Artboards panel showing for the next steps.

Reordering artboards

When you navigate your document, the order in which the artboards appear can be important, especially if you are navigating the document using the Next artboard (▶) and Previous artboard (◀) buttons. By default, artboards are ordered according to the order in which they are created, but you can change that order. Next, you will reorder the artboards in the Artboards panel.

1 With the Artboards panel open, double-click the number 1 to the left of the name "Inside" in the Artboards panel.

This makes the artboard named "Inside" the active artboard and fits it in the Document window.

2 Click and drag the "Front" artboard name up until a line appears above the artboard named "Inside." Release the mouse button.

This moves the artboard up in order so that it becomes the first artboard in the list.

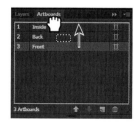

▶ **Tip:** You can also reorder the artboards by selecting an artboard in the Artboards panel and clicking the Move Up (⬆) or Move Down (⬇) button at the bottom of the panel.

3 Double-click to the right or left of the name "Front" in the Artboards panel to fit that artboard in the Document window, if necessary.

4 Click the Next artboard button () in the lower-left corner of the Document window to navigate to the next artboard (Inside). This fits the Inside artboard in the Document window.

If you had not changed the order, the next artboard would have been dimmed since the "Front" artboard was the last artboard in the Artboards panel (there was no artboard after it).

5 Choose File > Save.

Now that the artboards are set up, you will concentrate on transforming artwork to create the content for your project.

Editing document setup options

When working with artboards for the current document, you can change default setup options, like units of measure, bleed guides, type settings (such as language), and more in the Document Setup dialog box. Here's two ways you can access the Document Setup dialog box:

- Choose File > Document Setup.

- If nothing is selected in the Document window, click the Document Setup button in the Control panel.

There are two sets of options in the Document Setup dialog box that will be worth exploring: **General** and **Type**. In the General options, you can change the units and set bleed guides, among a host of other options.

Transforming content

In Lesson 4, "Editing and Combining Shapes and Paths," you learned how to take simple paths and shapes and create more complex artwork by editing and combining that content. That was a form of transforming artwork. In this lesson, you'll learn how to transform content by moving, rotating, reflecting, scaling, shearing, and either free distort or perspective distorting objects. Objects can be transformed using the Transform panel, selection tools, specialized tools, Transform commands, guides, Smart Guides, and more.

Working with rulers and guides

To start this lesson on transforming, you'll learn about aligning and measuring content using rulers and guides. *Rulers* help you accurately place and measure objects. They appear at the top and left in the Document window and can be shown and hidden. *Guides* are non-printing lines created from the rulers that help you align objects. Next, you'll create a few guides based on ruler measurements so that later you can more accurately align content.

1 Choose View > Rulers > Show Rulers, if you don't see the rulers along the top edge and left edge of the Document window.

2 Choose View > Fit All In Window.

3 With the Selection tool (▶) selected, click each of the artboards and, as you do, look at the horizontal and vertical rulers (along the top and left side of the Document window). Notice that 0 (zero) for each ruler is always in the upper-left corner of the active (selected) artboard (the last artboard you clicked in).

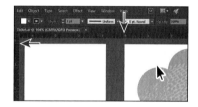

The point on each ruler (horizontal and vertical) where the 0 appears is called the *ruler origin*. By default, the ruler origin is in the upper-left corner of the active artboard. As you can see, the 0 point on both rulers corresponds to the edges of the active artboard.

There are two types of rulers in Illustrator: *artboard rulers* and *global rulers*. Artboard rulers, which are the default rulers that you are seeing, set the ruler origin at the upper-left corner of the *active* artboard. Global rulers set the ruler origin at the upper-left corner of the *first* artboard, or the artboard that is at the top of the list in the Artboards panel, no matter which artboard is active.

● **Note:** You could switch between artboard and global rulers by choosing View > Rulers > and selecting Change To Global Rulers or Change To Artboard Rulers, (depending on which option is currently chosen), but don't do that now.

4 With the Selection tool, click in the leftmost artboard, called "Front."

As you just saw, that sets the first artboard as the active artboard and sets the ruler origin at the upper-left corner of that same artboard.

5 Open the Layers panel by choosing Window > Layers, and select the layer named "Edit."

Guides are similar to drawn objects in that they can be selected and repositioned, or they can be deleted by pressing the Backspace/Delete key. They're also listed in the Layers panel on the active layer; that's why you selected the Edit layer.

6 Shift-drag from the left vertical ruler to the right to create a vertical guide at 1 inch on the horizontal ruler (the ruler above the artboard) on the "Front" artboard. When the guide reaches 1 inch on the ruler, release the mouse button, and then release the Shift key.

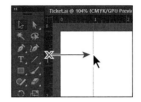

Dragging with the Shift key pressed "snaps" guides to the measurements on the ruler. The guide is selected, and when selected, its color matches the color of the layer that it's associated with (red in this case).

7 With the guide still selected (in this case it will be red in color), change the X value in the Control panel to **0.25 in**, and press Enter or Return.

Note: If you don't see the X value, you can click the word "Transform" in the Control panel or open the Transform panel (Window > Transform).

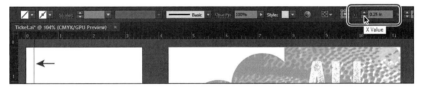

On the horizontal ruler, measurements to the right of 0 (zero) are positive and to the left are negative. On the vertical ruler, measurements below 0 (zero) are positive and above are negative.

Tip: To change the units for a document, you can right-click either ruler and choose the new units.

8 Position the pointer in the upper-left corner of the Document window, where the rulers intersect (⊞), drag the pointer to the lower-left corner of the artboard and release the mouse button.

As you drag, a crosshair in the window and in the rulers indicates the changing ruler origin. This sets the ruler origin (0,0) to the lower-left corner of the artboard. This can be very useful when you need to place content a set distance from the bottom edge of the artboard, for instance.

Tip: If you Command-drag (Mac OS) or Ctrl-drag (Windows) from the ruler intersect, you create a horizontal and vertical guide that intersects where you release the mouse button and then release the Ctrl or Command key.

Next, you'll add a guide using a different method that can sometimes be faster.

9 Select the Zoom tool (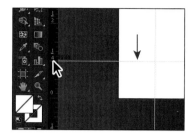) and click several times, slowly, on the lower-left corner of the artboard until you see 1/4-inch measurements on the ruler. I had to click at least four times.

10 Shift-double-click the vertical ruler at the 1/4-inch mark (the ruler to the left of the artboard), *above* the 0 on the ruler.

This creates a guide that crosses the bottom part of the artboard at –0.25 inches from the bottom.

11 Position the pointer in the upper-left corner of the Document window, where the rulers intersect (▦), and double-click to reset the ruler origin to the upper-left corner of the artboard.

12 Choose View > Guides > Lock Guides to prevent them from being accidentally moved.

The guides are no longer selected and are aqua in color by default.

▶ **Tip:** You can also hide and show guides by pressing Command+; (Mac OS) or Ctrl+; (Windows).

13 Choose View > Fit All In Window.

14 Select the Selection tool (▶), and click to select the white text "ALL CITY."

15 Choose View > Hide Edges so you only see the bounding box of the grouped paths. Drag the text group into the lower-left corner of the artboard with the guides. When it's roughly positioned in the guides, release the mouse button.

Choosing Hide Edges hides the inside edges of the shapes, but not the bounding box. It can make it easier to move and position artwork.

Positioning objects precisely

At times, you may want to position objects more precisely—either relative to other objects or to the artboard. You could use the alignment options, like you saw in Lesson 2, "Techniques for Selecting Artwork," but you can also use Smart Guides and the Transform panel to move objects to exact coordinates on the x- and y-axes and to control the position of objects in relation to the edge of the artboard.

Positioning artwork using the Transform panel

Next, you'll add content to the backgrounds of two artboards and then position that content precisely.

1 Press Command+– (Mac OS) or Ctrl+– (Windows) (or View > Zoom Out) *three times* to zoom out. You should see artwork off the bottom edge of the artboards.

2 Click the artboard with the guides on it (the artboard named "Front") to ensure that it is the active artboard (check the origin of the rulers and make sure that 0,0 starts in the upper-left corner of the artboard).

3 With the Selection tool (▶), click to select the large background shape on the far left, below the artboards (labeled "1").

4 Click the upper-left point of the reference point locator (▦) in the Control panel. Then, change the X value to **0** and the Y value to **0**.

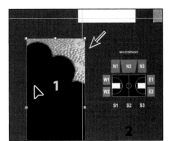

> **Note:** Again, depending on the resolution of your screen, the Transform options may not appear in the Control panel. If they do not appear, you can click the word "Transform" to see the Transform panel, or you can choose Window > Transform.

The content should now be precisely positioned on the artboard since it was the same size as the artboard to begin with.

5 In the Artboards panel, on the right side of the workspace, select the artboard named "Back" to make it the active artboard.

6 Select the group with the "City Arena" text in it labeled "6," below the artboards. You may need to either zoom out or scroll over and down to see it.

7 With the upper-left point of the reference point locator (⊞) selected in the Control panel, change the X value to **0** and the Y value to **0**.

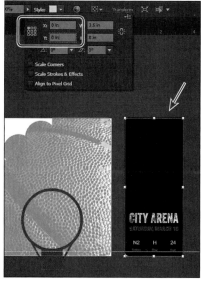

Positioning artwork using Smart Guides

Next, you will use Smart Guides to move content. When moving objects with Smart Guides turned on (View > Smart Guides), measurement labels appear next to the pointer and display the distance (X and Y) from the object's original location. You will use these to make sure that an object is a certain distance from the edge of the artboard.

1 With the Selection tool, select the basketball hoop and net directly beneath the "Back" artboard (labeled "5").

2 With the upper-left point of the reference point locator (⊞) in the Control panel selected, change the X value to **0** and the Y value to **0** to position the artwork into the upper-left corner of the artboard.

3 Choose View > Fit Artboard In Window.

● **Note:** You can also choose Illustrator CC > Preferences > Smart Guides (Mac OS) or Edit > Preferences > Smart Guides (Windows) and deselect the Measurement Labels option to turn off just the measurement labels when Smart Guides are on.

4 Using the Selection tool, position the pointer over the selected basketball hoop with the net and drag the group down and to the right. As you drag, press the Shift key to constrain the movement to 45°. When the measurement label shows *approximately* dX: 0.25 in and dY: 0.25 in, release the mouse button and then the Shift key. Leave the artwork selected.

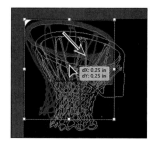

The dX indicates the distance moved along the x axis (horizontally), and dY indicates the distance moved along the y-axis (vertically). Don't worry if you can't get the exact values; it's difficult when zoomed out so far. Also, because there is other content on the canvas, Smart Guides are attempting to snap to it. You can always change the X and Y values in the Control panel or Transform panel.

5 Choose File > Save.

Scaling objects

So far in this book, you've scaled most content with the selection tools. In this lesson, you'll use several other methods for scaling artwork.

1 With the artwork (basketball hoop and net) still selected, click the word "Transform" to show the Transform panel and ensure that the upper-left point of the reference point locator (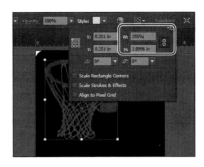) is selected. Click to select the Constrain Width And Height Proportions icon (⬚). Change the Width (W:) to **255%** (*make sure* to type the %). Press Enter or Return to accept the value.

● **Note:** The figure shows the Width value before pressing Enter or Return.

▶ **Tip:** When typing values to transform content, you can type different units such as percent (%) or pixels (px), and they will be converted to the default unit, which is inches (in) in this case.

2 Choose View > Fit All In Window.

3 Press Command+– (Mac OS) or Ctrl+– (Windows) (or View > Zoom Out) *two or three times* to zoom out. You should see content off the bottom edge of the artboards again. You may need to scroll down to see all of the content.

4 Select the basketball labeled "3" and double-click the Scale tool (⬚) in the Tools panel.

5 In the Scale dialog box, change Uniform to **61%**. Toggle Preview on and off to see the change in size. Click OK.

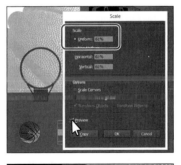

▶ **Tip:** You could also choose Object > Transform > Scale to access the Scale dialog box.

6 Select the Selection tool (▶), and drag the basketball onto the first artboard named "Front," like you see in the figure.

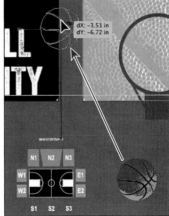

7 Select the basketball court group below the larger artboard (labeled "4"). Notice that the Stroke weight in the Control panel shows as 1 pt.

8 Select the Zoom tool (🔍) in the Tools panel, and click three or four times, *slowly*, to zoom in to it.

9 Choose View > Show Edges to show the inside edges of the artwork.

10 Open the Transform panel by clicking the X, Y, W, or H link in the Control panel (or the word "Transform" if that appears in the Control panel). Select Scale Strokes & Effects.

● **Note:** Depending on the resolution of your screen, the Transform options may not appear in the Control panel. If they do not appear, you can click the word "Transform" to see the Transform panel or you can choose Window > Transform.

11 In the Control panel, either click the word "Transform" to reveal the Transform panel or click the center reference point of the reference point locator (▦) in the Control panel. Ensure that the Constrain Width And Height Proportions is set (⊠), type **3.5** in the Width (W) field, and then press Enter or Return to increase the size of the artwork. Notice that the Stroke weight has scaled as well and is now 2 pt. Leave the artwork selected.

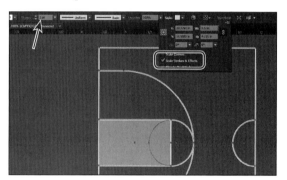

By default, strokes and effects, like drop shadows, are not scaled along with objects. For instance, if you enlarge a circle with a 1 pt stroke, the stroke remains 1 pt. But by selecting Scale Strokes & Effects before you scale—and then scaling the object—that 1 pt stroke would scale (change) relative to the amount of scaling applied to the object.

Reflecting objects

When you *reflect* an object, Illustrator flips the object across an invisible vertical or horizontal axis. In a similar way to scaling and rotating, when you reflect an object, you either designate the reference point or use the object's center point, by default.

Next, you'll use the Reflect tool (⚐) to flip the basketball court artwork 90° across the vertical axis and copy it.

1   Select the Reflect tool (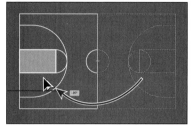), which is nested
    within the Rotate tool (⟳) in the Tools panel.
    Click the right edge of the basketball court group
    (the word "anchor" or "path" may appear).

    This sets the invisible axis that the shape will
    reflect around on the right edge of the selected
    artwork, rather than on the center, which is
    the default.

▶ **Tip:** If all you want
to do is flip content
in place, you can also
choose Flip Horizontal
or Flip Vertical from
the Transform panel
menu (▤).

2   With the basketball court artwork
    still selected, position the pointer off
    the right edge and drag clockwise.
    As you are dragging, hold down
    the Shift+Option (Mac OS) or
    Shift+Alt (Windows) keys. When the
    measurement label shows −90°, release
    the mouse button and then release the
    modifier keys.

▶ **Tip:** You can
reflect and copy in one
step. With the Reflect
tool (☑) selected,
Option-click (Mac OS)
or Alt-click (Windows)
to set a point to reflect
around and to open the
Reflect dialog box, in
one step. Select Vertical,
and then click Copy.

The Shift key constrains the rotation to 45° as the artwork is reflected, and the
Option (Alt) key will copy the artwork. Leave the new court artwork where it is
for now. You'll move it later.

3   Select the Selection tool (▶), drag across both groups, and then choose
    Object > Group.

Distorting objects with effects

You can distort the original shapes of objects in different ways, using various tools.
Now you'll distort the basketball net using the Pucker & Bloat effect. These are
different types of transformations because they are applied as effects, which means
you could ultimately edit the effect later or remove it in the Appearance panel.

● **Note:** To learn
more about effects, see
Lesson 12, "Exploring
Creative Uses of Effects
and Graphic Styles."

1   Choose 2 Inside from the Artboard Navigation menu to fit the larger artboard in
    the Document window.

2   Click the Layers panel icon (▨) to open the
    panel, click the visibility column (an arrow is
    pointing to it in the figure) to the left of the Net
    layer name to show that content, and click the
    eye icon (◉) to the left of the Background layer
    to hide its contents.

3   Click to select the red triangle shape on the
    artboard. Choose Effect > Distort & Transform >
    Pucker & Bloat.

4 In the Pucker & Bloat dialog box, select Preview and drag the slider to the left to change the value to roughly −20%, which distorts the triangle. Click OK.

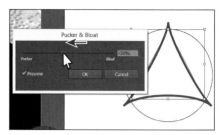

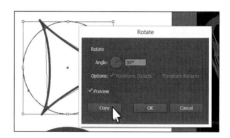

▶ **Tip:** To access the Rotate dialog box, you can also double-click the Rotate tool (↻) in the Tools panel. The Transform panel (Window > Transform) also has a rotate option.

5 Drag across the triangle and circle to select them both. Choose Object > Transform > Rotate. In the Rotate dialog box, change Angle to **30**, select Preview, and then click **Copy**.

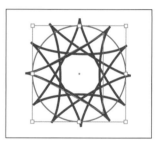

You will learn more about rotating artwork in the next section.

6 Choose Object > Transform > Transform Again to repeat the rotation and copy on the selected shapes.

7 Press Command+D (Mac OS) or Ctrl+D (Windows) once to apply the transformation one more time.

Command+D (Mac OS) or Ctrl+D (Windows) is simply the keyboard shortcut for the Object > Transform > Transform Again command.

8 Choose Select > Deselect; then drag across the edge of *just* the circle (see the following figure) to select all of the copies, and press Delete.

9 Drag across the triangles to select them all, and choose Object > Group.

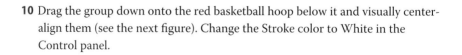

10 Drag the group down onto the red basketball hoop below it and visually center-align them (see the next figure). Change the Stroke color to White in the Control panel.

11 In the Layers panel, click the visibility column to the left of the Background and the Text layers to show the content for each.

12 Choose 3 Back from the Artboard Navigation menu, and select the basketball net above the "CITY ARENA" text.

13 Choose Effect > Distort & Transform > Free Distort.

14 In the Free Distort dialog box, drag the lower-left and lower-right points so they match the figure. Click OK.

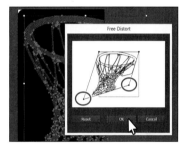

Note: To better see the transformed artwork, you can choose Select > Deselect.

▶ **Tip:** Later in this lesson, you will learn about the Free Transform tool (⧉) that has a free distort option. Applying a free distort via the Free Transform tool is permanent and affects the underlying artwork, whereas the Free Distort effect can be edited and even removed later because it's an effect.

Rotating objects

You rotate objects by turning them around a designated reference point. There are lots of ways to do this, including methods that range from more precise to more free-form rotation.

First, you'll rotate the basketball manually, using the Selection tool.

1 Choose 1 Front from the Artboard Navigation menu in the lower-left corner of the Document window.

2 With the Selection tool (▶), select the basketball. Option-drag (Mac OS) or Alt-drag (Windows) the basketball up and to the left to create a copy. When the artwork is positioned like you see in the figure, release the mouse button and then the modifier key.

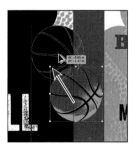

3 Position the pointer just off either the upper-right or lower-right corner points of the bounding box of the basketball you just created, and when the pointer changes to rotate arrows (↰), drag in a counterclockwise fashion (up). When the measurement label shows *approximately* 15°, release the mouse button.

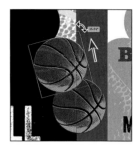

Next, you'll rotate content using the Rotate tool (⟳) and learn how this method can be different from rotating with the Selection tool.

4 With the Selection tool, Option-drag (Mac OS) or Alt-drag (Windows) the selected basketball up and to the left to create another copy. When the artwork is positioned like you see in the following figure, release the mouse button and then the modifier key.

5 Select the Rotate tool (⟳) in the Tools panel (it's under the Reflect tool). Notice the rotate-around point in the center of the basketball artwork. The Rotate tool allows you to rotate the object around a different reference point. Position the pointer to the right of the basketball, drag counterclockwise (up) until the measurement label shows approximately 15°, and then release the mouse button.

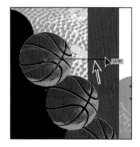

6 With the Selection tool, Option-drag (Mac OS) or Alt-drag (Windows) the selected basketball up and to the left to create a final copy. When the artwork is positioned like you see in the following figure, release the mouse button and then the modifier key.

7 With the last basketball selected, double-click the Rotate tool in the Tools panel. In the Rotate dialog box that appears, the last rotation value should be the value set for the Angle value. It should be approximately 15°. Make sure it's **15°** and click OK.

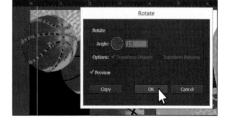

8 Choose View > Fit All In Window.

9 Press Command+− (Mac OS) or Ctrl+− (Windows) (or View > Zoom Out) *twice* to zoom out. You should see content off the bottom edge of the artboards again.

10 Choose File > Save.

Shearing objects

Shearing an object slants, or skews, the sides of the object along the axis you specify, keeping opposite sides parallel and making the object asymmetrical.

Next, you'll copy artwork and apply shear to it.

1 Select the Selection tool (▶). Click to select the grouped content below the first artboard labeled "2." You may need to scroll in the Document window to see it.

2 Choose Edit > Cut, and then choose "3 Back" from the Artboard Navigation menu in the lower-left corner of the Document window.

3 Press Cmd+R (Mac OS) or Ctrl+R (Windows) to hide the rulers.

4 Choose View > Fit Artboard In Window.

5 Select the basketball net, and choose Object > Hide > Selection.

6 Choose Edit > Paste to paste a copy in the center of the artboard.

7 Begin dragging the group of content up, and as you drag, press the Shift key to constrain the movement. Drag it up until it looks something like you see in the figure (the dY value in the measurement label will be approximately -1.5 in). Release the mouse button and then the Shift key.

8 Choose Object > Ungroup and then Select > Deselect.

9 Press Command++ (Mac OS) or Ctrl++ (Windows) once to zoom in to the artboard.

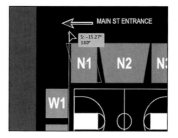

10 Select the gray rectangle beneath the "N1" text. Select the Shear tool (↗), nested within the Scale tool (⬚) in the Tools panel. Position the pointer above the shape; press the Shift key and drag to the left a bit. Release the mouse button and then the key.

The Shift key constrains the artwork to its original width. If you were shearing a single object and precision didn't matter, you could leave the object as is. But this artwork requires the shapes beneath "N1" and "N3" to have the same shearing applied.

11 Choose Edit > Undo Shear.

12 With the rectangle still selected, double-click the Shear tool. In the Shear dialog box, change the Shear Angle to **170**, turn Preview on and off a few times, and click OK.

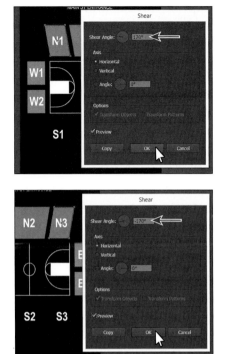

13 With the Selection tool, select the gray rectangle beneath the "N3" text. Double-click the Shear tool in the Tools panel, change Shear Angle to **–170**, select Preview, and click OK. Leave the rectangle selected.

▶ **Tip:** You can also apply shear numerically in the Transform panel (Window > Transform) or in the Shear dialog box (Object > Transform > Shear).

14 With the "N3" rectangle still selected, select the Selection tool, and with the Shift key pressed, select the gray rectangles behind the "N1" and "N2" text to select all three.

15 Choose Object > Group.

16 Select the Rotate tool (⟳) and position the pointer over the center of the circle below (circled in the figure). When the green word "center" appears, Option-click (Mac OS) or Alt-click (Windows). In the Rotate dialog box, change the Angle to **180**, and click **Copy**.

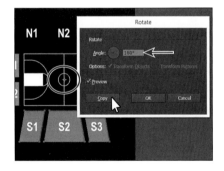

17 Choose Object > Show All to show the basketball net you hid earlier.

18 Choose Select > Deselect, and then choose File > Save.

Transforming with the Free Transform tool

The Free Transform tool (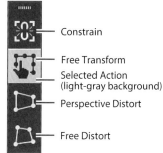) is a multipurpose tool that allows you to distort an object, combining functions like moving, scaling, shearing, rotating, and distorting (perspective or free). The Free Transform tool is also touch-enabled, which means you can control transformation using touch controls on certain devices. For more information on touch controls, see the sidebar at the end of this section.

Note: To learn more about the options for the Free Transform tool, search for "Free Transform" in Adobe Help (Help > Illustrator Help).

1 Select the Selection tool (➤) in the Tools panel. Press the spacebar to access the Hand tool (✋) temporarily. Drag up so you can see the basketball court group (labeled "4") beneath the artboards.

2 Click to select the basketball court group, and then select the Free Transform tool (▸) in the Tools panel.

After selecting the Free Transform tool, the Free Transform widget appears in the Document window. This widget, which is free-floating and can be repositioned, contains options to change how the Free Transform tool works. By default, the Free Transform tool allows you to move, shear, rotate, and scale objects. By selecting other options, like Perspective Distort, you can change how the tool transforms content.

— Constrain

— Free Transform
— Selected Action
(light-gray background)
— Perspective Distort

— Free Distort

First, you'll change the width of the selected artwork using the Free Transform tool.

3 Position the pointer over the left middle point of the artwork bounding box, and the pointer changes its appearance (↔), indicating that you can shear or distort. Begin dragging to the right. As you drag, press the Option (Mac OS) or Alt (Windows) key to change both sides at once. Notice that you can't drag the artwork up or down—the movement is constrained to horizontal by default. When a width of *approximately* 3.7 in shows in the measurement label, release the mouse button and then the key.

Note: If you were to drag the side bounding point up first to distort the artwork by shearing, the movement wouldn't be constrained, and you could move in any direction.

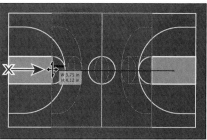

Next, you will rotate with the Free Transform tool around a specific point.

4 Position the pointer over the lower-left corner of the selected artwork and double-click when the pointer looks like this (⟲). This moves the reference point and ensures that the artwork will rotate around it. Press the Shift key, and drag the upper-right corner in a counterclockwise fashion until you see 90° in the measurement label. Release the mouse button and then the Shift key.

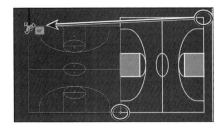

● **Note:** If you find that, by trying to rotate, you are instead scaling, stop dragging and choose Edit > Undo Scale and try again.

Like other transform tools, by holding down the Shift key while dragging with the Free Transform tool, you can constrain the movement for most of the transformations. If you don't want to hold down the Shift key, you can also select the Constrain option in the Free Transform widget before transforming to constrain movement automatically. After dragging, the Constrain option is deselected.

5 Position the pointer over the right middle point of the artwork bounding box, and drag to the right. Drag until a width of approximately 7.7 in shows in the measurement label.

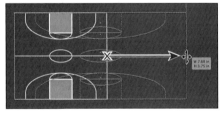

6 With the Free Transform tool still selected, click the Perspective Distort option in the Free Transform widget (circled in the following figure).

With this option selected, you can drag a corner point of the bounding box to distort the perspective.

7 Position the pointer over the upper-left corner of the bounding box, and the pointer changes in appearance (ᐟ▷). Drag to the right until it looks like the figure.

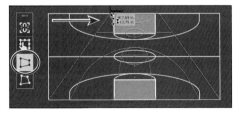

8 Change the Opacity to **60%** in the Control panel.

9 Press Command+− (Mac OS) or Ctrl+− (Windows) several times to zoom out, until you see the artboard with the basketballs on it.

10 Select the Selection tool and drag the artwork onto the artboard similar to what you see in the figure.

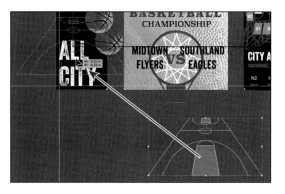

● **Note:** If the artwork appears on top of the text, choose Object > Arrange > Send To Back as many times as necessary to arrange it behind the text.

11 Choose View > Fit All In Window.

12 Select the Artboard tool (⊞) in the Tools panel. Drag the 1 Front artboard to the left until the basketball court is no longer overlapping the artboard to the right.

▶ **Tip:** You could also simply mask the content that is outside of the artboard. You will learn about clipping masks in Lesson 14, "Using Illustrator CC with Other Adobe Applications."

● **Note:** When you drag an artboard with content on it, the art moves with the artboard, by default. If you want to move an artboard but not the art on it, select the Artboard tool (⊞), and then click to deselect Move/Copy Artwork With Artboard (▨) in the Control panel.

13 Choose File > Save.

The Free Transform tool and touch-enabled devices

In Illustrator CC, the Free Transform tool is touch-enabled. This means that, if you are using either a Windows 7, 8, or 10 touchscreen PC or a touchscreen device like Wacom Cintiq 24HD Touch, you can utilize certain touch-enabled features.

Here are a few noteworthy examples:

- You can touch and drag from the center of an object and move the reference point.

- Double-tapping any of the corner points moves the reference point for the object to that point.

- Double-tapping the reference point resets it to the default position (if it's not already there).

- To constrain movement, you can tap the Constrain option in the widget before transforming.

Creating a PDF

Portable Document Format (PDF) is a universal file format that preserves the fonts, images, and layout of source documents created on a wide range of applications and platforms. Adobe PDF is the standard for the secure, reliable distribution and exchange of electronic documents and forms around the world. Adobe PDF files are compact and complete, and can be shared, viewed, and printed by anyone with free Adobe Reader software.

You can create different types of PDF files from within Illustrator. You can create multipage PDFs, layered PDFs, and PDF/x-compliant files. Layered PDFs allow you to save one PDF with layers that can be used in different contexts. PDF/X-compliant files ease the burden of color, font, and trapping issues in printing. Next, you will save this project as a PDF so that you can send it to someone else to view.

1   Choose File > Save As. In the Save As dialog box, choose Adobe PDF (pdf) from the Format menu (Mac OS) or Adobe PDF (*.PDF) from the Save As Type menu (Windows). Navigate to the Lessons > Lesson05 folder, if necessary. Notice that you have the option, at the bottom of the dialog box, to save all of the artboards in the PDF or a range of artboards. Click Save.

● **Note:** If you want to learn about the options and other presets in the Save Adobe PDF dialog box, choose Help > Illustrator Help and search for "Creating Adobe PDF files."

2   In the Save Adobe PDF dialog box, click the Adobe PDF Preset menu to see all of the different PDF presets available. Ensure that [Illustrator Default] is chosen and click Save PDF.

There are many ways to customize the creation of a PDF. Creating a PDF using the [Illustrator Default] preset creates a PDF in which all Illustrator data is preserved. PDFs created with this preset can be reopened in Illustrator without any loss of data. If you are planning on saving a PDF for a particular purpose, such as viewing on the web or printing, you may want to choose another preset or adjust the options.

3   Choose File > Save, if necessary, and then choose File > Close.

Review questions

1 Name two ways to change the size of an existing active artboard.

2 What is the *ruler origin*?

3 What is the difference between *artboard rulers* and *global rulers*?

4 Briefly describe what the Scale Strokes & Effects option in the Transform panel does.

5 Name at least three transformations that can be applied with the Free Transform tool.

Review answers

1 To change the size of an existing artboard, you can do the following:

   • Double-click the Artboard tool (⊞), and edit the dimensions of the active artboard in the Artboard Options dialog box.

   • Select the Artboard tool, position the pointer over an edge or corner of the artboard, and drag to resize.

   • Select the Artboard tool, click an artboard in the Document window, and change the dimensions in the Control panel.

2 The ruler origin is the point where 0 (zero) appears on each ruler. By default, the ruler origin is set to be 0 (zero) in the top-left corner of the active artboard.

3 There are two types of rulers in Illustrator: artboard rulers and global rulers. Artboard rulers, which are the default rulers, set the ruler origin at the upper-left corner of the active artboard. Global rulers set the ruler origin at the upper-left corner of the first artboard, no matter which artboard is active.

4 The Scale Strokes & Effects option, found in the Transform panel (or in Illustrator CC > Preferences > General [Mac OS] or Edit > Preferences > General [Windows]), scales any strokes and effects as the object is scaled. This option can be turned on and off, depending on the current need.

5 The Free Transform tool (⊞) can perform a multitude of transformation operations, including move, scale, rotate, shear, and distort (perspective distort and free distort).

6 CREATING AN ILLUSTRATION WITH THE DRAWING TOOLS

Lesson overview

In this lesson, you'll learn how to do the following:

- Understand paths and anchor points.
- Draw curved and straight lines with the Pen tool.
- Edit curved and straight lines.
- Add and delete anchor points.
- Draw with the Curvature tool.
- Delete and add anchor points.
- Convert between smooth points and corner points.
- Create dashed lines and add arrowheads.
- Draw and edit with the Pencil tool.
- Work with the Join tool.

 This lesson takes approximately 90 minutes to complete.

Download the project files for this lesson from the Lesson & Update Files tab on your Account page at www.peachpit.com and store them on your computer in a convenient location, as described in the "Getting Started" section of this book.

Your Account page is also where you'll find any updates to the chapters or to the lesson files. Look on the Lesson & Update Files tab to access the most current content.

Aside from creating artwork using shapes like in previous lessons, you can also create artwork using drawing tools such as the Pencil tool, Pen tool, and Curvature tool. With these tools, you can draw precisely, including drawing straight lines, curves, and complex shapes. You'll start with the Pen tool and use all of these tools and more to create an illustration.

Getting started

In the first part of this lesson, you'll understand paths and ease into drawing with the Pen tool with lots of practice.

● **Note:** If you have not already downloaded the project files for this lesson to your computer from your Account page, make sure to do so now. See the "Getting Started" section at the beginning of this book.

1 To ensure that the tools and panels function exactly as described in this lesson, delete or deactivate (by renaming) the Adobe Illustrator CC preferences file. See "Restoring default preferences" in the "Getting Started" section at the beginning of the book.

2 Start Adobe Illustrator CC.

3 Open the L6_practice.ai file in the Lessons > Lesson06 folder on your hard disk.

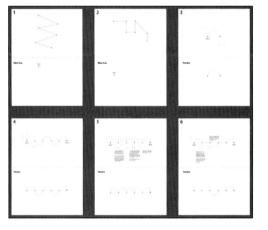

The document is made up of six artboards, numbered 1 through 6. As you progress through the first part of this lesson, you will be asked to move between artboards.

4 Choose File > Save As. In the Save As dialog box, navigate to the Lesson06 folder, and open it. Rename the file to **PenPractice.ai**. Choose Adobe Illustrator (ai) from the Format menu (Mac OS), or choose Adobe Illustrator (*.AI) from the Save As Type menu (Windows). Click Save.

5 In the Illustrator Options dialog box, leave the default settings, and then click OK.

6 Choose Window > Workspace > Reset Essentials.

● **Note:** If you don't see Reset Essentials in the menu, choose Window > Workspace > Essentials before choosing Window > Workspace > Reset Essentials.

An intro to drawing with the Pen tool

The Pen tool (✐) is one of the main drawing tools in Illustrator that's used to create both free-form and more precise artwork and also plays a role in editing existing vector artwork. It's important to have an understanding of a tool like the Pen tool when working with Illustrator. *Just know that it takes plenty of practice to feel comfortable with the Pen tool!*

In this first section, you'll begin to explore the Pen tool and later in the lesson, you'll create artwork using the Pen tool and other tools and commands.

1   Choose 1 from the Artboard Navigation menu in the lower-left corner of the Document window.

2   Choose View > Fit Artboard In Window.

3   Choose View > Smart Guides to turn off the Smart Guides. Smart Guides can be useful when you draw, but you won't need them now.

4   In the Control panel, click Fill color, and choose None (▱). Then, click the Stroke color and make sure that the Black swatch is selected. Make sure the Stroke weight is 1 pt in the Control panel.

When you begin drawing with the Pen tool, it's usually best to have no fill on the path you create because the fill can cover parts of the path you are trying to create. You can add a fill later, if necessary.

5   Select the Pen tool (✐) in the Tools panel. Position the pointer in the artboard area, and notice the asterisk next to the Pen icon (✎.), indicating that you'll create a new path if you begin drawing.

Note: If you see an X (✕) instead of the Pen icon (✎.), the Caps Lock key is active. Caps Lock turns the Pen tool icon into an X (✕) for increased precision.

6   In the area labeled "Work Area," click where the blue "start" square is to set the first anchor point.

After clicking and moving the pointer away from the point, notice that the asterisk has disappeared from next to the pointer, indicating that you are now drawing a path.

7   Move the pointer away from the original point, and you will see a line connecting the first point and the pointer, no matter where you move the pointer.

That line is called the Pen tool preview (or Rubber Band). Later, as you create curved paths, it will make drawing them easier because it is a preview of what the path will look like.

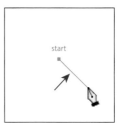

▷ **Tip:** You can toggle the Pen tool preview by choosing Illustrator CC > Preferences > Selection & Anchor Display (Mac OS) or Edit > Preferences > Selection & Anchor Display (Windows) to open the Preferences dialog box. In the dialog box, with the Selection & Anchor Display category options showing, deselect Enable Rubber Band for Pen Tool.

Note: If the path looks curved, you have accidentally dragged with the Pen tool; choose Edit > Undo Pen, and then click again without dragging.

8 Position the pointer down and to the right of the original point, and click to create the next anchor point in the path.

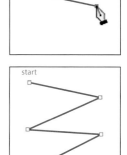

9 Click a third anchor point beneath the initial anchor point to begin creating a zigzag pattern. Create a zigzag that has a total of six anchor points, which means you will click the artboard three more times.

One of the many benefits of using the Pen tool is that you can create custom paths and continue to edit the anchor points that make up the path. Notice that only the last anchor point is filled (not hollow like the rest of the anchor points), indicating that it is selected.

10 Choose Select > Deselect.

Selecting paths

The type of anchor points you created in the previous section are called corner points. *Corner points* are not smooth like a curve; rather, they create an angle where the anchor point is. Now that you can create corner points, you will move on to adding other types of points such as smooth points to create curves in a path. But first, you will learn a few more techniques for selecting paths.

Back in Lesson 2, "Techniques for Selecting Artwork," you were introduced to selecting content with the Selection and Direct Selection tools. Next, you'll explore a few more options for selecting artwork with those same Selection tools.

Tip: You can also drag across a path to select it with the Selection tool.

1 Select the Selection tool (▶) in the Tools panel, and position the pointer directly over a straight line in the zigzag path. When the pointer shows a solid black box (▶.) next to it, click.

This selects the path and all of the anchor points. You can tell the anchor points are selected because they become filled.

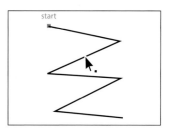

2 Position the pointer over one of the straight lines in the path. When the pointer changes (▶), drag to a new location anywhere on the artboard. All the anchor points travel together, maintaining the zigzag path.

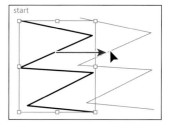

3 Deselect the zigzag path in one of the following ways:

- With the Selection tool, click an empty area of the artboard.

- Choose Select > Deselect.

4 In the Tools panel, select the Direct Selection tool (⟑). Position the pointer over a straight line in the path, and when the pointer changes (⟑.), click the path to reveal all of the anchor points.

You just selected the line segment (path). If you were to press Backspace or Delete (*don't*), only that portion of the zigzag path would be removed.

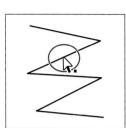

▶ **Tip:** If the Pen tool (✐) were still selected, you could Command-click (Mac OS) or Ctrl-click (Windows) in a blank area of the artboard to deselect the path. This temporarily selects a Selection tool. When you release the Ctrl or Command key, the Pen tool is selected again.

5 Position the pointer over one of the anchor points and the anchor point will become a little larger than the others, and the pointer will show a small box with a dot in the center (⟑▫) next to it (the figure shows this). Both of these indicate that if you click, you will select the anchor point. Click to select the anchor point, and the selected anchor point is filled (looks solid), whereas the deselected anchor points are still hollow.

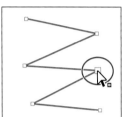

Note: When you position the pointer over a line segment that is not already selected, a black, solid square appears next to the Direct Selection tool pointer, indicating that you will select a line segment.

6 Drag the anchor point to the left a bit to reposition it.

The anchor point moves, but the others remain stationary. This is one method for editing a path, like you saw in Lesson 2.

7 Click in a blank area of the artboard to deselect

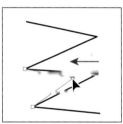

8 Position the Direct Selection pointer over a straight line segment in the middle of the zigzag shape. When the pointer changes (⟑.), click to select. Choose Edit > Cut. This cuts only the selected segment from the zigzag.

Note: If the entire zigzag path disappears, choose Edit > Undo Cut and try again.

9 Select the Pen tool (✐), and position the pointer over one of the end anchor points that was connected to the line segment that was cut. Notice that the Pen tool shows a forward slash (✎), indicating that if you click, you will continue drawing from that anchor point. Click the point.

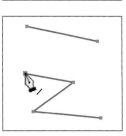

10 Position the pointer over the other anchor point that was connected to the cut line segment. The pointer now shows a merge symbol next to it (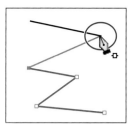), indicating that you are connecting to another path. Click the point to reconnect the paths.

Drawing straight lines with the Pen tool

In previous lessons, you learned that using the Shift key as well as Smart Guides in combination with shape tools constrains the shape of objects. The Shift key and Smart Guides can also constrain paths drawn with the Pen tool to create straight paths in angles of 45˚. Next, you will learn how to draw straight lines and constrain angles as you draw.

1 Choose 2 from the Artboard Navigation menu in the lower-left corner of the Document window.

2 Choose View > Smart Guides to turn on the Smart Guides.

3 With the Pen tool (✐) selected, in the area labeled Work Area, click where the blue "start" square is to set the first anchor point.

Don't worry if the Smart Guides are attempting to "snap" the anchor point you create to other content on the artboard, making it difficult to click directly on the "start" square. This is expected behavior and is sometimes why you might turn off the Smart Guides when drawing.

▶ **Tip:** If Smart Guides are turned off, you will need to press the Shift key and click to create constrained lines.

4 Move the pointer to the right of the original anchor point approximately 1.5 in, as indicated by the measurement label. It doesn't have to be exact. A magenta alignment guide appears when the pointer is vertically aligned with the previous anchor point. Click to set another anchor point.

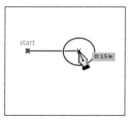

As you've learned in previous lessons, the measurement label and alignment guides are part of the Smart Guides. When working with the Pen tool, you can achieve finer measurements in the measurement labels when you zoom in.

● **Note:** The points you set don't have to be in exactly the same position as the path at the top of the artboard. Also, the measurement you see in your measurement label may not match what you see in the figure, and that's okay.

5 Click to set three more points, following the same generic shape as shown in the top half of the artboard. The new points are labeled 1, 2, and 3 in the figure.

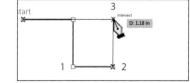

The magenta alignment guides that appear as you draw can be helpful for aligning points. Sometimes they align to content that you don't necessarily want to align to.

6 Press the Shift key, and move the pointer to the right and down. When the measurement label shows approximately 2 in, click to set an anchor point, and then release the modifier key.

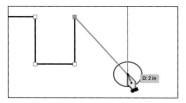

Notice that the new anchor point may not be where you clicked. That's because the line has been constrained to 45°. Pressing the Shift key creates angled lines constrained to 45°.

7 Position the pointer below the last point, and click to set the last anchor point for the shape (circled in the figure).

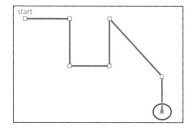

8 Choose View > Smart Guides to turn them off.

9 Choose Select > Deselect, and then choose File > Save.

Introducing curved paths

In this part of the lesson, you'll learn how to draw smooth, curved lines with the Pen tool. In vector drawing applications such as Illustrator, you can draw a curve, called a Bezier curve, with anchor points and direction handles. By setting anchor points and dragging direction handles, you can define the shape of the curve. This type of anchor point, with direction handles, is called a *smooth point*. Although drawing curves this way can take some time to learn, it gives you some of the greatest control and flexibility in creating paths.

The goal for this exercise is not to create anything specific but to get accustomed to the feel of creating Bezier curves. First, you'll just get the feel for how to create a curved path.

Smooth points vs. Corner points

Paths can have two kinds of anchor points: *corner points* and *smooth points*. At a corner point, a path abruptly changes direction. At a smooth point, path segments are connected as a continuous curve.

—From Illustrator Help

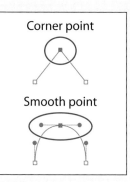

1 Choose 3 from the Artboard Navigation menu in the lower-left corner of the Document window. You will draw in the area labeled "Practice."

2 Select the Zoom tool (🔍) in the Tools panel, and click twice in the bottom half of the artboard to zoom in.

3 Select the Pen tool (✒) in the Tools panel. In the Control panel, make sure that the Fill color is None (▨) and the Stroke color is Black. Also, make sure the Stroke weight is still **1 pt** in the Control panel.

4 With the Pen tool selected, click in a blank area of the artboard to create a starting anchor point.

5 Move the pointer away from the original point you created, and click and drag away from the point to create a curved path.

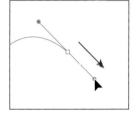

Notice that as you drag away from the point, direction handles appear. *Direction handles* consist of direction lines that end in round direction points. The angle and length of the direction handles determine the shape and size of the curve. Direction handles do not print and are not visible when the anchor point is inactive.

6 Move the pointer away from the anchor point you just created to see the rubber banding. Move the pointer around a bit to see how it changes.

7 Continue clicking and dragging in different areas to create a series of points.

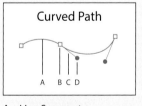

8 Choose Select > Deselect. Leave the file open for the next section.

Components of a path

As you draw, you create a line called a path. A path is made up of one or more straight or curved *segments*. The beginning and end of each segment is marked by *anchor points*, which work like pins holding a wire in place. A path can be closed (for example, a circle) or open, with distinct endpoints (for example, a wavy line). You change the shape of a path by dragging its anchor points, the *direction points* at the end of *direction lines* that appear at anchor points, or the path segment itself.

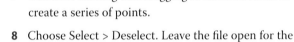

Curved Path

A. Line Segment
B. Anchor point
C. Direction line
D. Direction point

—From Illustrator Help

Drawing a curve with the Pen tool

In this part of the lesson, you'll use what you just learned about drawing curves to trace a curved shape with the Pen tool.

1   Press the spacebar to temporarily select the Hand tool (🖐), and drag down until you see the curve at the top of the current artboard (on Artboard 3).

2   Select the Pen tool (✒) in the Tools panel. Click and drag from the "start" square, up to the gold dot, and then release the mouse button.

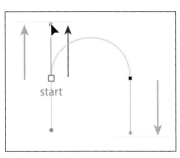

● **Note:** The artboard may scroll as you drag. If you lose visibility of the curve, choose View > Zoom Out until you see the curve and anchor point. Pressing the spacebar allows you to use the Hand tool to reposition the artwork.

This creates a direction line going in the same direction as the path. Up to this point, you've started your paths by simply clicking to create an anchor point, not dragging, like you did in this step. To create a more "curved" path, dragging out direction lines on the very first anchor point can be helpful.

3   Click the black point on the right side of the arch and drag down. Release the mouse button when the pointer reaches the gold dot and the path you are creating follows the arch.

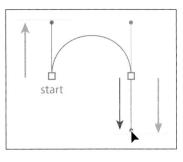

● **Note:** Pulling the direction handle longer makes a steeper curve; when the direction handle is shorter, the curve is flatter.

If the path you created is not aligned exactly with the template, select the Direct Selection tool (▷), and select the anchor points one at a time to show the direction handles. You can then drag the ends of the direction handles until your path follows the template more accurately.

4   Select the Selection tool (▶), and click the artboard in an area with no objects, or choose Select > Deselect.

Deselecting the first path allows you to create a new path. If you click somewhere on the artboard with the Pen tool while the path is still selected, the path connects to the next point you draw.

▶ **Tip:** While drawing with the Pen tool, to deselect objects, you can press the Command (Mac OS) or Ctrl (Windows) key to temporarily switch to the Selection or Direct Selection tool, whichever was last used, and then click the artboard where there are no objects. Another way to end a path is to press the Escape key when you are finished drawing.

If you want to try drawing the curve for more practice, scroll down to the Practice area in the same artboard and trace the curve.

Drawing a series of curves with the Pen tool

Now that you've experimented with drawing a curve, you will draw a shape that contains several continuous curves.

1 Choose 4 from the Artboard Navigation menu in the lower-left corner of the Document window. Select the Zoom tool (🔍), and click several times in the top half of the artboard to zoom in.

2 In the Control panel, make sure that the Fill color is None (◻) and the Stroke color is Black. Also, make sure the Stroke weight is still **1 pt** in the Control panel.

3 Select the Pen tool (✒️). Click the blue "start" square, and drag up in the direction of the arch, stopping at the gold dot.

● **Note:** Don't worry if the path you draw is not exact. You can correct the line with the Direct Selection tool (▶) when the path is complete.

4 Position the pointer over the black square to the right, and click and drag down to the gold dot, adjusting the first arch with the direction handle before you release the mouse button.

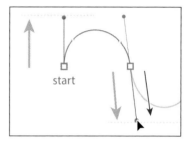

You'll find that you spend a lot of time focusing on the path segment *behind* (before) the current anchor point you are creating. Remember, by default there are two direction lines for a point. The previous direction line controls the shape of the previous segment.

▶ **Tip:** As you drag out the direction handles for an anchor point, you can press and hold the spacebar to reposition the anchor point. When the anchor point is where you want it, release the spacebar.

5 Continue along the path, alternating between dragging up and down. Put anchor points only where there are black squares (points) and finish with the red "end" point.

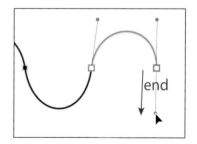

If you make a mistake as you draw, you can undo your work by choosing Edit > Undo Pen and then draw the last point again. Note that your direction lines may not match the figures, and that's okay.

6 When the path is complete, select the Direct Selection tool, and click to select an anchor point.

● **Note:** For more information about these attributes, see Lesson 7, "Using Color to Enhance Signage."

When the anchor point is selected, the direction handles appear, and you can readjust the curve of the path if necessary. With a curve selected, you can also change the stroke and fill of the curve. When you do this, the next line you draw will have the same attributes.

If you want to try drawing the shape again for more practice, scroll down to the bottom half of the same artboard (labeled Practice) and trace the shape down there.

7 Choose Select > Deselect, and then choose File > Save.

Converting smooth points to corner points

When creating curves, the direction handles help to determine the shape and size of the curved segments, as you've already seen. Removing the direction lines from an anchor point can convert a smooth curve into a corner. In the next part of the lesson, you will practice converting between smooth points and corner points.

1   Choose 5 from the Artboard Navigation menu in the lower-left corner of the Document window.

   On the top of the artboard, you can see the path that you will trace. You will use the top artboard as a template for the exercise, creating your paths directly on top of those. Use the Practice section at the bottom of the artboard for additional practice on your own.

2   In the top part of the artboard, use the Zoom tool (Q), and click several times to zoom in.

3   In the Control panel, make sure that the Fill color is None (▨) and the Stroke color is Black. Also, make sure the Stroke weight is still **1 pt** in the Control panel.

4   Select the Pen tool (✐), and pressing the Shift key, click the blue "start" square and drag up to the gold dot. Release the mouse button, and then release the Shift key.

   Pressing the Shift key when dragging constrains the direction handles to multiples of 45°.

5   Click the next black anchor point to the right, and pressing the Shift key, drag down to the red dot. When the curve looks correct, release the mouse button, and then release the Shift key. Leave the path selected.

   Now you need the curve to switch directions and create another arch. You will split the direction lines to convert a smooth point to a corner point.

6   Press the Option (Mac OS) or Alt (Windows) key, and position the pointer over the last anchor point created. When a convert-point icon (^) appears next to the Pen tool pointer (✎ₙ), click and drag a direction line up to the gold dot. Release the mouse button, and then release the modifier key. If you do not see the caret, you may create an additional loop.

▶ **Tip:** After you draw a path, you can also select single or multiple anchor points and click the Convert Selected Anchor Points To Corner button (⬧) or Convert Selected Anchor Points To Smooth button (⬧) in the Control panel.

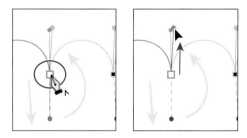

You can also Option-drag (Mac OS) or Alt-drag (Windows) the end of the direction handle (called the *direction point*). An arrow is pointing to it in the first part of the following figure. Either method "splits" the direction handles so they can go in different directions.

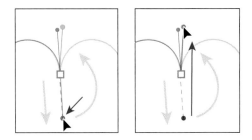

7   Position the Pen tool pointer over the next (third) black square point on the template path, and drag down to the red dot. Release the mouse button when the path looks similar to the template path.

8   Press the Option (Mac OS) or Alt (Windows) key, and after the convert-point icon (^) appears, position the pointer over the anchor point or direction point and drag up to the gold dot. Release the mouse button, and then release the modifier key.

For the next (fourth) point, you will not release the mouse button to split the direction handles, so pay close attention.

9   For the fourth anchor point, click the next black square on the template path, and drag down to the red dot until the path looks correct. This time, *do not release the mouse button*. Press the Option (Mac OS) or Alt (Windows) key, and drag up to the gold dot for the next curve. Release the mouse button, and then release the modifier key.

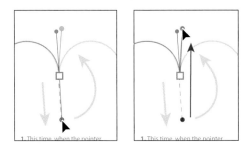

10 Continue this process using the Option (Mac OS) or Alt (Windows) key to create corner points until the path is completed.

11 Use the Direct Selection tool to fine-tune the path, and then deselect the path.

If you want to try drawing the same shape for more practice, scroll down to the Practice area in the same artboard and trace the shape down there.

Combining curves and straight lines

Of course in the real world, when you draw with the Pen tool, you won't just create either curves or straight lines. In this next section, you'll learn how to go from curves to straight lines and from straight lines to curves.

1 Choose 6 from the Artboard Navigation menu in the lower-left corner of the Document window. Select the Zoom tool (🔍), and click several times in the top half of the artboard to zoom in.

2 Select the Pen tool (✎). Click the blue "start" square, and drag up. Release the mouse button when the pointer reaches the gold dot.

Up to this point, you've been dragging to a gold or red dot in the templates. In the real world those obviously won't be there, so for the next point you will drag to create a point without much template guidance. Don't worry, you can always choose Edit > Undo Pen and try again!

3 Drag down from the second anchor point, and release the mouse button when the arch roughly matches the template. This method of creating a curve should be familiar to you by now.

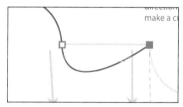

If you were to click the next black anchor point (*don't*), even pressing the Shift key (to produce a straight line), the path would be curved. The last point you created is a smooth anchor point and has a direction handle after the point. The figure at right shows what the path would look like if you clicked with the Pen tool on the next point.

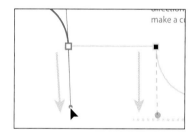

You will now continue the path as a straight line by removing the leading direction handle.

4 Position the pointer over the last point created (notice that the convert-point icon appears [^]), and click to delete the leading direction handle from the anchor point, as shown in the figure.

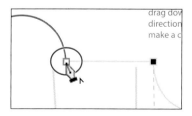

5 Press the Shift key, and click the next point in the template path to the right to set the next point, creating a straight segment.

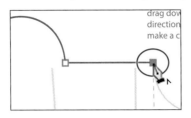

6 For the next arch, position the pointer over the last point created (notice that the convert-point icon appears [^]), and then drag down from that point to the gold dot. This creates a new direction line.

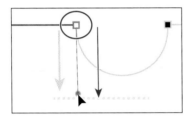

7 Click the next point, and drag up to complete the arch.

8 Click the last anchor point you just created to remove the direction line.

9 Shift-click the next point to create the second straight segment.

10 Click and drag up from the last point created to create a direction line, and then click and drag down on the end point to create the final arch.

If you want to try drawing the same shape for more practice, scroll down to the Practice area in the same artboard and trace the shape down there. Make sure you deselect the previous artwork first.

11 Choose File > Save, and then choose File > Close.

Remember, you can always go back and work on those Pen tool templates in the L6_practice.ai file as many times as you need. Take it as slow as you need and *practice, practice, practice.*

Creating artwork with the Pen tool

Next, you'll take what you've learned and create some artwork to be used in your project. To start, you'll draw a coffee cup, which combines curves and corners. Just take your time as you practice with this shape, and use the template guides provided to assist you in drawing it.

Tip: Don't forget, you can always undo a point you've drawn (Edit > Undo Pen) and then try again.

1 Choose File > Open, and open the L6_end.ai file in the Lessons > Lesson06 folder.

2 Choose View > Fit All In Window to see the finished artwork. (Use the Hand tool [🖑] to move the artwork to where you want it.) If you don't want to leave the artwork open, choose File > Close.

3 Choose File > Open. If a panel appears, click Open in the panel. You could also choose File > Open again. In the Open dialog box, navigate to the Lessons > Lesson06 folder and select the L6_start.ai file on your hard disk. Click Open to open the file.

4 Choose View > Fit All In Window.

5 Choose File > Save As, name the file **CoffeeShop.ai**, and select the Lesson06 folder in the Save As dialog box. Choose Adobe Illustrator (ai) from the Format menu (Mac OS) or choose Adobe Illustrator (*.AI) from the Save As Type menu (Windows), and click Save. In the Illustrator Options dialog box, leave the options set at the defaults, and then click OK.

6 Choose 1 Main from the Artboard Navigation menu in the lower-left corner of the Document window, if it's not already chosen.

7 Choose View > Fit Artboard In Window.

8 Select the Zoom tool (🔍), and zoom in to the cup at the bottom of the artboard.

9 In the Layers panel, select the layer named "Artwork" if it's not already selected.

10 In the Control panel, make sure that the Fill color is None (⬜) and the Stroke color is Black. Also make sure the Stroke weight is **1 pt** in the Control panel.

Drawing a coffee cup

Now that you have the file open and ready, you're going to put to use some of the Pen tool practice you did in previous sections, by drawing a coffee cup. This next section has more than the average number of steps, so take your time.

● **Note:** You do not have to start at the blue square (point A) to draw this shape. You can set anchor points for a path with the Pen tool in a clockwise or counterclockwise direction.

1   Select the Pen tool (✐), and drag from the blue square labeled "A" to the red dot above it to set the starting anchor point and direction of the first curve.

2   Continue on, dragging from point B to the red dot, to create the first curve.

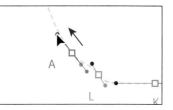

The next point you create will be a simple corner point.

3   Position the pointer over the point C, and click to set a corner point.

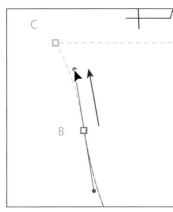
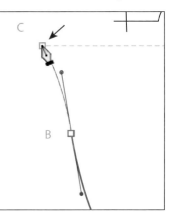

● **Note:** If you find that the path you are drawing has a fill of white, part of the template may be hidden. You can always change the fill to None (▨) for the path you are drawing.

4   Press the Shift key, and click point D to create a straight line.

5   Position the Pen tool pointer over point D again. When the convert-point icon appears [^] next to the pointer, drag down from that point to the red dot. This creates a new direction line.

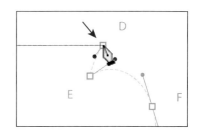

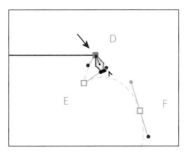
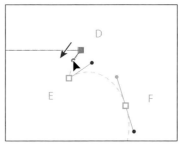

As you draw with the Pen tool, you may want to edit a curve you previously drew without ending the path you are drawing. Pressing a modifier key with the Pen tool selected, you can position the pointer over a previous path segment and drag to modify it, which is what you'll do next.

6   Position the pointer over the path between points C and D, and press the Option (Mac OS) or Alt (Windows) key. The pointer changes appearance (▶.). Drag the path down to make the path curved, like you see in the figure. Release the mouse button and then the key. Now, you can continue drawing the path.

Tip: You can also press the Option+Shift (Mac OS) or Alt+Shift (Windows) keys to constrain the handles to a perpendicular direction, which ensures that the handles are the same length.

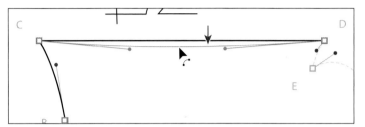

Dragging the path turns the path into a curve, rather than a straight line. This adds direction handles to the top anchor points.

7   Position the pointer over point E. Notice that as you move the pointer, you can see the Pen tool rubber banding, which means you are still drawing the path. Click point E to create a corner point and release the mouse button.

8   With the Pen tool pointer over point E, click and drag up and to the right from that point to the red dot. This creates a new direction line.

Note: After releasing the mouse button in the previous step, if you move the pointer away and then bring it back to point E, the convert-point icon [^] will appear next to the pointer.

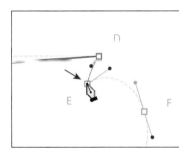
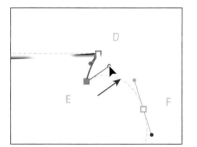

9   Continue drawing the point at F by dragging from the anchor point to the red dot.

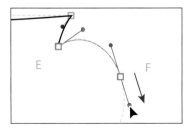

For the next point, G, you will create another smooth point, but you will edit the direction handles independently using a modifier key as you draw. For the next step, don't release the mouse button until you are told.

● **Note:** You could also create the point in this step by dragging and releasing the mouse button when the pointer reaches the red dot. You could then position the Pen tool icon over the anchor point. When the convert-point icon (^) appears next to the pointer, you could drag out a new direction handle.

10 Begin dragging from point G to the red dot. When the pointer reaches the red dot, *without letting go yet*, press the Option (Mac OS) or Alt (Windows) key, and continue dragging from the red dot to the gold dot to make just that one direction handle longer. When the pointer reaches the gold dot, release the mouse button, and then release the key.

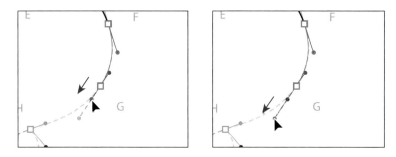

Next, you'll create a smooth point, and split the direction handles.

11 Continue drawing the point at H by first dragging from the anchor point to the gold dot, and then pressing the Option (Mac OS) or Alt (Windows) key and dragging from the gold dot to the red dot.

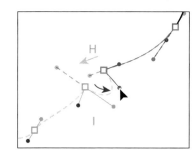
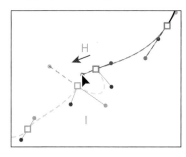

12 Continue drawing the point at I by first dragging from the anchor point to the gold dot and then pressing the Option (Mac OS) or Alt (Windows) key and dragging from the gold dot to the red dot.

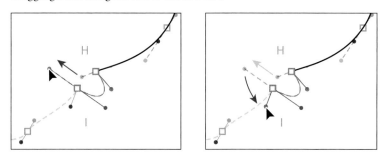

13 Continue drawing the point at J by dragging from the anchor point to the red dot.

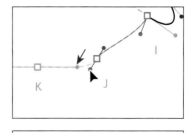

14 Begin dragging from point K to the red dot. As you drag, press the Shift key to constrain the direction handles. When you reach the red dot, release the mouse button and then the key.

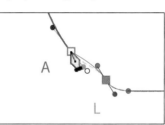

Note: If you press and hold the Shift key before you click and drag from a point, the point will be aligned with the previous point. That's not what you want in this case.

15 Continue drawing the point at L by dragging from the anchor point to the red dot.

Next, you'll complete the drawing of the coffee cup by closing the path.

16 Position the Pen tool over the starting point A without clicking.

Notice that an open circle appears next to the Pen tool pointer (✎), indicating that the path will close if you were to click the anchor point (don't click yet). If you were to click and drag, the direction handles on either side of the point would move as a single straight line. You need to split the direction handles so the final point is a corner point.

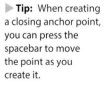

17 Press the Option (Mac OS) or Alt (Windows) key with the pointer still over point A. Click and drag up and to the left. Notice that a direction handle shows but is going in the opposite direction (it's going down and to the right). Drag until the curve looks right. Release the mouse button and then the key.

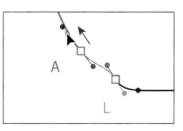

Tip: When creating a closing anchor point, you can press the spacebar to move the point as you create it.

As you drag up, another direction line appears above the point. Without the modifier key, as you drag away from closing point, you are reshaping the path before and after the anchor point. Pressing the Option/Alt modifier key on the closing point allows you to edit the previous direction handle independently.

18 Command-click (Mac OS) or Ctrl-click (Windows) away from the path to deselect it, and then choose File > Save.

Note: This is a shortcut method for deselecting a path while keeping the Pen tool selected. You could also choose Select > Deselect, among other methods.

Drawing with the Curvature tool

With the Curvature tool (), you can draw and edit paths quickly and visually to create paths with smooth refined curves and straight lines. Using the Curvature tool, you can also edit paths while drawing or after the path is complete using the same tool. The paths it creates are composed of anchor points and can be edited with any of the drawing or selecting tools. In this section, you'll explore the Curvature tool while creating a spoon.

1   Choose 3 Spoon from the Artboard Navigation menu in the lower-left corner of the Document window.

● **Note:** You may want to zoom in to the spoon template in this section.

2   Choose View > Fit Artboard In Window (if necessary).

Looking at the template path, you'll see a vertical guide running through points A and I. After you draw half of the spoon, you will copy and reflect it around the guide and then join the two halves together.

● **Note:** Like the Pen tool, you don't have to start at the blue square (point A) to draw this shape. You can set anchor points for a path with the Curvature tool in a clockwise or counterclockwise direction.

3   Select the Curvature tool () in the Tools panel. Click the blue square at point A to set the starting anchor point.

4   Click point B and move the pointer away from the point.

5   Move the pointer away from point B, and notice the preview of the curve before and after point B.

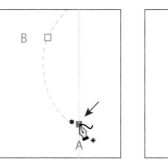

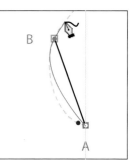

The Curvature tool works by creating anchor points where you click. The drawing curve will "flex" around the points dynamically. Direction handles are created when necessary to curve the path for you.

6   Click point C, and then click point D. Move the pointer away from point D.

At this point, the path between points A and B will no longer be affected by new points (E, F, etc.), but the path is not following the template. While drawing with the Curvature tool, you can go back and edit points as well as add points.

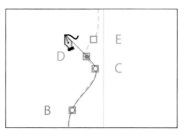

7 Hover the pointer over the path segment between the A and B points. When a plus (+) appears next to the pointer, click to create a new point. Drag the new point to the red dot in the template, repositioning it to match the shape of the dotted template.

● **Note:** The points you create with the Curvature tool can have three appearances, indicating its current state: selected (●), corner point (not selected [◉]), and smooth point (not selected [○]).

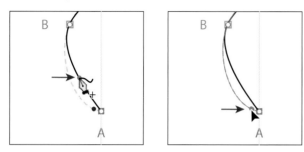

8 Click point E, and then click point F.

9 Shift-click to add point G.

Pressing the Shift key while clicking with the Curvature tool aligns the new point vertically (in this case) or horizontally with the previous point. Notice that the path segments before and after point F are curved, but they need to be straight to follow the template. To convert a default smooth point to a corner point, you can double-click a point you've made with the Curvature tool.

10 Hover the pointer over the anchor point at F. When the pointer changes (▶◦), double-click to convert the point to a corner point.

Double-clicking a point, which converts it to a corner point, has the effect of splitting the direction handles for the point.

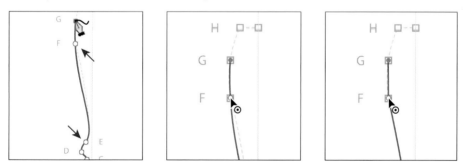

Next, you'll add a new point and convert it to a corner point in one step.

11 Option-click (Mac OS) or Alt-click (Windows) point H.

By Option-clicking (Mac OS) or Alt-clicking (Windows) when you create a point with the Curvature tool, you create a corner point instead of the default smooth point.

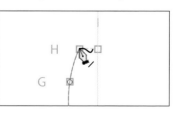

13 Press the Escape key to stop drawing, and then choose Select > Deselect.

Editing curves

In this part of the lesson, you'll adjust curves you've drawn using several methods learned previously and a few new ones.

Reflecting the spoon shape

Since the spoon you are creating is symmetrical, you drew only half of it. Now you'll copy, reflect, and join the spoon path to create a whole spoon.

1 Choose View > Smart Guides to turn them on.

2 Select the Selection tool, and click to select the spoon path.

3 In the Layers panel, click the visibility column (eye icon ⬤) for the layer named "Template" to hide the contents.

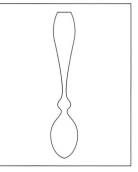

4 Press the Rotate tool (↻) in the Tools panel, and select the Reflect tool (⧗).

5 While holding down Option (Mac OS) or Alt (Windows), position the pointer over point I. When you see the word "anchor" appear, click with the modifier key held down.

6 In the Reflect dialog box, select Vertical if necessary, and click Preview. Click Copy to copy the shape and reflect it in one step.

7 Select the Selection tool and Shift-click the original path to select both and press Cmd+J (Mac OS) or Ctrl+J (Windows) *twice*, to join the paths together.

8 Choose Select > Deselect.

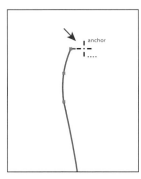
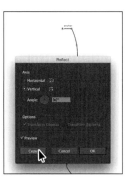
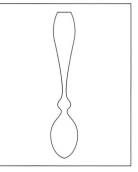

Rounding corner points

In Lesson 3, "Using Shapes to Create Artwork for a Postcard," you learned about live shapes and the ability to round corners. You can also round corner points on paths, which is what you'll do next.

1 Select the Zoom tool (🔍), and click a few times on the top of the spoon to zoom in.

2 Select the Direct Selection tool (🔧), and drag across the two points shown in the following figure to select them.

   Notice that a Live Corners widget (◉) shows next to each of the anchor points. With both points selected, you can edit the radius of both by dragging one of the Live Corners widgets or double-clicking one of them.

3 Drag the Live Corners widget on the right point toward the center of the spoon just a bit to make the corners round. When the measurement label shows a radius of roughly 0.1 in, release the mouse button.

4 Choose Select > Deselect.

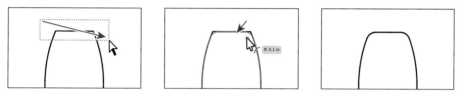

5 Choose View > Smart Guides to turn off the Smart Guides.

6 Select the Selection tool (▶), and click to select the spoon path.

7 Choose Edit > Copy.

Editing paths and points

Next, you'll edit a few of the paths and points for the coffee cup you created earlier.

1 Choose 1 Main from the Artboard Navigation menu in the lower-left corner of the Document window.

2 With the Selection tool, click in the artboard to make it the active artboard. Choose Edit > Paste to paste the spoon. Drag it off to the side for the moment.

● **Note:** You will need to select the spoon by its stroke since it doesn't have a fill.

3 Select the Direct Selection tool (🔧), and starting at the red X you see in the figure, drag across the "handle" of the coffee cup to select just that part of the path.

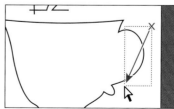

   Selecting with the Direct Selection tool in this way selects only the path segments and anchor points contained within the marquee selection. Clicking with the Selection tool (▶) selects the entire path.

4 Choose Edit > Copy and then Edit > Paste In Front.

5 Press Cmd+J (Mac OS) or Ctrl+J (Windows) to close the path.

6 Select the Selection tool, and Shift-drag the right, middle bounding point to the left to make it smaller. See the last part of the following figure.

  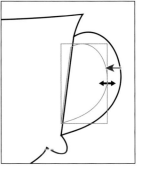

7 Select the Direct Selection tool, click the anchor point you see in the figure to select it. Drag the point to the right just a bit until it roughly matches the figure.

8 Position the pointer over the part of the path you see in the following figure, and click to select the path.

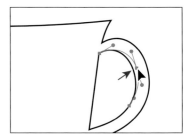

Notice that the pointer changes appearance (▶.) with the pointer over the path. This indicates that you can drag the path, which will adjust the anchor points and direction handles as you drag.

▶ **Tip:** As you are dragging a path with the Direct Selection tool, you can also press the Shift key to constrain the handles to a perpendicular direction, which ensures that the handles are the same length.

9 Drag the path up and to the left to make the curve a little less rounded. This is an easy way to make edits to a path.

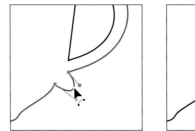 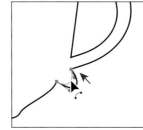

▶ **Tip:** If you wanted to adjust the direction handles instead of dragging the path and wanted to see the direction handles for all of the selected points, you could click Show Handles For Multiple Selected Anchor Points (▨) in the Control panel.

10 Choose Select > Deselect, and then choose File > Save.

Deleting and adding anchor points

Most of the time, the goal of drawing paths with a tool like the Pen tool or Curvature tool is to avoid adding more anchor points than necessary. You can reduce a path's complexity or change its overall shape by deleting unnecessary points (and therefore gain more control over the shape), or you can extend a path by adding points to it. Next, you will delete and add anchor points to the coffee cup path so that it has a flatter bottom.

1   Select the Zoom tool (🔍) in the Tools panel, and click twice, *slowly*, on the bottom of the cup to zoom in.

2   With the Direct Selection tool (▷) selected, click the edge of the coffee cup path.

3   Select the Pen tool (✐) in the Tools panel, and position the pointer over the anchor point at the bottom, center of the cup (see the figure). When a minus sign (−) appears to the right of the Pen tool pointer (✎₋), click to remove the anchor point.

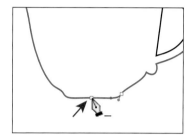

▶ **Tip:** With an anchor point selected, you can also click Remove Selected Anchor Points (✐) in the Control panel to delete the anchor point.

4   Position the Pen tool pointer over the bottom of the cup shape again. Look at the first part of the following figure for where. This time, when a plus sign (+) appears to the right of the Pen tool pointer (✎₊), click to add an anchor point.

5   Move the pointer over to the right a bit, and click the path to add another point. Leave this last point selected.

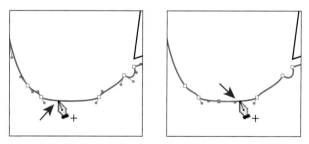

Adding points to a curved path means that the anchor points will most likely have direction lines and be considered smooth points.

Converting between smooth points and corner points

To more precisely control the path you create, you can convert points from smooth points to corner points and from corner points to smooth points, using several methods.

▶ **Tip:** You could also convert between corner and smooth points by double-clicking an anchor point (or Option-clicking [Mac OS], Alt-clicking [Windows]) with the Curvature tool, like you saw earlier.

1 Select the Direct Selection tool ( ), and with the last point still selected, Shift-click the other point you added to the left. Click the Convert Selected Anchor Points To Corner button ( ) in the Control panel.

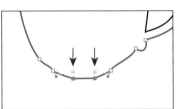

2 With both points selected, click the Vertical Align Bottom button ( ) in the Control panel to align one point to the other.

As you saw in Lesson 2, selected anchor points align to the last selected anchor point, which is known as the *key anchor*.

● **Note:** If the points align to the artboard after clicking the align button, try again. Make sure that Align To Key Anchor is selected in the Control panel first.

3 Press Down arrow *five times* to move both points down.

4 Choose Select > Deselect.

● **Note:** If you find it difficult to select the second anchor point, you can also drag a marquee across the bottom of the coffee cup to select the two anchor points.

5 With the Direct Selection tool, click the coffee cup shape to show all of the anchor points. Click the anchor point labeled 1 in the figure first, and then Shift-click the anchor point labeled 2. Click the Horizontal Align Left button ( ) to align them.

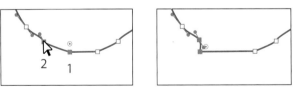

6 Click the anchor point labeled 3 in the figure first, and then Shift-click the anchor point labeled 4. Click the Horizontal Align Right button ( ) to align them. Leave the path (and points) selected.

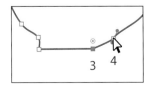
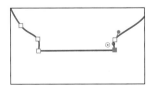

Working with the Anchor Point tool

Another way to convert anchor points between smooth and corner points is using the Anchor Point tool. Next, you'll convert anchor points using the Anchor Point tool (⌐) and see how to split direction handles using this tool.

1 Position the pointer over the Pen tool (✎), and click and hold down the mouse button to reveal more tools. Select the Anchor Point tool (⌐).

   You will also see the Add Anchor Point tool (✚✎) and the Delete Anchor Point tool (⌐✎), which are specifically for adding or removing anchor points.

2 Position the pointer over the point with an arrow pointing to it in the figure. Click to convert the point from a smooth point (with direction handles) to a corner point.

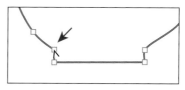

3 Position the pointer over the anchor point below the point you just converted. When the pointer looks like this ⌐, click and drag up. As you drag, press the Shift key. Drag up until you reach the anchor point above it. Release the mouse button, and then release the key.

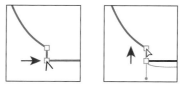

Tip: If you position the Anchor Point tool pointer over the end of a direction handle that is split, you can press the Option (Mac OS) or Alt (Windows) key and, when the pointer changes (▶), click to make the direction handles a single straight line again (not split).

● **Note:** If the pointer looks like this ▶., don't drag. This means that the pointer is not over the anchor point and if you drag, you will reshape the curve.

With the Anchor Point tool, you can perform tasks such as converting between smooth and corner points, split direction handles, and more.

Next, you'll do the same thing to the right side of the bottom of the coffee cup.

4 Position the pointer over the point with an arrow pointing to it in the figure. Click to convert the point from a smooth point (with direction handles) to a corner point.

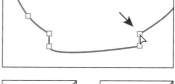

5 Position the pointer over the anchor point below the point you just converted. When the pointer looks like this ⌐, click and drag *down*. As you drag, press the Shift key. Drag down until the end of the opposite direction handle reaches the point above. Release the mouse button, and then release the key.

6 Choose Select > Deselect, and then choose File > Save.

Creating a dashed line

Dashed lines apply to the stroke of an object and can be added to a closed path or an open path. Dashes are created by specifying a sequence of dash lengths and the gaps between them. Next, add a dash to a line.

1 Choose View > Fit Artboard In Window.

2 In the Layers panel, click the visibility column for the layer named "Text" to show the layer contents.

3 Select the Zoom tool (🔍), and click twice to zoom in to the red circles that are now showing.

4 Select the Selection tool (▶) in the Tools panel, and click the dark gray path in the center of the red circles.

▶ **Tip:** The Preserves Exact Dash And Gap Lengths button (▦) allows you to retain the appearance of the dashes without aligning to the corners or the dash ends.

5 Click the word "Stroke" in the Control panel to show the Stroke panel. Change the following options in the Stroke panel:

- Weight: **8 pt**
- Dashed Line: **Selected** (By default, this creates a repeating dash pattern of 12 pt dash, 12 pt gap.)
- First Dash value: **4 pt** (This creates a 4 pt dash, 4 pt gap repeating pattern.)
- First Gap value: **2 pt** (This creates a 4 pt dash, 2 pt gap repeating pattern.)
- Aligns Dashes To Corners And Path Ends (▦): **Selected** (the default setting)

6 Press the Escape key to hide the Stroke panel.

7 Choose File > Save, and leave the line selected.

Adding arrowheads to a path

You can add arrowheads to both ends of a path using the Stroke panel. There are many different arrowhead styles to choose from in Illustrator, as well as arrowhead editing options. Next, you'll add different arrowheads to the dashed path.

1 With the dashed line still selected, click the word "Stroke" again in the Control panel to open the Stroke panel (or choose Window > Stroke). In the Stroke panel, change only the following options:

   • Choose **Arrow 21** from the menu directly to the right of the word "Arrowheads." This adds an arrowhead to the start (left end) of the line.

   • Scale (*beneath where you chose Arrow 21*): **30%**

   • Choose **Arrow 17** from the arrowheads menu to the far right of the word "Arrowheads." This adds an arrowhead to the end of the line.

   • Scale (*beneath where you chose Arrow 17*): **50%**

   • Click the Extend Arrow Tip Beyond End Of Path button ().

2 Click the edge of the coffee cup path, and change the Fill color to White.

3 Click the spoon shape, and change the Fill color to a light gray (I chose the color with the tooltip that shows C=0 M=0 Y=0 K=10).

4 With the spoon selected, choose Object > Transform > Rotate, change the Angle to **90**, select Preview, and then click OK.

5 Drag the spoon into the position you see in the following figure.

Working with the Pencil tool

The Pencil tool (✏) lets you draw free-form open and closed paths that contain curves and straight lines. As you draw with the Pencil tool, anchor points are created on the path where necessary and according to the Pencil tool options you set. The path can easily be adjusted when the path is complete.

Drawing freeform paths with the Pencil tool

Next, you will draw and edit a simple path using the Pencil tool.

1   Choose 2 Coffee Bean from the Artboard Navigation menu in the lower-left corner of the Document window.

2   Choose View > Fit Artboard In Window, if necessary.

3   In the Layers panel, click the visibility column for the layer named "Template" to show the layer contents.

4   Select the Zoom tool (🔍) in the Tools panel, and click a few times, slowly, on the top of the artboard to zoom in where you see "A."

5   Choose Select > Deselect. In the Control panel, make sure that the Fill color is None (▱) and the Stroke color is Black. Also make sure the Stroke weight is **1 pt** in the Control panel.

▶ **Tip:** When it comes to the Fidelity value, dragging the slider closer to Accurate usually creates more anchor points and more accurately reflects the path you've drawn. Dragging the slider toward Smooth makes fewer anchor points and a smoother, less complex path.

⬤ **Note:** A window may appear when clicking the Shaper tool. Close it.

6   Click and hold down on the Shaper tool (◕) in the Tools panel to select the Pencil tool (✏). Double-click the Pencil tool. In the Pencil Tool Options dialog box, set the following options, leaving the rest at their default settings:

   • Drag the Fidelity slider to the right, one position closer to Smooth. This will reduce the number of points on a path drawn with the Pencil tool and make the path smoother.

   • Keep Selected: **Selected**

   • Option Key (Alt Key on Windows) Toggles To Smooth Tool: **Selected** (The Smooth tool is used to smooth the path after it is drawn.)

   • Close Paths When Ends Are Within: **Selected**

7   Click OK.

   The asterisk (*) that appears next to the Pencil tool pointer indicates that you are about to create a new path. If you don't see the asterisk, it means that you are about to redraw a shape that the pointer is near.

8 Starting at the red X in the template, click and drag around the dashed template path. When the pointer gets close to the start of the path (at the red X), a small circle displays next to it (✐ₒ) to indicate that if you release the mouse button, the path will close. When you see the circle, release the mouse button to close the path.

Notice that as you are drawing, the path may not look perfectly smooth. After releasing the mouse button, the path is smoothed based on the Fidelity value that you set in the Pencil Tool Options dialog box.

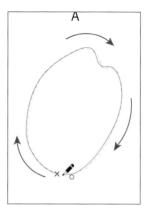

Note: If you see an X (✕) instead of the Pencil icon (✐), the Caps Lock key is active. Caps Lock turns the Pencil tool icon into an X for increased precision.

Note: When editing a path with the Pencil tool, you may find that a new path is created instead of editing the original shape. You can always undo and make sure that you finish back on the original path (or at least close to it).

9 Position the Pencil tool on or near the path to redraw it. When the asterisk disappears from the pointer, click and drag to reshape the path. Make sure you wind up back on the original path. Think of it as redrawing parts of the path.

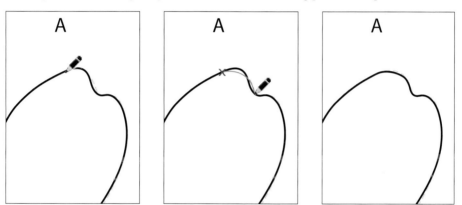

▶ **Tip:** If you wanted to "smooth" parts of the path you drew, you could press the Option key (Mac OS) or Alt key (Windows) and drag along the path. This can simplify the path and remove anchor points. This is possible because you selected Option key (Alt Key on Windows) Toggles To Smooth Tool option in the Pencil Tool Options dialog box earlier.

Drawing straight segments with the Pencil tool

Aside from drawing more free-form paths, you can also create straight lines that can be constrained to 45° angles with the Pencil tool. That's what you'll do next.

1 Scroll down the artboard to see the template shapes labeled "B" and "C," if you can't see them.

Note: When drawing the path, after reaching the blue X, you could have released the mouse button to stop drawing and then just started drawing from the same place later on. You can tell you are continuing a path with the Pencil tool when a line appears next to the Pencil tool pointer (✐), with the pointer positioned over the end of a path.

2 Position the pointer over the red X at the bottom of the path labeled "B." Click and drag around the left side of the shape and stop at the blue X, but *don't release the mouse button yet.*

3 With the mouse button still down, press Option (Mac OS) or Alt (Windows), and drag a straight line that follows the flat edge of the shape. When you reach the red X again and a small circle displays next to the Pencil tool pointer (✐), release the mouse button and then the key to close the path.

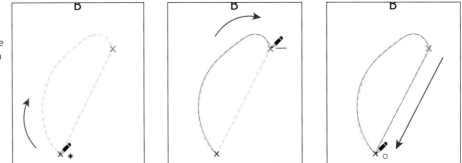

4 Position the pointer over the red X at the bottom of the path labeled "C" (it's below "B"). Click and drag down around the right side of the shape and stop at the blue X, but *don't release the mouse button yet.*

5 With the mouse button still down, press the Shift key, and drag a straight line that follows the flat edge of the shape. When you reach the red X again and a small circle displays next to the Pencil tool pointer (✐), release the mouse button and then the key to close the path.

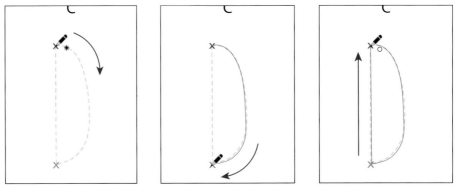

6 With shape "C" selected, choose Object > Transform > Rotate. In the Rotate dialog box, change the Angle to **-25**°, select Preview, and then click OK.

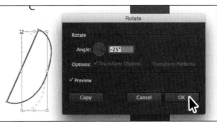

Finishing the coffee bean

1 Choose View > Fit Artboard In Window.

2 Select the Selection tool (▶), and click to select the top shape labeled "A."
Change the Fill color to the swatch named "CoffeeBean" in the Control panel.

3 Click to select shape B, and then Shift-click to select shape C. Change the Fill color for both to the swatch named "CoffeeBean2" in the Control panel.

4 Choose Select > Deselect.

5 Drag shape B and then shape C onto shape A, something like you see in the figure.

Feel free to adjust the individual shapes using any of the methods you've learned so far (I did).

6 Drag across all three shapes to select them and choose Object > Group.

7 Choose View > Fit All In Window.

8 Drag the coffee bean group on front of the coffee cup and spoon.

9 Choose Select > Deselect.

Joining with the Join tool

In this lesson and earlier lessons, you've used the Join command (Object > Path > Join) to join as well as close paths. Using the Join tool (✐), you can easily join paths that cross, overlap, or have open ends using scrubbing gestures.

1 Choose View > Steam. This command will zoom in to the shapes above the coffee cup and also hide the layer named "Template."

2 Click and hold down the mouse on the Pencil tool (✐), and select the Join tool (✐).

Unlike the Join command (Object > Path > Join) you learned about in Lesson 3, the Join tool can trim overlapping paths as it joins, and it doesn't simply create a straight line between the anchor points you are joining. The angle created by the two paths to be joined are taken into account.

● **Note:** If you were to instead join the ends of the open path by pressing Cmd+J (Mac OS) or Ctrl+J (Windows), a straight line would connect the ends.

3 With the Join tool selected, drag across the two ends of the path on the right (see the figure for which).

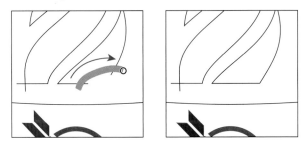

When dragging (also called *scrubbing*) across paths, they will be either "extended and joined" or "trimmed and joined." In this example, the paths were extended and joined. The Join tool works on paths that are selected or not, but the result of joining is not selected to continue working on more paths.

4 Drag across (or scrub) the excess part of the paths on the shape to the left to remove them and close the path. In this case, the path was "trimmed and joined."

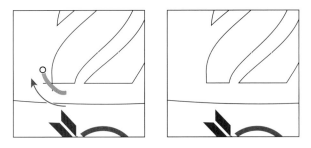

5 Choose View > Fit Artboard In Window.

6 Select the Selection tool, and drag across the "steam" shapes to select them.

7 Change the Fill color to the swatch named "Steam" and the Stroke weight to **0** in the Control panel.

8 Choose Object > Group, and drag the group down like the following figure.

9 Choose Select > Deselect, and take a step back to admire all that you've accomplished in this lesson!

10 Choose File > Save, and then choose File > Close.

Review questions

1   Describe how to draw straight vertical, horizontal, or diagonal lines using the Pen tool (✐).

2   How do you draw a curved line using the Pen tool?

3   Name two ways to convert a smooth point on a curve to a corner point.

4   Which tool would you use to edit a segment on a curved line?

5   How can you change the way the Pencil tool (✐) works?

6   How is the Join tool different from the Join command (Object > Path > Join)?

Review answers

1   To draw a straight line, click with the Pen tool (✐), and then move the pointer and click again. The first click sets the starting anchor point, and the second click sets the ending anchor point of the line. To constrain the straight line vertically, horizontally, or along a 45° diagonal, press the Shift key as you click to create the second anchor point with the Pen tool.

2   To draw a curved line with the Pen tool, click to create the starting anchor point, drag to set the direction of the curve, and then click to end the curve.

3   To convert a smooth point on a curve to a corner point, use the Direct Selection tool (⬚) to select the anchor point, and then use the Anchor Point tool (⌐) to drag a direction handle to change the direction. Another method is to choose a point or points with the Direct Selection tool and then click the Convert Selected Anchor Points To Corner button (⬚) in the Control panel.

4   To edit a segment on a curved line, select the Direct Selection tool, and drag the segment to move it, or drag a direction handle on an anchor point to adjust the length and shape of the segment. Dragging a path segment with the Direct Selection tool or pressing the Option/Alt key and dragging a path segment with the Pen tool is another way to reshape a path.

5   To change the way the Pencil tool (✐) works, double-click the Pencil tool in the Tools panel to open the Pencil Tool Options dialog box. There you can change the smoothness, fidelity, and other options.

6   Unlike the Join command, the Join tool can trim overlapping paths as it joins, and it doesn't simply create a straight line between the anchor points you are joining. The angle created by the two paths to be joined are taken into account.

7 USING COLOR TO ENHANCE SIGNAGE

Lesson overview

In this lesson, you'll learn how to do the following:

- Understand color modes and the main color controls.
- Create, edit, and paint with colors using a variety of methods.
- Name and save colors, and build a color palette.
- Work with color groups.
- Use the Color Guide panel.
- Explore the Edit Colors/Recolor Artwork features.
- Copy and paint appearance attributes from one object to another.
- Work with Live Paint.

This lesson takes approximately 90 minutes to complete.

Download the project files for this lesson from the Lesson & Update Files tab on your Account page at www.peachpit.com and store them on your computer in a convenient location, as described in the "Getting Started" section of this book.

Your Account page is also where you'll find any updates to the chapters or to the lesson files. Look on the Lesson & Update Files tab to access the most current content.

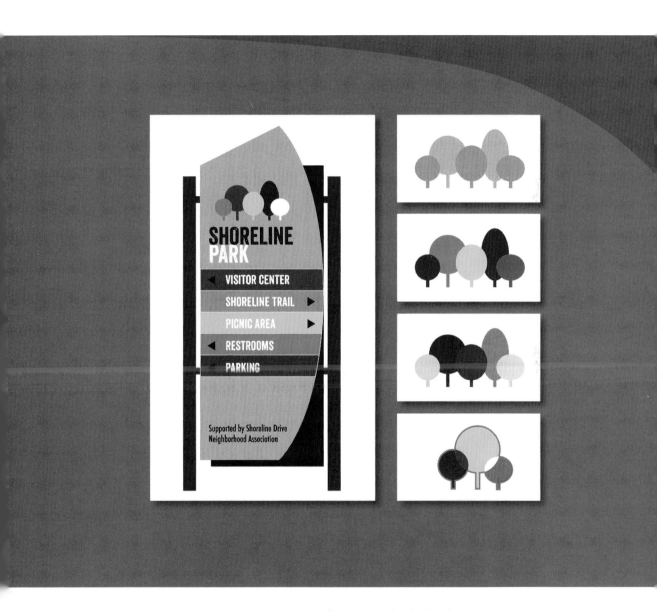

Spice up your illustrations with colors by taking advantage of color controls in Adobe Illustrator CC. In this information-packed lesson, you'll discover how to create and paint fills and strokes, use the Color Guide panel for inspiration, work with color groups, recolor artwork, and more.

Getting started

In this lesson, you will learn about the fundamentals of color and create and edit colors for a park sign and logo, using the Color panel, Swatches panel, and more.

1   To ensure that the tools and panels function exactly as described in this lesson, delete or deactivate (by renaming) the Adobe Illustrator CC preferences file. See "Restoring default preferences" in the "Getting Started" section at the beginning of the book.

● **Note:** If you have not already downloaded the project files for this lesson to your computer from your Account page, make sure to do so now. See the "Getting Started" section at the beginning of the book.

2   Start Adobe Illustrator CC.

3   Choose File > Open, and open the L7_end.ai file in the Lesson07 folder, located in the Lessons folder, to view a final version of the park sign you will paint.

4   Choose View > Fit All In Window.

    Leave the file open for reference.

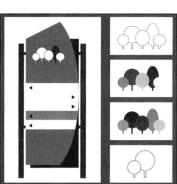

5   Choose File > Open. If a panel appears, click Open in the panel. You could also choose File > Open again. In the Open dialog box, navigate to the Lessons > Lesson07 folder and select the L7_start.ai file on your hard disk. Click Open to open the file. This file has all of the pieces already in it; they just need to be painted.

6   Choose View > Fit All In Window.

7   Choose File > Save As. In the Save As dialog box, navigate to the Lesson07 folder, and name it **ParkSign.ai**. Leave the Format option set to Adobe Illustrator (ai) (Mac OS) or the Save As Type option set to Adobe Illustrator (*.AI) (Windows), and click Save. In the Illustrator Options dialog box, leave the options at their default settings, and then click OK.

8   Choose Window > Workspace > Reset Essentials.

    ● **Note:** If you don't see Reset Essentials in the menu, choose Window > Workspace > Essentials before choosing Window > Workspace > Reset Essentials.

Exploring color modes

There are many ways to experiment with and apply color to your artwork in Adobe Illustrator CC. As you work with color, it's important to keep in mind the medium in which the artwork will be published, such as a print piece or a website. The colors you create need to be described in the correct way for the medium. This usually requires that you use the correct color mode and color definitions for your colors. The first part, color modes, will be described next.

Before starting a new illustration, you should decide which color mode the artwork should use, *CMYK* or *RGB*.

- **CMYK**—Cyan, magenta, yellow, and black are the colors used in four-color process printing. These four colors are combined and overlapped in a screen pattern to create a multitude of other colors. Select this mode for printing (in the New Document dialog box or the File > Document Color Mode menu).

- **RGB**—Red, green, and blue light are added together in various ways to create an array of colors. Select this mode if you are using images for onscreen presentations or the Internet.

When creating a new document by choosing File > New, each profile has a specific color mode. For instance, the Print profile uses the CMYK color mode. You can change the color mode by clicking the arrow to the left of Advanced and making a selection in the Color Mode menu.

Tip: To learn more about color and graphics, search for "About color" in Illustrator Help (Help > Illustrator Help).

When a color mode is selected, the applicable panels open, displaying colors in the selected color mode. You can change the color mode of a document, after a file is created, by choosing File > Document Color Mode and then selecting either CMYK Color or RGB Color in the menu.

ADOBE ILLUSTRATOR CC CLASSROOM IN A BOOK (2015 RELEASE) **189**

Working with color

In this lesson, you'll learn about the traditional methods of coloring (also called *painting*) objects in Illustrator using a combination of panels and tools, such as the Control panel, Color panel, Swatches panel, Color Guide panel, Color Picker, and the paint options in the Tools panel.

Note: The Tools panel you see may be a single column, and that just depends on the resolution of your screen.

Before you jump into color, though, let's discuss stroke and fill. In previous lessons, you learned that objects in Illustrator can have a fill, a stroke, or both. At the bottom of the Tools panel, notice the Fill and Stroke boxes. The Fill box is white (in this case), and the Stroke box is Black. If you click those boxes one at a time, you'll see that whichever you click is brought in front of the other and is selected. When a color is then chosen, it is applied to the fill or stroke, whichever is selected. As you explore more of Illustrator, you'll see these fill and stroke boxes in lots of other places like the Color panel, Swatches panel, and more.

As you will see in this section, Illustrator provides a lot of ways to arrive at the color you need. You'll start by applying an existing color to a shape and then work your way through the most widely used methods for creating and applying color.

Applying an existing color

Note: Throughout this lesson, you'll be working on a document with a color mode that was set to CMYK when the document was created, which means that the majority of colors you create will, by default, be composed of cyan, magenta, yellow, and black.

As was mentioned previously, every new document in Illustrator has a series of default colors available for you to use in your artwork in the form of swatches in the Swatches panel. The first method of working with color you will explore is to paint a shape with an existing color.

1 Click the ParkSign.ai document tab at the top of the Document window, if you did not close the L7_end.ai document.

2 Choose 1 from the Artboard Navigation menu in the lower-left corner of the Document window (if it's not chosen already), and then choose View > Fit Artboard In Window.

3 Choose Window > Workspace > Reset Essentials.

4 With the Selection tool (▶), click to select the large red shape.

5 Click the Fill color in the Control panel (■▾), and the Swatches panel appears. Position the pointer over swatches in the list to reveal a tooltip with the swatch name. Click to apply the swatch named "Sign Bg." Press the Escape key to hide the Swatches panel.

   By choosing the Fill color in the Control panel, you are telling Illustrator you want to change the color of the fill for the selected artwork.

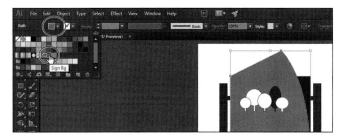

6 Choose Select > Deselect to ensure that nothing is selected.

Creating a custom color using the Color panel

There are a lot of ways to create your own custom color in Illustrator. Using the Color panel (Window > Color), you can apply color to an object's fill and stroke and also edit and mix colors using different color models (CMYK, for example). The Color panel displays the current fill and stroke of the selected content, and you can either visually select a color from the color spectrum bar at the bottom of the panel or mix your own colors, changing the color values in various ways.

Next, you'll create a custom color using the Color panel.

1 With the Selection tool (▶), click to select the white bar above the green bar on the sign, in the middle of the artboard.

2 Choose Window > Color to open the Color panel. Click the Color panel menu icon (▤) and choose CMYK from the menu (if it's not already selected), and then choose Show Options from the same menu.

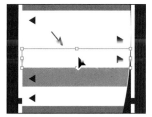

3 In the Color panel, click the white Fill box (if it's not selected). An arrow is pointing to it in the following figure. Click in the light green part of the color spectrum to sample a light green color and apply it to the fill.

Since the spectrum bar is so small, you most likely won't achieve the same color as I did. That's okay, because you'll edit it shortly to match.

> ▶ **Tip:** You can drag the bottom of the Color panel down to reveal more of the color spectrum bar.

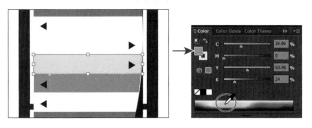

If artwork is selected when you create a color in the Color panel, the color is automatically applied.

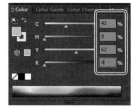

▶ **Tip:** Each CMYK value is a percentage of 100.

4 In the Color panel, type the following values in the CMYK text fields: C=**42**, M=**0**, Y=**62**, K=**0**. This ensures that we are all using the same color.

Colors created in the Color panel are not saved anywhere except for in the fill or stroke of the selected artwork. If you wanted to easily reuse the color you just created elsewhere in this document, you can save it as a swatch in the Swatches panel. All documents start with a set number of swatches, as mentioned earlier, but any colors in the Swatches panel are available to the current document only (by default), since each document has its own defined swatches.

Saving a color as a swatch

You can name and save different types of colors, gradients, and patterns in the Swatches panel as swatches so that you can apply and edit them later. Swatches are listed in the Swatches panel in the order in which they were created, but you can reorder or organize the swatches into groups to suit your needs.

Next, you'll save the green color you just created in the Color panel as a swatch.

1 Choose Window > Swatches to open the Swatches panel. Making sure that the green Fill box is selected (an arrow is pointing to it in the figure), click the New Swatch button (⊞) at the bottom of the panel to create a swatch from the fill color of the selected artwork.

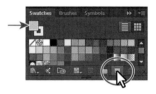

▶ **Tip:** Naming colors can be an art form. You can name them according to their value (C=45, ...), appearance (Light Green), or a descriptive name like "text header," among other attributes.

2 In the New Swatch dialog box, change the following options:

- Swatch Name: **Light Green**
- Add To My Library: **Deselected** (In Lesson 13 you'll learn all about libraries.)

3 Click OK.

Notice that the new Light Green swatch is highlighted in the Swatches panel (it has a white border around it). That's because it is applied to the selected shape automatically. You may need to scroll in the Swatches panel to see it.

4 With the Selection tool (▶), select the third white tree from the left, on the top of the sign.

5 In the Swatches panel on the right, drag the bottom of the panel down to see more swatches. Ensure that the Fill box at the top of the panel is selected to paint the fill of the shape, and select the swatch named "Light Green" to apply it.

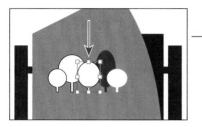
Select the tree.

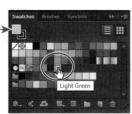
Apply the swatch named "Light Green."

When applying a swatch from the Swatches panel, it's always important to select the stroke or the fill *first* so that it paints the right part.

6 Click the Stroke box at the top of the Swatches panel to paint the stroke of the selected shape (an arrow is pointing to it in the figure). Select the None swatch (⬜) in the Swatches panel to remove the stroke.

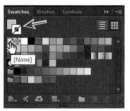

7 Choose Select > Deselect.

Creating a copy of a swatch

Next, you will create another swatch by copying and editing the Light Green swatch.

1 Click the green Fill box at the top of the Swatches panel.

2 Click the New Swatch button (▣) at the bottom of the Swatches panel.

Clicking the New Swatch button creates a swatch from the fill or stroke color (whichever is active or up front at the top of the Swatches panel). If the None swatch is applied, you won't be able to click the New Swatch button (it'll be dimmed).

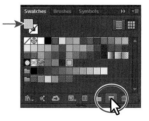

> **Tip:** In the New Swatch dialog box, the Color Mode menu lets you change the color mode of a specific color to RGB, CMYK, Grayscale, or another mode, when you create it.

3 In the New Swatch dialog box, change the name to **Orange**, change the values to C=**15**, M=**45**, Y=**70**, K=**0**, and make sure that Add To My Library is deselected. Click OK.

● **Note:** If the tree shape had still been selected, it would be filled with the new orange color.

4 With the Selection tool (▶), click the white bar above the Light Green–filled bar to select it. Click the Fill color in the Control panel, and click to select the color named "Orange."

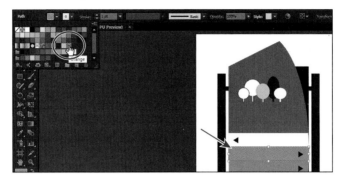

Editing a swatch

After a color is created and saved in the Swatches panel, you can later edit that color if you need to. Next, you'll edit the Sign Bg swatch.

1 With the Selection tool (▶) selected, click to select the large brown sign shape you first applied a fill color to.

2 Make sure that the Fill box is selected in the Swatches panel, and then double-click the swatch named "Sign Bg" in the Swatches panel. In the Swatch Options dialog box, change the K value to **0**, select Preview to see the change, and then click OK.

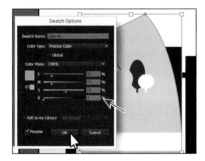

When you edit a swatch, artwork with the swatch color applied to the fill or stroke will not be updated unless the artwork is selected or the swatch is a global color (more about global colors in the next section). Editing a swatch will not update the colored objects by default.

Creating and editing a global swatch

Next, you will create a color and make it a *global color*. When you edit a global color, all artwork with that swatch applied, regardless of whether it's selected, is updated.

1 With the Selection tool (▶), click to select the white bar above the orange bar.

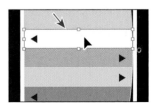

2 In the Swatches panel, click the New Swatch button () at the bottom of the panel. In the New Swatch dialog box, change the following options:

- Swatch Name: **Forest Green**
- Global: **Selected**
- Change the CMYK values to C=**91**, M=**49**, Y=**49**, K=**0**
- Add To My Library: **Deselected**

3 Click OK.

In the Swatches panel, notice that the new swatch is in the top row of colors, to the right of the white swatch. When you selected the shape, it was filled with white, so the white swatch was selected in the panel. When you click the New Swatch button to make a new color, it duplicates the selected swatch and puts the new swatch next to the original.

4 Click and drag the Forest Green swatch to the right of the Orange swatch to keep them together.

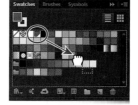

As you interact with the Forest Green swatch, notice the little white triangle in the lower-right corner. This indicates that it's a global swatch.

5 With the Selection tool, click the second white tree from the left (see the following figure). Make sure the Fill box is selected (active) in the Swatches panel, and apply the new "Forest Green" swatch to the fill.

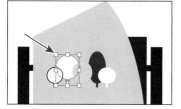

Select the tree.

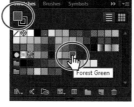

Apply the swatch.

6 Change the Stroke weight in the Control panel to **0** by either typing in the value or clicking the down arrow to remove it.

7 Choose Select > Deselect.

Now you'll see the power of a global swatch.

8   In the Swatches panel, double-click the Forest Green swatch. In the Swatch Options dialog box, change the K value to **24**, select Preview to see the changes (you may need to click in another field to see the change), and then click OK.

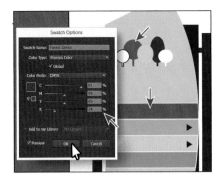

All of the shapes with the global swatch applied are updated, even though they weren't selected.

● **Note:** You can change an existing swatch into a global swatch, but it requires a bit more effort. You either need to select all of the shapes with that swatch applied before you edit the swatch and make it global, or you edit the swatch to make it global and then reapply the swatch to the content.

Using the Color Picker to create color

Another method for creating color is to use the Color Picker. The Color Picker lets you select color in a color field and in a spectrum either by defining colors numerically or by clicking a swatch, and it is found in other Adobe applications like InDesign and Photoshop. Next, you will create a color using the Color Picker and then save that color as a swatch in the Swatches panel.

1   With the Selection tool (▶), click the bottom white bar on the sign.

▶ **Tip:** You can also double-click the Fill box (or Stroke box) in the Color panel or at the bottom of the Tools panel to access the Color Picker.

2   Double-click the Fill box at the top of the Swatches panel to open the Color Picker.

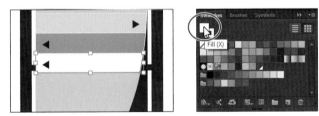

In the Color Picker dialog box, the larger color field shows saturation (horizontally) and brightness (vertically) and is labeled "A" in the next figure. The color spectrum bar (labeled "B" in the figure) shows the hue.

3   In the Color Picker dialog box, click and drag up and down in the color spectrum bar to change the color range. Make sure that you wind up with the triangles in an orange/brown hue (it doesn't have to be exact).

▶ **Tip:** You can also change the color spectrum you see by selecting H, S, B, R, G, or B.

4   Click and drag in the color field. As you drag right and left, you adjust the saturation, and as you drag up and down, you adjust the brightness. The color you create when you click OK (*don't yet*) appears in the New color rectangle, labeled "C" in the figure. Don't worry about matching the color in the figure yet.

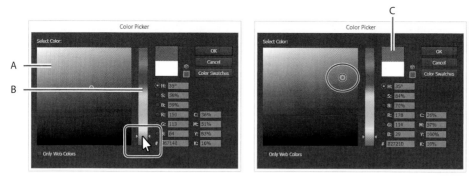

Drag in the color spectrum bar.   Drag in the color field.

5 In the CMYK fields, change the values to C=**40**, M=**65**, Y=**90**, and K=**33**.

6 Click OK, and you should see that the brown is applied to the fill of the shape.

● **Note:** The Color Swatches button in the Color Picker shows you the swatches in the Swatches panel and the default color books (the sets of swatches that come with Illustrator), and it lets you select a color from one. You can return to the color spectrum by clicking the Color Models button and then editing the swatch color values, if necessary.

7 In the Swatches panel, click the New Swatch button (■) at the bottom of the panel, and name the color **Dark Brown** in the New Swatch dialog box. Select Global, make sure that Add To My Library is deselected, and then click OK to see the color appear as a swatch in the Swatches panel.

8 Choose Select > Deselect, and then choose File > Save.

Using Illustrator swatch libraries

Swatch libraries are collections of preset colors, such as Pantone and TOYO, and thematic libraries, such as Earthtone and Ice Cream. Illustrator has default swatch libraries that appear as separate panels when you open them, and these cannot be edited. When you apply color from a library to artwork, the color in the library becomes a swatch that is saved in that document only and appears in the Swatches panel. Libraries are a great starting point for creating colors.

Next, you will create a spot color, which prints using a spot ink, using a Pantone Plus library. You will then apply that color to a logo. When color is defined in Illustrator and later printed, the appearance of the color could vary. This is why most printers and designers rely on a color-matching system, like the PANTONE system, to help maintain color consistency and, in some cases, to give a wider range of colors.

● **Note:** Sometimes it's practical to use process (typically CMYK) and spot inks (PANTONE, for instance) in the same job. For example, you might use one spot ink to print the exact color of a company logo on the same pages of an annual report where photographs are reproduced using process color. You can also use a spot-color printing plate to apply a varnish over areas of a process color job. In both cases, your print job would use a total of five inks—four process inks and one spot ink or varnish.

Adding a spot color

In this section, you will see how to load a color library, such as the PANTONE color system, and how to add a PANTONE MATCHING SYSTEM (PMS) color to the Swatches panel.

▶ **Tip:** You could also choose Window > Swatch Libraries > Color Books > PANTONE+ Solid Coated.

1 In the Swatches panel, click the Swatch Libraries Menu button (▨) at the bottom of the panel. Choose Color Books > PANTONE+ Solid Coated.

The PANTONE+ Solid Coated library appears in its own panel.

2 Type **755** in the Find field. As you type, the list is filtered, showing a smaller and smaller range of swatches. Type another **5** so that 7555 appears in the search field.

3 Click the swatch beneath the search field to add it to the Swatches panel. Click the X to the right of the search field to stop the filtering.

Open the color library.   Select the swatch after filtering the list.

4 Close the PANTONE+ Solid Coated panel.

● **Note:** If you exit Illustrator with the PANTONE library panel still open and then relaunch Illustrator, the panel does not reopen. To automatically open the panel whenever Illustrator opens, choose Persistent from the PANTONE+ Solid Coated panel menu (▾≡).

5 Choose 2 Artboard 2 from the Artboard Navigation menu in the lower-left corner of the Document window.

▶ **Tip:** Now that you know a number of ways to apply a fill and stroke (the Swatches panel and Control panel), you can use either of those methods to apply color swatches going forward.

6 With the Selection tool (▶), click the first white-filled tree shape on the left. Make sure the Fill box is selected (active) in the Swatches panel, and select the PANTONE 7555 C swatch to fill the shape.

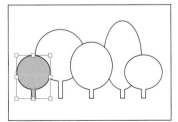 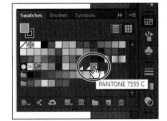

7 Change the Stroke weight to **0** in the Control panel.

8 Choose Select > Deselect, and then choose File > Save.

PANTONE swatches vs. other swatches in the Swatches panel

In the Swatches panel, you can identify spot-color swatches by the spot-color icon (⊙) when the panel is in List view or by the dot in the lower corner (⬚) when the panel is in Thumbnail view. Process colors do not have a spot-color icon or a dot. To learn more about color libraries and spot colors, search for "About color" in Illustrator Help (Help > Illustrator Help).

Creating and saving a tint of a color

A *tint* is a mixture of a color with white to make the color lighter. You can create a tint from a global process color, like CMYK, or from a spot color.

Next, you will create a tint of the Pantone swatch.

1   With the Selection tool (▶), click the white tree shape just to the right of the tree shape filled with the Pantone color (the tree second from the left).

2   In the Swatches panel, apply the new Pantone color to the fill of the shape.

● **Note:** Don't forget, you need to make sure that the Fill box is selected in the Swatches panel to apply the color to the fill! Also, the Fill and Stroke boxes in the Tools panel, Color panel, and Swatches panel are linked together. When you change one, they all change.

3   Click the Color panel icon (⬛) to expand the Color panel. Make sure that the Fill box is selected in the Color panel, and then drag the tint slider to the left to change the tint value to **70%**.

● **Note:** You may need to choose Show Options from the Color panel menu to see the slider.

4   Click the Swatches panel icon (⬛) on the right side of the workspace. Click the New Swatch button (⬛) at the bottom of the panel to save the tint. Notice the new tint swatch in the Swatches panel. Position the pointer over the swatch icon to see its name, PANTONE 7555 C 70%.

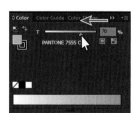
Create the tint.

See the tint swatch in the panel.

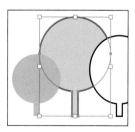
Notice the result.

5   Change the Stroke weight to **0** in the Control panel for the selected tree shape.

6 For the remaining three tree shapes, apply the PANTONE 7555 C swatch, the tint swatch (PANTONE 7555 C 70%), and then the PANTONE 7555 C swatch to their fills, in that order.

7 Change the Stroke weight to **0** in the Control panel for each of the tree shapes.

8 Choose Select > Deselect, and then choose File > Save.

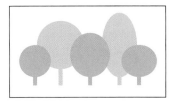

Adjusting colors

When working with colors, Illustrator offers an Edit Colors menu option (Edit > Edit Colors) that allows you to convert colors between color modes, blend colors, invert colors, and much more, for selected artwork. Next, you'll change the trees logo with the PANTONE 7555 C color applied to use CMYK colors instead of Pantone.

1 While still on Artboard 2, choose Select > All On Active Artboard to select all of the shapes with the Pantone color and tint applied.

2 Choose Edit > Edit Colors > Convert To CMYK.

The colors in the selected shapes are now composed of CMYK. Using this method for converting to CMYK does not affect the Pantone color swatches in the Swatches panel. It simply converts the selected *artwork* colors to CMYK. The swatches in the Swatches panel are no longer applied to the artwork.

● **Note:** Currently, Convert to RGB in the Edit Color menu is dimmed (you cannot select it). That's because the Document Color Mode is CMYK. To convert selected content color to RGB using this method, first choose File > Document Color Mode > RGB Color.

Copying appearance attributes

At times you may want to simply copy appearance attributes, such as character formatting, paragraph formatting, fill, and stroke, from one object to another. This can be done with the Eyedropper tool (✐) and can really speed up your creative process.

1 Choose 1 from the Artboard Navigation menu in the lower-left corner of the Document window to return to the artboard with the sign on it.

2 Using the Selection tool (▸), select the first white tree (on the left) at the top of the sign (the one with the black stroke applied).

▶ **Tip:** You can double-click the Eyedropper tool in the Tools panel, before sampling, to change the attributes that the Eyedropper picks up and applies.

3 Select the Eyedropper tool (✐) in the Tools panel. Click the green bar just above the bottom brown bar (see the figure).

The tree has the attributes from the painted bar applied, including a cream-colored stroke.

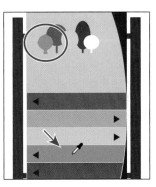

4 Click the Stroke color in the Control panel, and change the color to None (☐).

5 Choose Select > Deselect.

Creating a color group

In Illustrator, you can save colors in color groups, which consist of related color swatches in the Swatches panel. Organizing colors by their use, such as grouping all colors for a logo, can be helpful for organization and more, as you'll soon see. Color groups cannot contain patterns, gradients, the None color, or Registration color.

Next, you will create a color group of some of the swatches you've created for the logo to keep them organized.

1 Select the Selection tool (▶) in the Tools panel.

2 In the Swatches panel, click the swatch named "Aqua" to select it, if necessary. Holding down the Shift key, click the swatch named "Forest Green" to the right to select five color swatches.

3 Command-click (Mac OS) or Ctrl-click (Windows) the orange swatch to remove it from the selection.

4 Click the New Color Group button (▣) at the bottom of the Swatches panel. Change the Name to **Tree Logo** in the New Color Group dialog box, and click OK to save the group.

● **Note:** If objects are selected when you click the New Color Group button, an expanded New Color Group dialog box appears. In this dialog box, you can create a color group from the colors in the artwork and convert the colors to global colors.

5 With the Selection tool (▶) selected, click a blank area of the Swatches panel to deselect the color group you just created.

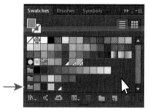

Each swatch in a color group can still be edited independently by double-clicking a swatch in the group and editing the values in the Swatch Options dialog box.

For the next step, you may want to drag the bottom of the Swatches panel down so that you can see all of the swatches in the panel.

6 Click the white swatch in the top row of the Swatches panel, and drag it to the right of the Forest Green swatch in the tree logo color group.

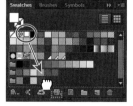

When dragging a color into a color group, make sure that you see a line appear on the right edge of the Forest Green swatch. Otherwise, you may drag the white swatch to the wrong place. You can always choose Edit > Undo Move Swatches and try again. Aside from dragging colors in or out of a color group, you can rename a color group, reorder the colors in the group, and more.

Creative inspiration with the Color Guide panel

The Color Guide panel can provide you with color inspiration as you create your artwork. You can use it to pick color tints, analogous colors, and much more, and then apply them directly to artwork, edit them using several methods, or save them as a group in the Swatches panel.

Next, you will use the Color Guide panel to select different colors for a version of a tree logo, and then you'll save those colors as a color group in the Swatches panel.

1   Choose 3 Artboard 3 from the Artboard Navigation menu in the lower-left corner of the Document window.

2   With the Selection tool ( ), click the first tree on the left (with the aqua color fill). Make sure that the Fill box is selected in the Tools panel or Swatches panel.

3   Choose Window > Color Guide to open the panel. Click the Set Base Color To The Current Color button ( ) (see the following figure).

    This allows the Color Guide panel to suggest colors based on the color showing in the Set Base Color To The Current Color button. The colors you see in the Color Guide panel may differ from what you see in the figure. That's okay.

    Next, you'll experiment with colors using Harmony Rules.

▶ **Tip:** You can also choose a different color variation (different from the default Tints/Shades), such as Show Warm/Cool, by clicking the Color Guide panel menu icon ( ) and choosing one.

4   Choose Analogous from the Harmony Rules menu (circled in the figure) in the Color Guide panel.

    A base group of colors is created to the right of the base color (aqua), and a series of tints and shades of those colors appears in the body of the panel. There are lots of harmony rules to choose from, each instantly generating a color scheme based on any color you want. The base color you set (aqua) is the basis for generating the colors in the color scheme.

Select the tree.

Set the base color.

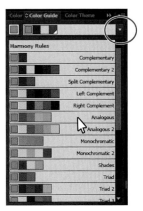

Choose the harmony rule.

5 Click the Save Color Group To Swatch Panel button () at the bottom of the Color Guide panel to save the base colors (the five colors at the top) in the Swatches panel as a group.

6 Click the Swatches panel icon (▦).
Scroll down to see the new group added.

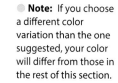

Next, you'll experiment with the colors in the color group that you just created to create an alternate group of colors.

7 Choose Select > Deselect.

8 Click the Color Guide panel icon (▨) to open the Color Guide panel.

9 In the list of swatches in the Color Guide panel, select the fifth color from the left in the third row (see the figure). If the tree were still selected, it would now be filled with the blue.

● **Note:** If you choose a different color variation than the one suggested, your color will differ from those in the rest of this section.

10 Click the Set Base Color To The Current Color button (▤) (circled in the following figure) to ensure that all colors that the panel creates are based on that same blue.

11 Choose Complementary 2 from the Harmony Rules menu.

12 Click the Save Color Group To Swatch Panel button (▥) to save the colors as a group in the Swatches panel.

13 Choose File > Save.

Working with Adobe Color Themes

The Color Themes panel (Window > Color Themes) displays color themes you have created and synced with your account on the Adobe Color website (http://color.adobe.com). The Adobe ID used in Illustrator CC is automatically used to sign in to the Adobe Color CC website, and the Color Themes panel is refreshed with your Adobe Color themes. For more information about working with the Color Themes panel, search for "Color themes" in Illustrator Help (Help > Illustrator Help).

Editing a color group in the Edit Colors dialog box

When you create color groups in the Swatches panel or in the Color Guide panel, you can edit the swatches in the group either individually from the Swatches panel, or together. In this section, you will learn how to edit the colors of a color group in the Swatches panel using the Edit Color dialog box. Later, you will apply those colors to a version of the logo.

1   Choose Select > Deselect (if it's available), and then click the Swatches panel icon (■) to show the panel.

Deselecting right now is important! If artwork is selected when you edit the color group, the edits can apply to the selected artwork.

2   Click the Color Group icon (■) to the left of the colors in the *bottom color group* (the one you just saved) to select the group. It's circled in the following figure.

▶ **Tip:** With no artwork selected, you could also double-click the Color Group icon (the folder) to open the Edit Colors dialog box.

3   Click the Edit Color Group button (●) at the bottom of the Swatches panel to open the Edit Colors dialog box.

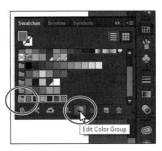

The Edit Color Group button appears in multiple locations, like the Swatches and Color Guide panels. The Edit Colors dialog box allows you to edit a group of colors in various ways or even to create new color groups. On the right side of the Edit Colors dialog box, under the Color Groups section, all of the existing color groups in the Swatches panel are listed.

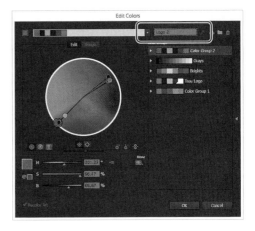

4   Select the name "Color Group 2" in the field above the Color Groups section if not already selected, (circled in the figure), and rename the group **Logo 2**. This is one way you can rename a color group.

Next, you will make a few changes to the colors in the Logo 2 group. On the left side of the Edit Colors dialog box, you can edit the colors of each color group, either individually or together, and edit them visually or precisely using specific color values. In the color wheel, you'll see markers (circles) that represent each color in the selected group.

5 In the color wheel on the left side of the dialog box, drag the largest blue circle, called a *marker*, in the lower-left section of the color wheel, down and to the right just a little bit. The largest marker is the base color of the color group that you set in the Color Guide panel initially.

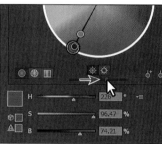

▶ **Tip:** You'll notice that all of the colors in the group move and change together. This is because they are linked together by default.

Moving the color markers away from the center of the color wheel increases saturation, and moving them toward the center decreases saturation. Moving a color marker around the color wheel (clockwise or counterclockwise) edits the hue.

6 Drag the Adjust Brightness slider below the color wheel to the right to brighten all the colors at once.

Next, you will edit the colors in the group independently and then save the colors as a new named group.

Note: You can match the H, S, B (hue, saturation, brightness) values below the color wheel in the Edit Colors dialog box to mimic what you see in the figure, if you want to match exactly the color I achieved.

7 Click the Unlink Harmony Colors button (![icon]) in the Edit Colors dialog box to edit the colors independently.

The lines between the color markers (circles) and the center of the color wheel become dotted, indicating that you can edit the colors independently.

Next, you will edit just one of the colors, since they are now unlinked. You will edit that color by using specific color values rather than by dragging the color in the color wheel.

8 Click the Color Mode icon (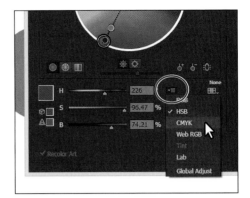) to the right of the H, S, B values below the color wheel, and choose CMYK from the menu, if the CMYK sliders are not already visible.

9 Click to select the lightest orange marker in the color wheel, as shown in the figure. Change the CMYK values to C=**10**, M=**50**, Y=**100**, and K=**0**. Notice that the marker has moved in the color wheel, and it's the only one that moved. Leave the dialog box open.

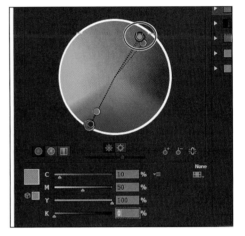

● **Note:** It's okay if the color markers in your Edit Colors dialog box are different from those shown in the figure.

10 Click the Save Changes To Color Group button () in the upper-right corner of the Edit Colors dialog box to save the changes to the color group.

If you decide to make changes to colors in another color group, you can select the color group you want to edit on the right side of the Edit Colors dialog box and edit the colors on the left side. You can then save the changes to the group by clicking the Save Changes To Color Group button (●) in the upper-right corner of the dialog box.

● **Note:** If a dialog box appears after clicking OK, click Yes to save the changes to the color group in the Swatches panel.

11 Click OK to close the Edit Colors dialog box.

The subtle changes to the colors in the group should show in the Swatches panel.

12 Choose File > Save.

Editing colors in artwork

You can also edit the colors in selected artwork using the Recolor Artwork command. It's really useful when global swatches weren't used in the artwork. Without using global colors in your artwork, updating a series of colors in selected artwork may take a lot of time. Next, you will edit the colors for one of the logos that was created with colors that were not saved in the Swatches panel.

1   Choose 4 Artboard 4 from the Artboard Navigation menu in the lower-left corner of the Document window.

2   Choose Select > All On Active Artboard to select all of the artwork.

3   Click the Recolor Artwork button (⬤) in the Control panel to open the Recolor Artwork dialog box.

Tip: You can also access the Recolor Artwork dialog box by selecting the artwork and then choosing Edit > Edit Colors > Recolor Artwork.

The Recolor Artwork dialog box options allow you to edit, reassign, or reduce the colors in your selected artwork and to create and edit color groups. You'll probably notice that it looks an awful lot like the Edit Colors dialog box. The big difference is that instead of editing color and creating color groups to apply later, you are dynamically editing colors in the selected artwork.

4   In the Recolor Artwork dialog box, click the Hide Color Group Storage icon (◀) on the right side of the dialog box (circled in the following figure).

Like in the Edit Colors dialog box, all of the color groups in the Swatches panel appear on the right side of the Recolor Artwork dialog box (in the Color Groups storage area). In the Recolor Artwork dialog box, you can apply colors from these color groups to the selected artwork.

5   Click the Get Colors From Selected Art icon (▧) to make sure that the colors from the selected artwork are showing in the Recolor Artwork dialog box.

6   Click the Edit tab to edit the colors in the artwork using the color wheel.

7   Make sure that the Link Harmony Colors icon (▦) is disabled so that you can edit all of the colors independently.

The lines between the color markers (circles) and the center of the color wheel should be dotted. If it looks like this (▦), click it to unlink.

When you created a color group, you worked with the color wheel and the CMYK sliders to edit color. This time, you will adjust color using a different method.

8 Click the Display Color Bars button () to show the colors in the selected artwork as bars. Click the cream color bar in the middle to select it.

▶ **Tip:** If you want to return to the original logo colors, click the Get Colors From Selected Art button ().

9 At the bottom of the dialog box, change the CMYK values to C=**5**, M=**10**, Y=**40**, K=**0**. If the Recolor Artwork dialog box isn't in the way, you should see the artwork changing.

10 Click the green color bar to select it instead of the cream color bar. With the pointer over the green color bar, right-click and choose Select Shade from the menu that appears. Click in the shade menu, and drag to change the color of the color bar.

Editing the colors as bars is just another way to view and edit the colors, and there are so many options for editing. To learn more about these options, search for "Color groups (harmonies)" in Illustrator Help (Help > Illustrator Help).

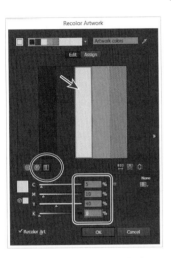
Click the cream color bar and edit it.

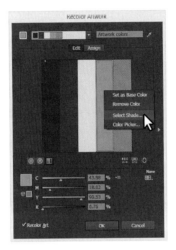
Choose Select Shade with the green color bar selected.

Change the shade.

▶ **Tip:** You can save the edited colors as a color group by clicking the Show Color Group Storage icon (▶) on the right side of the dialog box and then clicking the New Color Group button (■).

11 Click OK in the Recolor Artwork dialog box.

12 Choose Select > Deselect, and then choose File > Save.

Assigning colors to your artwork

As you've seen, clicking the Recolor Artwork button (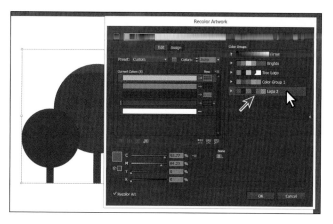) with artwork selected opens the Recolor Artwork dialog box. In the Recolor Artwork dialog box, you can edit colors in existing artwork, as you've seen, but you can also "assign" colors from an existing color group to your artwork. Next, you will assign a color group to create a version of the logo.

1 Choose 3 Artboard 3 from the Artboard Navigation menu in the lower-left corner of the Document window.

2 Choose Select > All On Active Artboard to select the logo trees.

3 Click the Recolor Artwork button ( ) in the Control panel.

4 Click the Show Color Group Storage icon ( ) on the right side of the dialog box to show the color groups, if they aren't already showing. Make sure that, in the top left of the dialog box, the Assign button is selected.

On the left side of the Recolor Artwork dialog box, notice that the five colors of the selected logo are listed in the Current Colors column, in what is called *hue-forward* sorting. That means they are arranged, from top to bottom, in the ordering of the color wheel: red, orange, yellow, green, blue, indigo, and violet.

5 Under Color Groups in the Recolor Artwork dialog box, select the Logo 2 color group you created earlier. The selected artwork on the artboard should change in color.

Note: If the colors of the logo do not change, make sure that Recolor Art is selected in the lower-left corner of the Recolor Artwork dialog box.

On the left side of the Recolor Artwork dialog box, notice that the colors of the Logo 2 color group are *assigned* to the colors in the logo. The Current Colors column shows what the color was in the logo, and an arrow to the right of each of those colors points to the New column, which contains what the color has become (or has been *reassigned to*). Notice that the white color has not been modified and that there is no arrow pointing to a color in the New column. That's because white, black, and grays are typically *preserved*, or unchanged.

6 Click the Hide Color Group Storage icon (◀) to hide the color groups. Drag the dialog box by the title bar at the top so that you can see the artwork.

7 Click the small arrow to the right of the dark green bar in the Current Colors column (see the figure).

This tells Illustrator *not* to change that specific green color in the logo. You can see that reflected in the logo on the artboard.

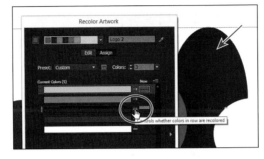

Now suppose that you wanted to change the white color in the Logo 2 color group. That's what you'll do next.

8 Click the line to the right of the white color in the Current Colors column, and the line will change into an arrow that looks dimmed.

The arrow indicates to Illustrator that you want the white color to be different, but there currently is no color in the New column to change it to.

9 Click the Show Color Group Storage icon (▶) to show the color groups.

10 Click another color group in the Color Groups area on the right side of the panel, and then click to select the Logo 2 color group again.

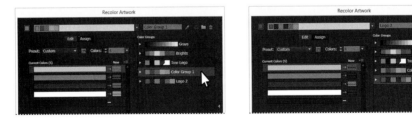

This is one of the easiest ways to reapply the color group colors, and it will fill in the missing color to the right of the white in the Current Colors column. You might not like how it assigned the colors to your artwork, and that's what you'll edit next.

11 In the New column of the Recolor Artwork dialog box, drag the top blue color box in the column down on top of the brown color and release the mouse button.

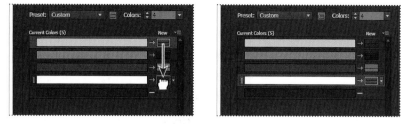

This is one way that you can reassign the Logo 2 group colors to the colors in the logo. The colors in the New column show what you see in the artwork. If you click one of the colors in the New column, notice that the CMYK sliders at the bottom of the dialog box let you edit that one color.

12 Double-click the brown color box at the top of the New column. In the Color Picker dialog box, click the Color Swatches button (on the right side) and select the color named "Light Green." You may need to scroll in the list of color swatches. Click OK to return to the Recolor Artwork dialog box.

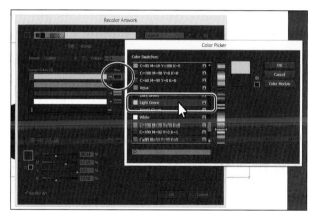

13 In the Recolor Artwork dialog box, click the Save Changes To Color Group button (⬛) to save the changes to the color group without closing the dialog box. Click OK. The color changes that you made to the color group are saved in the Swatches panel.

14 Choose Select > Deselect, and then choose File > Save.

There are many kinds of color edits that can be made to selected artwork in the Recolor Artwork dialog box, including reducing the number of colors, applying other colors (like Pantone colors), and much more.

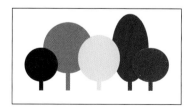

● **Note:** To learn more, search for "Working with color groups" in Illustrator Help.

Working with Live Paint

● **Note:** To learn more about Live Paint and all that it can do, search for "Live Paint groups" in Illustrator Help (Help > Illustrator Help).

Live Paint lets you paint vector graphics intuitively, by automatically detecting and correcting gaps that might otherwise affect the application of fills and strokes. Paths divide the drawing surface into areas that can be colored, whether the area is bounded by a single path or by segments of multiple paths. Painting objects with Live Paint is like coloring in a coloring book or using watercolors to paint a sketch, and the underlying shapes are not edited.

Creating a Live Paint group

Next, you will paint a simpler version of the logo using the Live Paint Bucket tool.

1   Choose 5 Artboard 5 from the Artboard Navigation menu in the lower-left corner of the Document window.

2   With the Selection tool (▶) selected, choose Select > All On Active Artboard.

3   Choose View > Zoom Out, several times, until you see the tree shape off the right edge of the artboard.

    That shape is not selected, but you will add it to the rest of the shapes soon.

4   Select the Live Paint Bucket tool (▨) from the Shape Builder tool (▨) group in the Tools panel.

● **Note:** Positioning the pointer over a color group will show you the name of the color group in a tooltip.

5   Click the Swatches panel icon (▦) to show the panel. Select the first (dark) blue swatch in the Logo 2 color group in the Swatches panel.

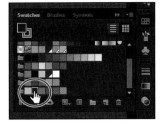

6   Position the pointer over the first tree shape (on the left), and click to convert the selected shapes to a Live Paint group.

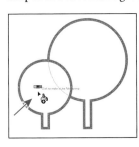 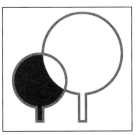

You can click any of the shapes to convert it to a Live Paint group, but the shape you click is filled with the dark blue color. Clicking selected shapes with the Live Paint Bucket tool creates a Live Paint group that you can paint with that same tool. Once a Live Paint group is created, the paths are fully editable, but they are treated like a group. Colors are automatically reapplied to new regions created when you move or adjust a path's shape.

Painting with the Live Paint Bucket tool

After objects are converted to a Live Paint group, you can paint them using several methods, which is what you'll do next.

1 Position the pointer over the second tree from the left in the Live Paint group (not where the trees overlap).

   A red highlight appears around the shape that will be painted, and three color swatches appear above the pointer. The selected color (dark blue) is in the middle, and the two adjacent colors in the Swatches panel are on either side.

2 Press the left arrow key once to select the lighter-green swatch (shown in the three swatches above the pointer).

   As you press the arrow key to change colors, notice, in the Swatches panel, that the color is highlighted. You can press the up or down arrow key, along with right or left arrow keys to select a new swatch to paint with. Click to apply the lighter-green color to the tree shape.

3 In the Swatches panel, click to select the swatch named "Dark Brown." Click to fill the overlapping (white) shape between the trees.

 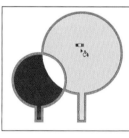  

4 Double-click the Live Paint Bucket tool () in the Tools panel. This opens the Live Paint Bucket Options dialog box. Select the Paint Strokes option, and then click OK.

   Next, you'll remove the inner gray stroke from the shapes and retain the outer strokes.

5 Select None (⊘) from the Stroke color in the Control panel. Press the Escape key to hide the Swatches panel.

6 Position the tip (▶) of the pointer directly over the gray stroke, between the two tree shapes, as shown in the figure. When the pointer changes to a paintbrush (↘), click the stroke to remove the stroke color (by applying the None swatch).

7 Choose Select > Deselect, and then choose File > Save.

Note: To learn more about the Live Paint Bucket Options dialog box, including working with Gap Options, search for "Paint with the Live Paint Bucket tool" in Illustrator Help (Help > Illustrator Help).

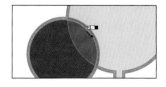

Note: I exaggerated the red line in the figure so you could more easily see it.

Modifying a Live Paint group

When you make a Live Paint group, each path remains editable. When you move or adjust a path, the colors that were previously applied don't just stay where they were, like they do in natural media paintings or with image-editing software. Instead, the colors are automatically reapplied to the new regions that are formed by the intersecting paths. Next, you will edit the paths by adding another shape.

1 Select the Selection tool (▶), and click to select the white tree shape off the right edge of the artboard. Drag it so that it overlaps the rightmost tree shape.

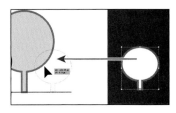

2 With the Selection tool, Shift-click the Live Paint group to select both objects.

3 Click the Merge Live Paint button in the Control panel to add the new white shape to the Live Paint group.

4 Select the Live Paint Bucket tool (🔲) in the Tools panel. In the Swatches panel (▦), click to select one of the brown colors in the Logo 2 group. Click to paint the part of the new tree that is not overlapping the other tree.

5 Select another swatch (I chose white), and click to paint the part of the circle that overlaps the light green tree.

Note: If you find that the stroke is not going away, try selecting the None swatch again for the Stroke color, positioning the pointer over the stroke, and clicking again when you see the paintbrush icon.

6 Select None (▱) from the Stroke color in the Control panel. Press the Escape key to hide the panel. Position the pointer directly over the stroke, between the tree shapes. When the paintbrush (↘) appears, click the stroke to remove it.

7 Select the Selection tool, and with the Live Paint object selected, you will see the words "Live Paint" on the left end of the Control panel. Double-click the Live Paint object (the trees) to enter Isolation mode.

▶ **Tip:** You could also edit the anchor points of the selected artwork using the Direct Selection tool (▷), for instance. The paths are still editable, and the colors are reapplied to the new regions that are formed by edited paths.

8 Drag the rightmost tree shape to the left to reposition it.

Notice how the color fill and stroke changes every time you release the mouse button.

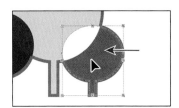

9 Choose Select > Deselect, and then press the Escape key to exit Isolation mode.

10 Choose View > Fit All In Window.

11 Choose File > Save, and then choose File > Close.

Review questions

1 Describe what a *global color* is.

2 How can you save a color?

3 Describe what a *tint* is.

4 How can you choose color harmonies for color inspiration?

5 Name two things that the Recolor Artwork dialog box allows you to do.

6 Explain what Live Paint allows you to do.

Review answers

1 A global color is a color swatch that, when you edit it, automatically updates all artwork to which it is applied. All spot colors are global; however, process colors can be either global or local.

2 You can save a color for painting other objects in your artwork by adding it to the Swatches panel by doing one of the following:

   - Drag the color from a Fill box, and drop it over the Swatches panel.
   - Click the New Swatch button () at the bottom of the Swatches panel.
   - Choose New Swatch from the Swatches panel menu ().
   - Choose Create New Swatch from the Color panel menu ().

3 A *tint* is a mixture of a color with white to make the color lighter. You can create a tint from a global process color, like CMYK, or from a spot color.

4 You can choose color harmonies from the Color Guide panel. Color harmonies are used to generate a color scheme based on a single color.

5 You use the Recolor Artwork dialog box to change the colors used in selected artwork, create and edit color groups, or reassign or reduce the colors in your artwork, among other functions.

6 Live Paint lets you paint vector graphics intuitively, by automatically detecting and correcting gaps that might otherwise affect the application of fills and strokes. Paths divide the drawing surface into areas, any of which can be colored, regardless of whether the area is bounded by a single path or by segments of multiple paths.

8 ADDING TYPE TO A POSTER

Lesson overview

In this lesson, you'll learn how to do the following:

- Create and edit area and point type.
- Import text.
- Create columns of text.
- Change text attributes.
- Modify text with the Touch Type tool.
- Create and edit paragraph and character styles.
- Copy and apply text attributes by sampling type.
- Wrap type around an object.
- Reshape text with a warp.
- Create type on a path and on shapes.
- Create text outlines.

This lesson takes approximately 75 minutes to complete.

Download the project files for this lesson from the Lesson & Update Files tab on your Account page at www.peachpit.com and store them on your computer in a convenient location, as described in the "Getting Started" section of this book.

Your Account page is also where you'll find any updates to the chapters or to the lesson files. Look on the Lesson & Update Files tab to access the most current content.

Text as a design element plays a major role in your illustrations. Like other objects, type can be painted, scaled, rotated, and more. In this lesson, you'll discover how to create basic text and interesting text effects.

Getting started

You'll be adding type to a poster and postcard during this lesson, but before you begin, restore the default preferences for Adobe Illustrator CC. Then open the finished art file for this lesson to see the illustration.

Note: If you have not already downloaded the project files for this lesson to your computer from your Account page, make sure to do so now. See "Getting Started" at the beginning of the book.

1 To ensure that the tools and panels function exactly as described in this lesson, delete or deactivate (by renaming) the Adobe Illustrator CC preferences file. See "Restoring default preferences" in the "Getting Started" section at the beginning of the book.

2 Start Adobe Illustrator CC.

3 Choose File > Open. Locate the file named L8_end.ai in the Lessons > Lesson08 folder. Click Open. You will most likely see a Missing Fonts dialog box since the file is using a specific Typekit font. Simply click Close in the Missing Fonts dialog box. You will learn all about Typekit fonts later in this lesson.

Leave the file open for reference later in the lesson, if you like. I closed it.

4 Choose File > Open. If a panel appears, click Open in the panel. You could also choose File > Open again. In the Open dialog box, navigate to the Lessons > Lesson08 folder and select the L8_start.ai file on your hard disk. Click Open to open the file.

This file already has non-text components in it. You will add all of the text elements to complete the poster and card (front and back).

5 Choose File > Save As. In the Save As dialog box, navigate to the Lesson08 folder and name the file **BuzzSoda.ai**. Leave the Format option set to Adobe Illustrator (ai) (Mac OS) or Save As Type option set to Adobe Illustrator (*.AI) (Windows), and then click Save.

6 In the Illustrator Options dialog box, leave the Illustrator options at their default settings, and then click OK.

Note: If you don't see Reset Essentials in the Workspace menu, choose Window > Workspace > Essentials before choosing Window > Workspace > Reset Essentials.

7 Choose View > Smart Guides to turn off the Smart Guides. Turning off the Smart Guides will make it easier to create text without snapping to existing content.

8 Choose Window > Workspace > Reset Essentials.

Adding type to the poster

Type features are some of the most powerful tools in Illustrator. You can add a single line of type to your artwork, create columns and rows of text like you do in Adobe InDesign, flow text into a shape or along a path, and work with letterforms as graphic objects. In Illustrator, you can create text in three different ways: as point type, area type, and type on a path.

Adding text at a point

Point type is a horizontal or vertical line of text that begins where you click and expands as you enter characters. Each line of text is independent—the line expands or shrinks as you edit it but doesn't wrap to the next line unless you add a paragraph return or a soft return. Entering text this way is useful for adding a headline or a few words to your artwork. Next, you will enter some text in the poster as point type.

1 Ensure that 1 Poster is chosen in the Artboard Navigation menu in the lower-left corner of the Document window.

2 Select the Zoom tool (🔍) in the Tools panel, and click in the top half of the large artboard twice, *slowly*.

3 Choose Window > Layers to show the panel. Select the layer named "Text," if it's not already selected. Click the Layers panel tab to collapse it.

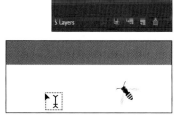

Note: Selecting a layer means any content you create going forward will be on that layer.

4 Select the Type tool (**T**), and click (*don't drag*) in the white area near the top of the artboard. The cursor appears on the artboard. Type **BUZZ soda** (make sure BUZZ is uppercase).

5 Select the Selection tool (▶) in the Tools panel, and notice the bounding box that appears around the text. Drag the lower-right bounding point, away from the center of the text (see the figure). The text will stretch if you drag any bounding point.

Note: Scaling point type this way may result in a font size that is not a round number (12.93 pt, for instance).

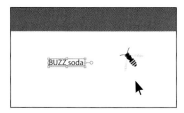

6 Choose Edit > Undo Scale, and then choose View > Fit Artboard In Window.

Adding area type

Area type uses the boundaries of an object (like a rectangle) to control the flow of characters, either horizontally or vertically. When the text reaches a boundary, it automatically wraps to fit inside the defined area. Entering text in this way is useful when you want to create one or more paragraphs, such as for a poster or a brochure.

To create area type, you click with the Type tool (**T**) where you want the text and drag to create an area type object (also called a *text area*). You can also convert an existing shape or object to a type object by clicking the edge of an object (or inside the object) with the Type tool. When the cursor appears, you can type. Next, you will create an area type object and enter more text.

1   Choose View > Smart Guides to turn on the Smart Guides.

2   Choose 2 CardFront from the Artboard Navigation menu in the lower-left corner of the Document window.

3   Select the Type tool (**T**). Position the cursor roughly in the middle of the artboard. Click and drag down and to the right to create a text area with a width and height of roughly 1 inch.

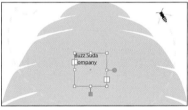

4   With the cursor in the new text area, type **Buzz Soda Company**.

Notice how the text wraps horizontally to fit within the type area.

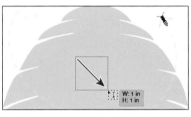

5   Select the Selection tool (**↖**) and drag the lower-right bounding point to the left and then back to the right to see how the text wraps within.

You can drag any of the eight bounding points on the text area to resize it, not just the lower-right.

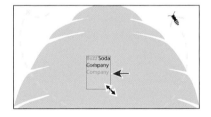

6   Before you continue, make sure that the area type looks like you see in the figure.

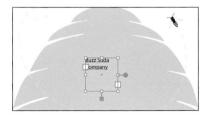

Working with Auto Sizing

By default, when you create area type by dragging with the Type tool, the type area will not resize to fit the text within (similar to how InDesign treats text frames by default). If there is too much text, the text that doesn't fit will not be visible and will be considered overset. For each type area, you can enable a feature called *Auto Sizing* so that area type will resize to fit the text within, and that's what you'll do next.

1. With the text area selected, look at the bottom, middle bounding point and you'll see a widget (⬇) indicating that the type area is *not* set to auto size. Hover the pointer over the box at the end of the widget (the pointer will change [🖥]), and double-click.

   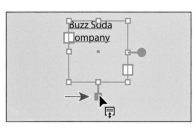

   ● **Note:** The figure shows just before double-clicking.

   By double-clicking the widget, you turn Auto Sizing on. As the text is edited and re-edited, the frame shrinks and grows vertically (only) to accommodate the changing amount of copy and eliminates overset text without manually sizing and resizing frames.

   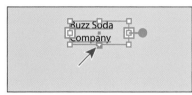

   ▷ **Tip:** If Auto Sizing is enabled for a selected type area, dragging one of the bottom bounding points on the type area down, disables Auto Sizing for the type area.

2. Select the Type tool, and insert the cursor after the word "Company." Press Enter or Return, and type **Raleigh, North Carolina**.

   ▷ **Tip:** If you double-click text with the Selection tool (▶) or Direct Selection tool (▷), the Type tool becomes selected.

   The type area will expand vertically to fit the new text. If you were to double click the Auto Sizing widget, Auto Sizing would be turned off for the area type. The type area would remain the current size no matter how much text was added.

3. Select the Type tool (T), and select all of the text, except for "Buzz Soda Co," and delete it.

   Buzz Soda Co

   Notice that the type area shrank vertically to fit around the text. Leave the text where it is for now.

4. Choose Select > Deselect, and then choose File > Save.

   In the next section, you'll continue editing the text on the 2 CardFront artboard.

Converting between area and point type

You can easily convert between area and point type objects. This method can be useful if you type a headline by clicking (creating point type) but later wish to resize and add more text without stretching the text inside. This method is also useful if you paste text from InDesign into Illustrator because text pasted from InDesign into Illustrator (with nothing selected) is pasted as point type. Most of the time, it would be better suited as an area type object so that you could flow the text within.

Next, you will convert the "Buzz Soda Co" text object on the 2 CardFront artboard from area type to point type. In this instance, you want the text to resize when you resize the bounding box to make it easier on us later.

1   While still on the 2 CardFront artboard with the text "Buzz Soda Co" on it, select the Type tool and insert the cursor right before the "S" in "Soda Co." Press Backspace or Delete to remove the space between "Buzz" and "Soda." Press Shift+Enter or Shift+Return to add a soft return.

▶ **Tip:** With a text object selected, you can also choose Type > Convert To Point Type or Convert To Area Type, depending on what the selected text area is.

2   Select the Selection tool (▶), and position the pointer over the annotator (━●) off the right edge of the type object. A filled end on the annotator indicates that it's area type. When the pointer changes (▶▁ᴛ), click once to see the message "Double-click to convert to Point Type." Double-click the annotator to convert the area type to point type.

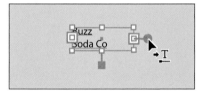

The annotator end should now be hollow (━○), indicating that it is a point type object. If you were to resize the bounding box, the text would scale as well.

3   Press the Shift key and drag the lower-right bounding point down and to the right until you see a width of 2.5 inches in the measurement label next to the pointer. Release the mouse button and then the key.

As you saw earlier, because the text is now point type, it stretches when the type area is resized. Pressing the Shift key is very important because otherwise the text will most likely be distorted.

4   Choose Select > Deselect, and then choose File > Save.

Importing a plain-text file

You can import text into artwork from a file that was created in another application. Illustrator supports DOC, DOCX, RTF, Plain text (ASCII) with ANSI, Unicode, Shift JIS, GB2312, Chinese Big 5, Cyrillic, GB18030, Greek, Turkish, Baltic, and Central European encoding. One of the advantages of importing text from a file, rather than copying and pasting it, is that imported text retains its character and paragraph formatting (by default). For example, text from an RTF file retains its font and style specifications in Illustrator, unless you choose to remove formatting when you import the text. In this section, you'll place text from a plain-text file into your design.

1. Choose 1 Poster from the Artboard Navigation menu in the lower-left corner of the Document window.

2. Choose File > Place. In the Lessons > Lesson08 folder, select the L8_text.txt file, select Show Import Options, and click Place.

3. In the Text Import Options dialog box, you can set some options prior to importing text. Leave the default settings, and then click OK.

4. Position the loaded text pointer over the upper-left corner of the aqua guide box on the left side of the artboard. When the word "anchor" appears, click and drag down and to the right. As you drag, notice that the width and height are constrained (always the same proportion). Drag until the pointer reaches the right edge of the aqua guide box, and then release the mouse button.

Note: The figures are from Mac OS, so the Platform options that you see may be different, and that's okay.

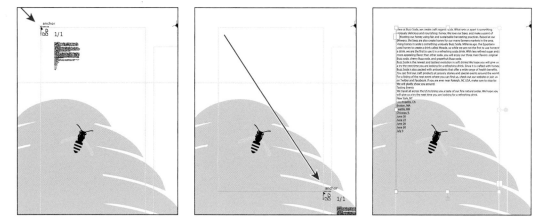

If you were to simply click with the loaded text pointer, an area type object would be created that was smaller than the size of the artboard.

5 With the Selection tool (▶), drag the bottom bounding point of the type object up to the horizontal guide. An overset text icon (⊞) appears in the out port.

6 Leave the area type object selected.

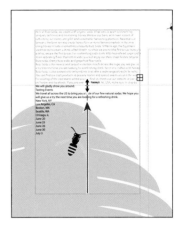

Placing Microsoft Word documents

When you place (File > Place) RTF (Rich Text Format) or Word documents (DOC or DOCX) in Illustrator, the Microsoft Word Options dialog box appears.

In this dialog box, you can select to keep the generated table of contents, footnotes and endnotes, and index text, and you can even choose to remove the formatting of the text before you place it (the styles and formatting are brought in from Word by default).

Threading text

When working with area type (*not* point type), each area type object contains an *in port* and an *out port*. The ports enable you to link type objects and flow text between them.

An empty out port indicates that all the text is visible and that the object isn't linked. An arrow in a port indicates that the type object is linked to another type object. A red plus sign (⊞) in an out port indicates that the object contains additional text, which is called *overflow text*. To show all of the overflow text, you can thread the text to another type object, resize the type object, or adjust the text. To *thread*, or continue, text from one object to the next, you have to link the objects. Linked type objects can be of any shape; however, the text must be entered in an object or along a path, not as point type (by simply clicking to create text).

Next, you will practice threading text a few times.

1   With the Selection tool (↖), click the out port (larger box) in the lower-right corner of the type object that has the red plus sign in it (⊞). The pointer changes to a loaded text icon (▦) when you move it away.

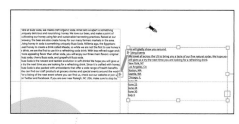

● **Note:** It may be difficult to click the out port because of the guides. You can always zoom in, remembering to zoom out again for the next steps.

● **Note:** If you double-click an out port, a new type object appears. If this happens, you can either drag the new object where you would like it to be positioned or choose Edit > Undo Link Threaded Text, and the loaded text icon reappears.

2   Position the pointer in the upper-left corner of the aqua guide box to the right and click when the word "anchor" appears. An area type object is created that is as wide and tall as the original.

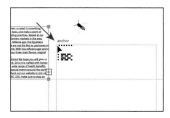

With the second type object still selected, notice the line between the two objects. This line is the thread that tells you that the two objects are connected. If you don't see this thread (line), choose View > Show Text Threads.

▶ **Tip:** Another way to thread text between objects is to select an area type object, select the object (or objects) you want to link to, and then choose Type > Threaded Text > Create.

The out port (▶) of the type object that is the first (left) column on the artboard and the in port (▶) of the type object that is the second (right) column on the artboard have small arrows in them indicating how the text is flowing from one to the other. If you delete the second type object, the text is pulled back into the original object as overflow text. Although not visible, the overflow text is *not* deleted.

3   Click the out port in the lower-right corner of the second type object. It may have a red plus sign in it (⊞) indicating overset text, or it may be empty (☐). Mine was empty. Move the pointer away after clicking and you should see the loaded text icon like before.

4   Choose 3 CardBack from the Artboard Navigation menu in the lower-left corner of the Document window.

5   Click and drag to create a blank text area on the artboard within the aqua guide box.

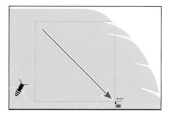

The new text area most likely will not contain any text. If it does, that's okay. In the next section, you'll learn how to format the text so that it is more readable. The text will begin to flow between the type areas as the formatting (like font size) changes, and that's what you want.

▶ **Tip:** You can split the threaded text so that each type area is no longer connected to the next by selecting one of the threaded text areas and choosing Type > Threaded Text > Remove Threading.

Formatting type

You can format text using character and paragraph formatting, apply fill and stroke attributes to it, and change its transparency (how see-through it is). You can apply these changes to one character, a range of characters, or all characters in a type object that you select. As you'll soon see, selecting the type object, rather than selecting the text inside, lets you apply global formatting options to all of the text in the object, including options from the Character and Paragraph panels, fill and stroke attributes, and transparency settings.

In this section, you'll discover how to change text attributes, such as size and font, and later learn how to save that formatting as text styles.

Changing font family and font style

● **Note:** The Creative Cloud desktop application must be installed on your computer and you must have an Internet connection to initially sync fonts. The Creative Cloud desktop application is installed automatically when you install your first Creative Cloud application, like Illustrator.

In this section, you'll apply a font to text. Aside from applying local fonts to text from your machine, Creative Cloud users can apply Typekit fonts that have been synced with their computer. Typekit is a subscription service offering access to a library of fonts for use in desktop applications such as InDesign or Microsoft Word and on websites. A Typekit Portfolio plan is included with your Creative Cloud subscription, and trial Creative Cloud members have access to a selection of fonts from Typekit for web and desktop use. The fonts appear alongside other locally installed fonts in the fonts list in Illustrator, as you'll soon see. By default, Typekit is turned on in the Creative Cloud desktop application (version 1.9 and later) so that it can sync fonts and make them available in your desktop applications.

● **Note:** For questions about Typekit font licensing, visit http://help.typekit.com/customer/portal/articles/1341590-typekit-font-licensing. For more information on working with Typekit fonts, visit https://helpx.adobe.com/creative-cloud/help/add-fonts-typekit.html.

Sync Typekit fonts

Next, you'll select and sync a few Typekit fonts to your machine so that you may use them in Illustrator.

1   Ensure that the Creative Cloud for desktop application is launched and you are signed in with your Adobe ID (*this requires an Internet connection*).

2   In Illustrator, choose 1 Poster from the Artboard Navigation menu in the lower-left corner of the Document window.

3   Press Command++ (Mac OS) or Ctrl++ (Windows) twice to zoom into the text in the center of the artboard.

● **Note:** If you miss the text when you attempt to insert the cursor, you will create point type. Choose Edit > Undo Type, if that's the case, and try again.

4   Select the Type tool ($\mathbf{T}$) in the Tools panel, and with the pointer over the text, click to insert the cursor in either column of text. Choose Select > All or press Command+A (Mac OS) or Ctrl+A (Windows) to select all the text in the threaded text objects.

5 Click the arrow to the right of the Font menu in the Control panel, and notice the fonts that appear in the menu. These fonts are those that are installed locally. Click the Add Fonts From Typekit button.

Note: You may see the word "Character" instead of the Font menu listed in the Control panel. Click the word "Character" to reveal the Character panel, and then click the Font menu.

A browser will open and should open the Typekit.com website and log you in using your Adobe ID. If you do not have an Internet connection, you can choose any other font in the font menu instead.

6 Once the Typekit.com website is open in your browser, click the Sans Serif button in the Classification options to sort the fonts, showing only available sans serif fonts.

Note: If you are taken to the Typekit.com home page, you can simply click the Browse Fonts button.

7 Make sure that the Sync button is selected to show all fonts that are available for use in desktop applications.

8 Hover over the font "Adelle Sans" or another font, and click +Use Fonts.

Note: If you don't see +Use Fonts, you will most likely need to log in to the Typekit site using your Adobe ID.

9 In the pop-up that appears, click Sync Selected Fonts. After the fonts have synced, click Close to return to the main Typekit web page.

▶ **Tip:** The fonts are synced to all computers where you've installed the Creative Cloud application and logged in. To view fonts, open the Creative Cloud desktop application, and click the Assets > Fonts panel.

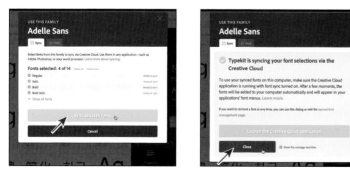

10 Type **Copal** in the Search Typekit field above the font list. Click the search glass (🔍) or press Enter or Return to search the site for the Copal font.

● **Note:** The font order you see may be different, and that's okay.

11 Position the pointer over the Copal Std Outline font, and click + Use Fonts.

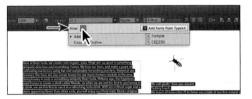

12 Follow the same process as before by clicking Sync Selected Fonts and then clicking Close. You can close the browser and return to Illustrator.

Once the fonts are synced to your computer (be patient, it may take a few minutes), a quick notification is typically displayed in your OS, indicating how many fonts have been added.

Apply the Typekit fonts to text in Illustrator

Now that the Typekit fonts are synced with your machine, you can use them in any application, and that's what you'll do next.

1 Back in Illustrator, with the threaded text still selected, click the arrow to the right of the Font menu in the Control panel, and click the Apply Typekit Filter button (Tk) to filter the font list and show only the Typekit fonts you just synced.

● **Note:** You may see other Typekit fonts in your menu (aside from the Adelle Sans font), and that's okay.

2 Click the arrow to the left of Adelle Sans in the menu, and choose Regular.

3 Choose View > Fit Artboard In Window.

4 With the Selection tool (▶), click the "BUZZ soda" text at the top of the artboard to select the object.

If you want to apply the same font to all of the text in a point type or area type object, you can simply select the object, not the text, and then apply the font.

5 Choose Type > Font > Adelle Sans > Bold (or another font).

▶ **Tip:** You could also use the arrow keys (Up and Down) to navigate the list of fonts. When the font you want is chosen, you can press Enter or Return to apply it.

Your font list probably won't be the same as you see in the figure, and that's okay.

Next, you will use Font search to locate a font. This next method is the most dynamic method for selecting a font.

6 Select the Zoom tool (🔍) in the Tools panel, and click twice on the "BUZZ soda" text to zoom in.

7 Select the Type tool, and double-click the word "BUZZ" to select it.

8 With the text selected, select the Adelle Sans font name in the Control panel. Begin typing the letters **cop**.

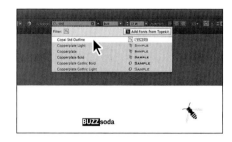

▶ **Tip:** With the cursor in the font name field, you can also click the X on the right side of the Font Family field to remove the current font shown.

Notice that a menu appears beneath where you are typing. Illustrator filters through the list of fonts and displays the font names that contain "cop," regardless of where "cop" is in the font name and regardless of whether it's capitalized. The Typekit font filter is still turned on from before, so you will turn it off next.

9 Click the Clear Filter button (Tk) in the menu that is showing to see all of the available fonts (see previous figure). In the menu that appears beneath where you are typing, click to select Copal Std Outline to apply the font to the selected text. Leave the text selected.

▶ **Tip:** You can click the Eyeglass icon (🔍) to the left of the Font Name field and choose to search the first word only. You can also open the Character panel (Window > Type > Character) and search for a font by typing the name.

When the menu of fonts appears, you'll notice an icon to the right of the name indicating what type of font it is (Tk is Typekit, *O* is OpenType, TT is TrueType, and a is Adobe Postscript). Notice that each of the fonts in the list also shows sample text with the font applied. Font styles are specific to each font family. For instance, although you may have the Adobe Garamond Pro font family on your system, you may not have the bold or italic styles of that family.

▶ Tip: You'll learn about the Package command in Lesson 14, "Using Illustrator CC with Other Adobe Applications."

Illustrator Package (File > Package) and Typekit fonts

In Illustrator, you can package the content associated with an Illustrator document using the File > Package command. Illustrator CC will not package Typekit desktop fonts but will continue to package conventionally licensed fonts, except Chinese, Japanese, and Korean fonts, which have never been packaged by Illustrator. Recipients who are Creative Cloud members or Typekit subscribers can easily obtain the fonts through their online service when the file is opened.

—From Illustrator Help

Changing font size

By default, typeface size is measured in points (a point equals 1/72 of an inch). In this section, you will change the font size of text and also see what happens to point type that is scaled.

Note: You may see the word "Character" instead of the Font Size field in the Control panel. Click the word "Character" to reveal the Character panel.

1   With the "BUZZ" text at the top of the artboard and Type tool (**T**) still selected, choose 72 pt from the preset sizes in the Font Size menu in the Control panel. The figure shows the font size applied.

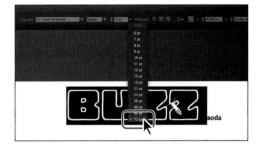

2   Select 72 pt in the Font Size field in the Control panel, and type **88**. Press Enter or Return.

▶ Tip: You can dynamically change the font size of selected text using keyboard shortcuts. To increase the font size in increments of 2 points, press Command+Shift+> (Mac OS) or Ctrl+Shift+> (Windows). To reduce the font size, press Command+Shift+< (Mac OS) or Ctrl+Shift+< (Windows).

3   Insert the cursor before the "S" in "Soda." Press Backspace or Delete to remove the space between "BUZZ" and "soda." Press Enter or Return so that "soda" is on its own line.

4   Drag across the word "soda" to select it.

5   Choose 72 pt from the preset sizes in the Font Size menu in the Control panel, and leave the "soda" text selected.

Changing font color

You can change the appearance of text by applying fills, strokes, and more. In this example, you will change the stroke and then the fill of the selected text.

1 Click the Layers panel icon () to expand the panel. Click the visibility column to the left of the layer named "Poster Heading." Click the Layers panel tab to collapse it.

2 With the "soda" text still selected, click the Stroke color in the Control panel. When the Swatches panel appears, select the swatch named "BuzzBrown."

3 Change the Stroke weight of the text to **2 pt** in the Control panel.

4 Click the Fill color in the Control panel. When the Swatches panel appears, select the swatch named "Gold."

5 Choose Select > Deselect.

6 Choose File > Save.

Changing additional character formatting

In Illustrator you can change a lot of text attributes besides font, font size, and color. Like in InDesign, text attributes are split between character and paragraph formatting and can be found in two panels: the Character panel and the Paragraph panel.

The Character panel, which you can access by clicking the underlined word "Character" in the Control panel or by choosing Window > Type > Character, contains formatting for selected text such as font, font size, kerning, and more. In this section, you will apply some of the many possible attributes to experiment with the different ways you can format text.

1   Open the Character panel by choosing Window > Type > Character. Click the double arrow on the left side of the Character panel tab to show more options.

    The following are the formatting options available in the Character panel when all options are showing.

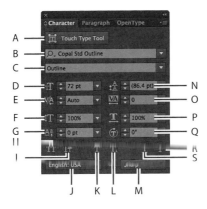

A. Touch Type tool	**K.** Superscript
B. Font Family	**L.** Subscript
C. Font Style	**M.** Text Anti-Aliasing
D. Font Size	**N.** Leading
E. Kerning	**O.** Tracking
F. Vertical Scale	**P.** Horizontal Scale
G. Baseline Shift	**Q.** Character Rotation
H. All Caps	**R.** Strikethrough
I. Small Caps	**S.** Underline
J. Language	

2   Press the spacebar to access the Hand tool temporarily. Drag the artboard up just enough to see the threaded text below.

3   With the Type tool (**T**) selected, click in either of the threaded text objects on the artboard that contain the placed text. Choose Select > All.

▶ **Tip:** You could also click the word "Character" in the Control panel to show the Character panel.

4   In the Character panel, change the following options:

    • Font Size: **11 pt**

    • Leading (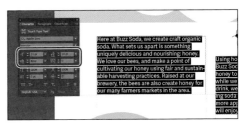): **14 pt** (Leading is the vertical space between lines of text. Adjusting the leading can be useful for fitting text into a text area.)

5   Choose View > Fit Artboard In Window.

6 Double-click in the word "soda" in "BUZZ soda" toward the top of the artboard to select it.

7 With the text selected, change the following formatting in the Character panel:

- Leading (): **60 pt**.

- Click the Tracking icon () in the Character panel to select the value in the Tracking field, and type **40**. Press Enter or Return. *Tracking* changes the spacing between characters. A positive value pushes the letters apart horizontally; a negative value pulls the letters closer together.

- Click the All Caps button () to make the word uppercase. Changing case this way is not a permanent change since it is styling applied and can be removed later.

▶ **Tip:** If you want to permanently change the case of text, you can choose Type > Change Case and choose a method.

8 With the text object still selected, click the Vertical Scale icon () in the Character panel to select the value and type **80**. Press Enter or Return to accept the value. Change Horizontal Scale to **110**.

9 Leave the Character panel open.

10 Choose Select > Deselect.

Working with glyphs

Glyphs are characters within a certain typeface that may be harder to find, like a bullet point or a registration symbol. In Illustrator, the Glyphs panel (Type > Glyphs) is used to insert type characters, like trademark symbols (™). The panel shows all of the characters (glyphs) available for a given font.

To learn more about working with glyphs in Illustrator, search for "Glyphs" in Illustrator Help (Help > Illustrator Help).

Changing paragraph formatting

As with character formatting, you can set paragraph formatting, such as alignment or indenting, before you enter new type or change the appearance of existing type. Paragraph formatting applies to entire paragraphs rather than just selected content. Most of this type of formatting is done in the Paragraph panel, which you can access by clicking the underlined word "Paragraph" in the Control panel or by choosing Window > Type > Paragraph.

▶ **Tip:** You could also click the word "Paragraph" in the Control panel to show the Paragraph panel.

1   Open the Paragraph panel by clicking the Paragraph tab in the Character panel group. Click the double arrow on the left side of the Paragraph panel tab to show more options, if necessary.

The following are the formatting options available in the Paragraph panel.

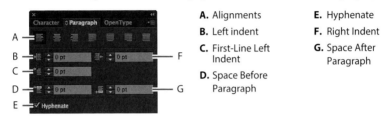

A. Alignments
B. Left indent
C. First-Line Left Indent
D. Space Before Paragraph
E. Hyphenate
F. Right Indent
G. Space After Paragraph

2   Select the Zoom tool (⌕) in the Tools panel, and click twice on the "BUZZ SODA" text at the top of the larger artboard.

▶ **Tip:** You will accidentally click with the Type tool and create a type object from time to time and want to get rid of the ones you aren't using. Illustrator has an easy way to clean up those objects: Object > Path > Clean Up.

3   Select the Type tool (T), and insert the cursor in the "BUZZ SODA" text. Press Cmd+A (Mac OS) or Ctrl+A (Windows) to select the text.

4   Click the Align Center button (▣) to center align the text.

Since the text is point type, it appears to jump to the left. Text is aligned according to the leftmost edge of the point type object, by default.

5   Select the Selection tool, and drag the text object into the center of the artboard. Use the figure for placement.

6   Choose View > Fit All In Window.

7   Select the Type tool (T), and insert the cursor in the threaded text below "BUZZ SODA." Press Cmd+A (Mac OS) or Ctrl+A (Windows) to select the text.

8 Change the Space After Paragraph to **6 pt** in the Paragraph panel.

Setting a spacing value after paragraphs, rather than pressing the Return key, is useful for maintaining consistency and ease of editing later.

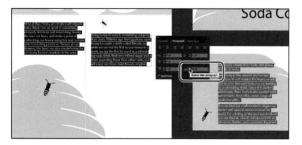

9 Leave the Paragraph panel group open for later use.

10 Choose Select > Deselect, and then choose File > Save.

Resizing and reshaping type objects

You can create unique type object shapes by reshaping them using a variety of methods, including adding columns to area type objects or reshaping text objects using the Direct Selection tool.

In this next section, you'll reshape and resize type objects to better fit text in them.

1 Using the Selection tool (![arrow]), click the text in the right column on the larger artboard to select it. Drag the bottom middle handle down until the text "...We will gladly show you around." is the last text in the object.

2 Select the Type tool (T), and click three times on the "Tasting Events" text on the 2 CardBack artboard to select it.

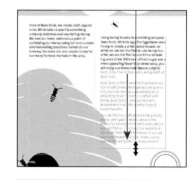

Tip: Clicking once in text inserts the cursor. Clicking twice on text selects a word. Clicking three times selects the entire paragraph in Illustrator.

3 Change the Font Size to **20 pt** in the Control panel.

4 Select the Selection tool (![arrow]), and click in a blank area of the artboard with the "Tasting Events" text on it to deselect the type areas.

5 Choose View > Fit Artboard In Window to fit the 3 CardBack artboard in the Document window.

6 Click the text "Tasting Events" to select the type area. Drag the bottom middle handle of the type area up so that it looks like the figure. There will be overset text (⊞) when you are finished.

7 Select the Type tool (T), and click three times on the text that begins with "We travel all..." to select the paragraph.

8 Change the Font Size to **10 pt** in the Control panel.

9 Select the Direct Selection tool (⬉). Click the upper-right corner of the type object to select the anchor point. Drag that point to the left to adjust the shape of the path to fit the yellow shape. As you drag, press the Shift key. Release the mouse button and then the Shift key when finished.

Change the font size.	Select the anchor point.	Drag the anchor point.

Creating columns of text

You can easily create columns and rows of text by using the Type > Area Type Options command. This can be useful for creating a single area type object with multiple columns or for organizing text, such as a table or simple chart, for instance. Next, you'll add a few columns to the area type object you create.

1 Choose Select > Deselect.

2 Select the Selection tool (⬆), and click the text to select the area type object. Click the out port (larger box) in the lower-right corner of the type object that has the red plus sign in it (⊞) (circled in the following figure). The pointer changes to a loaded text icon (▤) when you move it away.

3 Click and drag to draw a type area below, roughly in the size of the aqua guide box.

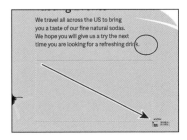

4 With the area type object still selected, choose Type > Area Type Options. In the Area Type Options dialog box, change the Number to **2** in the Columns section, and select Preview. Click OK. The text is now flowing between two columns.

▶ **Tip:** To learn more about the large number of options in the Area Type Options dialog box, search for "Creating Text" in Illustrator Help (Help > Illustrator Help).

5 Drag the bottom middle bounding point up and down to see the text flow between the columns. Drag so that the text in the columns is even (see the previous figure).

6 Choose Select > Deselect, and then choose File > Save.

Modifying text with the Touch Type tool

Using the Touch Type tool (⬚), you can modify the properties of a character, such as size, scale, and rotation, using a mouse cursor or touch controls. This is a very visual (and personally more fun) way of applying the character formatting properties: baseline shift, horizontal and vertical scale, rotation, and kerning.

1 Choose 1 Poster from the Artboard Navigation menu in the lower-left corner of the Document window.

2 Select the Zoom tool (🔍), and click the headline "BUZZ SODA" several times to zoom in closely. Make sure you can see all of the "BUZZ SODA" text.

3 With the Selection tool (▶), click to select the "BUZZ SODA" type object.

4 Select the Touch Type tool (⬚) by pressing and holding down on the Type tool (**T**) in the Tools panel and then selecting the Touch Type tool.

After selecting the Touch Type tool, a message briefly appears at the top of the Document window telling you to click a character to select it.

5 Click the letter "B" in "BUZZ" to select it.

A box with a dot above it appears around the letter after you select it. The different points around the box allow you to adjust the character in different ways, as you'll see.

● **Note:** You may still see a bounding box around the "BUZZ SODA" text after clicking the letter. The figures in this section do not show it.

6 Click and drag the upper-right corner of the box away from the center to make the letter larger. Stop dragging when you see roughly 140% for width (W:) and height (H:) in the measurement label.

Notice that width and height change together proportionally. You just adjusted the horizontal scale and the vertical scale for the letter "B." If you look in the Character panel you would see that the Horizontal Scale and Vertical Scale values are roughly 140%.

7 Click the "U" to the right of the "B," and drag the lower-right point of the box to the left until you see an H. Scale (horizontal scale) of approximately 85%.

8 Drag the rotate handle (the circle above the letter "U") counterclockwise until you see approximately 20° in the measurement label.

> **Tip:** You can also nudge a selected letter with the arrow keys or press Shift+arrow key to move the letter in bigger increments.

9 With the letter "U" still selected, position the pointer in the center of the letter. Click and drag the letter to the left and a little down until the Baseline value shows approximately −1 pt in the gray measurement label.

Change the horizontal scale. · Rotate the letter. · Drag the letter.

> **Note:** There are limits to how far you can drag in any direction. Those limits are based on the kerning and baseline shift value limits.

You just visually edited the horizontal scale, rotation, kerning, and baseline shift of the letter "U."

10 Click the first "Z" to the right of the "U," and drag the upper-left point of the box up until you see a V. Scale (vertical scale) of approximately 120%.

11 Drag that same "Z" to the left, closer to the "U." See the figure for help.

> **Tip:** You can always experiment a bit with the letters if you like, just know that they may not match the figures going forward.

Change the vertical scale. · Drag the "Z" into position.

12 If the Character panel group is open, close it.

Creating and applying text styles

Styles allow you to format text consistently and are helpful when text attributes need to be updated globally. Once a style is created, you only need to edit the saved style, and then all text formatted with that style is updated.

Illustrator provides two types of text styles.

- **Paragraph**—Retains character and paragraph attributes and applies them to an entire paragraph.

- **Character**—Retains character attributes and applies them to selected text.

Creating and applying a paragraph style

First, you will create a paragraph style for the body copy.

1   Choose View > Fit Artboard In Window.

2   Select the Type tool (**T**) in the Tools panel (it's under the Touch Type tool [**⊞**]), and insert the cursor anywhere in the first paragraph in the first column of text that starts with "Here at Buzz Soda...."

    By inserting the cursor in text when you create a paragraph style, the formatting attributes from the paragraph are saved.

3   Choose Window > Type > Paragraph Styles, and click the Create New Style button (**⊞**) at the bottom of the Paragraph Styles panel.

    This creates a new paragraph style in the panel, called "Paragraph Style 1." This style captures the character and paragraph formatting from the paragraph.

4   Double-click directly on the style name "Paragraph Style 1" in the list of styles. Change the name of the style to **Body**, and press Enter or Return to edit the name inline.

    By double-clicking the style to edit the name, you are also applying the new style to the paragraph (where the cursor is). This means that if you edit the Body paragraph style, this paragraph will update as well.

5   With the Type tool selected, click and drag to select the text in both columns, making sure *not* to select the text on the 3 CardBack artboard.

6 Click the Body style in the Paragraph Styles panel.

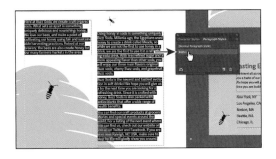

Notice that a plus sign (+) appears to the right of the Body style name. The plus sign indicates that the style has an override. An *override* is any formatting that doesn't match the attributes defined by the style, for example, if you changed the font size for the selected paragraph.

●Note: If you place a Microsoft Word document and choose to keep the formatting, the styles used in the Word document may be brought into the Illustrator document and may appear in the Paragraph Styles panel.

7 Press the Option (Mac OS) or Alt (Windows) key, and select the Body style again in the Paragraph Styles panel to overwrite existing attributes on the selected text.

The plus sign (+) should go away after clicking the "Body" style name with the key held down.

8 Choose Select > Deselect.

Editing a paragraph style

After creating a paragraph style, you can easily edit the style formatting. Then anywhere the style has been applied, the formatting will be updated automatically.

Next, you'll edit the Body style to see firsthand why you can use paragraph styles to save time and maintain consistency.

▶ Tip: You can also choose Paragraph Style Options from the Paragraph Styles panel menu (▾☰).

1 Double-click to the right of the style name "Body" in the Paragraph Styles panel list to open the Paragraph Style Options dialog box, select the Indents And Spacing category on the left side of the dialog box, and change the following, if necessary:

▶ Tip: There are many more options for working with paragraph styles, most of which are found in the Paragraph Styles panel menu, including duplicating, deleting, and editing paragraph styles. To learn more about these options, search for "paragraph styles" in Illustrator Help (Help > Illustrator Help).

- Space After: **8 pt**
- Add To My Library: **Deselected**

Since Preview is selected by default, you can move the dialog box out of the way to see the text change everywhere that the Body style is applied.

2 Click OK.

3 Choose File > Save.

Creating and applying a character style

Character styles, unlike paragraph styles, can be applied only to selected text and can contain only character formatting. Next, you will create a character style from text styling within the columns of text.

1 Choose View > Zoom In, twice, to zoom into the threaded text in the center.

2 Using the Type tool (T), in the first column, select Buzz Soda.

3 Change the Fill color to the swatch named "BuzzBrown" in the Control panel.

4 Click the word "Character" in the Control panel, click the Underline button (T) to underline the text. Choose Italic from the Font Style menu.

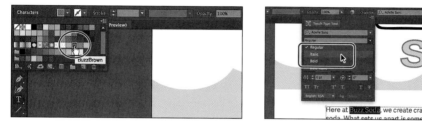

Note: If you chose a font other than Adelle Sans and don't see Italic, try choosing another font style.

5 In the Paragraph Styles panel group, click the Character Styles panel tab.

6 In the Character Styles panel, Option-click (Mac OS) or Alt-click (Windows) the Create New Style button ( ) at the bottom of the Character Styles panel.

   Option-clicking (Mac OS) or Alt-clicking (Windows) the Create New Style button in the Character or Paragraph Styles panel allows you to edit the style options before it is added to the panel.

7 In the Character Styles Options dialog box, change the following options:

   • Style Name: **Emphasis**

   • Add To My Library: **Deselected**

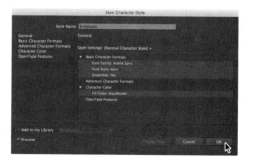

8 Click OK.

   The style records the attributes applied to your selected text.

Note: If you apply the character style and a plus appears next to the style name, you can Option-click (Mac OS) or Alt-click (Windows) the style name to apply it.

9 With the text still selected, click the style named "Emphasis" in the Character Styles panel to assign the style to that text so that it will update if the style formatting changes.

10 In the next column (text object), anytime you see the text "Buzz Soda," select it, and click the Emphasis style in the Character Styles panel to apply it.

11 Choose Select > Deselect.

Note: You must select the entire phrase rather than just placing the cursor in the text.

Editing a character style

After creating a character style, you can easily edit the style formatting, and, anywhere the style is applied, the formatting will be updated automatically.

Note: If the Font Family field is blank, choose Adelle Sans (or the font you chose), and then you can select a font style.

1 Double-click to the right of the Emphasis style name in the Character Styles panel (not the style name itself). In the Character Style Options dialog box, click the Basic Character Formats category on the left side of the dialog box, and change the following:

- Choose **Regular** from the Font Style menu
- Add To My Library: **Deselected**
- Preview: **Selected**

2 Click OK.

Sampling text formatting

Using the Eyedropper tool (✒), you can quickly sample type attributes and copy them to text without creating a style.

1 Using the Type tool (**T**), select the text "Raleigh, NC USA" toward the bottom of the second column of text. You may need to scroll in the Document window.

2 Select the Eyedropper tool (✒) in the Tools panel, and click in any "Buzz Soda" text (they all are gold and underlined) when a letter "T" appears above the Eyedropper pointer.

This applies the Emphasis character style (and its formatting) to your selected text.

Note: Clicking [Normal Character Style] ensures that any new text you add to the document will not have the style named "Emphasis" applied.

3 Choose Select > Deselect, and then click the style named [Normal Character Style] in the Character Styles panel. Close the Character Styles panel group.

Wrapping text

In Illustrator, you can easily wrap text around objects, such as type objects, imported images, and vector artwork, to avoid text running over those objects or to create interesting design effects. Next, you'll wrap text around part of the artwork. In Illustrator, like InDesign, you apply text wrap to the content that the text will wrap around.

1 Choose View > Fit Artboard In Window.

2 Select the Selection tool (▶), and click the yellow "beehive" shape under the bees in the lower-left corner of the artboard.

3 Choose Object > Text Wrap > Make. Click OK if a dialog box appears.

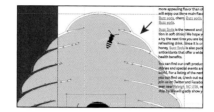

To wrap text around an object, the object that the text is to wrap around must be in the same layer as the text and must be located above the text in the layer hierarchy.

4 With the yellow shape still selected, choose Object > Arrange > Bring To Front.

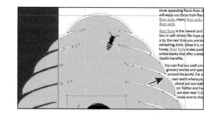

The text should now be wrapping around that yellow shape.

5 Choose Object > Text Wrap > Text Wrap Options. In the Text Wrap Options dialog box, change Offset to **15 pt**, and select Preview to see the change. Click OK.

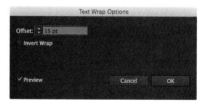

6 With the Selection tool (▶) selected, click the second column of text and drag the bottom middle point down to make sure that the text "We will gladly show you around." is the last showing.

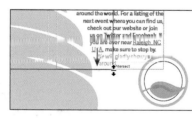

Note: Your text may wrap differently, and that's okay.

Warping text

You can create some great design effects by warping text into different shapes using envelopes. You can make an envelope out of an object on your artboard, or you can use a preset warp shape or a mesh grid as an envelope. As you explore warping with envelopes, you'll also discover that you can use envelopes on any object except graphs, guides, or linked objects.

Tip: There are several additional ways to warp content like text, including with a mesh and with an object you create. To learn more about these other methods, search for "Reshape using envelopes" in Illustrator Help (Help > Illustrator Help).

Reshaping text with a preset envelope warp

Illustrator comes with a series of preset warp shapes that you can warp text with. Next, you'll apply one of the preset warp shapes that Illustrator provides.

1 Choose 2 CardFront from the Artboard Navigation menu in the lower-left corner of the Document window.

2   Choose View > Fit Artboard In Window, if necessary.

3   With the Type tool (T), select the word "BUZZ," and change the Font Size to **92 pt** in the Control panel.

4   Choose Type > Change Case > UPPERCASE to change the case of the word.

5   Select the words "Soda Co," and change the Font Size to **62 pt** in the Control panel.

Note: The same visual result can be achieved by choosing Object > Envelope Distort > Make With Warp. For more information about envelopes, see "Reshape using envelopes" in Illustrator Help (Help > Illustrator Help).

6   Select the Selection tool (↖), and make sure that the text object is selected. Click the Make Envelope button (▦) in the Control panel (*not* the arrow to the right of the button).

7   In the Warp Options dialog box that appears, select Preview. The text appears as an arc, by default. Make sure Arc is chosen in the Style menu. Drag the Bend, Horizontal, and Vertical Distortion sliders to see the effect on the text. When you are finished experimenting, drag both Distortion sliders to **0%**, make sure that the Bend is **24%**, and then click OK.

Editing the envelope warp

If you want to make any changes, you can edit the text and shape that make up the envelope warp object separately. Next, you will edit the text and then the warp shape.

1   With the envelope object still selected, click the Edit Contents button (▦) on the left end of the Control panel. This is one way you can edit the text in the warped shape.

▶ **Tip:** If you double-click with the Selection tool instead of with the Type tool, you enter Isolation mode. This is another way to edit the text within the envelope warp object. Press the Escape key to exit Isolation mode if that is the case.

2   Using the Type tool (T), position the cursor over the warped text. Notice that the unwarped text appears in blue. Insert the cursor in the words "Soda Co," and click three times to select those words.

3   In the Character panel (Window > Type > Character). Change Leading to **50 pt**.

You can also edit the preset shape, which is what you'll do next.

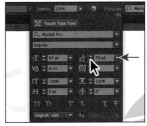

4 Select the Selection tool (▶), and make sure that the envelope object is still selected. Click the Edit Envelope button (▦) in the Control panel.

Notice the options for the envelope warp object in the Control panel. You can choose another warp shape from the Style menu and then change the warp options, like Horizontal, Vertical, and Bend. These are the same options you saw in the Warp Options dialog box when you first created the envelope warp.

Note: Changing the warp style will most likely move the warp object on the artboard.

5 Change Bend to **12%** in the Control panel. Make sure that H (horizontal) Distortion is **0** and V (vertical) Distortion is **0**.

▶ **Tip:** To take the text out of the warped shape, select the text with the Selection tool, and choose Object > Envelope Distort > Release. This gives you two objects: the type object and an arc upper shape.

6 With the Selection tool, drag the envelope object (warped text) into the approximate center of the yellow shape. Make sure to closely match the vertical position you see in the figure. In the next section, you are going to add text to the dotted path beneath the text.

Working with type on a path

In addition to having text in point and type areas, you can have type along a path. Text can flow along the edge of an open or closed path and can lead to some really creative ways to display text.

Creating type on a path

In this section, you'll add some text to an open path.

1 With the Selection tool (▶), select the dashed curved path next to the bee.

2 Choose Edit > Copy, and then choose Edit > Paste In Front to paste a copy of the path directly on top of the original.

3 With the Type tool (**T**), position the cursor over the middle of the path to see an insertion point with an intersecting wavy path (⤢) (see the figure). Click when this cursor appears.

The text starts where you click the path. Also, the stroke attributes of the path change to None (which is why you copied the line), and a cursor appears.

4 Choose Window > Type > Paragraph Styles to open the panel. Option-click (Mac OS) or Alt-click (Windows) [Normal Paragraph Style] to apply the style.

Note: If the text is brown and underlined, it means that the character style is applied. Select the text and Option-click (Mac OS) or Alt-click (Windows) [Normal Character Style] in the Character Styles panel.

5 Type the text **Honey Infused Natural Sodas**. Note that the new text follows the path.

6 With the Type tool, click three times on the new text to select it.

7 Change Font Size to **18 pt** in the Control panel.

8 Change the Fill color to BuzzBrown in the Control panel.

Next, you'll reposition the text on the path so that all of the text appears.

Tip: With the path or the text on the path selected, you can choose Type > Type On A Path > Type On A Path Options to set more options.

9 Select the Selection tool, and position the pointer over the line on the left edge of the text (just to the left of the "H" in "Honey"). When you see this cursor (▸̟), click and drag to the right—just a bit. Use the figure as a guide.

From where you click a path to the end of the path is where the text can flow. If you align the text left, center, or right, it's aligned within that area on the path.

10 Choose Select > Deselect, and then choose File > Save.

Creating type on a closed path

Next, you will add text around a circle.

1 Choose 1 Poster from the Artboard Navigation menu in the lower-left corner of the Document window.

2 Select the Zoom tool (Q) in the Tools panel, and click the green circle in the lower-right corner of the artboard three times to zoom in.

3 Select the Type tool (T), and position the pointer over the edge of the white circle. The Type cursor (I) changes to a Type cursor with a circle (☉). This indicates that if you click (*don't click*), text will be placed inside of the circle, creating a type object in the shape of a circle.

Instead of adding text to the inside of a shape, we want to add text to the path, which is what you'll do next.

4 While pressing the Option (Mac OS) or Alt (Windows) key, position the pointer over the left side of the white circle with black stroke (use the figure as a guide). The insertion point with an intersecting wavy path (⌶⁓) appears. Click and type **CERTIFIED ORGANIC**. If you accidentally click on the leaf, choose Edit > Undo Type and try again.

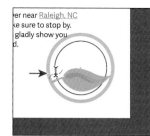

Note: Instead of pressing the Option (Mac OS) or Alt (Windows) key to allow the Type tool to type on a path, you can select the Type On A Path tool (⤳) by holding down the Type tool in the Tools panel.

5 Click three times on the text to select it. Change the font size to **12 pt**, the font to Adelle Sans Regular (if it isn't already), and the Fill color to the swatch named BuzzBrown.

Next, you'll edit the type on a path options for the text on the circle.

6 Select the Selection tool (▸) in the Tools panel. With the path type object selected, choose Type > Type On A Path > Type On A Path Options. In the Type On A Path Options dialog box, select Preview, and change the following options:

Note: To learn about the Type On A Path options like "Flip," search for "Creating type on a path" in Illustrator Help (Help > Illustrator Help).

- Effect: **Rainbow**.
- Align To Path: **Ascender**
- Spacing: **−11 pt**

7 Click OK.

8 Position the pointer over the line on the left end of the word "CERTIFIED." That line you see is called a *bracket*. When you see this cursor (▸⌶), with an arrow pointing to the right, drag up around the circle just a little in a clockwise fashion. See the figure for position.

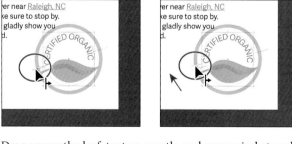

Note: Brackets appear at the beginning of the type, at the end of the path, and at the midpoint between the start and end brackets. All of these brackets can be adjusted to reposition the text in the path.

9 Drag across the leaf, text on a path, and green circle to select them all. Drag the leaf (which drags all three objects) down away from the column of text so that they aren't touching, if necessary.

Creating text outlines

Converting text to outlines means converting text into *vector* shapes that you can edit and manipulate as you would any other graphic object. Text outlines are useful for changing the look of large display type, but they are rarely useful for body text or other type at small sizes. The file recipient doesn't need to have your fonts installed to open and view the file correctly if you convert all text to outlines.

When you create outlines from text, you should consider that text is no longer editable. Also, bitmap fonts and outline-protected fonts cannot be converted to outlines, and outlining text that is less than 10 points in size is not recommended. When type is converted to outlines, the type loses its *hints*—instructions built into outline fonts to adjust their shape to display or print optimally at many sizes. You must also convert all type in a selection to outlines; you cannot convert a single letter within a type object.

Next, you will convert the main heading to outlines and position content.

1   Choose View > Fit Artboard In Window.

● **Note:** The original text is still there; it's just hidden. This way, you can always choose Object > Show All to see the original text if you need to make changes.

2   With the Selection tool (▶) selected, click the heading text "BUZZ SODA" at the top of the artboard to select it.

3   Choose Edit > Copy, and then choose Object > Hide > Selection.

4   Choose Edit > Paste In Front.

5   Choose Type > Create Outlines. Drag it into position like you see in the figure (if it's not already there).

The text is no longer linked to a particular font. Instead, it is now artwork, much like any other vector art in your illustration.

6   Choose View > Guides > Hide Guides, and then choose Select > Deselect.

7   Choose View > Fit All In Window to take a look at what you've created.

8   Choose File > Save, and then choose File > Close.

Review questions

1 Name two methods for creating text in Adobe Illustrator.

2 What does the Touch Type tool (⌶) let you do?

3 What is *overflow text*?

4 What is *text threading*?

5 What is the difference between a *character style* and a *paragraph style*?

6 What is the advantage of converting text to outlines?

Review answers

1 The following methods can be used for creating text areas:

- With the Type tool (T), click the artboard and start typing when the cursor appears. A point type object is created to accommodate the text.

- With the Type tool, drag to create a text area. Type when a cursor appears.

- With the Type tool, click a path or closed shape to convert it to text on a path, or click in a text area. Option-clicking (Mac OS) or Alt-clicking (Windows) when crossing over the stroke of a closed path creates text around the shape.

2 The Touch Type tool (⌶) allows you to visually edit certain character formatting options for individual characters in text. You can edit the character rotation, kerning, baseline shift, and horizontal and vertical scale of text and the text remains editable.

3 Overflow text is text that does not fit within an area type object or path. A red plus sign (⊞) in an out port indicates that the object contains additional text.

4 Text threading allows you to flow text from one object to another by linking type objects. Linked type objects can be of any shape; however, the text must be entered in an area or along a path (not at a point).

5 A character style can be applied to selected text only. A paragraph style is applied to an entire paragraph. Paragraph styles are best for indents, margins, and line spacing.

6 Converting text to outlines eliminates the need to send the fonts along with the Illustrator file when sharing with others and makes it possible to add effects to type that aren't possible when the type is still editable (live).

9 ORGANIZING YOUR ARTWORK WITH LAYERS

Lesson overview

In this lesson, you'll learn how to do the following:

- Work with the Layers panel.

- Create, rearrange, and lock layers and sublayers.

- Move objects between layers.

- Copy and paste objects and their layers from one file to another.

- Merge layers into a single layer.

- Locate objects in the Layers panel.

- Isolate content in a layer.

- Make a layer clipping mask.

- Apply an appearance attribute to objects and layers.

This lesson takes approximately 45 minutes to complete.

Download the project files for this lesson from the Lesson & Update Files tab on your Account page at www.peachpit.com and store them on your computer in a convenient location, as described in the "Getting Started" section of this book.

Your Account page is also where you'll find any updates to the chapters or to the lesson files. Look on the Lesson & Update Files tab to access the most current content.

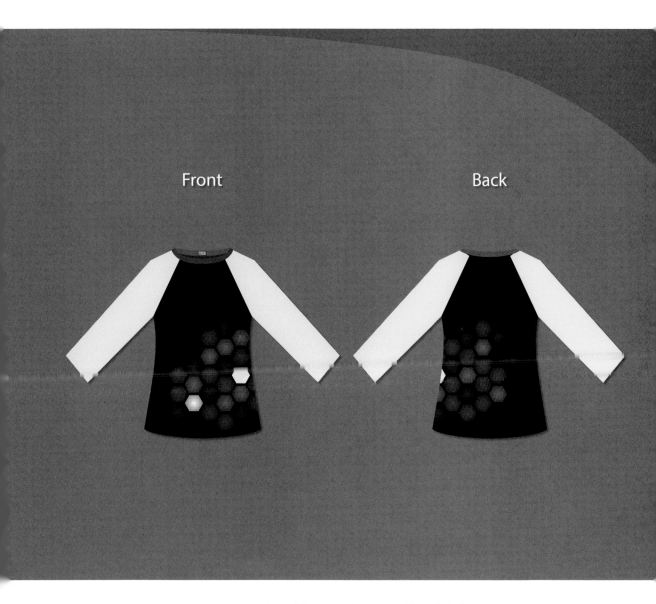

Front

Back

Layers let you organize your work into distinct
levels that can be edited and viewed individually or
together. Every Adobe Illustrator CC document has
at least one layer. Creating multiple layers in your
artwork lets you easily control how artwork is printed,
displayed, selected, and edited.

Getting started

In this lesson, you'll organize the artwork for several shirts as you explore the various ways to use the Layers panel.

Note: If you have not already downloaded the project files for this lesson to your computer from your Account page, make sure to do so now. See the "Getting Started" section at the beginning of this book.

1 To ensure that the tools and panels function exactly as described in this lesson, delete or deactivate (by renaming) the Adobe Illustrator CC preferences file. See "Restoring default preferences" in the "Getting Started" section at the beginning of the book.

2 Start Adobe Illustrator CC.

3 Choose File > Open, and open the L9_end.ai file in the Lessons > Lesson09 folder, located on your hard disk.

4 Choose View > Fit Artboard In Window.

5 Choose Window > Workspace > Reset Essentials.

Note: If you don't see Reset Essentials in the Workspace menu, choose Window > Workspace > Essentials before choosing Window > Workspace > Reset Essentials.

Understanding layers

Layers are like invisible folders to help you hold and manage all of the items (some of which can be difficult to select or track) that make up your artwork. If you shuffle those folders, you change the stacking order of the items in your artwork. (You learned about stacking order in Lesson 2, "Techniques for Selecting Artwork.")

The structure of layers in your document can be as simple or as complex as you want. When you create a new Illustrator document, all of the content you create is organized in a single layer. However, you can create new layers and sublayers (like subfolders) to organize your artwork, as you'll learn about in this lesson.

1 Click the Layers panel icon (⬗) on the right side of the workspace, or choose Window > Layers.

In addition to organizing content, the Layers panel offers an easy way to select, hide, lock, and change your artwork's appearance attributes. In the next figure, the Layers panel you see will not look exactly the same, and that's okay. You can refer to this figure as you progress through the lesson.

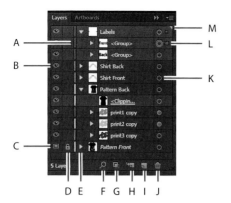

A. Layer color
B. Visibility column
C. Template Layer icon
D. Edit column (lock/unlock)
E. Disclosure triangle (expand/collapse)
F. Locate Object
G. Make/Release Clipping Mask
H. Create New Sublayer
I. Create New Layer
J. Delete Selection
K. Target column
L. Selection column
M. Current layer indicator (the small triangle)

To begin working, you'll open an existing art file that is incomplete.

2 Choose File > Open. If a panel appears, click Open in the panel. You could also choose File > Open again. In the Open dialog box, navigate to the Lessons > Lesson09 folder and select the L9_start.ai file on your hard disk. Click Open to open the file.

The Missing Fonts dialog box will most likely appear, indicating that a font (CreteRound-Regular) was used in the file that Illustrator can't find. The file uses a Typekit font that you most likely don't have synced with your machine, so you will fix the missing font before moving on.

3 In the Missing Fonts dialog box, ensure that Sync is selected in the Sync column (circled in the figure), and click Sync Fonts. The font should be synced with your machine, and you should see a success message in the Missing Fonts dialog box. Click Close.

This will sync the Typekit font to your computer and ensure that the font shows as intended in Illustrator.

Note: If the font is unable to sync, you may not have an Internet connection or you may need to launch the Creative Cloud desktop application, sign in with your Adobe ID, choose Assets > Fonts, and click Turn Typekit On. If you went through Lesson 8, "Adding Type to a Poster," you would have this already turned on. For more information, visit http://helpx.adobe.com/creative-cloud/help/add-fonts-typekit.html.

Note: If you see a warning message in the Missing Fonts dialog box or cannot select Sync, you can click Find Fonts to replace the font with a local font. In the Find Font dialog box, make sure that CreteRound-Regular is selected in the Fonts in Document section, and choose System from the Replace With Font From menu. This shows all the local fonts that are available to Illustrator. Select a font from the Fonts In System section, and click Change All to replace the font. Click Done.

4 Choose File > Save As, name the file **Shirts.ai**, and select the Lesson09 folder. Leave the Format option set to Adobe Illustrator (ai) (Mac OS) or the Save As Type option set to Adobe Illustrator (*.AI) (Windows), and then click Save. In the Illustrator Options dialog box, leave the Illustrator options at their default settings, and then click OK.

5 Choose Select > Deselect (if available).

6 Choose View > Fit Artboard In Window.

Creating layers and sublayers

By default, every document begins with one layer, named "Layer 1." As you create artwork, you can rename and add layers and sublayers at any time. Placing objects on separate layers lets you more easily select and edit them. For example, by placing type on a separate layer, you can change the type all at once without affecting the rest of the artwork.

Create new layers

Next, you'll change the default layer name and then create new layers using different methods. The idea for this project is to organize the artwork so you can more easily work with it later.

1 If the Layers panel isn't visible, click the Layers panel icon () on the right side of the workspace, or choose Window > Layers. Layer 1 (the default name for the first layer) is highlighted, indicating that it is active.

2 In the Layers panel, double-click the layer name "Layer 1" to edit it inline. Type **Shirt Front**, and then press Enter or Return.

● **Note:** If you double-click just to the right or left of a layer name, the Layer Options dialog box will open. You can also change the layer name there.

Instead of keeping all the content on one single layer, you'll create several layers and sublayers to better organize the content and to make it easier to select content later.

3 Click the Create New Layer button () at the bottom of the Layers panel.

Layers and sublayers that aren't named are numbered in sequence. For example, the second layer is named Layer 2. When a layer or sublayer in the Layers panel contains other items, a disclosure triangle (▶) appears to the left of the layer or sublayer name. You can click the disclosure triangle to show or hide the contents. If no triangle appears, the layer has no content on it.

▶ **Tip:** You can easily delete a layer by selecting the layer or sublayer and clicking the Delete Selection button (🗑) at the bottom of the Layers panel. This deletes the layer or sublayer and all content on it.

4 Double-click to the right or left of the layer name "Layer 2" to open the Layer Options dialog box. Change the name to **Shirt Back**, and notice all the other options available. Click OK.

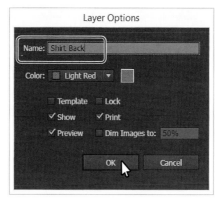

By default, the new layer is added above the currently selected layer (Shirt Front) in the Layers panel and becomes active. Notice that the new layer has a different layer color (a light red) to the left of the layer name. This will become more important later, as you select content.

Next, you will create a few layers and name them in one step, using a modifier key.

5 Option-click (Mac OS) or Alt-click (Windows) the Create New Layer button (⬛) at the bottom of the Layers panel. In the Layer Options dialog box, change the name to **Pattern Front**, and then click OK.

6 Option-click (Mac OS) or Alt-click (Windows) the Create New Layer button (⬛) at the bottom of the Layers panel. In the Layer Options dialog box, change the name to **Labels**, and then click OK.

▶ **Tip:** Choosing New Layer from the Layers panel menu (▼≡) will also create a new layer and open the Layer Options dialog box.

7 Drag the Pattern Front layer to the Create New Layer button. This creates a copy of the layer and names it "Pattern Front copy." Double-click directly on the new layer name in the panel, and change it to **Pattern Back**.

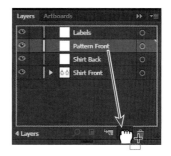

Create sublayers

Next, you'll create a sublayer, which is a layer nested within a layer.

● **Note:** Depending on your operating system, the selection color of objects (the bounding box) may be different colors, and that's okay.

1   Click the layer named Shirt Front to select it, and then click the Create New Sublayer button (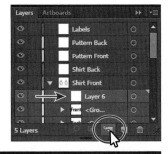) at the bottom of the Layers panel to create a new sublayer in the Shirt Front layer.

2   Drag the left edge of the Layers panel to the left to make it wider so that you can more easily read the layer names.

3   Double-click the new sublayer name (Layer 6, in our case), change the name to **Front Collar**, and then press Enter or Return.

The new sublayer appears directly beneath its main layer, Shirt Front, and is selected. Creating a new sublayer opens the selected layer to show existing sublayers. Sublayers are used to organize content within a layer without grouping or ungrouping content.

● **Note:** To create a new sublayer and name it in one step, Option-click (Mac OS) or Alt-click (Windows) the Create New Sublayer button or choose New Sublayer from the Layers panel menu to open the Layer Options dialog box.

4   Click the disclosure triangle (▶) to the left of the Shirt Front layer to hide the content of the layer.

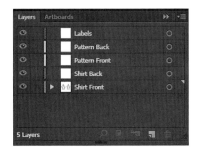

Layers and color

By default, Illustrator assigns a unique color to each layer in the Layers panel. The color displays next to the layer name in the panel. The same color displays in the artwork bounding box, path, anchor points, and center point of a selected object.

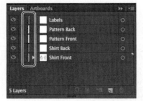

You can use this color to quickly locate an object's corresponding layer in the Layers panel, and you can change the layer color to suit your needs.

—From Illustrator Help

Editing layers and objects

By rearranging the layers in the Layers panel, you can change the stacking order of objects in your artwork. On an artboard, objects in layers that are higher in the Layers panel list are in front of objects located on layers lower in the list, and each layer has its own stacking order as well. Layers are useful for a variety of reasons, including the ability to move objects between layers and sublayers to organize and more easily select your artwork.

Locating layers

When working in artwork, there may be times when you select content on the artboard and then want to locate that same content in the Layers panel. This can help you to determine how content is organized.

1   With the Selection tool (▸), click to select the yellow/green sleeves on the shirt below the word "Front." Click the Locate Object button (◉) at the bottom of the Layers panel to reveal the group of objects within the Layers panel.

Clicking the Locate Object button will open the layer so that the layer content can be seen, and the Layers panel will scroll, if necessary, to reveal the selected content. With an Illustrator file that has a lot of layered content, this can be helpful. In the Layers panel, you will see the selection indicator to the far right of the <Group> object (it's the small colored box to the far right in the figure that the arrow is pointing to), as well as the two <Path> objects in the group.

2   In the Layers panel, double-click the <Group> text, and rename it **Front Sleeves**.

By default, when content is grouped, a group object is created that contains the grouped content. Look on the left end of the Control panel to see the word "Group" in the selection indicator. Renaming a group doesn't change the fact that it's a group, but it can make it easier to find in the Layers panel.

3 Choose Select > Deselect.

4 Click the disclosure triangle () for the main Shirt Front layer to hide the contents of the layer (you most likely will need to scroll up in the Layers panel to see it).

The Shirt Front layer is the only layer with a disclosure triangle because it's currently the only layer with content on it.

Moving layers and content between layers

Next, you'll move the artwork to the different layers so that the artwork is better organized and later add content from another Illustrator file.

1 Choose View > Outline to enter Outline mode.

2 In the artwork, using the Selection tool (↖), drag a marquee selection across the artwork for the Back shirt content to select it (see the figure for what to select).

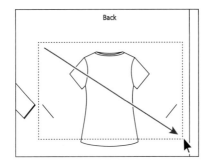
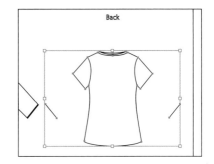

In the Layers panel, notice that the Shirt Front layer name has the selected-art indicator (color square); an arrow is pointing to it in the figure.

Also notice that the color of the bounding box, paths, and anchor points of the selected artwork matches the color of the layer. If you want to move selected artwork from one layer to another, you can either drag the selected-art indicator to the right of each sublayer or drag the selected-art indicator to the right of the layer name.

3 Drag the selected-art indicator (the little blue box) from the right of the Shirt Front layer name straight up to the right of the target icon (⊙) on the Shirt Back layer.

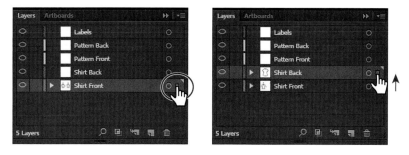

This action moves all of the selected artwork to the Shirt Back layer. The color of the bounding box, paths, and anchor points in the artwork changes to the color of the Shirt Back layer, which is red.

4 Choose Select > Deselect.

5 Choose View > GPU Preview if available or View > Preview on CPU if not.

6 Click the disclosure triangle (▶) to the left of the Shirt Front layer to show the layer content. Drag the bottom of the Layers panel down to see more layers.

7 Click the <Group> layer that contains the Front type shapes, press the Shift key and click the Back <Group> object to select both sublayers without selecting the artwork on the artboard. Drag either <Group> object to the Labels layer at the top of the list. When the Labels layer is highlighted, release the mouse button.

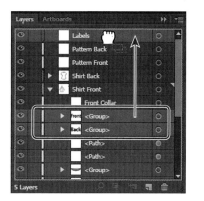
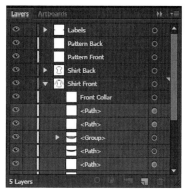

This is another way to move artwork between layers. Any content that is dragged to another layer is automatically at the top of the layer stack on that layer.

8 Click the disclosure triangle (▼) to the left of the Shirt Front layer to hide the layer contents.

▶ **Tip:** Keeping layers and sublayers closed can make it easier to navigate content in the Layers panel.

Note: Be careful
not to drag the layer
into one of the other
layers. If the Shirt Back
and Shirt Front layers
disappear, you can
choose Edit > Undo
Reorder Layers and then
try again.

9 Shift-click the Shirt Front and Shirt Back
layers to select them. Drag either of them
up, below the Labels layer in the Layers
panel. When a line appears below the
Labels layer, release the mouse button to
reorder the layers.

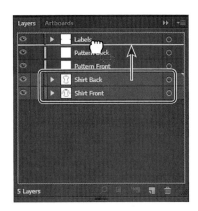

10 With the Selection tool, click the white
shirt shape for the shirt labeled Front on
the artboard. Choose Edit > Cut.

11 Select the Pattern Front layer in the
Layers panel, and choose Edit > Paste
In Front.

The cut artwork is pasted onto the layer named "Pattern Front" in the same location.

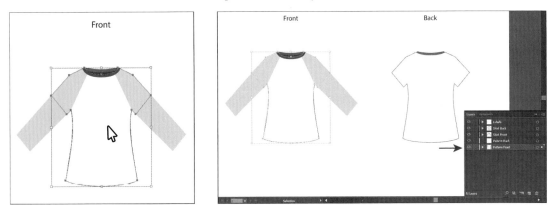

12 Click to select the other white shirt shape under the Back label on the artboard.

13 Choose Edit > Cut, select the Pattern Back layer, and then choose Edit > Paste
In Front.

14 Choose Select > Deselect, and you can
see what the Layers panel should now
look like in the figure.

Duplicating layer content

In previous lessons, you've worked with the Edit > Copy and Edit > Cut commands. You can also use the Layers panel as another method for duplicating layers and other content. Next, you'll duplicate content between layers.

1   Click the disclosure triangle (▶) to the left of the Shirt Front layer to show the layer content.

2   Press the Option (Mac OS) or Alt (Windows) key, and click the Front Sleeves sublayer to select the content on the artboard. You may need to scroll down in the panel or make the panel taller to see it (I made it taller).

3   While still pressing the Option (Mac OS) or Alt (Windows) key, drag the Front Sleeves row up onto the Shirt Back layer. When the layer is highlighted and a plus sign (+) appears to the right of the pointer, release the mouse button, and then release the key. Leave the artwork selected on the artboard.

This copies the Front Sleeves content onto the Shirt Back layer. Notice that the new copied artwork has a red color on the bounding box, paths, and anchor points, indicating that it's on the Shirt Back layer now. Dragging with the modifier key copies the selected content. This is the same as selecting the content on the artboard, choosing Edit > Copy, selecting the Shirt Back layer in the Layers panel, and then choosing Edit > Paste In Place.

▶ **Tip:** You can also Option-drag (Mac OS) or Alt-drag (Windows) the selected-art indicator to duplicate content. You can also select the Front Sleeves row in the Layers panel and choose Duplicate "Front Sleeves" from the Layers panel menu to create a copy of the same content.

4   Click the disclosure triangle to the left of the Shirt Front layer to hide the contents, and click the disclosure triangle to the left of the Shirt Back layer to see its contents.

5   With the yellow/green sleeves artwork still selected on the artboard, Shift-click the white shirt shape on the right side of the artboard (under Back) to select both objects. Release the Shift key. Click again on the white shirt shape to make it the key object. Click the Horizontal Align Center button (▤) in the Control panel to align the objects to each other.

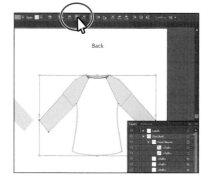

6 Choose Object > Arrange > Send To Back. In the Layers panel, notice that the stacking order of the sublayers on the Shirt Back layer is now different, reflecting how the artwork is arranged on the artboard.

7 Choose Select > Deselect.

Merging layers

To streamline your artwork, you can merge layers, sublayers, content, or groups to combine the contents into one layer or sublayer. Note that items will be merged into the layer or group that you selected last. Next, you will merge content into a new layer and then merge a few sublayers into one.

▶ **Tip:** You can also Command-click (Mac OS) or Ctrl click (Windows) layers or sublayers in the Layers panel to select multiple, nonsequential layers.

1 In the content for the Shirt Back layer in the Layers panel, click the top <Path> object in the Layers panel to highlight it, and then Shift-click the bottom <Path> object in the layer to select four <Path> objects.

● **Note:** Layers can merge only with other layers that are on the same hierarchical level in the Layers panel. Likewise, sublayers can only merge with other sublayers that are in the same layer and on the same hierarchical level. Objects can't be merged with other objects.

2 Click the Layers panel menu icon (▼≣), and choose Collect In New Layer to create a new sublayer (in this case) and put the <Path> objects in it.

The objects in the new sublayer retain their original stacking order.

3 Double-click the thumbnail to the left of or directly to the right of the new layer name (mine is Layer 7). In the Layer Options dialog box, change the name to **Shirt Back Stitching**, and choose Light Red from the Color menu. Click OK.

▶ **Tip:** Choose Merge Selected from the Layers panel menu to merge selected content into a single layer. The last layer you select determines the name and color of the merged layer.

Changing the layer color to match the main layer isn't necessary. The Layer Options dialog box has a lot of the options you've already worked with, including naming layers, Preview or Outline mode, locking layers, and showing and hiding layers. You can also deselect the Print option in the Layer Options dialog box, and any content on that layer will not print.

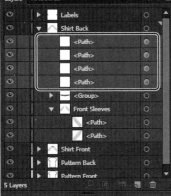

Select the objects.

Collect the objects in a new layer.

The new layer renamed.

Next, you'll do the same thing to the stitching artwork on the Shirt Front layer.

4   Click the disclosure triangle to the left of the Shirt Back layer to hide its contents, and click the disclosure triangle to the left of the Shirt Front layer to show the contents.

5   Command-click (Mac OS) or Ctrl-click (Windows) the four <Path> objects on the Shirt Front layer, like you see in the first part of the following figure, to select them all (they have shaded circles to the far right of their names).

6   Choose Collect In New Layer from the Layers panel menu (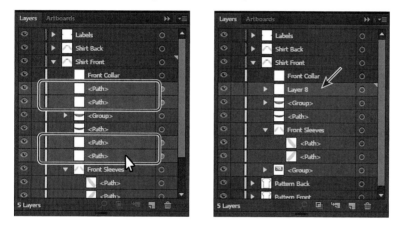) to create a new sublayer (in this case), and put the <Path> objects in it.

7   Double-click the new sublayer name (mine is Layer 8; see the previous figure), and change the name to Shirt Front Stitching by double-clicking the name in the Layers panel. Press Enter or Return to accept the name.

8   In the Shirt Front layer, drag the remaining <Path> object up into the <Group> object above it.

The <Path> object is now a part of the group (<Group>), but it appears on top of the other objects in the group.

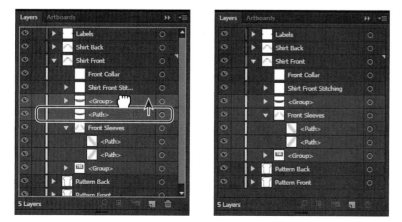

Look at the collar on the shirt under the word "Front" (on the artboard). After completing the next step, take a look at it again.

9 Click the disclosure triangle to the left of the <Group> object to show the contents. Drag the top <Path> object to just below the bottom <Path> object in the group. When a line appears, release the mouse button.

This changes the stacking order of the artwork in your project and is the same as choosing Object > Arrange > Send To Back.

10 Click the disclosure triangle to the left of the <Group> object to hide the contents of the group.

▶ **Tip:** If you want to merge layers or groups, you could also select the layers or content to merge in the Layers panel and then choose Merge Selected from the Layers panel menu (▼≣). In the case of the two groups you selected, it simply creates a single group that contains the artwork from the original two groups. If you were to merge selected sublayers, a single sublayer would be created.

11 Click the top <Group> object to select it in the Shirt Front layer. Command-click (Mac OS) or Ctrl-click (Windows) the other <Group> beneath it in the layer to select both (see the figure for what to select). Drag the selected <Group> objects onto the Front Collar sublayer to move them.

12 Click the disclosure triangle to the left of the Shirt Front layer to hide the contents.

13 Choose File > Save.

● **Note:** You cannot merge selected content that is not either a layer, sublayer, or group. For instance, if you were to select a <Path> object and a sublayer or group in the Layers panel, the Merge Selected command would be available, but it wouldn't work.

Pasting layers

To complete the shirts, you'll copy and paste the remaining pieces of artwork from another file. You can paste a layered file into another file and even keep the layers intact. In this section, you'll also learn a few new things, including how to apply appearance attributes to layers and reordering layers.

1 Choose Window > Workspace > Reset Essentials.

2 Choose File > Open. If a panel appears, click Open in the panel. You could also choose File > Open again. Open the Pattern.ai file in the Lessons > Lesson09 folder on your hard disk.

3 Choose View > Fit Artboard In Window.

4 Click the Layers panel icon ( ) to show the panel. To see how the objects in each layer are organized, Option-click (Mac OS) or Alt-click (Windows) the eye icon ( ) for each layer in the Layers panel to show one layer and hide the others. You can also click the disclosure triangle ( ) to the left of each layer name to expand and collapse the layers for further inspection. When you're finished, make sure that all the layers are showing and that they are collapsed.

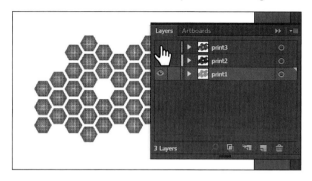

5 Choose Select > All, and then choose Edit > Copy to select and copy the content to the clipboard.

6 Choose File > Close to close the Pattern.ai file without saving any changes. If a warning dialog box appears, click No (Windows) or Don't Save (Mac OS).

7 In the Shirts.ai file, choose Paste Remembers Layers from the Layers panel menu ( ). A checkmark next to the option indicates that it's selected.

When Paste Remembers Layers is selected, artwork is pasted into the layer(s) from which it was copied, regardless of which layer is active in the Layers panel. If the option is not selected, all objects are pasted into the active layer, and the layers from the original file are not pasted in.

● **Note:** If the target document has a layer of the same name, Illustrator combines the pasted content into a layer of the same name.

8 Choose Edit > Paste to paste the pattern content into the center of the artboard.

The Paste Remembers Layers option causes the Pattern.ai layers to be pasted as three separate layers at the top of the Layers panel (print3, print2, print1).

Now you'll move the newly pasted layers into the Pattern Front layer and then change the ordering of the layers.

9 Drag the bottom of the Layers panel down so that you can see the new layers (print3, print2, print1) and the Pattern Front layer.

10 In the Layers panel, select the print3 layer (if it's not already selected), and Shift-click the print1 layer name. Drag any of the three selected layers down on top of the Pattern Front layer to move it to the new layer.

The three pasted layers become sublayers of the Pattern Front layer. Notice that they keep their individual layer colors.

11 Choose Select > Deselect, and then choose File > Save.

Changing layer order

As you've seen, you can easily drag layers, sublayers, groups, and other content in the Layers panel to reorganize the layer ordering. There are also several Layers panel options for commands like reversing layer ordering and more that can make reorganizing layers easier.

1 Click the print3 layer, and Shift-click the print1 layer names to select all three layers again.

2 Choose Reverse Order from the Layers panel menu (▾≣) to reverse the layer ordering.

The layers before reversing

The layers after reversing

3 Choose Select > Deselect (if available), and then click the disclosure triangle for the Pattern Front and Shirt Front layers, if need be, to hide their contents.

Viewing layers

The Layers panel lets you hide layers, sublayers, or individual objects from view. When a layer is hidden, the content on the layer is also locked and cannot be selected or printed. You can also use the Layers panel to display layers or objects individually, in either Preview or Outline mode. In this section, you'll learn how to view layers in Outline mode to make artwork potentially easier to select.

1 Select the Zoom tool (🔍), and click three times on the gray collar (top part of the shirt) for the Front shirt to zoom in.

2 Choose View > Outline. This displays the artwork so that only its outlines (or paths) are visible and you can see the "TEE" text that is hidden.

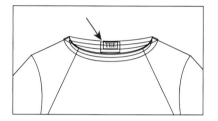

3 Choose View > GPU Preview if available or View > Preview on CPU if not.

Sometimes, you may want to view part of the artwork in outline mode while retaining the strokes and fills for the rest of the artwork. This can be useful if you need to see all artwork in a given layer, sublayer, or group.

4 In the Layers panel, click the disclosure triangle for the Shirt Front layer to reveal the layer content. Command-click (Mac OS) or Ctrl-click (Windows) the eye icon (👁) to the left of the Front Collar layer name to show the content for that layer in Outline mode.

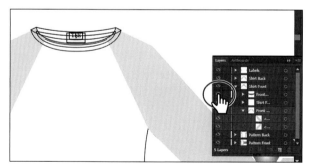

> **Tip:** To view layer artwork in Outline mode, you can also double-click either the layer thumbnail or just to the right of the layer name to open the Layer Options dialog box. You can then deselect Preview and click OK.

Displaying a layer in Outline mode is also useful for selecting the anchor points or center points on objects.

5 Select the Selection tool (▶), and attempt to click the "TEE" text. You'll most likely select the group of content that is on top of it.

6 Click the Locate Object () button at the bottom of the Layers panel to see where the selected group is in the Layers panel. Drag the left edge of the Layers panel to the left so you can see more of the layer names.

7 Choose Object > Arrange > Send To Back to send the selected group to the bottom of the Front Collar layer.

8 Command-click (Mac OS) or Ctrl-click (Windows) the eye icon ( ) to the left of the Front Collar layer name to show the content for that layer in Preview mode again.

9 Choose View > Fit Artboard In Window.

● **Note:** This will hide and show all other layers, even sublayers on the Shirt Back layer.

10 Option-click (Mac OS) or Alt-click (Windows) the eye icon ( ) to the left of the Shirt Back layer to hide the other layers.

Hiding all layers except those that you want to work with can be very useful.

11 Choose Show All Layers from the Layers panel menu ( ).

12 Click the disclosure triangle to the left of each of the layers to ensure that they are all closed.

Applying appearance attributes to layers

● **Note:** To learn more about working with appearance attributes, see Lesson 12, "Exploring Creative Uses of Effects and Graphic Styles."

You can apply appearance attributes, such as styles, effects, and transparency, to layers, groups, and objects, using the Layers panel. When an appearance attribute is applied to a layer, any object on that layer takes on that attribute. If an appearance attribute is applied only to a specific object on a layer, it affects only that object, not the entire layer.

Next, you'll apply an effect to an object on one layer, and then you'll copy that effect to another layer to change all objects on that layer.

1 Click the disclosure triangle to the left of the Pattern Front layer name to show its contents, and then click the target icon ( ) to the right of the print1 layer in the target column.

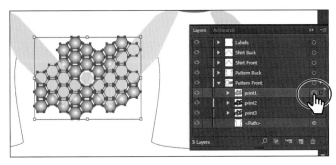

● **Note:** Clicking the target icon also selects the object(s) on the artboard. You could simply select the content on the artboard to apply an effect.

Clicking the target icon indicates that you want to apply an effect, style, or transparency change to that layer, sublayer, group, or object. In other words, the layer, sublayer, group, or object is *targeted*. The content is also selected in the Document window. When the target button appears as a double-ring icon (either 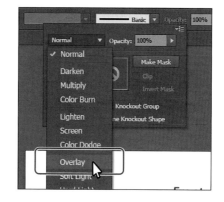 or), the item is targeted; a single-ring icon indicates that the item is not targeted.

2   Click the Opacity link in the Control panel to show the Transparency panel. Choose Overlay from the Blending Mode menu, which shows as Normal by default.

For the print1 layer, the target icon ( ) in the Layers panel is now shaded, indicating that the layer has at least one appearance attribute (a blending mode) applied to it.

3   Click the target icon ( ) to the right of the print2 layer in the Layers panel.

4   Click the Opacity link in the Control panel to show the Transparency panel. Choose Luminosity from the Blending Mode menu, which shows as Normal by default. Change the Opacity to **20**.

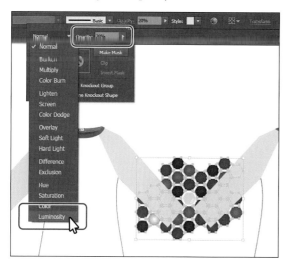

5   Choose Select > Deselect.

6   Choose Window > Workspace > Reset Essentials.

Creating a clipping mask

The Layers panel lets you create clipping masks to control whether artwork on a layer (or in a group) is hidden or revealed. A *clipping mask* is an object or group of objects that masks (with its shape) artwork below it in the same layer or sublayer, so that only artwork within the shape is visible. In Lesson 14, "Using Illustrator CC with Other Adobe Applications," you will learn about creating clipping masks that are independent of the Layers panel.

Now you'll create a clipping mask for the pattern for each shirt. As you create the clipping mask, you'll learn about working with Isolation mode so that you can focus on specific parts of the artwork.

1   Choose Window > Layers to open the Layers panel. Click the disclosure triangle to the left of all main layers to hide their content. Select the layer named Pattern Front, and choose Enter Isolation Mode from the Layers panel menu (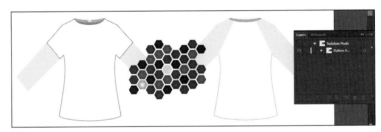).

When a layer is in Isolation mode, objects on all layers except that layer are dimmed and temporarily locked, much like when you enter Isolation mode for a group, so that you can easily edit items being isolated without affecting other layers. The Layers panel now shows a layer called Isolation Mode and a layer that contains the Pattern Front layer content.

2   In the Layers panel, click the disclosure triangle for the Pattern Front layer to reveal the layer contents. Choose Select > All, and then Shift-click the selection column (little red box) to the right of the <Path> object (the shirt shape) in the Layers panel to deselect it.

3   With the Selection tool selected, drag any of the selected shapes on the artboard to the left and onto the shirt shape until it's positioned roughly as in the figure.

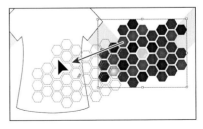

In the Layers panel, a masking object must be above the objects it masks. You can create a clipping mask for an entire layer, a sublayer, or a group of objects. You want to mask the content in the Pattern Front layer, so the clipping object needs to be at the top of the Pattern Front layer, which is what you did in the previous section.

4   Choose Object > Arrange > Send To Back.

The white shirt shape will now be on top of the pattern artwork on the Pattern Front layer.

5   Select the Pattern Front layer to highlight it in the Layers panel. Click the Make/Release Clipping Mask button (⬚) at the bottom of the Layers panel.

Note: Deselecting the artwork on the artboard is not necessary to complete the next steps, but it can be helpful for viewing the artwork.

The name of the <Path> sublayer is underlined to indicate that it is the masking shape, and it has been renamed to "Clipping Path." On the artboard, the <Path> sublayer has hidden the parts of the pattern content that extended outside of the shape.

Tip: To release the clipping mask, you can select the Pattern Front layer again and click the same Make/Release Clipping Mask button (⬚).

6   Click the selection column for the <Clipping Path> layer to select the shirt path. Change the Fill color to Black in the Control panel.

7   Press the Escape key to exit Isolation mode.

Next, you will practice creating a clipping mask by performing the same steps on the Back shirt.

Note: You can also double-click in a blank area of the artboard to exit Isolation mode.

8   In the Pattern Front layer, click the print1 layer, and Shift-click the print3 layer to select all three layers.

9 Option-drag (Mac OS) or Alt-drag (Windows) any of the layers to the Pattern Back layer to copy them there. Make sure you release the mouse button and then the modifier key.

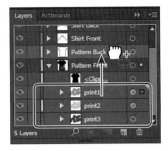

10 Select the Pattern Back layer, and choose Enter Isolation Mode from the Layers panel menu (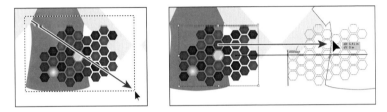...).

11 Drag a selection marquee across the pattern objects to select them all. Begin dragging to the right, and as you drag, press the Shift key to constrain the movement. Drag them into position like you see in the figure. Release the mouse button and then the key.

12 Choose Object > Arrange > Send To Back to put the pattern content behind the white shirt.

13 Select the Pattern Back layer to highlight it in the Layers panel. Click the Make/Release Clipping Mask button (■) at the bottom of the Layers panel.

14 Click the selection column for the <Clipping Path> layer to select the shirt path. Change the Fill color to Black in the Control panel.

15 Double-click in a blank area of the artboard to exit Isolation mode.

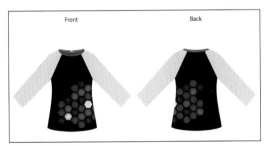

Note: For a complete list of shortcuts that you can use with the Layers panel, see "Keyboard shortcuts" in Illustrator Help (Help > Illustrator Help).

Now that the artwork is complete, you may want to combine all the layers into a single layer and then delete the empty layers. This is called *flattening* artwork. Delivering finished artwork in a single-layer file can prevent accidents, such as hiding layers or omitting parts of the artwork during printing. To flatten specific layers without deleting hidden layers, you can select the layers you want to flatten and then choose Merge Selected from the Layers panel menu.

16 Choose File > Save, and then choose File > Close.

Review questions

1 Name at least two benefits of using layers when creating artwork.

2 How do you hide layers? How do you show individual layers?

3 Describe how to reorder layers in a file.

4 What is the purpose of changing the color for a layer?

5 What happens if you paste a layered file into another file? Why is the Paste Remembers Layers option useful?

6 How do you create a layer clipping mask?

7 How do you apply an effect to a layer? How can you edit that effect?

Review answers

1 The benefits of using layers when creating artwork include organizing content, selecting content more easily, protecting artwork that you don't want to change, hiding artwork that you aren't working with so that it's not distracting, and controlling what prints.

2 To hide a layer, click to deselect the eye icon (⊙) to the left of the layer name in the Layers panel. Select the blank, leftmost column (the Visibility column) to show a layer.

3 You reorder layers by selecting a layer name in the Layers panel and dragging the layer to its new location. The order of layers in the Layers panel controls the document's layer order—topmost in the panel is frontmost in the artwork.

4 The color for a layer controls how selected anchor points and direction lines are displayed on a layer and helps you identify which layer an object resides on in your document.

5 The paste commands paste layered files or objects copied from different layers into the active layer by default. The Paste Remembers Layers option keeps the original layers intact when the objects are pasted.

6 Create a clipping mask on a layer by selecting the layer and clicking the Make/Release Clipping Mask button (▣) in the Layers panel. The topmost object in the layer becomes the clipping mask.

7 Click the target icon for the layer to which you want to apply an effect. Then, choose an effect by using the Effect menu or by clicking the Add New Effect button (fx.) in the Appearance panel. To edit the effect, make sure that the layer is selected, and then click the name of the effect in the Appearance panel. The effect's dialog box opens, and you can change the values.

10 GRADIENTS, BLENDS, AND PATTERNS

Lesson overview

In this lesson, you'll learn how to do the following:

- Create and save a gradient fill.
- Apply and edit a gradient on a stroke.
- Apply and edit a radial gradient.
- Add colors to a gradient.
- Adjust the direction of a gradient.
- Adjust the opacity of color in a gradient.
- Blend the shapes of objects in intermediate steps.
- Create smooth color blends between objects.
- Modify a blend and its path, shape, and color.
- Create and paint with patterns.

This lesson takes approximately 60 minutes to complete.

Download the project files for this lesson from the Lesson & Update Files tab on your Account page at www.peachpit.com and store them on your computer in a convenient location, as described in the "Getting Started" section of this book.

Your Account page is also where you'll find any updates to the chapters or to the lesson files. Look on the Lesson & Update Files tab to access the most current content.

To add texture and interest to your artwork in Illustrator, you can apply gradient fills, which are graduated blends of two or more colors, patterns, and blends of shapes and colors. In this lesson, you'll explore how to work with each of these to complete a project.

Getting started

In this lesson, you'll explore various ways to work with gradients, blend shapes and colors, and also create and apply patterns.

Before you begin, you'll restore the default preferences for Adobe Illustrator CC. Then you'll open the finished art file for this lesson to see what you'll create.

Note: If you have not already downloaded the project files for this lesson to your computer from your Account page, make sure to do so now. See the "Getting Started" section at the beginning of this book.

1   To ensure that the tools and panels function exactly as described in this lesson, delete or deactivate (by renaming) the Adobe Illustrator CC preferences file. See "Restoring default preferences" in the "Getting Started" section at the beginning of the book.

2   Start Adobe Illustrator CC.

3   Choose File > Open, and open the L10_end.ai file in the Lessons > Lesson10 folder on your hard disk.

4   Choose View > Zoom Out to make the finished artwork smaller, if you want to leave it on your screen as you work. (Use the Hand tool [✋] to move the artwork where you want it in the window.) If you don't want to leave the document open, choose File > Close.

To begin working, you'll open an existing art file.

5   Choose File > Open. If a panel appears, click Open in the panel. You could also choose File > Open again. In the Open dialog box, navigate to the Lessons > Lesson10 folder and select the L10_start.ai file on your hard disk. Click Open to open the file.

6   Choose View > Fit Artboard In Window.

7   Choose File > Save As, name the file **Sailing.ai**, and select the Lesson10 folder in the Save As menu. Leave the Format option set to Adobe Illustrator (ai) (Mac OS) or the Save As Type option set to Adobe Illustrator (*.AI) (Windows), and then click Save.

8   In the Illustrator Options dialog box, leave the Illustrator options at their default settings, and then click OK.

9   Choose Reset Essentials from the workspace switcher in the Application bar.

Note: If you don't see Reset Essentials in the workspace switcher menu, choose Window > Workspace > Essentials before choosing Window > Workspace > Reset Essentials.

Working with gradients

A *gradient fill* is a graduated blend of two or more colors, and it always includes a starting color and an ending color. You can create different types of gradient fills in Illustrator, including *linear*, in which the beginning color blends into the ending color along a line, and *radial*, in which the beginning color radiates outward, from the center point to the ending color. You can use the gradients provided with Adobe Illustrator CC or create your own gradients and save them as swatches for later use.

You can use the Gradient panel (Window > Gradient) or the Gradient tool (■) to apply, create, and modify gradients. In the Gradient panel, the Gradient Fill or Stroke box displays the current gradient colors and gradient type applied to the fill or stroke of an object.

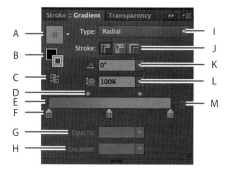

A. Gradient
B. Fill box/ Stroke box
C. Reverse Gradient
D. Gradient midpoint
E. Gradient slider
F. Color stop

G. Opacity
H. Location
I. Gradient type
J. Stroke gradient type
K. Angle
L. Aspect ratio
M. Delete Stop

Note: The Gradient panel you see will not match the figure, and that's okay.

In the Gradient panel under the gradient slider, the leftmost gradient stop labeled "F" in the previous figure is also called a *color stop*. This marks the starting color; the right gradient stop marks the ending color. A *gradient color stop* is the point at which a gradient changes from one color to the next. You can add more color stops by clicking below the gradient slider, and double-clicking a color stop opens a panel where you can choose a color from swatches, color sliders, or the eyedropper.

Applying a linear gradient to a fill

With the simplest, two-color linear gradient, the starting color (leftmost color stop) blends into the ending color (rightmost color stop) along a line. To begin the lesson, you'll create a gradient fill for the yellow background shape to simulate a blue sky.

1 Using the Selection tool (▶), click to select the large yellow rectangle in the background.

2 Change the Fill color to the gradient swatch named "White, Black" in the Control panel. The default black-and-white gradient is applied to the fill of the selected background shape.

Editing a gradient

Next, you'll edit the colors in the default black and white gradient you applied.

1 Open the Gradient panel (Window > Gradient), and perform the following:

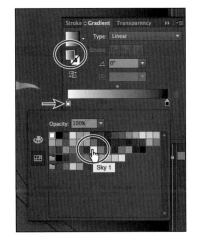

- Make sure that the Fill box is selected (circled in the figure).

- Double-click the white, leftmost gradient stop to select the starting color of the gradient (an arrow is pointing to it in the figure).

- Click the Swatches button (▦) in the panel that appears.

- Click to select the light-gray swatch named "Sky 1."

2 Press the Escape key or click in a blank area of the Gradient panel to close the Swatches panel.

3 In the Gradient panel, perform the following:

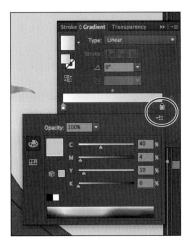

- Double-click the black color stop on the right side of the gradient slider to edit the color in the Gradient panel (circled in the figure). In the panel that appears, click the Color button (🎨) to open the Color panel.

- Click the menu icon (▼≡), and choose CMYK from the menu, if CMYK values aren't showing.

- Change the CMYK values to C=**40**, M=**4**, Y=**10**, and K=**0**.

- After entering the last value, click in a blank area of the Gradient panel to return to the Gradient panel.

The following figure shows the gradient so far.

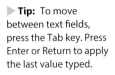

Tip: To move between text fields, press the Tab key. Press Enter or Return to apply the last value typed.

FOR THE ADVENTURE OF A LIFETIME
SAIL WITH A WHALE >

Saving a gradient

Next, you'll save the gradient in the Swatches panel.

1 Click the Gradient menu arrow (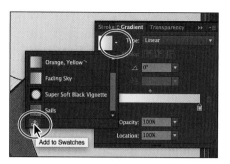) to the left of the word "Type," and then click the Add To Swatches button () at the bottom of the panel that appears.

The Gradient menu lists all the default and saved gradients that you can apply.

2 Click the Swatches panel icon () on the right side of the workspace to open the Swatches panel. In the Swatches panel, double-click the "New Gradient Swatch 1" thumbnail to open the Swatch Options dialog box.

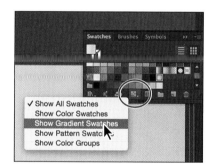

3 In the Swatch Options dialog box, type **Sky** in the Swatch Name field, and then click OK.

4 Click the Show Swatch Kinds Menu button () at the bottom of the Swatches panel, and choose Show Gradient Swatches from the menu to display only gradient swatches in the Swatches panel.

The Swatches panel lets you sort colors based on type. So if you want to only show gradient swatches in the panel, for instance, you can temporarily sort the swatches in the panel.

> **Tip:** Like most things in Illustrator, there is more than one method for saving a gradient swatch. You can also save a gradient by selecting an object with a gradient fill or stroke, clicking the Fill box or Stroke box in the Swatches panel (whichever the gradient is applied to), and then clicking the New Swatch button () at the bottom of the Swatches panel.

5 With the rectangle still selected on the artboard, apply some of the different gradients to the shape fill by selecting them in the Swatches panel.

6 Click the gradient named "Sky" (the one you just saved) in the Swatches panel to make sure it is applied before continuing to the next step.

7 Click the Show Swatch Kinds Menu button () at the bottom of the Swatches panel, and choose Show All Swatches from the menu.

8 Choose File > Save, and leave the rectangle selected.

Adjusting a linear gradient fill

Once you have painted an object with a gradient, you can adjust the direction, the origin, and the beginning and end points of the gradient using the Gradient tool.

Now you'll adjust the gradient fill in the background shape.

1 Select the Gradient tool () in the Tools panel.

With the Gradient tool, you can apply a gradient to the fill of an object or edit an existing gradient fill. Notice the horizontal gradient annotator (bar) that appears in the middle of the rectangle. The bar indicates the direction of the gradient. The larger circle on the left shows the starting point of the gradient (the first color stop), and the smaller square on the right is the ending point (the last color stop).

▶ **Tip:** You can hide the gradient annotator (bar) by choosing View > Hide Gradient Annotator. To show it again, choose View > Show Gradient Annotator.

● **Note:** If you move the pointer to different areas of the gradient slider, the appearance of the pointer may change. This indicates that different functionality has been activated.

2 Position the pointer over the bar in the gradient annotator.

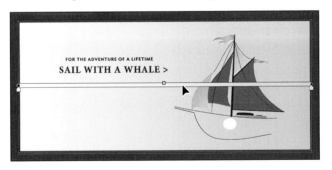

The bar turns into the gradient slider, much like the one found in the Gradient panel. You can use the gradient slider to edit the gradient without opening the Gradient panel.

3 With the Gradient tool, Shift-click the top of the artboard and drag down to the bottom of the artboard to change the position and direction of the starting and ending colors of the gradient in the background rectangle. Release the mouse button, and then release the key.

Holding down the Shift key constrains the gradient to 45-degree angles.

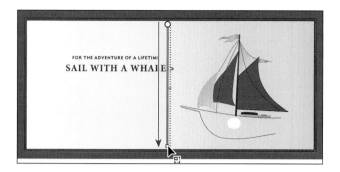

4 With the Gradient tool, Shift-click below the bottom of the artboard, and drag up to just past the top of the artboard to change the position and direction of the starting and ending colors of the gradient in the background rectangle. Release the mouse button, and then release the key.

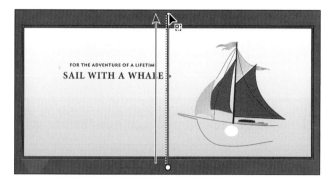

5 With the Gradient tool, position the pointer just off the small white square at the top of the gradient annotator. A rotation icon (⟳) appears. Drag to the right to rotate the gradient in the rectangle, and then release the mouse button.

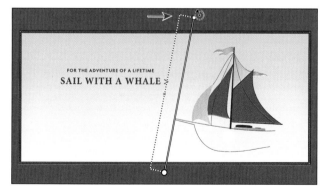

Note: Entering the gradient rotation in the Gradient panel, rather than adjusting it directly on the artboard, is useful when you want to achieve consistency and precision.

6 Double-click the Gradient tool in the Tools panel to show the Gradient panel. Ensure that the Fill box is selected in the panel (circled in the figure), and then change the rotation angle in the Angle field to **80** and press Enter or Return.

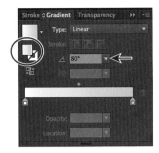

7 Choose Object > Lock > Selection to lock the rectangle.

8 Choose File > Save.

Applying a linear gradient to a stroke

You can also apply a gradient blend to the stroke of an object. Unlike a gradient applied to the fill of an object, you cannot use the Gradient tool to edit a gradient on the stroke of an object. A gradient on a stroke, however, has more options available in the Gradient panel than a gradient fill. Next, you will add a series of colors to a stroke gradient to create a frame for the artwork.

1 Select the Selection tool (➤) in the Tools panel, and click the red stroke on the edge of the artboard to select that rectangle. Choose **18 pt** from the Stroke Weight menu in the Control panel.

Note: Depending on the resolution of your screen, you may see a double-column Tools panel.

2 Click the Stroke box at the bottom of the Tools panel, and click the Gradient box below the Fill box to apply the last used gradient (the light gray to blue for the rectangle fill).

Note: Depending on the resolution of your screen, the Transform options may appear directly in the Control panel.

3 Click the word "Transform" or X, Y, W, or H in the Control panel to show the Transform panel. Make sure that Constrain Width And Height Proportions is turned off (▨) and that the center point of the reference point locator (▦) is selected. Change Width to **14.75 in** and Height to **6.25 in**.

This will ensure that the stroke fits within the bounds of the artboard.

4 Select the Zoom tool (🔍) in the Tools panel, and drag across the upper-right corner of the selected rectangle to zoom in to it.

Edit a gradient on a stroke

For a gradient on a stroke, you can choose how to align the gradient to the stroke: within, along, or across. In this section, you'll explore how to align to a stroke and also edit the colors of the gradient.

1 In the Gradient panel, click the Stroke box (if not already selected) circled in the following figure to edit the gradient applied to the stroke. Leave Type as Linear, and click the Apply Gradient Across Stroke button (⬛) to change the gradient type.

Note: You can apply a gradient to a stroke in three ways: within a stroke (default) (⬛), along a stroke (⬛), and across a stroke (⬛).

2 Double-click the blue color stop on the right, and click the Swatches button (⬛) to show the swatches. Click to select the swatch named "Border 2." Click outside the panel to accept the selection.

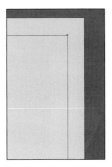
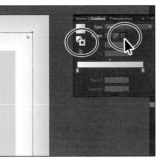

Zoom into the corner. | Edit the stroke gradient type. | Adjust the color stop color.

3 Double-click the leftmost color stop (the white color), and with the Swatches button (⬛) selected, click to select the swatch named "Border 3." Press the Escape key to hide the swatches and return to the Gradient panel.

4 Position the pointer below the color ramp and between the two color stops, to add another color stop. When the pointer with a plus sign (⬛₊) appears, click to add another color stop like you see in the middle part of the following figure.

5 Double-click that new color stop and, with the swatches selected (⬛), click the swatch named "Border 1." Press the Escape key to hide the swatches and return to the Gradient panel.

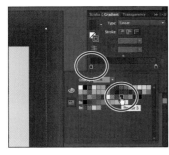
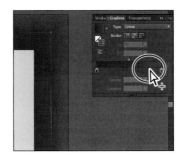
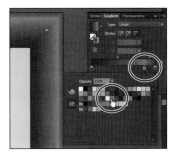

Edit the leftmost color stop. | Add a new color stop. | Change the color of the color stop.

6 With the color stop still selected, change the Location to **80%**.

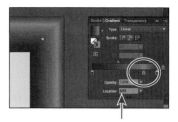

For the next few steps, you'll discover how to add more colors to the gradient by dragging copies of color stops in the Gradient panel.

7 Pressing the Option (Mac OS) or Alt (Windows) key, drag the selected (middle) color stop to the left (closer to the leftmost color stop), release the mouse button when you see *roughly* 25% in the Location value, and then release the modifier key. See the first part of the following figure.

▶ **Tip:** You can delete a color in the color ramp by selecting a color stop and clicking the Delete Stop button (🗑) or by dragging the color stop downward and out of the Gradient panel. Remember that the gradient must contain at least two colors!

8 Pressing the Option (Mac OS) or Alt (Windows) key, drag the rightmost (Border 3) color stop to the left. Release the mouse button, and then release the modifier key when it is positioned at roughly 35%, as you see in the second part of the following figure.

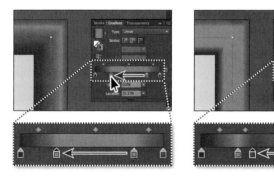

Duplicate a color stop.   Duplicate a second color stop.

9 Choose Select > Deselect, and then choose File > Save.

Applying a radial gradient to artwork

As previously noted, with a *radial gradient*, the starting color (leftmost color stop) of the gradient defines the center point of the fill, which radiates outward to the ending color (rightmost color stop).

Next, you will create and apply a radial gradient fill to the windows of the ship (called *portholes*).

1 Choose View > Fit Artboard In Window.

2 With the Zoom tool (🔍) selected, drag from left to right across the white ellipse, below the red sails on the ship, to zoom in very closely.

3 Select the Selection tool (▶) in the Tools panel, and click the white ellipse.

4 In the Control panel, change the Fill color to the White, Black gradient. Press the Escape key to hide the Swatches panel.

5 Click the Gradient panel icon (■) to show the Gradient panel (if necessary). In the Gradient panel, make sure the Fill box is selected. Choose Radial from the Type menu to convert the linear gradient in the shape to a radial gradient. Keep the ellipse selected and the Gradient panel showing.

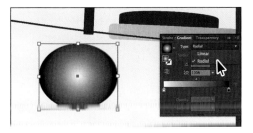

Editing the colors in the radial gradient

Next, you'll use the Gradient tool to adjust the colors in the radial gradient.

1 In the Gradient panel, with the ellipse still selected, click the Reverse Gradient button (▤) to swap the white and black colors in the gradient.

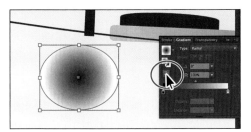

2 Select the Gradient tool (▦) in the Tools panel.

3 Position the pointer over the gradient annotator (bar) in the ellipse to reveal the gradient slider, and perform the following operations:

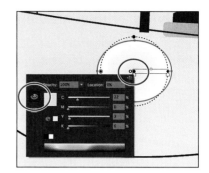

- Double-click the black color stop in the center of the ellipse to edit the color.

- In the panel that appears, click the Color button (), if it's not already selected.

- Choose CMYK from the panel menu (if necessary) to show the CMYK sliders.

- Change the color values to C=**22**, M=**0**, Y=**3**, K=**0**. Press the Escape key to hide the panel.

Note: For the next steps, I zoomed in a little further into the artwork to more easily see the color stops in the gradient.

Notice that the gradient annotator starts from the center of the ellipse and points to the right. The dashed circle around the gradient annotator when the pointer is over it, indicates that it is a radial gradient. You can set additional options for radial gradients, as you'll soon see.

4 Position the pointer beneath the gradient slider, a little to the left of the white color stop at the right end of the color ramp. When the pointer with a plus sign (▸₊) appears, click to add another color to the gradient (circled in the first part of the following figure).

5 Double-click the new color stop. In the panel that appears, click the Swatches button (▦), and select the swatch named "Window 1." Change the Location to **87%**. Press the Escape key to close the panel.

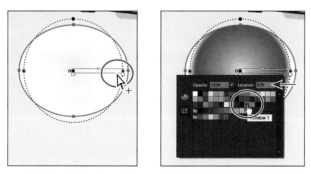

6 Pressing the Option (Mac OS) or Alt (Windows) key, drag the color stop you just created to the left (see the following figure for how far). Release the mouse button, and then release the modifier key.

7 Double-click the new color stop, and change the Location value to **80%** in the panel that appears. Press Enter or Return to change the value and hide the panel.

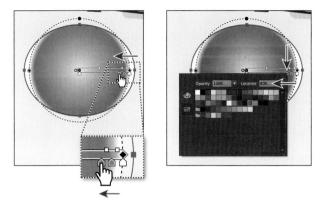

Once the colors are set in the gradient, you can always delete, add more, or even change the order of colors.

▷ **Tip:** When you edit a color stop that has a swatch applied, you can easily see which swatch is applied because it is highlighted in the panel.

8 Double-click the leftmost light-blue color stop, and change the Location value to **70%** in the panel that appears. Press Enter or Return to change the value and hide the panel.

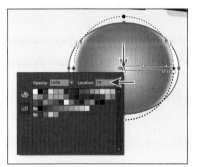 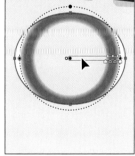

9 Choose File > Save.

Adjusting the radial gradient

Next, you will change the aspect ratio of the radial gradient, adjust the position, and change the radius and the origin of the radial gradient.

Note: You may not see the dotted circle as you drag the end of the gradient annotator. That's okay. It appears if you position the pointer over the gradient annotator bar first, before dragging the right end point.

1 With the Gradient tool (▨) selected and the ellipse still selected, position the pointer over the right end of the gradient annotator. Click and drag the black diamond shape (◆), to the right, stopping just before the right edge of the ellipse shape, and release the mouse button.

Make sure that you still see some white on the edges of the gradient. If you don't, you can drag the diamond shape back to the left a bit. This lengthens the gradient slightly.

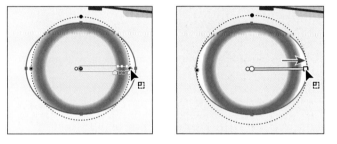

2 In the Gradient panel, ensure that the Fill box is selected, and then change the Aspect Ratio (▣) to **80%** by selecting it from the menu.

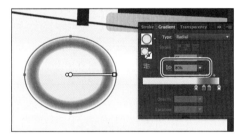

The aspect ratio changes a radial gradient into an elliptical gradient and makes the gradient better match the shape of the artwork. Another way to edit the aspect ratio is to do so visually. If you position the pointer over the gradient on the selected artwork with the Gradient tool selected and then position the pointer over the top black circle that appears on the dotted path, the pointer changes to ▸○. You can then drag to change the aspect ratio of the gradient.

Note: The aspect ratio is a value between 0.5% and 32,767%. As the aspect ratio gets smaller, the ellipse flattens and widens.

Next, you will drag the gradient slider to reposition the gradient in the ellipse.

3 With the Gradient tool, click and drag the gradient slider up a little bit to move the gradient in the ellipse. See the figure for approximately where to drag to.

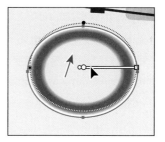

▶ **Tip:** You can drag the small white dot to the left of the larger white dot to reposition the center of the gradient without moving the entire gradient bar. This also changes the radius of the gradient.

4 Select the Selection tool (⬆), and double-click the Scale tool (⬕) in the Tools panel. Change the Uniform Scale value to **60%**, and click OK.

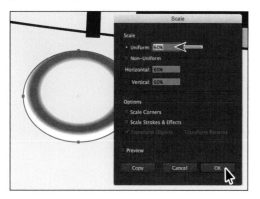

If you transform a shape with a gradient applied, such as scale or rotate the shape (among other types of transformations), the gradient transforms as well.

5 Select the Selection tool in the Tools panel, and Option-drag (Mac OS) or Alt-drag (Windows) the window to the right to create a copy. Position it to the right of the original, like you see in the figure.

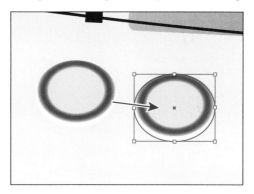

6 Choose Select > Deselect, and then choose File > Save.

Applying gradients to multiple objects

You can apply a gradient to multiple objects by selecting all the objects, applying a gradient color, and then dragging across the objects with the Gradient tool.

Now you'll apply a linear gradient fill to the sails and edit the colors in it.

1 Choose View > Fit Artboard In Window.

2 With the Selection tool (▶) selected, click to select the leftmost red sail shape. Shift-click the red sail to the right of it to select both shapes.

3 In the Control panel, choose the gradient named "Sails" from the Fill color. Press the Escape key to hide the Swatches panel, if necessary.

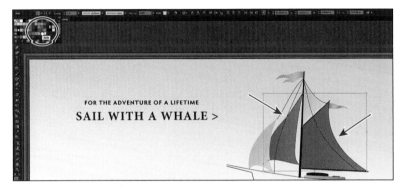

When you apply a gradient to the fill or stroke of multiple selected objects, they are applied independently.

Now you'll adjust the gradient on the shapes so that the gradient blends across all of them as one object.

4 Make sure that the Fill box at the bottom of the Tools panel or in the Swatches panel is selected.

5 Select the Gradient tool (▮) in the Tools panel.

Notice that there is a gradient annotator (a bar) on each of the sails. This shows that by applying a gradient to multiple selected objects, the gradients are applied to each object *independently*.

6 Drag from the center of the leftmost sail shape to the rightmost edge of the sail on the right, as shown in the figure, to apply the gradient uniformly as a single gradient across both shapes.

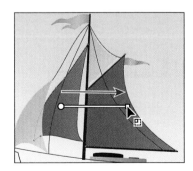

7 Choose Select > Deselect, and then choose File > Save.

Adding transparency to gradients

By specifying varying opacity values for the different color stops in your gradient, you can create gradients that fade in or out and that show or hide underlying images. Next, you will apply a gradient that fades to transparent.

1 Open the Layers panel, and click the visibility column to the left of the Water layer to show its contents as well. Make sure that the Water layer is selected. You may need to scroll down in the panel or collapse the layers.

2 Select the Rectangle tool (▦) in the Tools panel, and click anywhere in the Document window. In the Rectangle dialog box, change Width to **15 in** and Height to **2 in**. Click OK to create a rectangle.

● **Note:** Since the units for the document are set to inches, you don't need to enter the "in."

3 Press the letter D to ensure that the rectangle has the default fill of white and stroke of black.

4 Click the Gradient panel icon (▦) to open the panel. Ensure that the Fill box is selected, click the Gradient menu arrow (▾), and then select White, Black to apply the generic gradient to the fill.

5 Select the Selection tool (▸), and choose Align To Artboard from the Align To menu in the Control panel (if necessary). Click the Horizontal Align Center button (▦) and the Vertical Align Bottom button (▦) to align the rectangle to the center and bottom of the artboard.

● **Note:** Depending on your screen resolution, you may need to click the word "Align" in the Control panel to access the Align panel.

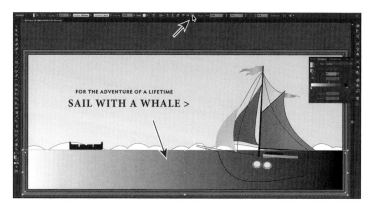

6 Change Stroke Weight to **0** in the Control panel, and leave the shape selected.

7 In the Gradient panel, change Angle to **−90°** by choosing it from the menu.

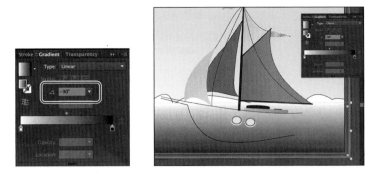

8 Double-click the white color stop in the Gradient panel. In the panel that appears, make sure that the Swatches button (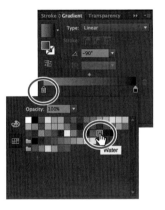) is selected, and select the color swatch named "Water." Press the Escape key once to hide the swatches.

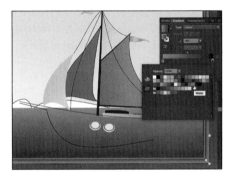

9 With the leftmost color stop still selected in the Gradient panel, change Opacity to **0%**.

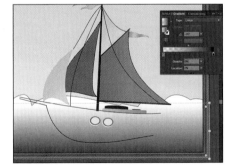

10 Double-click the rightmost color stop (the black color). In the panel that appears, with the Swatches button (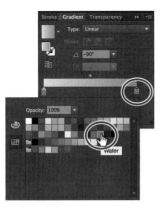) selected, select the color swatch named "Water." Press the Escape key once to hide the swatches.

11 Drag the gradient midpoint (the diamond shape) to the right until you see a value of approximately 60% in the Location field. Click the Gradient panel tab to collapse the Gradient panel group.

12 Choose Object > Lock > Selection.

13 Choose File > Save.

Working with blended objects

You can blend two distinct objects to create and distribute shapes evenly between two objects. The two shapes you blend can be the same or different. You can also blend between two open paths to create a smooth transition of color between objects, or you can combine blends of colors and objects to create color transitions in the shape of a particular object.

The following are examples of different types of blended objects you can create:

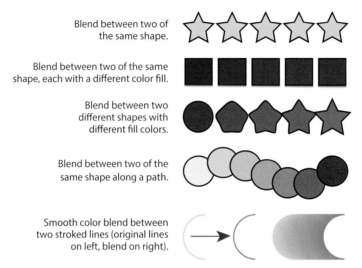

Blend between two of the same shape.

Blend between two of the same shape, each with a different color fill.

Blend between two different shapes with different fill colors.

Blend between two of the same shape along a path.

Smooth color blend between two stroked lines (original lines on left, blend on right).

When you create a blend, the blended objects are treated as one object, called a *blend object*. If you move one of the original objects or edit the anchor points of the original object, the blend changes accordingly. You can also expand the blend to divide it into distinct objects.

Creating a blend with specified steps

Next, you'll use the Blend tool ( ) to blend two shapes that you will later use to create a pattern fill for the water beneath the ship.

1   Scroll down in the Document window so that you can see shapes off the bottom of the artboard. You will create a blend between those two shapes.

2   Select the Zoom tool ( ) in the Tools panel, and drag from left to right, across the large and small white shapes off the bottom of the artboard, to zoom in.

> **Tip:** You can add more than two objects to a blend.

3   Select the Blend tool ( ) in the Tools panel, and position the pointer over the larger shape on the left. Click when the pointer displays an asterisk ( ). Then, hover over the small shape on the right until the pointer displays a plus sign ( ), indicating that you can add an object to the blend. Click to create a blend between these two objects.

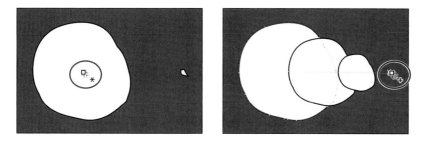

● **Note:** If you wanted to end the current path and blend other objects, you would first click the Blend tool in the Tools panel and then click the other objects, one at a time, to blend them.

4   With the blended object still selected, choose Object > Blend > Blend Options. In the Blend Options dialog box, choose Specified Steps from the Spacing menu, change Specified Steps to **10**, and then click OK.

▶ **Tip:** To edit the blend options for an object, you can also select the blend object and then double-click the Blend tool. You can also double-click the Blend tool (🖾) in the Tools panel to set tool options before you create the blend object.

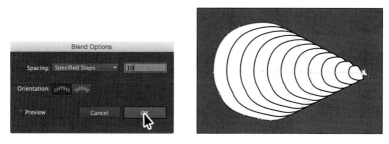

5   Select the Selection tool (▶) in the Tools panel, and double-click anywhere on the blend object to enter Isolation mode.

This temporarily ungroups the blended objects and lets you edit each original shape, as well as the spine (path).

6   Choose View > Outline.

In Outline mode, you can see the outlines of the two original shapes and a straight path between them. The straight path you see, called the *spine*, is the path along which the steps in a blend object are aligned. These three objects are what a blend object is composed of, by default. It can be easier to edit the path between the original objects in Outline mode.

7   Click to select the edge of the smaller shape.

8   Choose View > GPU Preview if supported or View > Preview On CPU if not.

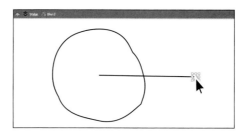

9 Drag the smaller shape roughly into the center of the larger shape, and you will see the blend change.

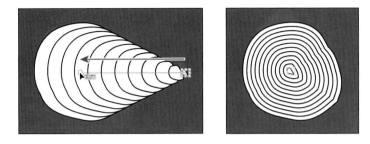

Make sure you drag the shape and not the path (the spine). You may want to zoom in (Command++ [Mac OS] or Ctrl++ [Windows]) to make it easier to select.

10 Choose Select > Deselect, and press the Escape key to exit Isolation mode.

Modifying a blend

Now you'll create another blend and edit the shape of the straight path, called the *spine*, which the objects blend along. You will create a blend between two copies of the blended object you just created. Blending between two objects that are also blended objects can produce unexpected results. That's why you will expand the blended object first (and understand what that means).

1 Choose View > Fit Artboard In Window.

2 Select the Zoom tool ($\mathcal{Q}$) in the Tools panel, and drag to the right, across the orange flag off the right side of the ship to zoom in.

3 With the Selection tool ($\blacktriangle$) selected, click to select the flag. Option-drag (Mac OS) or Alt-drag (Windows) the flag down along the edge of the orange sail, like you see in the figure.

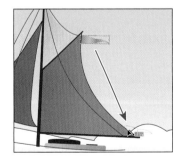 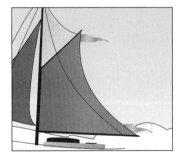

4 Double-click the Blend tool () in the Tools panel to open the Blend Options dialog box. Change the specified steps to **6**. Click OK.

5 With the Blend tool selected, position the pointer over the top flag. Click when the pointer displays an asterisk (⬚₊). Then, hover over the bottom flag until the pointer displays a plus sign (⬚₊). Click to blend the objects. There is now a blend between these two objects.

▶ **Tip:** Expanding a blended object divides the blend into distinct objects, which you can edit individually like any object. The objects are grouped together by default.

To expand a blend, you can choose Object > Blend > Expand. You can no longer edit the blended object as a single object because it has become a group of individual shapes.

6 Choose View > Outline.

7 Choose Select > Deselect.

8 Select the Pen tool (✎) in the Tools panel. Press the Option key (Mac OS) or Alt key (Windows), and position the pointer over the path between the flags. When the pointer changes (▶·), drag the path to the left, like in the first part of the figure.

9 Choose View > GPU Preview if supported or View > Preview On CPU if not to see the change. Press Option (Mac OS) or Alt (Windows), and drag the selected path a bit more (if needed) so that the flags appear to come from behind the sail (see the following figure).

▶ **Tip:** Another way to reshape the spine of a blend is to blend the shapes along another path. You can draw another path, select the blend as well, and then choose Object > Blend > Replace Spine.

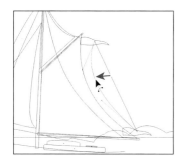 

10 Choose Select > Deselect.

Creating and editing a smooth color blend

You can choose several options for blending the shapes and colors of objects to create a new object. When you choose the Smooth Color blend option in the Blend Options dialog box, Illustrator combines the shapes and colors of the objects into many intermediate steps, creating a smooth, graduated blend between the original objects. If objects are filled or stroked with different colors, the steps are calculated to provide the optimum number of steps for a smooth color transition. If the objects contain identical colors or if they contain gradients or patterns, the number of steps is based on the longest distance between the bounding box edges of the two objects.

Now you'll combine two shapes into a smooth color blend to make the ship.

1 Choose View > Fit Artboard In Window.

2 Select the Zoom tool, and click twice to zoom into the windows on the ship.

You will now blend the two paths that will become the ship. Both paths have a stroke color and no fill. Objects that have strokes blend differently than those that have no stroke.

3 Select the Blend tool (⊞) in the Tools panel, and position the pointer (⊞₊) over the top line beneath the sails and click. Position the pointer (⊞₊) over the bottom line, and click. Leave the blend object selected.

The blend you created is using the last settings from the Blend Options dialog box (Specified Steps: 6).

Next, you'll change the blend settings for the ship so that it blends as smooth color, rather than in specified steps.

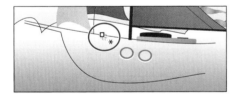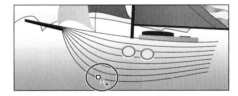

4 Double-click the Blend tool in the Tools panel. In the Blend Options dialog box, choose Smooth Color from the Spacing menu to set up the blend options, which will remain set until you change them. Select Preview, and then click OK.

5 Choose Select > Deselect.

When you make a smooth color blend between objects, Illustrator automatically calculates the number of intermediate steps necessary to create the transition between the objects. Once you've applied a smooth color blend to objects, you can edit it.

● **Note:** Creating smooth color blends between paths can be difficult in certain situations. For instance, if the lines intersect or the lines are too curved, unexpected results can occur.

Next, you will edit the paths that make up the blend.

6 Using the Selection tool ( ), double-click the color blend (the ship) to enter Isolation mode. Click the top path to select it, and change the Stroke color in the Control panel to any color you want. Press the Escape key to hide the panel. Notice how the colors are blended.

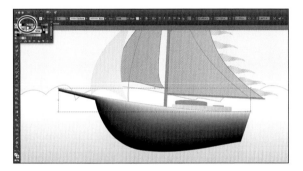

7 Choose Edit > Undo Apply Swatch until the original stroke color is showing.

8 Double-click away from the blend to exit Isolation mode and deselect the ship.

9 Choose View > Fit Artboard In Window.

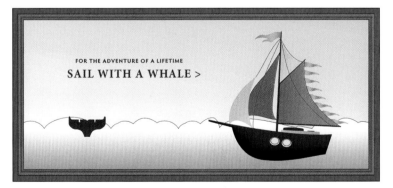

10 Choose File > Save.

Painting with patterns

In addition to process and spot colors, the Swatches panel can also contain pattern and gradient swatches. Illustrator provides sample swatches of each type in the default Swatches panel as separate libraries and lets you create your own patterns and gradients. In this section, you will focus on creating, applying, and editing patterns.

Applying an existing pattern

A *pattern* is artwork saved in the Swatches panel that can be applied to the stroke or fill of an object. You can customize existing patterns and design patterns from scratch with any of the Illustrator tools. All patterns start with a single tile that is *tiled* (repeated) within a shape, starting at the ruler origin and continuing to the right. Next, you will apply an existing pattern to a shape.

1 Choose Object > Unlock All, and then choose Select > Deselect.

2 With the Selection tool (▶) selected, click to select the rectangle with the blue gradient that represents the sky (behind the text and ship).

3 Choose Window > Appearance to open the Appearance panel. Click the Add New Fill button at the bottom of the panel. This adds a second gradient fill to the rectangle and layers it on top of the first.

● **Note:** You'll learn all about the Appearance panel in Lesson 12, "Exploring Creative Uses of Effects and Graphic Styles."

4 In the Appearance panel, click the top word "Fill:" to select the top Fill row. An arrow is pointing to it in the figure.

5 Choose Window > Swatch Libraries > Patterns > Decorative > Vonster Patterns to open the pattern library.

▶ **Tip:** You can type the word "diadem" in the Find field to sort the pattern swatches or choose Small List View from the panel menu to see the names of the pattern swatches.

6 In the Vonster Patterns panel, select the Diadem pattern swatch to fill the path with the pattern. Close the Vonster Patterns panel.

The pattern swatch fills the shape as a second fill on top of the first and is added to the list in the Swatches panel for this document.

7 Click the word "Opacity" in the Control panel above the artwork to open the Transparency panel (or choose Window > Transparency). Choose Screen from the blending mode menu, and change the opacity value to **30**. Press the Escape key to hide the panel.

8 Choose Object > Lock > Selection, and then choose File > Save.

Creating your own pattern

In this section, you'll create your own custom pattern and add it as a swatch to the Swatches panel for this document.

1 Press the spacebar, and drag the artboard up just enough to see the blend object off the bottom of the artboard, if necessary.

2 With the Selection tool (), click to select the blend object, and choose Object > Pattern > Make. Click OK in the dialog box that appears.

Note: You don't need to have anything selected to start with a blank pattern.

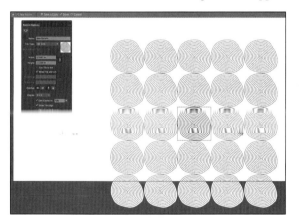

When you create a pattern, Illustrator enters Pattern Editing mode, which is similar to the group Isolation mode you've worked with in previous lessons. Pattern Editing mode allows you to create and edit patterns interactively, while previewing the changes to the pattern on the artboard. All other artwork is dimmed and cannot be edited while in this mode. The Pattern Options panel (Window > Pattern Options) also opens, giving you all the necessary options to create your pattern.

3 With the Selection tool, click the artwork in the center to select it.

The blend object is now a group of objects. In a pattern, blend objects are expanded and grouped, which means you can no longer edit the artwork as a blend object. Going forward, I'll refer to the blend object as a group.

Note: A pattern can be composed of shapes, symbols, or embedded raster images, among other objects. For instance, to create a flannel pattern for a shirt, you can create three overlapping rectangles or lines, each with varying appearance options.

4 Press Command++ (Mac OS) or Ctrl++ (Windows) several times to zoom in.

The series of lighter-colored objects around the center shape are the pattern repeat. They are there for a preview and are dimmed to let you focus on the original. The blue box around the original group of objects is the *pattern tile* (the area that repeats).

5 In the Pattern Options panel, change the Name to **Waves**, and choose Hex By Column from the Tile Type menu.

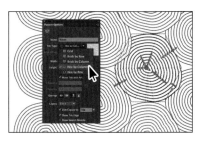

The name appears in the Swatches panel as a tooltip and can be useful to distinguish multiple pattern swatches. The Tile Type determines how the pattern is tiled. You have three main Tile Type choices: the default grid pattern, a brick-style pattern, or the hex pattern.

6 Choose 1 x 1 from the Copies menu at the bottom of the Pattern Options panel. This will remove the repeat and let you temporarily focus on the main pattern artwork.

7 With the Selection tool selected, drag the group over a little. After you have finished dragging, notice that the blue tile moves with the artwork.

▶ **Tip:** Because the blend objects are repeating in Pattern Editing mode, it may be difficult to select the three original objects. You can choose View > Outline to enter Outline mode to see the original blend objects only.

8 With the artwork group selected, Option-drag (Mac OS) or Alt-drag (Windows) it twice to make three of them. Change the size of each to make them a little different in size and arrange them something like you see in the figure.

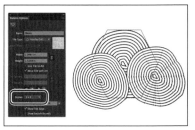

9 In the Pattern Options panel, change the following options (use the following figure as a guide):

- Choose 5 x 5 from the Copies menu to see the repeat again.

- Select the Size Tile To Art option in the middle of the panel.

  The Size Tile To Art selection fits the tile area (the blue hex shape) to the bounds of the artwork, changing the spacing between the repeated objects. With Size Tile To Art deselected, you could manually change the width and the height of the pattern definition area in the Width and Height fields to include more content or to edit the spacing between. You can also edit the tile area manually with the Pattern Tile Tool button (▦) in the upper-left corner of the Pattern Options panel.

▶ **Tip:** The spacing values can be either positive or negative values to move the tiles apart or to bring them closer together.

- Change H Spacing to **–0.25 in**, and change V Spacing to **–1 in**.

- For Overlap, click the Bottom In Front button (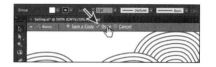), and notice the change in the pattern.

  The artwork in a pattern may begin to overlap due to the size of the tile or the spacing values. By default, when objects overlap horizontally, the left object is on top; when objects overlap vertically, the top object is on top.

Note: The Pattern Options panel has a host of other pattern-editing options, including the ability to see more or less of the pattern, called Copies. To learn more about the Pattern Options panel, search for "Create and edit patterns" in Illustrator Help (Help > Illustrator Help).

10 Select Show Swatch Bounds at the bottom of the Pattern Options panel to see the dotted area that will be saved in the swatch. Deselect Show Swatch Bounds.

11 Click Done in the bar along the top of the Document window. If a dialog box appears, click OK.

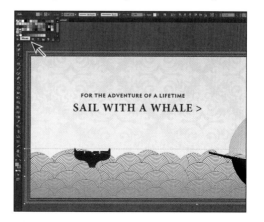

12 Choose File > Save.

Tip: If you want to create pattern variations, you can click Save A Copy in the bar along the top of the Document window when in Pattern Editing mode. This saves the current pattern in the Swatches panel as a copy and allows you to continue creating.

Applying your pattern

You can assign a pattern using a number of different methods. In this section, you'll apply your pattern using the Fill color in the Control panel.

1 Choose View > Fit Artboard In Window.

2 With the Selection tool (▶), click the scalloped white shape behind the ship.

3 Select the swatch named "Waves" from the Fill color in the Control panel.

4 Choose File > Save.

● **Note:** Your pattern may look different, and that's okay.

FOR THE ADVENTURE OF A LIFETIME
SAIL WITH A WHALE >

Editing your pattern

Next, you will edit the Waves pattern swatch in Pattern Editing mode.

▶ Tip: You can also select an object filled with a pattern swatch and, with the Fill box selected in the Swatches, Color, or Tools panel, choose Object > Pattern > Edit Pattern.

1 In the Swatches panel, double-click the Waves pattern swatch to edit it.

2 In Pattern Editing mode, with the Selection tool (▶) selected, choose Select > All to select all three of the objects.

3 In the Control panel, change the Stroke color to the swatch named "Window 1."

4 Click Done in the gray bar along the top of the Document window to exit Pattern Editing mode.

5 Click the waves shape to select it, if necessary.

▶ Tip: In the Scale dialog box, if you wanted to scale the pattern *and* the shape, you can select Transform Objects and select Transform Patterns. You can also transform patterns in the Transform panel by choosing Transform Pattern Only, Transform Object Only, or Transform Both from the panel menu (▾) before applying a transformation.

6 With the shape selected, double-click the Scale tool (⬚) in the Tools panel to scale the pattern but not the shape. In the Scale dialog box, change the following options (if not already set):

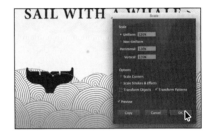

- Uniform Scale: **120%**
- Scale Corners: **Deselected** (the default setting)
- Scale Strokes & Effects: **Deselected** (the default setting)
- Transform Objects: **Deselected**
- Transform Patterns: **Selected**

7 Select Preview to see the change. Click OK, and leave the shape selected.

8 Choose Object > Show All to show a hidden shape on top of the boat. You'll use that shape to mask the boat so that it looks like it's in the water.

9 With the Selection tool and the new shape selected, Shift-click the boat shape. Choose Object > Clipping Mask > Make.

10 Choose Select > Deselect, and then choose File > Save.

11 Choose File > Close.

Review questions

1 What is a *gradient*?

2 How do you adjust the blend between colors in a gradient?

3 Name two ways you can add colors to a gradient.

4 How can you adjust the direction of a gradient?

5 What is the difference between a gradient and a blend?

6 When you save a pattern in Illustrator, where is it saved?

Review answers

1 A gradient is a graduated blend of two or more colors or of tints of the same color. Gradients can be applied to the stroke or fill of an object.

2 To adjust the blend between colors in a gradient, with the Gradient tool (■) selected and with the pointer over the gradient annotator or in the Gradient panel, you can drag the diamond icons or the color stops of the gradient slider.

3 To add colors to a gradient, in the Gradient panel, click beneath the gradient slider to add a gradient stop to the gradient. Then, double-click the color stop to edit the color, using the panel that appears to mix a new color or to apply an existing color swatch. You can select the Gradient tool in the Tools panel, position the pointer over the gradient-filled object, and then click beneath the gradient slider that appears in the artwork to add a color stop.

4 Drag with the Gradient tool to adjust the direction of a gradient. Dragging a long distance changes colors gradually; dragging a short distance makes the color change more abrupt. You can also rotate the gradient using the Gradient tool and change the radius, aspect ratio, starting point, and more.

5 The difference between a gradient and a blend is the way that colors combine together—colors blend together within a gradient and between objects in a blend.

6 When you save a pattern in Illustrator, it is saved as a swatch in the Swatches panel. By default, swatches are saved with the current document open.

11 USING BRUSHES TO CREATE A POSTER

Lesson overview

In this lesson, you'll learn how to do the following:

- Use four brush types: Calligraphic, Art, Bristle, and Pattern.

- Apply brushes to paths.

- Paint and edit paths with the Paintbrush tool.

- Create an Art brush from a raster image.

- Change brush color and adjust brush settings.

- Create new brushes from Adobe Illustrator artwork.

- Work with the Blob Brush tool and the Eraser tool.

This lesson takes approximately 60 minutes to complete.

Download the project files for this lesson from the Lesson & Update Files tab on your Account page at www.peachpit.com and store them on your computer in a convenient location, as described in the "Getting Started" section of this book.

Your Account page is also where you'll find any updates to the chapters or to the lesson files. Look on the Lesson & Update Files tab to access the most current content.

The variety of brush types in Adobe Illustrator CC lets you create a myriad of effects simply by painting or drawing using the Paintbrush tool or the drawing tools. You can work with the Blob Brush tool; choose from the Art, Calligraphic, Pattern, Bristle, or Scatter brushes; or create new brushes based on your artwork.

Getting started

In this lesson, you will learn how to work with the different brush types in the Brushes panel and how to change brush options and create your own brushes. Before you begin, you'll restore the default preferences for Adobe Illustrator CC. Then you'll open the finished art file for the lesson to see the finished artwork.

● **Note:** If you have not already downloaded the project files for this lesson to your computer from your Account page, make sure to do so now. See "Getting Started" at the beginning of the book.

1   To ensure that the tools and panels function exactly as described in this lesson, delete or deactivate (by renaming) the Adobe Illustrator CC preferences file. See "Restoring default preferences" in the "Getting Started" section at the beginning of the book.

2   Start Adobe Illustrator CC.

3   Choose File > Open, and open the L11_end.ai file in the Lessons > Lesson11 folder on your hard disk.

4   If you want, choose View > Zoom Out to make the finished artwork smaller, and then adjust the window size and leave the artwork on your screen as you work. (Use the Hand tool [✋] to move the artwork to where you want it in the Document window.) If you don't want to leave the artwork open, choose File > Close.

To begin working, you'll open an existing art file.

5   Choose File > Open. If a panel appears, click Open in the panel. You could also choose File > Open again. In the Open dialog box, navigate to the Lessons > Lesson11 folder and select the L11_start.ai file on your hard disk. Click Open to open the file.

6   Choose View > Fit Artboard In Window.

7   Choose File > Save As. In the Save As dialog box, name the file **CruisePoster.ai**, and select the Lesson11 folder. Leave the Format option set to Adobe Illustrator (ai) (Mac OS) or the Save As Type option set to Adobe Illustrator (*.AI) (Windows), and then click Save.

● **Note:** If you don't see Reset Essentials in the workspace switcher menu, choose Window > Workspace > Essentials before choosing Window > Workspace > Reset Essentials.

8   In the Illustrator Options dialog box, leave the Illustrator options at their default settings, and then click OK.

9   Choose Reset Essentials from the workspace switcher in the Application bar to reset the workspace.

Working with brushes

Using brushes you can decorate paths with patterns, figures, brush strokes, textures, or angled strokes. You can modify the brushes provided with Illustrator and create your own brushes.

You can apply brush strokes to existing paths, or you can use the Paintbrush tool to draw a path and apply a brush stroke simultaneously. You can change the color, size, and other features of a brush, and you can edit paths after brushes are applied (including adding a fill).

Types of brushes

A. Calligraphic brush

B. Art brush

C. Bristle brush

D. Pattern brush

E. Scatter brush

There are five types of brushes that appear in the Brushes panel (Window > Brushes): Calligraphic, Art, Bristle, Pattern, and Scatter. In this lesson, you will discover how to work with all of these except for the Scatter brush.

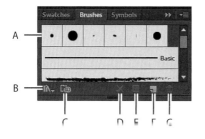

A. Brushes

B. Brush Libraries Menu

C. Libraries Panel

D. Remove Brush Stroke

E. Options Of Selected Object

F. New Brush

G. Delete Brush

Using Calligraphic brushes

The first type of brush I'll discuss is Calligraphic brushes. Calligraphic brushes resemble strokes drawn with the angled point of a calligraphic pen. Calligraphic brushes are defined by an elliptical shape whose center follows the path, and you can use these brushes to create the appearance of hand-drawn strokes made with a flat, angled pen tip.

Calligraphic brush examples

Applying a Calligraphic brush to artwork

To get started, you'll filter the type of brushes shown in the Brushes panel so that it shows only Calligraphic brushes.

1 Click the Brushes panel icon (▉) on the right side of the workspace to show the Brushes panel. Click the Brushes panel menu icon (▉), and choose List View.

2 Click the Brushes panel menu icon (▾≡) again, and deselect Show Art Brushes, Show Bristle Brushes, and Show Pattern Brushes, leaving only the Calligraphic brushes visible in the Brushes panel. You can't deselect them all at once, so you'll have to keep clicking the menu icon (▾≡) to access the menu.

3 Select the Selection tool (▸) in the Tools panel, and Shift-click both of the two curved pink paths above the orange/yellow shape of a ship to select both of them.

4 Click the 5 pt. Flat brush in the Brushes panel to apply it to the pink paths.

5 Change the Stroke weight to **6 pt**, and change the Stroke color to White in the Control panel. Press the Escape key to hide the Swatches panel, if necessary.

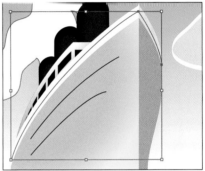

6 Choose Select > Deselect.

7 With the Selection tool, click the smaller of the white paths (the path on the right) that you just applied the brush to. Change the Stroke color to a light gray in the Control panel (I chose the color with the tooltip values C=0, M=0, Y=0, K=10).

8 Choose Select > Deselect, and then choose File > Save.

Drawing with the Paintbrush tool

As mentioned earlier, the Paintbrush tool allows you to apply a brush as you paint. Painting with the Paintbrush tool creates vector paths that you can edit with the Paintbrush tool or other drawing tools. Next, you'll use the Paintbrush tool to paint waves in the water with a calligraphic brush from a default brush library. Your waves won't look identical to what you see in the lesson, and that's okay—*just have some fun.*

1   With the Selection tool (➤), click the darker blue water shape below the ship.

2   Choose Select > Deselect.

The water shape is on a sublayer behind the ship. Selecting the water shape selects that sublayer in the Layers panel, which means that all of the waves you create will also be on the same sublayer as the water shape.

3   Select the Paintbrush tool (✔) in the Tools panel.

4   Click the Brush Libraries Menu button (▣) at the bottom of the Brushes panel, and choose Artistic > Artistic_Calligraphic. A brush library panel with various brushes appears.

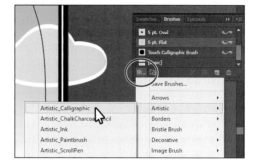

Illustrator comes with a host of brush libraries that you can use in your artwork. Each of the brush types discussed previously has a series of libraries to choose from.

5   Click the Artistic_Calligraphic panel menu icon (▤), and choose List View. Click the brush named "50 pt. Flat" to add it to the Brushes panel. Close the Artistic_Calligraphic brush library.

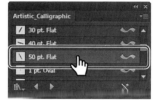

Selecting a brush from a brush library, such as the Artistic_Calligraphic library, adds that brush to the Brushes panel for the active document only.

6   Change the Fill color to None (▨), the Stroke color to the swatch named "Dark Blue," and the Stroke weight to **1 pt** (if necessary) in the Control panel.

Notice that the Paintbrush pointer has an asterisk next to it (✔ₓ), indicating that you are about to draw a new path.

7   Position the pointer off the left side of the artboard, just below the ship. Paint a long, curving path from left to right, stopping about halfway across the water (see the figure). Try creating three more paths, painting from left to right, going all the way across the water. You can see the figure for ideas on how I painted.

● **Note:** This Calligraphic brush creates random angles on the paths, so yours may not look like what you see in the figures, and that's okay.

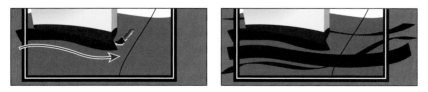

8   Choose Select > Deselect (if necessary), and then choose File > Save.

Editing paths with the Paintbrush tool

Now you'll use the Paintbrush tool to edit one of the paths you painted.

▶ **Tip:** You can also edit paths drawn with the Paintbrush tool using the Smooth tool (✏) and the Path Eraser tool (✏), located under the Pencil tool (✏) in the Tools panel.

1 Select the Selection tool (▶) in the Tools panel, and click to select the first path you drew on the water (the one that is just below the bottom of the ship).

2 Select the Paintbrush tool (✒) in the Tools panel. Position the pointer near the right end of the selected path. An asterisk will not appear next to the pointer when it's positioned over a selected path. Drag to the right to extend the path all the way to the right edge of the artboard. The selected path is edited from the point where you began drawing.

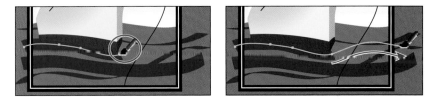

3 Press and hold the Command (Mac OS) or Ctrl (Windows) key to toggle to the Selection tool, and click to select another curved path you drew with the Paintbrush tool. After clicking, release the key to return to the Paintbrush tool.

4 With the Paintbrush tool, move the pointer over some part of the selected path. When the asterisk disappears next to the pointer, drag to the right to redraw the path.

5 Choose Select > Deselect (if necessary), and then choose File > Save.

Next, you will edit the Paintbrush tool options.

6 Double-click the Paintbrush tool (✒) in the Tools panel to display the Paintbrush Tool Options dialog box, and make the following changes:

- Fidelity: Drag the slider all the way to Smooth (to the right).

- Keep Selected: Selected.

7 Click OK.

The Paintbrush Tool Options dialog box changes the way the Paintbrush tool functions. For the Fidelity option, the closer to Smooth you drag the slider, the smoother the path will be with fewer points. Also, because you selected Keep Selected, the paths remain selected after you finish drawing them.

8 Change the Stroke color to the swatch named "Medium Blue," and change the Stroke weight to **0.5 pt** in the Control panel.

9 With the Paintbrush tool selected, paint three or four more paths from either left to right or right to left across the water shape below the ship.

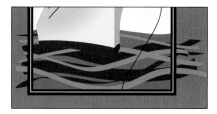

Notice that, after painting each path, the path is still selected, so you could edit it if you needed. I already deselected in the figure.

10 Double-click the Paintbrush tool in the Tools panel. In the Paintbrush Tool Options dialog box, deselect the Keep Selected option, and then click OK.

Now the paths will *not* remain selected after you finish drawing them, and you can draw overlapping paths without altering previously drawn paths.

● **Note:** When the Keep Selected option is deselected, you can edit a path by selecting it with the Selection tool (▶) or by selecting a segment or point on the path with the Direct Selection tool (▷) and then redrawing part of the path with the Paintbrush tool, like you saw previously.

11 Choose Select > Deselect, and then choose File > Save.

Editing a brush

To change the options for a brush, you can double-click the brush in the Brushes panel. When you edit a brush, you can also choose whether to change artwork to which the brush has been applied. Next, you'll change the appearance of the 50 pt. Flat brush you've been painting with.

1 In the Brushes panel, double-click the brush thumbnail for the brush named "50 pt. Flat" to open the Calligraphic Brush Options dialog box. In the dialog box, make the following changes:

- Name: **30 pt. Flat**

- Angle: **0°**

- Choose Fixed from the menu to the right of Angle. (When Random is chosen, a random variation of brush angles is created every time you draw.)

- Roundness: **5%** (the default setting)

- Size: **30 pt**

2 Click OK.

▶ **Tip:** The Preview window in the dialog box (below the Name field) shows the changes that you make to the brush.

● **Note:** The edits you make will change the brush for this document only.

3 In the dialog box that appears, click Leave Strokes so as not to apply the brush change to the existing waves that have the brush applied.

4 Change the Stroke color to the swatch named "Light Blue," and change the Stroke weight to **1 pt** in the Control panel.

5 Click the 30 pt. Flat brush in the Brushes panel to ensure that you will paint with it applied. With the Paintbrush tool ( ) selected, paint three paths across the water to create more waves, overlapping the existing waves. Use the figure as a guide, if you like.

6 Choose Select > Deselect, if necessary, and then choose File > Save.

The artwork should be deselected already, and, if it is, the Deselect command will be dimmed (you can't select it).

Removing a brush stroke

You can easily remove a brush stroke applied to artwork where you don't want it. Now you'll remove the brush stroke on the cloud.

1 Select the Selection tool ( ), and click the blue cloud with the white stroke in the sky.

2 Click the Remove Brush Stroke button ( ) at the bottom of the Brushes panel.

Removing a brush stroke doesn't remove the stroke color and weight; it just removes the brush applied.

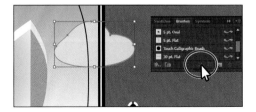

3 Change the Stroke weight to **0 pt** in the Control panel.

4 Choose Select > Deselect, and then choose File > Save.

Using Art brushes

Art brushes stretch artwork or an embedded raster image evenly along the length of a path. As with other brushes, you can edit the brush options to affect how the brush is applied to artwork.

Art brush examples

Applying an existing Art brush

Next, you will apply an existing Art brush to waves at the front of the boat.

1 In the Brushes panel, click the Brushes panel menu icon (), and deselect Show Calligraphic Brushes. Then select Show Art Brushes from the same panel menu to make the art brushes visible in the Brushes panel.

2 Click the Brush Libraries Menu button () at the bottom of the Brushes panel, and choose Artistic > Artistic_Paintbrush.

3 Click the Artistic_Paintbrush panel menu icon (), and choose List View. Click the brush named "Brush 3" in the list to add the brush to the Brushes panel for this document. Close the Artistic_Paintbrush panel group.

4 Select the Paintbrush tool () in the Tools panel.

5 Change the Stroke color to White (if necessary) and the Stroke weight to **1 pt**, and make sure that the Fill color is None () in the Control panel.

6 Click the Layers panel icon () on the right side of the workspace to open the Layers panel. Click the Spray/Tree sublayer so that the new artwork is on that layer. Click the Layers panel icon to collapse the panel.

7 Position the Paintbrush pointer () at the bottom front of the ship in the red area (marked with an X in the figure). Drag to the left along the bottom of the red strip on the ship, just along the water line. See the figure for how I painted it, and don't worry about being exact. You can always choose Edit > Undo Art Stroke and repaint the path.

▶ **Tip:** With the Paintbrush pointer selected, press the Caps Lock key to see a precise cursor (X). In certain situations, this can help to paint with more precision.

8 Paint a path from the same starting point (the red X in previous figure), but drag to the right this time. Then paint a "U" shape around the starting point (from left to right) to cover any red showing. The figure shows both paths. (See the figure—start at the X in the figure for the "U" shape.)

9 Try adding a few more painted paths, always starting from the same point as the end of the original path you painted.

10 Choose File > Save.

Creating an Art brush using a raster image

● **Note:** To learn about guidelines for creating brushes, see "Create or modify brushes" in Illustrator Help (Help > Illustrator Help).

In this section, you'll place a raster image, embedding it, to use in a new Art brush. When you create a new brush (for any of the brush types), it appears in the Brushes panel of the current document only.

1 Choose File > Place. In the Place dialog box, navigate to the Lesson11 folder, and select the image named tree.psd. Make sure to deselect the Link option. Click Place.

2 Position the pointer off of the artboard on the right. Click to place the image.

Next, you will make an Art brush from the selected artwork. You can make an Art brush from vector artwork or from embedded raster images, but that artwork must not contain gradients, blends, other brush strokes, mesh objects, graphs, linked files, masks, or text that has not been converted to outlines.

● **Note:** When dealing with embedded images and brushes, there is a direct impact on the performance of the document in Illustrator. There is a fixed limit to the size of the embedded image that can be used for a brush. You may see a dialog box telling you that the image needs to be resampled before you can make a brush from it.

3 Select the Selection tool (▶). Choose Window > Brushes to open the Brushes panel and click the New Brush button (▣) at the bottom of the Brushes panel. This begins the process of creating a new brush from the selected raster artwork.

4 In the New Brush dialog box, select Art Brush, and then click OK.

5 In the Art Brush Options dialog box that appears, change Name to **Palm Tree**. Click OK.

6 Delete the image you placed off the right side of the artboard since you don't need it anymore.

7 With the Selection tool selected, click to select the curved black line to the right of the ship.

8 Click the brush named "Palm Tree" in the Brushes panel to apply it.

Notice that the original tree image is stretched along the shape. This is the default behavior of an Art brush.

Editing an Art brush

Next, you'll edit the Palm Tree Art brush and update the appearance of the palm tree on the artboard.

▶ **Tip:** To learn more about the Art Brush Options dialog box, see "Art brush options" in Illustrator Help (Help > Illustrator Help).

1 With the curved path still selected on the artboard, double-click the brush thumbnail to the left of the text "Palm tree" or to the right of the name in the Brushes panel to open the Art Brush Options dialog box.

2 In the Art Brush Options dialog box, select Preview to see the changes as you make them, and move the dialog box so you can see the curvy line with the brush applied. Make the following changes:

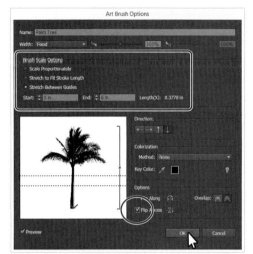

- Stretch Between Guides: Selected

- Start: **5 in**

- End: **6 in**

- Flip Across: **Selected**

3 Click OK.

4 In the dialog box that appears, click Apply To Strokes to apply the change to the curvy line that has the Palm Tree brush applied.

5 Click the word "Opacity" in the Control panel, and choose Multiply from the Blend Mode menu. Press Enter or Return to close the Transparency panel.

6 Choose Select > Deselect, and then choose File > Save.

Using Bristle brushes

Bristle brushes allow you to create strokes with the appearance of a natural brush with bristles. Painting with a Bristle brush, using the Paintbrush tool, creates vector paths with the Bristle brush applied.

In this section, you'll start by adjusting options for a brush to change how it appears in the artwork and then paint with the Paintbrush tool and a Bristle brush to create smoke.

Bristle brush examples

Changing Bristle brush options

As you've seen, you can change the appearance of a brush by adjusting its settings in the Brush Options dialog box, either before or after brushes have been applied to artwork. In the case of Bristle brushes, it's usually best to adjust the brush settings prior to painting since it can take some time to update the brush strokes.

1 In the Brushes panel, click the panel menu icon (), choose Show Bristle Brushes, and then deselect Show Art Brushes.

2 Double-click the thumbnail for the default Mop brush or double-click directly to the right of the brush name to open the Bristle Brush Options dialog box for that brush. In the Bristle Brush Options dialog box, make the following changes:

- Shape: **Round Fan** (the default setting)

- Size: **7 mm** (The brush size is the diameter of the brush.)

- Bristle Length: **150%** (the default setting) (The bristle length starts from the point where the bristles meet the handle of the bristle tip.)

- Bristle Density: **20%** (The bristle density is the number of bristles in a specified area of the brush neck.)

- Bristle Thickness: **75%** (the default setting) (The bristle thickness can vary from fine to coarse [between 1% and 100%].)

- Paint Opacity: **75%** (the default setting) (This option lets you set the opacity of the paint being used.)

- Stiffness: **50%** (the default setting) (Stiffness refers to the rigidity of the bristles).

3 Click OK.

Note: To learn more about the Bristle Brush Options dialog box and its settings, see "Using the Bristle brush" in Illustrator Help (Help > Illustrator Help).

Tip: Illustrator comes with a series of default Bristle brushes. Click the Brush Libraries Menu button () at the bottom of the Brushes panel, and choose Bristle Brushes > Bristle Brush Library.

Painting with a Bristle brush

Now you'll use the Mop brush to draw some smoke above the ship. Painting with a Bristle brush can create an organic, fluid path. To constrain the painting, you will paint inside a shape. This will mask (hide) part of the painting to be in the shape of smoke.

1 Select the Zoom tool (🔍) in the Tools panel, and click a few times, slowly, on the smoke shape above the ship (not the cloud) to zoom in on it.

2 Select the Selection tool (▸) in the Tools panel, and click to select the smoke shape. This selects the layer that the shape is on so that any artwork you paint will be on the same layer.

● **Note:** To learn more about the drawing modes, see Lesson 3, "Using Shapes to Create Artwork for a Postcard."

3 Click the Draw Inside button (▣) at the bottom of the Tools panel.

● **Note:** If the Tools panel appears as one column, click the Drawing Modes button (▣) at the bottom of the Tools panel, and then choose Draw Inside from the menu that appears.

4 With the smoke shape still selected, change the Fill color to None (⬜) in the Control panel (press the Escape key to hide the Swatches panel). Leave the stroke as is.

5 Choose Select > Deselect to deselect the smoke shape.

The dotted lines on the corners of the shape indicate that any paths you paint will be masked by the smoke shape.

6 Select the Paintbrush tool (🖌) in the Tools panel. Choose the Mop brush from the Brush Definition menu in the Control panel, if it's not already chosen.

▶ **Tip:** If you want to edit paths as you draw, you can select the Keep Selected option in the Paintbrush Tool Options for the Paintbrush tool or you can select paths with the Selection tool. You don't need to completely fill the shape.

7 Make sure that the Fill color is None (⬜) and the Stroke color is White in the Control panel. Press the Escape key to hide the Swatches panel. Make sure that the Stroke weight is **1 pt** in the Control panel.

▶ **Tip:** If you don't like what you just painted, you can choose Edit > Undo Bristle Stroke.

8 Position the pointer at the top of the largest smokestack. (See the red X in the following figure.) Drag up and then down and to the left to loosely follow the edge of the smoke shape. Release the mouse button when you reach the end of the smoke shape.

When you release the mouse button, notice that the path you just painted is masked by the smoke shape.

9 Use the Paintbrush tool to paint more paths inside the smoke shape, using the Mop brush. Try drawing from each of the smokestacks, following the smoke shape. The idea is to fill up the smoke shape with the paths you paint.

● **Note:** In the first part of the figure, I dimmed the shape paths so you could more easily see the smoke paths.

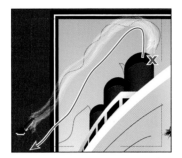 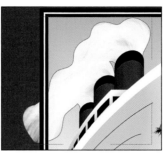

Paint the first path. Note the result after painting more.

10 Choose View > Outline to see all of the paths you just created when painting.

11 Choose Select > Object > Bristle Brush Strokes to select all of the paths created with the Paintbrush tool using the Mop brush.

12 Choose Object > Group, and then choose View > GPU Preview if supported or View > Preview On CPU if not.

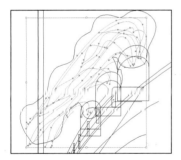 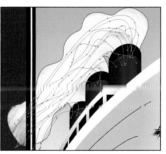

View the artwork in Outline mode. Note the result in Preview mode.

13 Click the Draw Normal button () at the bottom of the Tools panel.

14 Select the Selection tool in the Tools panel. Choose Select > Deselect.

15 Double-click the edge of the smoke shape to enter Isolation mode. Click the edge of the same smoke shape to select it. Change the Stroke color to None (▨) in the Control panel.

● **Note:** If the Tools panel appears as one column, click the Drawing Modes button at the bottom of the Tools panel, and then choose Draw Normal from the menu that appears.

Tip: You can also double-click away from the artwork to exit Isolation mode.

16 Press the Escape key several times to hide the panel and to exit Isolation mode.

17 Click the Layers panel icon (▨) on the right side of the workspace to open the Layers panel. Click the eye icon (◉) to the left of the Spray/Tree sublayer name to hide the artwork on that layer. Click the Layers panel icon to collapse the panel.

18 Choose Select > Deselect, and then choose File > Save.

When saving, you may see a warning dialog box indicating that the document contains multiple Bristle brush paths with transparency. As mentioned earlier, painting with a Bristle brush creates a series of individual vector paths with the brush applied. This can lead to issues with printing or saving to EPS/PDF or legacy versions of Illustrator documents. In order to reduce the complexity and number of the Bristle Brush paths, you can rasterize paths with a Bristle brush applied. Select the path(s) with the Bristle brush applied, and choose Object > Rasterize.

The Bristle brush and graphic tablets

When you use Bristle brush with a graphic tablet, Illustrator interactively tracks the movements of the stylus over the tablet. It interprets all aspects of its orientation and pressure input at any point along a drawing path. Illustrator provides the output that is modeled on the stylus's x-axis position, y-axis position, pressure, tilt, bearing, and rotation.

—From Illustrator Help

Using Pattern brushes

Pattern brushes paint a pattern made up of separate sections, or *tiles*. When you apply a Pattern brush to artwork, different tiles of the pattern are applied to different sections of the path, depending on where the section falls on the path—the end, middle, or corner. There are hundreds of interesting Pattern brushes that you can choose from when creating your own projects, from grass to cityscapes. Next, you'll apply an existing Pattern brush to a path to create windows on the ship.

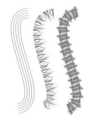

Pattern brush examples

1 Choose View > Fit Artboard In Window.

2 In the Brushes panel, click the panel menu icon (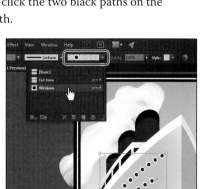), choose Show Pattern Brushes, and then deselect Show Bristle Brushes. The Windows brush that appears in the Brushes panel is a brush that I created and saved with the file.

Next, you will apply a Pattern brush and then edit its properties.

3 With the Selection tool (▶) selected, Shift-click the two black paths on the orange shape of the ship to select them both.

4 Choose the Windows Pattern brush from the Brush Definition menu in the Control panel or the Brushes panel to apply the Pattern brush.

Next, you will edit the brush properties for the selected paths.

5 Choose Select > Deselect.

6 Click the bottommost path with the Windows brush applied to select it.

▶ **Tip:** Just like other brush types, there is a series of default Pattern brush libraries that come with Illustrator. To access them, click the Brush Libraries Menu button (▣) and choose a library from one of the menus (the Decorative menu, for example).

7 Click the Options Of Selected Object button (▣) at the bottom of the Brushes panel to edit the brush options for only the selected path on the artboard.

This opens the Stroke Options (Pattern Brush) dialog box.

8 Select Preview in the Stroke Options (Pattern Brush) dialog box. Change the Scale to **110%** either by dragging the Scale slider or by typing in the value. Click OK.

▶ **Tip:** To change the size of the windows, you can also change the stroke weight of the lines on the artboard, with the brush applied.

When you edit the brush options of the selected object, you only see some of the brush options. The Stroke Options (Pattern Brush) dialog box is used to edit the properties of the brushed path without updating the corresponding brush.

9 Choose Select > Deselect, and then choose File > Save.

Creating a Pattern brush

You can create a Pattern brush in several ways. For a simple pattern applied to a straight line, for instance, you can select the content that you're using for the pattern and click the New Brush button (⬛) at the bottom of the Brushes panel.

To create a more complex pattern to apply to objects with curves and corners, you can select artwork in the Document window to be used in a pattern brush, create swatches in the Swatches panel from the artwork that you are using in the Pattern brush, and even have Illustrator auto-generate the Pattern brush corners. In Illustrator, only the side tile needs to be defined. Illustrator automatically generates four different types of corners based on the art used for the side tile. These four auto-generated options fit the corners perfectly.

Next, you'll create a Pattern brush for the border around the poster.

● **Note:** You'll find Pattern Objects at the bottom of the View menu.

1 Choose View > Pattern objects. This should show you a zoomed-in view of the life preserver and the rope off the right edge of the artboard.

2 With the Selection tool (▶) selected, click to select the brown rope group.

3 Click the Brushes panel icon (▦) to expand the panel, if necessary. Click the panel menu icon (▤), and choose Thumbnail View.

   Notice that Pattern brushes in Thumbnail view are segmented in the Brushes panel. Each segment corresponds to a pattern tile. The side tile is repeated in the Brushes panel thumbnail preview.

4 In the Brushes panel, click the New Brush button (⬛) to create a pattern out of the rope.

5 In the New Brush dialog box, select Pattern Brush. Click OK.

   A new Pattern brush can be made regardless of whether artwork is selected. If you create a Pattern brush without artwork selected, it is assumed that you will add artwork by dragging it into the Brushes panel later or by selecting the artwork from a pattern swatch you create as you edit the brush. You will see the latter method later in this section.

● **Note:** Some brushes have no corner tiles because they are designed for curved paths.

6 In the Pattern Brush Options dialog box, name the brush **Border**.

   Pattern brushes can have up to five tiles—the side, start, and end tiles, plus an outer-corner tile and an inner-corner tile to paint sharp corners on a path.

   You can see all five tiles as buttons below the Spacing option in the dialog box. The tile buttons let you apply different artwork to different parts of the path. You can click a

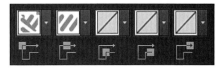

tile button for the tile you want to define, and then you select an auto-generated selection (if available) or a pattern swatch from the menu that appears.

7   Under the Spacing option, click the Side Tile box (the second tile from the left). The artwork that was originally selected is in the menu that appears, along with None and any pattern swatches found in the Swatches panel. Choose Pompadour from the menu.

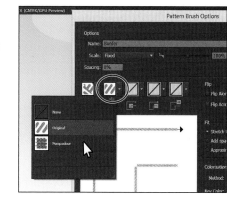

In the Preview area below the tiles, you will see how the new artwork affects a path.

Tip: Position the pointer over the tile squares in the Pattern Brush Options dialog box to see a tooltip indicating which tile it is.

Tip: Selected artwork becomes the side tile, by default, when creating a Pattern brush.

8   Click the Side Tile box again, and choose the Original option.

9   Click the Outer Corner Tile box to reveal the menu.

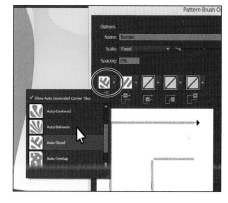

The outer-corner tile has been generated automatically by Illustrator, based on the original rope artwork. In the menu, you can choose from four types of corners that are generated automatically:

Tip: To save a brush and reuse it in another file, you can create a brush library with the brushes you want to use. For more information, see "Work with brush libraries" in Illustrator Help.

- **Auto-Centered.** The side tile is stretched around the corner and centered on it.

- **Auto-Between.** Copies of the side tile extend all the way into the corner, with one copy on each side. Folding elimination is used to stretch them into shape.

- **Auto-Sliced.** The side tile is sliced diagonally, and the pieces come together, similar to a miter joint in a wooden picture frame.

- **Auto-Overlap.** Copies of the tiles overlap at the corner.

10 Choose Auto-Between from the menu. This generates the outer corner of any path that the Pattern brush will be applied to from the rope.

11 Click OK. The Border brush appears in the Brushes panel.

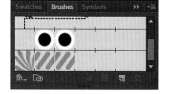

Applying a Pattern brush

In this section, you'll apply the Border Pattern brush to a rectangular border around the artwork. As you've seen, when you use drawing tools to apply brushes to artwork, you first draw the path with the drawing tool and then select the brush in the Brushes panel to apply the brush to the path.

1 Choose View > Fit Artboard In Window.

2 With the Selection tool (➤) selected, click the white stroke of the rectangle on the border.

3 In the Tools panel, click the Fill box, and make sure that None (▢) is selected. Then click the Stroke box and select None (▢).

4 With the rectangle selected, click the Border brush in the Brushes panel.

5 Choose Select > Deselect.

The rectangle is painted with the Border brush, with the side tile on the sides and the outer-corner tile on each corner.

Editing the Pattern brush

▶ **Tip:** For more information on creating pattern swatches, see "About patterns" in Illustrator Help.

Now you'll edit the Border Pattern brush using a pattern swatch that you create.

1 Click the Swatches panel icon (▦) to expand the Swatches panel, or choose Window > Swatches.

2 Choose View > Pattern objects to zoom in to the life preserver off the right edge of the artboard.

3 With the Selection tool (➤), drag the life preserver into the Swatches panel. The new pattern swatch appears in the Swatches panel.

After you create a pattern brush, you can delete the pattern swatches from the Swatches panel, if you don't plan to use them for additional artwork.

4 Choose Select > Deselect.

5 In the Swatches panel, double-click the pattern swatch that you just created. In the Pattern Options dialog box, name the swatch **Corner**, and choose 1 x 1 from the Copies menu.

6 Click Done in the gray bar, along the top of the Document window, to finish editing the pattern.

7 Choose View > Fit Artboard In Window.

8 In the Brushes panel, double-click the Border Pattern brush to open the Pattern Brush Options dialog box.

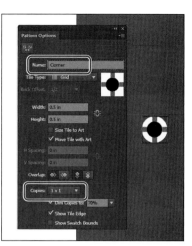

▶ **Tip:** You can also change the pattern tiles in a Pattern brush by pressing the Option (Mac OS) or Alt (Windows) key and dragging artwork from the artboard onto the tile of the Pattern brush you want to change in the Brushes panel.

9 Click the Outer Corner Tile box, and choose the Corner pattern swatch from the menu that appears (you'll need to scroll). Change the Scale to **70%**, and click OK. The figure shows choosing the outer-corner tile.

10 In the dialog box that appears, click Apply To Strokes to update the border on the artboard.

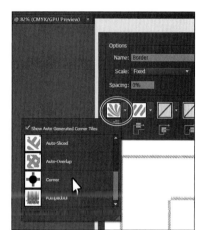

11 With the Selection tool selected, click to select one of the paths that contains a row of windows. Click the Border brush in the Brushes panel to apply it.

Notice that the life preservers are not applied to the path. The path is painted with the side tile from the Border brush. Because the path does not include sharp corners, outer-corner and inner-corner tiles are not applied to the path.

12 Choose Edit > Undo Apply Pattern Brush to remove the brush from the path.

13 Choose Select > Deselect, and then choose File > Save.

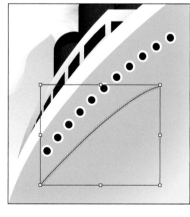

Note: Earlier in the lesson, you learned how to remove a brush from an object by clicking the Remove Brush Stroke button (▨) in the Brushes panel. In this case, you chose Edit > Undo Apply Pattern Brush instead, because clicking the Remove Brush Stroke button would strip the previous formatting from the path, leaving it with a default fill and stroke.

Working with the Blob Brush tool

You can use the Blob Brush tool () to paint filled shapes that intersect and merge with other shapes of the same color. With the Blob Brush tool, you can draw with Paintbrush tool artistry. Unlike the Paintbrush tool, which lets you create open paths, the Blob Brush tool lets you create a closed shape with a fill only (no stroke) that you can then easily edit with the Eraser or Blob Brush tool. Shapes that have a stroke cannot be edited with the Blob Brush tool.

Path created with the
Paintbrush tool

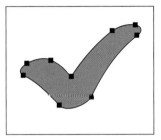

Shape created with the
Blob Brush tool

Drawing with the Blob Brush tool

Next, you'll use the Blob Brush tool to create part of a cloud.

1   Click the Layers panel icon () on the right side of the workspace to expand the Layers panel. Click the eye icon () to the left of the Ship sublayer to hide the contents of the layer. Click the Background sublayer to select it.

2   Change the Fill color to the swatch named "Light Blue," and change the Stroke color to None () in the Control panel.

When drawing with the Blob Brush tool, if a fill and stroke are set before drawing, the stroke color becomes the fill color of the shape made by the Blob Brush tool. If only a fill is set before drawing, it ultimately becomes the fill of the shape created.

3 Click and hold down on the Paintbrush tool ( ) in the Tools panel, and select the Blob Brush tool ( ). Double-click the Blob Brush tool in the Tools panel. In the Blob Brush Tool Options dialog box, select the Keep Selected option, and change the Size to **70 pt** in the Default Brush Options area. Click OK.

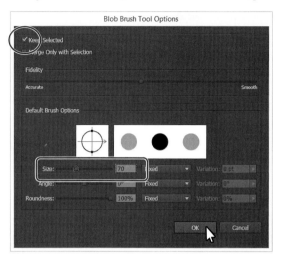

4 Position the pointer to the left of the little blue cloud in the sky. Drag to create a cloud shape that doesn't touch the little cloud to the right of it (see the figure).

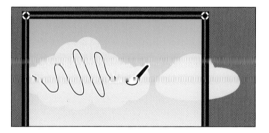

▶ **Tip:** You can also change the Blob Brush size by pressing the right bracket key ( ]) or left bracket key ([ ) several times to increase or decrease the size of brush.

When you draw with the Blob Brush tool, you create filled, closed shapes. Those shapes can contain any type of fill, including gradients, solid colors, patterns, and more. Notice that the Blob Brush pointer has a circle around it before you begin painting. That circle indicates the size of the brush (70 pt, which you set in the previous step).

Merging paths with the Blob Brush tool

In addition to drawing new shapes with the Blob Brush tool, you can use it to intersect and merge shapes of the same color. Objects merged with the Blob Brush tool need to have the same appearance attributes, have no stroke, be on the same layer or group, and be adjacent to each other in the stacking order.

● **Note:** To learn more about Blob Brush tool guidelines, search for "Painting with fills and strokes" in Illustrator Help (Help > Illustrator Help). On that Help page, go to the section titled "Draw and merge paths with the Blob Brush tool."

Next, you will merge the cloud you just created with the little cloud to the right of it to create one big cloud.

1 Choose Select > Deselect.

● **Note:** In the figure, the cloud you drew has a blue outline. You may not see that, and that's okay.

2 With the Blob Brush tool () selected, drag from inside the cloud shape you created to the inside of the little cloud to the right, connecting the two shapes.

● **Note:** If you find that the shapes are not merging, it may be that they have different strokes and fills. You can select both the cloud you created and the small cloud with the Selection tool (▶) and ensure that the Fill color is the light blue swatch and the stroke is None, in the Control panel. Then you can select the Blob Brush tool and try dragging from one cloud to the other.

3 Continue drawing with the Blob Brush tool to make the two clouds look more like a single cloud.

If you find that new shapes are being made instead of the existing cloud shape being edited, undo what you've created. Then, with the Selection tool (▶), reselect and deselect the cloud shape and continue.

4 Choose Select > Deselect, and then choose File > Save.

Editing with the Eraser tool

As you draw and merge shapes with the Blob Brush tool, you may draw too much and want to edit what you've done. You can use the Eraser tool () in combination with the Blob Brush tool to mold the shape and to correct any changes you don't like.

▶ **Tip:** As you draw with the Blob Brush and Eraser tools, it is recommended that you use shorter strokes and release the mouse button often. You can undo the edits that you make, but if you draw in one long stroke without releasing the mouse button, an undo removes the entire stroke.

1   With the Selection tool (▶), click to select the cloud shape.

Selecting the shape(s) before erasing limits the Eraser tool to erasing only the selected shape(s).

2   Double-click the Eraser tool () in the Tools panel. In the Eraser Tool Options dialog box, change the Size to **40 pt**, and click OK.

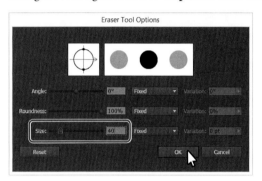

3   Position the pointer over the edge of the cloud shape and, with the Eraser tool, drag along the bottom of the cloud shape to remove some of it. Try switching between the Blob Brush tool and the Eraser tool to edit the cloud.

The Blob Brush and Eraser tools both have pointers that include a circle, indicating the diameter of the brush.

4   Choose Select > Deselect.

5   Click the Layers panel icon () on the right side of the workspace to expand the Layers panel, if necessary. Click the visibility columns to the left of all the sublayers to ensure that they are all showing. Click to select the main layer named "Mask" at the top of the Layers panel. Click the Make/Release Clipping Mask button (⬚) at the bottom of the Layers panel.

By clicking the Make/Release Clipping Mask button, you are taking an existing rectangle shape and using it to mask content. To learn more about masking, see Lesson 14, "Using Illustrator CC with Other Adobe Applications."

6   Click the Layers panel tab to collapse the panel group.

7   Choose Object > Show All to show some poster text.

8   Choose Select > Deselect.

9   Choose File > Save, and close all open files.

Review questions

1 What is the difference between applying a brush to artwork using the Paintbrush tool ( ) and applying a brush to artwork using one of the drawing tools?

2 Describe how artwork in an Art brush is applied to content.

3 Describe how to edit paths with the Paintbrush tool as you draw. How does the Keep Selected option affect the Paintbrush tool?

4 What must be done to a raster image in order for it to be used in certain brushes?

5 For which brush types must you have artwork selected on the artboard before you can create a brush?

6 What does the Blob Brush tool ( ) allow you to create?

Review answers

1 When painting with the Paintbrush tool ( ), if a brush is chosen in the Brushes panel and you draw on the artboard, the brush is applied directly to the paths as you draw. To apply brushes using a drawing tool, you select the tool and draw in the artwork. Then you select the path in the artwork and choose a brush in the Brushes panel. The brush is applied to the selected path.

2 An Art brush is made from artwork (vector or embedded raster). When you apply an Art brush to the stroke of an object, the artwork in the Art brush, by default, is stretched along the selected object stroke.

3 To edit a path with the Paintbrush tool, drag over a selected path to redraw it. The Keep Selected option keeps the last path selected as you draw with the Paintbrush tool. Leave the Keep Selected option selected when you want to easily edit the previous path as you draw. Deselect the Keep Selected option when you want to draw layered paths with the paintbrush without altering previous paths. When Keep Selected is deselected, you can use the Selection tool ( ) to select a path and then edit it.

4 In order to be used in certain brushes (Art, Pattern, and Scatter), a raster image must be embedded.

5 For Art and Scatter brushes, you need to have artwork selected in order to create a brush using the New Brush button ( ) in the Brushes panel.

6 Use the Blob Brush tool ( ) to edit filled shapes that you can intersect and merge with other shapes of the same color or to create artwork from scratch.

12 EXPLORING CREATIVE USES OF EFFECTS AND GRAPHIC STYLES

Lesson overview

In this lesson, you'll learn how to do the following:

- Work with the Appearance panel.

- Edit and apply appearance attributes.

- Copy, disable and enable, and remove appearance attributes.

- Reorder appearance attributes.

- Apply and edit an effect.

- Apply a variety of effects.

- Save and apply an appearance as a graphic style.

- Apply a graphic style to a layer.

- Scale strokes and effects.

 This lesson takes approximately 60 minutes to complete.

Download the project files for this lesson from the Lesson & Update Files tab on your Account page at www.peachpit.com and store them on your computer in a convenient location, as described in the "Getting Started" section of this book.

Your Account page is also where you'll find any updates to the chapters or to the lesson files. Look on the Lesson & Update Files tab to access the most current content.

You can change the look of an object without changing its structure simply by applying attributes, such as fills, strokes, and effects, from the Appearance panel. And because the effects themselves are live, they can be modified or removed at any time. This allows you to save the appearance attributes as graphic styles and apply them to another object.

Getting started

In this lesson, you'll change the appearance of artwork using the Appearance panel, various effects, and graphic styles. Before you begin, you'll need to restore the default preferences for Adobe Illustrator. Then you'll open a file containing the finished artwork to see what you'll create.

1 To ensure that the tools and panels function exactly as described in this lesson, delete or deactivate (by renaming) the Adobe Illustrator CC preferences file. See "Restoring default preferences" in the "Getting Started" section at the beginning of the book.

● **Note:** If you have not already downloaded the project files for this lesson to your computer from your Account page, make sure to do so now. See "Getting Started" at the beginning of the book.

2 Start Adobe Illustrator CC.

3 Choose File > Open, and open the L12_end.ai file in the Lessons > Lesson12 folder on your hard disk.

This file displays a completed illustration of a flyer for a music event.

● **Note:** You will need an Internet connection to sync the font.

4 In the Missing Fonts dialog box that most likely will appear, click Sync Fonts to sync all of the missing fonts from the FranklinGothicURW-Hea family to your computer. After it is synced and you see the message stating that there are no more missing fonts, click Close.

If you can't get the fonts to sync, you can go to the Creative Cloud desktop application and choose Assets > Fonts to see what the issue may be (refer to the section "Changing font family and font style" in Lesson 8, "Adding Type to a Poster," for more information on how to resolve it).

You can also just click Close in the Missing Fonts dialog box and ignore the missing fonts as you proceed. A third method is to click the Find Fonts button in the Missing Fonts dialog box and replace the fonts with a local font on your machine. You can also go to Help (Help > Illustrator Help) and search for "Find missing fonts."

5 Choose View > Zoom Out to make the finished artwork smaller. Adjust the window size, and leave it on your screen as you work. (Use the Hand tool [✋] to move the artwork where you want it in the window.) If you don't want to leave the image open, choose File > Close.

To begin working, you'll open an existing art file.

6 Choose File > Open. If a panel appears, click Open in the panel. You could also choose File > Open again. In the Open dialog box, navigate to the Lessons > Lesson12 folder and select the L12_start.ai file on your hard disk. Click Open to open the file.

● **Note:** For more help on resolving the missing font, refer to step 4.

The L12_start.ai file uses the same FranklinGothicURW-Hea font as the L12_end.ai file. If you synced the font once, you don't need to do it again. If you didn't open the L12_end.ai file, then the Missing Fonts dialog box will most likely will appear for this step. Click Sync Fonts to sync all of the missing fonts from the FranklinGothicURW-Hea family to your computer. After it is synced and you see the message stating that there are no more missing fonts, click Close.

7 Choose File > Save As, name the file **JazzFestival.ai**, and select the Lesson12 folder. Leave the Format option set to Adobe Illustrator (ai) (Mac OS) or the Save As Type option set to Adobe Illustrator (*.AI) (Windows), and then click Save.

8 In the Illustrator Options dialog box, leave the Illustrator options at their default settings, and then click OK.

9 Choose Reset Essentials from the workspace switcher in the Application bar to reset the workspace.

● **Note:** If you don't see Reset Essentials in the workspace switcher menu, choose Window > Workspace > Essentials before choosing Window > Workspace > Reset Essentials.

10 Choose View > Fit Artboard In Window.

Using the Appearance panel

An *appearance attribute* is an aesthetic property—such as a fill, stroke, transparency, or effect—that affects the look of an object but does not affect its basic structure. Up to this point, you've been changing appearance attributes in the Control panel, Swatches panel, and more. These attributes and more can also be found in the Appearance panel for selected artwork. In this lesson, you'll focus on using the Appearance panel to apply and edit appearance attributes.

1   Choose Window > Appearance to see the Appearance panel.

● **Note:** Depending on your operating system, the selection color of objects (the bounding box) may be different colors, and that's okay.

2   Select the Selection tool (▶), and click to select the largest of the shapes that make up the trumpet (see the arrow in the next figure).

The Appearance panel shows what the object is (a Path) and the appearance attributes applied to it (Stroke, Fill, Drop Shadow effect, and Opacity).

The different options available in the Appearance panel are described here:

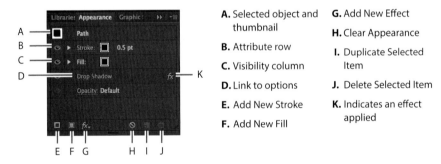

A. Selected object and thumbnail

B. Attribute row

C. Visibility column

D. Link to options

E. Add New Stroke

F. Add New Fill

G. Add New Effect

H. Clear Appearance

I. Duplicate Selected Item

J. Delete Selected Item

K. Indicates an effect applied

The Appearance panel (Window > Appearance) can be used to view and adjust the appearance attributes for a selected object, group, or layer. Fills and strokes are listed in stacking order; top to bottom in the panel correlates to front to back in the artwork. Effects applied to artwork are listed from top to bottom in the order in which they are applied to the artwork. An advantage of using appearance attributes is that they can be changed or removed at any time without affecting the underlying artwork or any other attributes applied to the object in the Appearance panel.

Editing appearance attributes

You'll start by changing the basic appearance of artwork using the Appearance panel.

1   With the trumpet shape still selected (see steps in previous section), choose Select > Same > Fill Color to select the rest of the black trumpet shapes.

Notice that the same appearance properties are listed in the Appearance panel. If you were to select multiple objects that had different fills, for instance, the Appearance panel would show "Mixed Appearance," indicating that the selected artwork has at least one appearance attribute that is different.

2   In the Appearance panel, click the black Fill color box in the Fill attribute row until the Swatches panel appears. Select the swatch named "Trumpet" to apply it to the Fill. Press the Escape key to hide the Swatches panel.

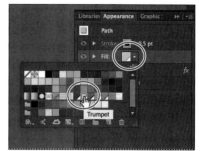

● **Note:** You may need to click the Fill box more than once to open the Swatches panel. The first click on the Fill box selects the Fill row in the panel, and the next click shows the Swatches panel.

You will find that you can change appearance attributes, like Fill color, in the Appearance panel or elsewhere in the workspace.

3   Click the words "0.5 pt" in the Stroke row to show the Stroke Weight option. Change the Stroke weight to **0** to remove it.

4   Click the underlined word "Stroke" to reveal the Stroke panel.

Clicking underlined words in the Appearance panel, as in the Control panel, shows more formatting options—usually a panel such as the Swatches or Stroke panel. Appearance attributes, such as Fill or Stroke, can have other options, such as Opacity or an effect applied to only that attribute. These additional options are listed as a subset under the attribute row and can be shown or hidden by clicking the disclosure triangle (▶) on the left end of the attribute row.

5 Press the Escape key to hide the Stroke panel.

6 Click the disclosure triangle (▶) to the left of the word "Fill" in the Appearance panel to reveal the options for the Fill. Click the word "Opacity" to reveal the Transparency panel. Change the Opacity value to **100%**. Press the Escape key to hide the Transparency panel and to return to the Appearance panel.

The Opacity you just changed affects only the fill of the selected artwork.

7 Click the visibility column (👁) to the left of the Drop Shadow attribute name in the Appearance panel.

Appearance attributes can be deleted or temporarily hidden so that they no longer are applied to the selected artwork.

▶ **Tip:** You may want to drag the bottom of the Appearance panel group up to make it shorter.

8 With the Drop Shadow row selected (click to the right of the link "Drop Shadow" if it isn't selected), click the Delete Selected Item button (🗑) at the bottom of the panel to completely remove the shadow, rather than just turning off the visibility.

Hide the drop shadow.   Delete the drop shadow.

▶ **Tip:** You can view all hidden attributes by choosing Show All Hidden Attributes from the Appearance panel menu (☰).

9 With the trumpet shapes still selected, choose Object > Group, and leave the new group selected for the next section.

In the Appearance panel, the word "Group" appears at the top. With the group selected, you can now apply appearance attributes to the group, and they will appear in the panel. The word "Contents" also appears below the word "Group." If you were to double-click the word "Contents" in the Appearance panel, you would see the appearance attributes of the individual items in the group.

Adding another stroke and fill

Artwork in Illustrator can have more than one stroke and fill applied to it to add interesting design elements. You'll now add another fill to an object using the Appearance panel.

1   With the trumpet group still selected, click the Add New Fill button (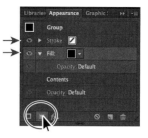) at the bottom of the Appearance panel.

● **Note:** The figure has the Fill row toggled open revealing the content. Yours may not look like that, and that's okay.

The figure shows what the panel looks like after clicking the Add New Fill button. New Stroke and Fill rows are added to the Appearance panel and are applied to the group as a whole (in this case). The fill and stroke attributes tend to be applied on top of the fill and stroke attributes applied to the individual objects in the group.

2   Click the black Fill color box in the Fill attribute row until the Swatches panel appears. Click the pattern swatch named "Paper" to apply it to the Fill. Press the Escape key to hide the Swatches panel.

3   Click the disclosure triangle (▶) to the left of the word "Fill," if necessary, to show the Opacity option. Click the word "Opacity" (under the Fill row) to show the Transparency panel, and choose Multiply from the Blending Mode menu.

▶ **Tip:** Other ways to close panels that appear when clicking an underlined word, like "Stroke," include pressing the Escape key, clicking the Stroke attribute row, or by pressing Return.

In the Appearance panel, appearance attributes with a disclosure triangle have options such as Opacity that affect only that appearance attribute.

Change the fill.

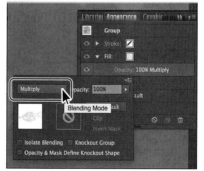

Edit the blending mode of the fill.

4   Choose Select > Deselect, and then choose File > Save.

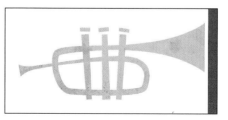

Now you'll add another stroke to text using the Appearance panel. This can be a great way to achieve interesting design effects with just one object.

5 In the Layers panel (Window > Layers), click the visibility column to the left of the Text layer to show its contents.

6 Select the Type tool (**T**) in the Tools panel, and click twice on the black "JAZZ" text to select it.

In the Appearance panel, notice the Stroke (none) and the Fill (black). Also notice that you cannot add another stroke or fill to the text since the Add New Stroke and Add New Fill buttons are dimmed at the bottom of the panel.

7 Select the Selection tool and notice that "Type" shows at the top of the Appearance panel.

With the type object selected (and not the text), you can now add multiple fills and strokes to text.

● **Note:** I dragged the bottom of the Appearance panel down to see more of the appearance attributes.

8 Click the Add New Fill button (▣) at the bottom of the Appearance panel.

A new fill row and stroke row are added above the word "Characters" in the Appearance panel. The "Characters" content is the formatting for the text within the text object.

9 With the new Fill attribute row selected, click the black Fill color box and select the blue/green gradient swatch named "Jazz." This new fill will cover the existing black text fill. Press the Escape key to hide the swatches.

10 Click the Add New Fill button () at the bottom of the Appearance panel once more to add another fill.

A duplicate of the existing Fill row appears.

11 Click the bottom Fill attribute row to select it. Click the Fill color box, and select the pattern swatch named "Paper." Press the Escape key to hide the swatches.

Notice that the paper swatch doesn't show in the artwork. That's because it is beneath the Fill attribute row with the "Jazz" gradient applied. As mentioned earlier, the ordering of the attribute rows is important, much like the ordering of layers is important. The top appearance row shows on top of the appearance attributes beneath it.

12 Click the disclosure triangle (▼) to the left of all the appearance rows in the Appearance panel to hide their properties.

▶ **Tip:** Depending on which attribute row is selected in the Attributes panel, the options in panels, such as the Control panel, Gradient panel, and others, will affect the attribute selected.

Reordering appearance attributes

The ordering of the appearance attribute rows can greatly change how your artwork looks. In the Appearance panel, fills and strokes are listed in stacking order—top to bottom in the panel correlates to front to back in the artwork. You can reorder attribute rows in a way similar to dragging layers in the Layers panel to rearrange the stacking order. Next, you'll change the appearance of the artwork by reordering attributes in the Appearance panel.

Tip: You can also apply blending modes and opacity changes to each Fill row to achieve different results.

1 Drag the bottom Fill attribute row (with the Paper pattern swatch applied) up above the original Fill attribute row with the blue/green gradient.

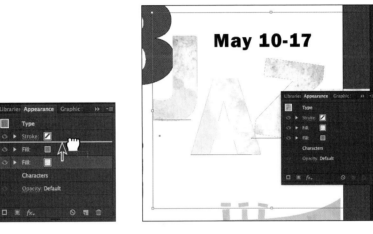

Moving the new Fill attribute above the original Fill attribute changes the look of the artwork. The pattern fill is now covering the gradient fill.

2 Click the disclosure triangle to the left of the Fill attribute row that has the "Paper" pattern fill. Click the word "Opacity" to show the Transparency panel, and choose Multiply from the Blending Mode menu.

3 Choose Select > Deselect, and then choose File > Save.

Now that you've begun to explore the options in the Appearance panel, you'll begin adding effects to the artwork and use the Appearance panel for those as well.

Applying an appearance attribute to a layer

You can also apply appearance attributes to layers or sublayers. For example, to make everything on a layer 50% opaque, you can target that layer and change the opacity. Every object on that layer will have the 50% opacity applied (even if you add the object to the layer later).

For more information on applying an appearance attribute to a layer, check out the section "Applying appearance attributes to layers" in Lesson 9, "Organizing Your Artwork with Layers."

Using live effects

Effects alter the appearance of an object without changing the underlying artwork. Applying an effect adds the effect to the object's appearance attribute, which you can edit, move, delete, or duplicate, at any time, in the Appearance panel.

There are two types of effects in Illustrator: *vector effects* and *raster effects*. In Illustrator, click the Effect menu item to see the different types of effects available.

Artwork with a Drop Shadow effect applied.

● **Note:** When you apply a raster effect, the original vector data is rasterized using the document's raster effects settings, which determine the resolution of the resulting image. To learn about document raster effects settings, search for "Document raster effects settings" in Illustrator Help.

- **Illustrator Effects (vector):** The top half of the Effect menu contains vector effects. You can apply these effects only to vector objects or to the fill or stroke of a bitmap object in the Appearance panel. The following vector effects can be applied to both vector and bitmap objects: 3D effects, SVG filters, Warp effects, Transform effects, Drop Shadow, Feather, Inner Glow, and Outer Glow.

- **Photoshop Effects (raster):** The bottom half of the Effect menu contains raster effects. You can apply them to either vector or bitmap objects.

In this section, you will first explore how to apply and edit effects. You will then explore a few of the more widely used effects in Illustrator to get an idea for the range of effects available.

Applying an effect

Effects are applied using the Effect menu or the Appearance panel and can be applied to objects, groups, or layers. You are first going to learn how to apply an effect using the Effect menu, and then you will apply an effect using the Appearance panel.

● **Note:** You may find it difficult to select the trumpet group with the other artwork showing and on top.

1   With the Selection tool (▶) selected, click the trumpet group on the artboard.

2   Choose Effect > Stylize > Drop Shadow from the Illustrator Effects section of the menu that appears.

3   In the Drop Shadow dialog box, change the following options:

- Mode: **Multiply** (the default setting)
- Opacity: **100%**
- X Offset: **.03 in**
- Y Offset: **.03 in**
- Blur: **.04 in**
- Darkness: **Selected**, **50%**

4   Select Preview to see the drop shadow applied to the artwork. Click OK.

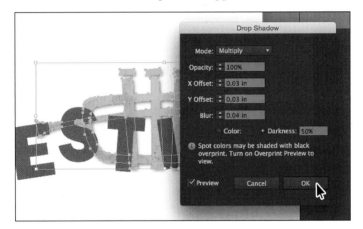

5   Choose File > Save, and leave the trumpet group selected.

Editing an effect

Effects are live, so they can be edited after they are applied to an object. You can edit the effect in the Appearance panel by selecting the object with the effect applied and then either clicking the name of the effect or double-clicking the attribute row in the Appearance panel. This displays the dialog box for that effect. Changes you make to the effect update in the artwork. In this section, you will edit the Drop Shadow effect applied to the trumpet group.

1   With the trumpet group still selected and the Appearance panel showing, click the orange text "Drop Shadow" in the Appearance panel.

2   In the Drop Shadow dialog box, change Opacity to **75%**. Select Preview to see the change, and then click OK.

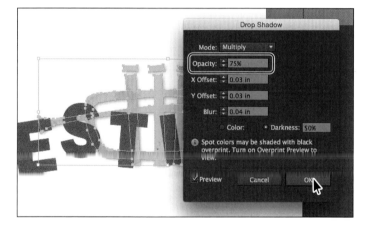

3   Choose Object > Ungroup to ungroup the trumpet shapes.

Notice that the drop shadow is no longer applied to the trumpet group. When an effect is applied to a group, it affects the group as a whole. If the objects are no longer grouped together, the effect is no longer applied.

▶ **Tip:** In the Appearance panel, you can drag an attribute row, such as Drop Shadow, to the Delete Selected Item button (🗑) to delete it, or you can select the attribute row and click the Delete Selected Item button.

4   Choose Edit > Undo Ungroup to regroup the artwork and apply the drop shadow again.

Styling text with a Warp effect

Text can have all sorts of effects applied, including a Warp, like you saw in Lesson 8, "Adding Type to a Poster." Next, you will use a Warp effect to warp the date text. The difference between the Warp you applied in Lesson 8 and this Warp effect is that this Warp is an effect and can be turned on and off, edited, or removed easily.

1   With the Selection tool (▶) selected, select the text "May 10-17."

2   Choose Effect > Warp > Flag.

3   In the Warp Options dialog box, to create an arcing effect, set Bend to **20%**. Select Preview to preview the changes. Try choosing other styles from the Style menu, and then return to Flag. Try adjusting the Horizontal and Vertical Distortion sliders to see the effect. Make sure that the Distortion values are returned to **0**, and then click OK.

4   With the warped text object still selected, click the visibility icon (◉) to the left of the "Warp: Flag" row in the Appearance panel to turn off visibility for the effect. Notice that the text is no longer warped on the artboard (see the following figure).

5   Select the Type tool (**T**) in the Tools panel, select the text "10-17" on the artboard, and change it to **10-18**.

6   Select all of the text "May 10-18," and change the Fill color to White in the Control panel.

If the Appearance panel is still open and the cursor is in the text, notice that the effect isn't listed in the panel. That's because the effect was applied to the type area, not to the text within.

7 Select the Selection tool (▸) in the Tools panel. Click the visibility column to the left of the Warp: Flag row in the Appearance panel to turn on visibility for the effect so that the text is once again warped.

Since the text is white on a white background (for now), you won't be able to see the warp.

8 Choose Select > Deselect, and then choose File > Save.

Applying the Offset Path effect

Next, you will offset the stroke for the "JAZZ" text. This process allows you to create the appearance of multiple stacked shapes.

1 With the Selection tool (▸) selected, click the "JAZZ" text object to select it.

2 Click the Stroke color (▨) in the Appearance panel, and make sure that the White swatch is selected in the Swatches panel. Press Enter or Return to close the Swatches panel, and return to the Appearance panel.

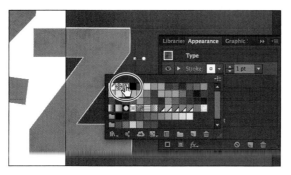

3 Make sure that the Stroke weight is **1 pt**.

4 With the Stroke attribute row selected in the Appearance panel, choose Effect > Path > Offset Path.

5 In the Offset Path dialog box, change the Offset to **−0.04 in**, select Preview, and then click OK.

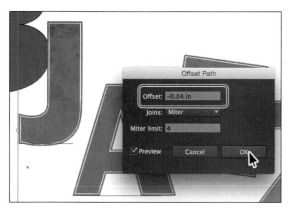

6 In the Appearance panel, click the disclosure triangle to the left of the words "Stroke: 1 pt" to toggle it open (if it's not already open).

Notice that the "Offset Path" effect is a subset of Stroke. This indicates that the Offset Path effect is applied to only that Stroke.

7 Choose Select > Deselect, and then choose File > Save.

Applying a Photoshop Effect

As described earlier in the lesson, raster effects generate pixels rather than vector data. Raster effects include SVG Filters, all of the effects in the bottom portion of the Effect menu, and the Drop Shadow, Inner Glow, Outer Glow, and Feather commands in the Effect > Stylize submenu. You can apply them to either vector or bitmap objects.

Next, you will apply a Photoshop effect (raster) to the "FESTIVAL" text.

1 With the Selection tool (▶), click to select the "FESTIVAL" text.

2 Choose Effect > Texture > Texturizer.

When you choose most of the raster (Photoshop) effects (not all), the Filter Gallery dialog box opens. Similar to working with filters in Adobe Photoshop, where you can also access a Filter Gallery, in the Illustrator Filter Gallery, you can try different raster effects to see how they affect your artwork.

3 With the Filter Gallery dialog box open, you can see the type of filter (Texturizer) showing at the top. Choose Fit In View from the view menu in the lower-left corner of the dialog box. That should fit the artwork in the preview area, so you can see how the effect alters the artwork.

The Filter Gallery dialog box, which is resizable, contains a preview area (labeled A), effect thumbnails that you can click to apply (labeled B), settings for the currently selected effect (labeled C), and the list of effects applied (labeled D). If you want to apply a different effect, expand a category in the middle panel of the dialog box, click a thumbnail, or choose an effect name from the menu in the upper-right corner of the dialog box.

4   Change the Texturizer settings in the upper-right corner of the dialog box as follows (if necessary):

- Texture: **Canvas** (the default setting)
- Scaling: **110**
- Relief: **5**
- Light: **Top** (the default setting)

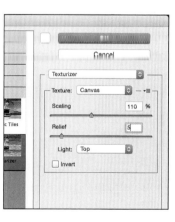

● **Note:** The Filter Gallery lets you apply only one effect at a time. If you want to apply multiple Photoshop effects, you can click OK to apply the current effect and then choose another from the Effect menu.

5   Click OK to apply the raster effect.

▶ **Tip:** You can click the eye icon ( ) to the left of the name Texturizer in the section labeled "D" above to see the artwork without the effect applied.

Working with 3D effects

Using Illustrator 3D effects, you can create three-dimensional (3D) objects from your two-dimensional (2D) artwork. You can control the appearance of 3D objects with lighting, shading, rotation, and other attributes, such as mapping artwork to each surface of the three-dimensional object (mapping is allowed with Extrude & Bevel or Revolve). There are three 3D effects that you can apply to artwork: Extrude & Bevel, Revolve, and Rotate. The following are visual examples of each type of 3D effect.

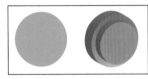  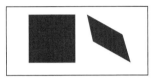

Extrude & Bevel 3D effect   Revolve 3D effect   Rotate 3D effect

Applying a 3D Rotate effect

The Rotate effect is a simple way to rotate artwork in 3D. Next, you are going to rotate the "JAZZ" text.

1   With the Selection tool (▶), click to select the JAZZ text object.

2   Choose Effect > 3D > Rotate.

3   In the 3D Rotate Options dialog box, set the following options:

● **Note:** 3D objects may display anti-aliasing artifacts onscreen, but these artifacts generally won't print or appear in artwork optimized for the web.

- X axis: **10°**
- Y axis: **–20°**
- Z axis: **10°**
- Perspective: **0°** (the default setting)
- Surface: **No Shading** (the default setting)

4   Select Preview to see the effect applied (if it's not selected).

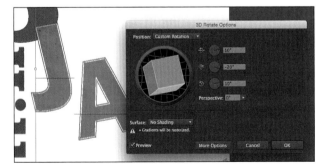

Notice the warning near the bottom of the 3D Rotate Options dialog box that states "Gradients will be rasterized." This means that the gradient used in the "JAZZ" text fill will be rasterized (that is, displayed and printed as a bitmap graphic). The resolution (PPI) of the rasterized portion of the artwork is based on the settings in the Document Raster Effects Settings dialog box (Effect > Document Raster Effects Settings).

5   Click and drag the left edge of the face of the track cube (it's blue in color) to the right (see the figure). Notice the text rotate as you drag.

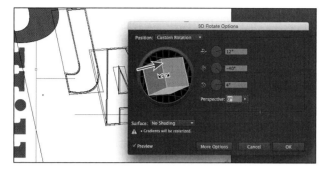

Note: Depending on the speed of the computer you are working on and the amount of RAM available, it may take some time to process changes made. If that's the case, you can deselect Preview, change the options, and then select Preview at the end.

For unconstrained rotation, you can drag a track cube face. The front of the object is represented by the track cube's blue face, the object's top and bottom faces are light gray, the sides are medium gray, and the back face is dark gray.

6   Choose Off-Axis Front from the Position menu, and click OK.

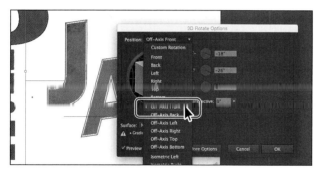

7   With the Selection tool, drag the text up to position it, like you see in the following figure.

8   Choose Select > Deselect, and then choose File > Save.

Note: Notice that every time you release the mouse button, Illustrator needs to process the change and redraw the 3D text. You will not see the 3D text as you drag; instead, you will see the text without the effect.

Using graphic styles

A *graphic style* is a saved set of appearance attributes that you can reuse. By applying graphic styles, you can quickly and globally change the appearance of objects and text.

The Graphic Styles panel (Window > Graphic Styles) lets you create, name, save, apply, and remove effects and attributes for objects, layers, and groups. You can also break the link between an object and an applied graphic style to edit that object's attributes without affecting other objects that use the same graphic style.

The different options available in the Graphic Styles panel are described here:

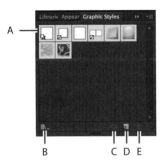

A. Graphic Style thumbnail

B. Graphic Styles Libraries menu

C. Break Link To Graphic Style

D. New Graphic Style

E. Delete Graphic Style

For example, if you have a map that uses a shape to represent a city, you can create a graphic style that paints the shape green and adds a drop shadow. You can then use that graphic style to paint all the city shapes on the map. If you decide to use a different color, you can change the fill color of the graphic style to blue. All the objects that use that graphic style are then updated to blue.

Applying an existing graphic style

You can apply graphic styles to your artwork from graphic style libraries that come with Illustrator. Now you'll add a graphic style to some of the text in the design.

1   Click the Graphic Styles panel tab. Click the Graphic Styles Libraries Menu button (■) at the bottom of the panel, and choose Vonster Pattern Styles.

> ▶ **Tip:** Use the arrows at the bottom of the Vonster Pattern Styles library panel to load the previous or next Graphic Styles library in the panel.

2   With the Selection tool (▶), select the number 3 shape in the upper-left corner of the artboard. Make sure not to select the "JAZZ" text.

3   Click the "Alyssa 1" graphic style in the Vonster Pattern Styles panel. Close the Vonster Pattern Styles panel.

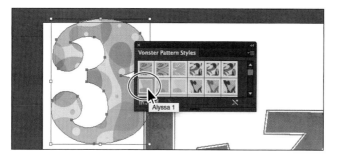

Clicking that style applies the appearance attributes to the selected "3" artwork and adds the graphic style to the Graphic Styles panel for the active document.

4 With the number 3 still selected, look in the Appearance panel to see the stroke and multiple fills applied to the selected artwork. Also notice Path: Alyssa 1 at the top of the panel. This indicates that the graphic style Alyssa 1 is applied.

Note: You may see a warning icon appear on the left end of the Control panel. That's okay. This is a helpful indicator that the topmost fill/stroke is not active in the Appearance panel.

5 Click the Graphics Style panel tab to show the panel again.

6 With the Selection tool, select the JAZZ text, and then right-click and hold down the mouse button on the Alyssa 1 graphic style thumbnail in the Graphic Styles panel to preview the graphic style on the artwork. When you're finished previewing, release the mouse button.

Previewing a graphic style is a great way to see how it will affect the selected object, without actually applying it.

7 Choose File > Save.

Creating and applying a graphic style

Now you'll create a new graphic style and apply that graphic style to artwork.

1 Click the number 3 again, and click the Appearance panel tab to show the panel. Click the Add New Fill button (▣) at the bottom of the Appearance panel.

There should now be a total of three fills applied to the number 3. Also notice that Alyssa 1 is gone from the Path toward the top of the panel. This means that the graphic style is no longer applied to the artwork. The number 3 will not update if the Alyssa 1 graphic style is edited.

Note: You can drag the bottom of the Appearance panel down to see more of the attributes.

2 Make the following changes to the Fill attribute rows, using the figure as a guide:

- **Top Fill attribute row:** Click the Fill color, and select the pattern swatch named "Lines." Press the Escape key to hide the swatches.

- **Middle Fill attribute row:** Click the Fill color, and select the pattern swatch named "Paper." Click the disclosure triangle to the left of the same Fill row, and click the Opacity link below the Paper fill row to show the Transparency panel. Choose Luminosity from the Blending Mode menu. Press the Escape key to hide the Transparency panel.

- **Bottom Fill attribute row:** Click the Fill color, and select the orange swatch named "Festival." Press the Escape key to hide the swatches.

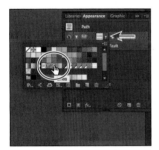
Top Fill attribute row

Middle Fill attribute row

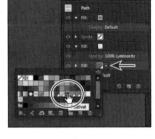
Bottom Fill attribute row

The number 3 should now have a series of textures and an orange color applied to the fill. Remember that the order of the attribute rows in the Appearance panel is important. This is especially important when you change the Opacity blending modes and want to blend the appearance attributes to achieve certain visual effects. Blending modes affect attribute rows below the attribute row that the blend mode is applied to in the Appearance panel.

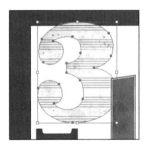

▶ **Tip:** To create a graphic style, you can also click to select the object that you are using to make the graphic style. In the Appearance panel, drag the appearance thumbnail at the top of the listing into the Graphic Styles panel. The panels can't be in the same panel group.

3 Leave the number 3 shape selected.

4 Click the Graphic Styles panel tab to show the Graphic Styles panel. Click the New Graphic Style button (▢) at the bottom of the panel.

The appearance attributes from the number 3 artwork are saved as a graphic style.

5 In the Graphic Styles panel, double-click the new graphic style thumbnail. In the Graphic Style Options dialog box, name the new style **Number**. Click OK.

6 Click the Appearance panel tab, and at the top of the Appearance panel you will see "Path: Number."

This indicates that a graphic style named Number is applied to the selected artwork (a path). You could now apply the Number graphic style to other artwork.

7 Open the Layers panel (Window > Layers), and click the visibility column for the Background layer to show the black shape behind the other content on the artboard. Click the lock icon in the edit column to unlock the Background layer as well.

8 With the Selection tool, click the black rectangle in the background. In the Graphic Styles panel, click the graphic style named "Number" to apply the styling.

9 Choose Select > Deselect, and then choose File > Save.

Applying a graphic style to text

When you apply a graphic style to a type area, the fill color of the graphic style overrides the fill color of the text by default. If you deselect Override Character Color from the Graphic Styles panel menu (⊟), the fill color (if there is one) in the text will override the color of the graphic style.

If you choose Use Text For Preview from the Graphic Styles panel menu (⊟), you can then right-click and hold down the mouse button on a graphic style to preview the graphic style on the text.

Updating a graphic style

Once you create a graphic style, you can still edit the object that the style is applied to. You can also update a graphic style, and all artwork with that style applied will update its appearance as well.

● **Note:** The number 3 may be difficult to see since it has the same fill as the background shape.

1   With the Selection tool (▶) selected, click the number 3 to select it.

Look in the Graphic Styles panel; you will see that the Number graphic style thumbnail is highlighted (has a border around it), indicating that it is applied.

2   Click the Appearance panel tab. Notice the text "Path: Number" at the top of the panel, indicating that the Number graphic style is applied. This is another way to tell whether a graphic style is applied to selected artwork.

3   Click the Fill color for the bottom appearance row (the one with the orange color). Select the purple swatch named "Hills." Press the Escape key to hide the swatches.

Notice that the "Path: Number" text at the top of the Appearance panel is now just "Path," telling you that the graphic style is no longer applied to the selected artwork.

4   Click the Graphic Styles panel tab to see that the Number graphic style no longer has a highlight (border) around it, which means that the graphic style is no longer applied.

5 Press the Option (Mac OS) or Alt (Windows) key, and drag the selected number 3 shape on top of the Number graphic-style thumbnail in the Graphic Styles panel. Release the mouse button, and then release the modifier key when the thumbnail is highlighted. The number 3 and the background rectangle now look the same since the Number graphic style has been applied to both objects.

6 Choose Select > Deselect.

7 Click the Appearance panel tab. You will see "No Selection: Number" at the top of the panel (you may need to scroll up).

When you apply appearance settings, graphic styles, and more to artwork, the next shape you draw will have the appearance settings listed in the Appearance panel.

8 Click to select the rectangle in the background that has the Number graphic style applied.

Next, you will remove all formatting from the rectangle and then add a black fill again.

9 Click the Clear Appearance button () at the bottom of the Appearance panel.

▶ **Tip:** If you were to click the Clear Appearance button with nothing selected, you would set the default appearance for new artwork to no fill and no stroke.

● **Note:** The figure shows the result after clicking the Clear Appearance button

With artwork selected, the Clear Appearance button removes all appearance attributes applied to selected artwork, including any stroke or fill.

10 Click the Fill color for the Fill appearance row, and in the Swatches panel that appears, select the Black swatch.

11 Choose Select > Deselect, and then choose File > Save.

Applying a graphic style to a layer

When a graphic style is applied to a layer, everything added to that layer has that same style applied to it. Now you'll apply a Drop Shadow graphic style that comes with Illustrator to the Text layer; this will apply the style to all the contents of that layer at once.

● **Note:** If you apply a graphic style to artwork and then apply a graphic style to the layer (or sublayer) that it's on, the graphic style formatting is added to the appearance of the artwork—it's cumulative. This can change the artwork in ways you didn't expect since applying a graphic style to the layer will be added to the formatting of the artwork.

1 In Layers panel, click the target icon (◉) for the Text layer.

This selects the layer content and targets the layer for any appearance attributes.

▶ **Tip:** In the Layers panel, you can drag a target icon to the Trash button (🗑) at the bottom of the Layers panel to remove the appearance attributes.

2 Click the Graphic Styles panel icon (), and then click the Drop Shadow graphic style thumbnail to apply the style to the layer and all its contents.

The target icon in the Layers panel for the Text layer is now shaded.

3 Click the Appearance panel tab, and you should see, with all of the artwork on the Text layer still selected, the words "Layer: Drop Shadow."

This is telling you that the layer target icon is selected in the Layers panel and that the Drop Shadow graphic style is applied to that layer.

▶ **Tip:** In the Graphic Styles panel, graphic-style thumbnails that show a small box with a red slash (⬜) indicate that the graphic style does not contain a stroke or fill. It may just be a drop shadow or outer glow, for instance.

4 Choose Select > Deselect, and then choose File > Save.

Applying multiple graphic styles

You can apply a graphic style to an object that already has a graphic style applied. This can be useful if you want to add properties to an object from another graphic style. After you apply a graphic style to selected artwork, you can then Option-click (Mac OS) or Alt-click (Windows) another graphic style thumbnail to add the graphic style formatting to the existing formatting, rather than replacing it.

Scaling strokes and effects

In Illustrator, when scaling (resizing) content, any strokes and effects that are applied do not change. For instance, suppose you scale a circle with a 2-pt. stroke from small to the size of the artboard. The shape may change size, but the stroke will remain 2 pt. by default. That can change the appearance of scaled artwork in a way that you didn't intend, so you'll need to watch out for that when transforming artwork. Next, you will make the trumpet group larger, but you will also scale the drop shadow effect applied to it proportionally.

1 Click the trumpet group to select it.

Note: If you choose Window > Transform to open the Transform panel, you may need to choose Show Options from the panel menu.

2 Click X, Y, W, or H in the Control panel to reveal the Transform panel (Window > Transform), and make the following edits in the panel:

- Select Scale Strokes & Effects at the bottom of the Transform panel.

- Click the Constrain Width And Height Proportions button () to ensure it's active.

- Change the Width (W) to **12.7 in**. Press the Tab key to tab to the next field. The height should change proportionally with the width.

Note: If you were to open the Drop Shadow options in the Appearance panel for the trumpet group, you would see that the values have adjusted according to the sizing. If Scale Strokes & Effects weren't selected, the drop shadow values would be the same before and after the transformation.

3 Choose Select > Deselect.

4 Choose File > Save, and then choose File > Close.

Review questions

1 How do you add a second stroke to artwork?

2 What's the difference between applying a graphic style to a *layer* versus applying it to *selected artwork*?

3 Name two ways to apply an effect to an object.

4 When you apply a Photoshop (raster) effect to vector artwork, what happens to the artwork?

5 Where can you access the options for effects applied to an object?

Review answers

1 To add a second stroke to an object, click the Add New Stroke button (■) in the Appearance panel, or choose Add New Stroke from the Appearance panel menu. A stroke is added to the top of the appearance list. It has the same color and stroke weight as the original.

2 When a style is applied to a single object, other objects on that layer are not affected. For example, if a triangle object has a Roughen effect applied to its path and you move it to another layer, it retains the Roughen effect.

   After a graphic style is applied to a layer, everything you add to the layer has that style applied to it. For example, if you create a circle on Layer 1 and then move that circle to Layer 2, which has a Drop Shadow effect applied, the circle adopts that effect.

3 You can apply an effect to an object by selecting the object and then choosing the effect from the Effect menu. You can also apply an effect by selecting the object, clicking the Add New Effect button (*fx.*) at the bottom of the Appearance panel, and then choosing the effect from the menu that appears.

4 Applying a Photoshop effect to artwork generates pixels rather than vector data. Photoshop effects include SVG Filters, all of the effects in the bottom portion of the Effect menu, and the Drop Shadow, Inner Glow, Outer Glow, and Feather commands in the Effect > Stylize submenu. You can apply them to either vector or bitmap objects.

5 You can edit effects applied to selected artwork by clicking the effect link in the Appearance panel to access the effect options.

13 CREATING ARTWORK FOR A T-SHIRT

Lesson overview

In this lesson, you'll learn how to do the following:

- Work with existing symbols.

- Create, modify, and redefine a symbol.

- Store and retrieve artwork in the Symbols panel.

- Understand Creative Cloud Libraries.

- Work with Creative Cloud Libraries.

- Understand perspective drawing.

- Use grid presets and adjust the grid.

- Draw and transform content in perspective.

- Edit grid planes and content.

- Create text and bring it into perspective.

 This lesson takes approximately 60 minutes to complete.

Download the project files for this lesson from the Lesson & Update Files tab on your Account page at www.peachpit.com and store them on your computer in a convenient location, as described in the "Getting Started" section of this book.

Your Account page is also where you'll find any updates to the chapters or to the lesson files. Look on the Lesson & Update Files tab to access the most current content.

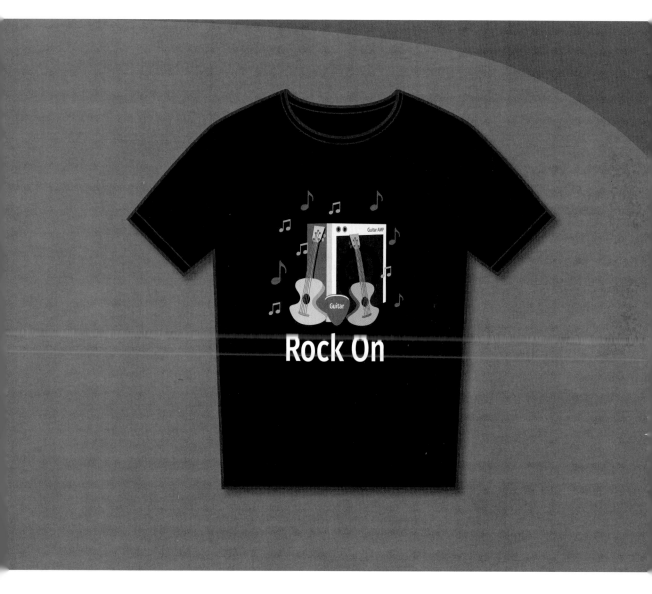

In this lesson, you'll explore a variety of useful concepts, including using symbols and the Symbols panel, working with Libraries to make your design assets available anywhere, and finally understanding how to work with the perspective grid to render artwork in perspective.

Getting started

In this lesson, you'll explore several concepts such as symbols, the Libraries panel, and working with the perspective grid by creating artwork for a T-shirt. Before you begin, you'll restore the default preferences for Adobe Illustrator. Then, you'll open the finished art file for this lesson to see what you'll create.

● **Note:** If you have not already downloaded the project files for this lesson to your computer from your Account page, make sure to do so now. See the "Getting Started" section at the beginning of this book.

● **Note:** If the Missing Fonts dialog box appears, click Close.

1 To ensure that the tools and panels function exactly as described in this lesson, delete or deactivate (by renaming) the Adobe Illustrator CC preferences file. See "Restoring default preferences" in the "Getting Started" section at the beginning of the book.

2 Start Adobe Illustrator CC.

3 Choose File > Open, and open the L13_end.ai file in the Lessons > Lesson13 folder on your hard disk.

You are going to create artwork for a T-shirt design.

4 Choose View > Fit Artboard In Window and leave the file open for reference, or choose File > Close.

5 Choose File > Open. If a panel appears, click Open in the panel. You could also choose File > Open again. In the Open dialog box, navigate to the Lessons > Lesson13 folder and select the L13_start.ai file on your hard disk. Click Open to open the file.

6 Choose View > Fit All In Window.

7 Choose File > Save As. In the Save As dialog box, navigate to the Lesson13 folder, and name the file **TShirt.ai**. Leave the Format option set to Adobe Illustrator (ai) (Mac OS) or the Save As Type option set to Adobe Illustrator (*.AI) (Windows), and then click Save.

8 In the Illustrator Options dialog box, leave the Illustrator options at their default settings, and then click OK.

9 Choose Reset Essentials from the workspace switcher in the Application bar.

● **Note:** If you don't see Reset Essentials in the menu, choose Window > Workspace > Essentials before choosing Window > Workspace > Reset Essentials.

Working with symbols

A *symbol* is a reusable art object that is stored in the Symbols panel (Window > Symbols). For example, if you create a symbol from a fish you drew, you can then quickly add multiple *instances* of that fish symbol to your artwork, which saves you from having to draw each fish again. All instances in the document are linked to the original symbol in the Symbols panel. When you edit the original symbol, all instances of the fish that are linked to it are updated. You can turn that fish from blue to green instantly! Not only do symbols save time, but they also greatly reduce file size.

Click the Symbols panel icon (⬛) on the right side of the workspace. The different options available in the Symbols panel are described here:

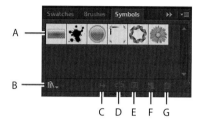

A. Symbol thumbnail

B. Symbol Libraries Menu

C. Place Symbol Instance

D. Break Link To Symbol

E. Symbol Options

F. New Symbol

G. Delete Symbol

● **Note:** The figure shows the default Symbols panel with a print document displaying in the Document window.

Illustrator comes with a series of symbol libraries, which range from tiki icons to hair to web icons. You can access those symbol libraries in the Symbols panel or by choosing Window > Symbol Libraries and easily incorporate them into your own artwork.

Using existing Illustrator symbol libraries

You will start by adding a symbol from an existing symbol library to the artwork.

1 Open the Artboards panel by choosing Window > Artboards. Double-click the "2" to the left of the name "T-Shirt" to show the middle artboard.

2 Choose View > Smart Guides to deselect (turn off) the Smart Guides.

3 Click the Layers panel tab to show the Layers panel. Click the Content layer to make sure it is selected. Make sure that both of the layers are collapsed by clicking the disclosure triangles to the left of the layer names (if necessary).

When adding symbols to a document, the layer that is selected when they are added is the same layer they become a part of.

4 Click the Symbols panel icon (⬛) on the right side of the workspace to show the panel.

5 In the Symbols panel, click the Symbol Libraries Menu button () at the bottom of the panel, and choose Tiki.

The Tiki library opens as a free-floating panel. This library is external to the file that you are working on, but you can import any of the symbols into the document and use them in the artwork.

▶ **Tip:** If you want to see the symbol names along with the symbol pictures, click the Symbols panel menu icon (▤), and then choose Small List View or Large List View.

6 Position the pointer over the symbols in the Tiki panel to see their names as tooltips. Click the symbol named "Guitar" to add it to the Symbols panel for the document. Close the Tiki panel.

Every document has a default set of symbols in the Symbols panel. When you add symbols to the panel, as you just did, they are saved with the active document only.

▶ **Tip:** You can also copy a symbol instance on the artboard and paste as many as you need. This is the same as dragging a symbol instance out of the Symbols panel onto the artboard.

7 Using the Selection tool (➤), drag the Guitar symbol from the Symbols panel onto the artboard into the center of the black T-shirt. Do this twice to create two instances of the guitar on the T-shirt.

Each time you drag a symbol onto the artboard, an *instance* of the Guitar symbol is created. Next, you will resize one of the symbol instances on the page.

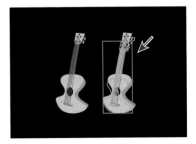

● **Note:** Although you can transform symbol instances in many ways, specific properties of instances from static symbols like the guitar cannot be edited. For example, the fill color is locked because it is controlled by the original symbol in the Symbols panel.

8 Click to select the Guitar instance on the right, if it's not already selected. Shift-drag the upper-right bounding point of the selected Guitar symbol instance toward the center to make it a little smaller, while constraining its proportions. Release the mouse button, and then release the Shift key.

A symbol instance is treated like a group of objects and can have only certain transformation and appearance properties changed (such as scale, rotate, move, transparency, etc). You cannot edit the individual artwork that makes up an instance without breaking the link to the original symbol. With the symbol instance still selected on the artboard, notice that, in the Control panel, you see the word "Symbol" and symbol-related options.

9   With the same instance still selected, choose Object > Transform > Reflect. In the Reflect dialog box, select Vertical, and then select Preview. Click OK.

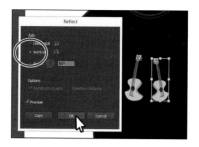

Editing a symbol

In this next section, you will edit the Guitar symbol, and all instances in the document will be updated. There are several ways to edit a symbol, and in this section you will focus on one.

1   With the Selection tool (▶) selected, double-click the Guitar symbol instance you just resized. A warning dialog box appears, stating that you are about to edit the original symbol and that all instances will update. Click OK to continue.

This takes you into Symbol Editing mode, so you can't edit any other objects on the page. The Guitar symbol instance you double-clicked will appear larger and will no longer be reflected. That's because in Symbol Editing mode, you are looking at the original symbol artwork. You can now edit the artwork that makes up the symbol.

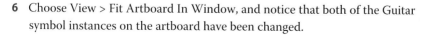

3   Select the Direct Selection tool (▶), and click to select the blue neck of the guitar artwork. See the figure.

4   Change the Fill color to the brown swatch with the tooltip "C=30 M=50 Y=75 K=10" in the Control panel.

5   Double-click away from the symbol content, or click the Exit Symbol Editing Mode button (◀) in the upper-left corner of the artboard until you exit Symbol Editing mode so that you can edit the rest of the content.

6   Choose View > Fit Artboard In Window, and notice that both of the Guitar symbol instances on the artboard have been changed.

▶ **Tip:** Another way to edit a symbol is to select the symbol instance on the artboard, and then click the Edit Symbol button in the Control panel.

● **Note:** It may be difficult to select the shape. You may want to zoom in closer.

Working with dynamic symbols

As you just saw, editing a symbol updates all of the instances in your document. Symbols can also be dynamic, which means you can change certain appearance properties of instances using the Direct Selection tool (⟨k⟩) without editing the original symbol. In this section, you'll edit the properties of the Guitar symbol so that it is dynamic, and then you'll edit each instance separately.

1   In the Symbols panel, click the Guitar symbol thumbnail to select it, if it's not already selected. Click the Symbol Options button (▣) at the bottom of the Symbols panel.

▶ **Tip:** You can tell if a symbol is dynamic by looking at the thumbnail in the Symbols panel. If there is a small plus (+) in the lower-right corner of the thumbnail, it is a dynamic symbol.

2   In the Symbol Options dialog box, select Dynamic Symbol, and click OK. The symbol and its instances are now dynamic.

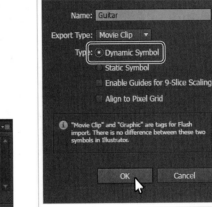

3   Select the Zoom tool (🔍), and drag across the symbol content (guitars) to zoom in.

4   Select the Direct Selection tool (⟨k⟩) in the Tools panel. Click to select the larger body shape of the guitar instance on the right.

With part of the symbol selected, notice the words "Symbol (Dynamic)" on the left end of the Control panel telling you it's a dynamic symbol.

▶ **Tip:** After making edits to a dynamic symbol instance with the Direct Selection tool, you can reselect the entire instance with the Selection tool and click Reset in the Control panel to reset the appearance to the same as the original symbol.

5   Change the Fill color to the lighter brown swatch with the tooltip "C=25 M=40 Y=65 K=0" in the Swatches panel (Window > Swatches).

Try clicking some of the other blue parts of the same guitar and changing their fill as well.

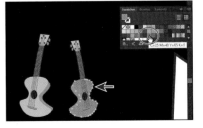

6   Select the Selection tool (▶), and double-click the guitar on the right again to edit the original symbol. Click OK in the dialog box that appears.

7 In Symbol Editing mode, click the guitar, and choose Object > Ungroup.

8 Choose Select > Deselect.

9 Select the larger shape at the top of the guitar. Drag the top-middle bounding point up a bit to make it taller.

10 Double-click away from the symbol content, or click the Exit Symbol Editing Mode button () in the upper-left corner of the artboard until you exit Symbol Editing mode so that you can see the change.

You'll see that the top shape changed for both symbol instances, but the color is still different.

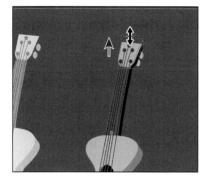
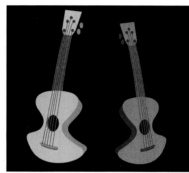

Note: The guitar on the right might look different than yours, and that's okay. I changed the fill for all the blue shapes in a previous step using the Direct Selection tool and the Swatches panel.

Symbol Options

In the Symbol Options dialog box, you will encounter several options. These options are briefly described here.

- **Export Type**: Movie Clip is the default symbol type in Flash and in Illustrator. This option will not affect the artwork while in Illustrator. If the artwork is imported from Flash or exported for use in Flash, a movie-clip symbol in Flash can contain reusable animation, while a graphic symbol in Flash will remain static.

- **Dynamic Symbol**: Selecting this option allows for local appearance overrides in dynamic symbol instances, but the relation with the master symbol is left intact.

- **Static Symbol**: Selecting this option does not allow for local appearance overrides; only certain operations are possible like transformations, opacity, and more.

- Specify a location on the Registration grid where you want to set the symbol's anchor point. The location of the anchor point affects the position of the symbol within the screen coordinates.

- Select Enable Guides For 9-Slice Scaling if you want to utilize 9-Slice scaling in Illustrator or Flash.

—From Illustrator Help

Creating a symbol

Illustrator also lets you create your own symbols. You can make symbols from objects, including paths, compound paths, text, embedded (not linked) raster images, mesh objects, and groups of objects. Symbols can even include active objects, such as brush strokes, blends, effects, or other symbol instances.

Next, you'll create your own symbol from existing artwork.

1 Choose 3 Symbol Artwork from the Artboard menu in the lower-left corner of the Document window.

2 With the Selection tool (▶) selected, click the top "musical note" shape on the artboard to select it.

▶ **Tip:** You can also drag the selected content into a blank area of the Symbols panel to create a symbol.

3 Click the New Symbol button (▣) at the bottom of the Symbols panel to make a symbol from the selected artwork.

▶ **Tip:** By default, the selected artwork becomes an instance of the new symbol. If you don't want the artwork to become an instance of the symbol, press the Shift key as you create the new symbol.

4 In the Symbol Options dialog box, change the name to **Note1,** and choose Graphic as Export Type. Ensure that Dynamic Symbol is also selected, just in case you want to edit the appearance of one of the instances later. Click OK to create the symbol.

In the Symbol Options dialog box, you'll see a note that explains that there is no difference between a movie clip and a graphic type in Illustrator, and so if you do not plan on exporting this content to Adobe Flash, you don't need to worry about choosing an export type.

After creating the symbol, the "Note" artwork on the artboard is converted to an instance of the Note1 symbol. The symbol also appears in the Symbols panel.

▶ **Tip:** You can drag the symbol thumbnails in the Symbols panel to change their ordering. Reordering symbols in the Symbols panel has no effect on the artwork. It can simply be a way to organize your symbols.

5 Delete the original "Note" artwork on the artboard.

6 Choose 2 T-Shirt from the Artboard menu in the lower-left corner of the Document window.

7   Drag the Note1 symbol from the Symbols panel onto the artboard four times, and position the instances around the guitars like you see in the following figure.

8   Try resizing a few of the Note1 instances on the artboard like you did earlier (the figure shows the result after I resized a few).

9   Choose Select > Deselect, and then choose File > Save.

Duplicating symbols

Often you will want to add a series of symbol instances to your artwork. After all, one of the reasons why you use symbols is for storing and updating frequently used content like trees or clouds. In this section, you'll create, add, and duplicate a symbol that happens to be another musical note.

1   Choose 3 Symbol Artwork from the Artboard menu in the lower-left corner of the Document window.

2   Using the Selection tool (▶), click and drag the bottom "musical note" shape from the artboard into a blank area of the Symbols panel to create a new symbol. In the Symbol Options dialog box, change the name to **Note2**, and choose Graphic as the Export Type. Leave the remaining settings at their defaults, and click OK to create the symbol.

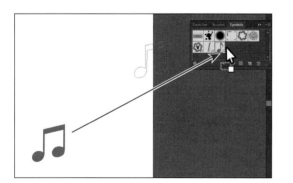 

3   Delete the original note artwork on the artboard.

4   Choose 2 T-Shirt from the Artboard menu in the lower-left corner of the Document window.

5 Drag one instance of the Note2 symbol from the Symbols panel onto the T-shirt, near the other notes.

Note: Your symbol instance may not be in the same position on the artboard, and that's fine. You will reposition them shortly anyway.

6 Press Option (Mac OS) or Alt (Windows), and drag the Note2 symbol instance on the artboard to create a copy. When the new instance is in position (see the figure), release the mouse button, and then release the modifier key.

7 Create a few more copies by pressing Option (Mac OS) or Alt (Windows) and dragging any of the note symbol instances. Drag them around the guitars and position them how you like. Know that later you will create artwork to go behind the guitars and cover the area between the guitars.

8 Resize a few of the symbol instances, making some smaller and some a bit larger, so they look different from each other.

9 Choose File > Save.

Replacing symbols

You can easily replace a symbol instance in the document with another symbol. Next, you will replace a few of the note symbol instances.

1 With the Selection tool (▶), select one of the Note2 symbol instances on the artboard.

When you select a symbol instance, you can tell which symbol it came from by looking for "Instance Of: Note2" in the Control panel. Also, in the Symbols panel, the symbol for the selected instance is highlighted (has a border around it).

Note: This option does not work for symbols in perspective.

2 In the Control panel, click the arrow to the right of the Replace Instance With Symbol field to open a panel showing the symbols in the Symbols panel. Click the Note1 symbol in the panel.

If the original symbol instance you were replacing had a transformation applied, such as a rotation, the symbol instance replacing it would have the same transformations applied.

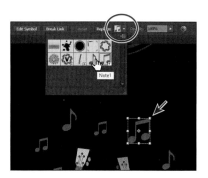

3 Double-click the Note2 symbol thumbnail in the Symbols panel to edit the symbol.

   A temporary instance of the symbol appears in the center of the Document window. Editing a symbol by double-clicking the symbol in the Symbols panel hides all artboard content except the symbol artwork. This is just another way to edit a symbol.

4 Press Command++ (Mac OS) or Ctrl++ (Windows) several times to zoom in.

5 Select the Selection tool (▶) in the Tools panel, and click the note shape.

6 Change the Fill color in the Control panel to the light gray swatch with the tooltip that shows "C=0 M=0 Y=0 K=40."

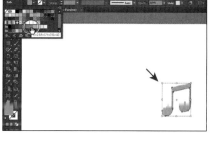

Note: The color of the path selection you see may be different than what shows in the figure, and that's okay.

7 Double-click away from the symbol content to exit Symbol Editing mode so that you can edit the rest of the content.

8 Choose View > Fit Artboard In Window.

9 Select the Selection tool (▶), and click one of the note symbol instances. It doesn't matter which symbol (Note1 or Note 2) it is. Choose Select > Same > Symbol Instance.

   This is a great way to select all instances of a symbol in the document.

10 Choose Object > Group to group the instances of that note symbol together.

11 Choose Select > Deselect.

Note: If you want to, you can select an instance of the other note symbol on the artboard and group those too. It's good to practice what you learn, right?

Symbol layers

When you edit a symbol using any of the methods described, open the Layers panel, and you will see that the symbol has its own layering.

Similar to working with groups in Isolation mode, you see the layers associated with that symbol only, not the document's layers. In the Layers panel, you can rename, add, delete, show/hide, and reorder content for a symbol.

Breaking a link to a symbol

At times, you need to edit specific instances on the artboard. As you've learned, you can only make changes, such as scaling, opacity, and flipping, to a symbol instance, and saving the symbol as dynamic only lets you edit certain appearance attributes using the Direct Selection tool. In certain cases you may need to break the link between a symbol and an instance. This breaks the instance into the original artwork on the artboard, and that instance will no longer update if the symbol is edited.

Next, you will break the link to one of the guitar symbol instances.

1   With the Selection tool (▶) selected, click to select the Guitar symbol instance on the left. In the Control panel, click the Break Link button.

This object is now a series of paths, as indicated by the words "Mixed Objects" on the left side of the Control panel, and can be edited directly. You should be able to see the anchor points of the shapes. This content will no longer update if the Guitar symbol is edited.

▶ **Tip:** You can also break the link to a symbol instance by selecting the symbol instance on the artboard and then clicking the Break Link To Symbol button (▦) at the bottom of the Symbols panel.

2 Select the Zoom tool (🔍), and drag across the top of the selected guitar artwork on the artboard to zoom in.

3 Choose Select > Deselect.

4 With the Selection tool selected, click the top small blue circle toward the top of the guitar. Option-drag (Mac OS) or Alt-drag (Windows) the circle up to create a copy. Release the mouse button and the modifier key.

5 Choose Select > Deselect.

6 Choose File > Save.

The Symbolism Tools

The Symbol Sprayer tool (🖌) in the Tools panel allows you to spray symbols on the artboard, creating symbol sets.

A symbol set is a group of symbol instances that you create with the Symbol Sprayer tool. This can be really useful if, for instance, you were to create grass from individual blades of grass. Spraying the blades of grass speeds up this process greatly and makes it much easier to edit individual instances of grass or the sprayed grass as a group. You can create mixed sets of symbol instances by using the Symbol Sprayer tool with one symbol and then using it again with another symbol.

You use the symbolism tools to modify multiple symbol instances in a set. For example, you can disperse instances over a larger area using the Symbol Scruncher tool or gradually tinting the color of instances to make them look more realistic.

Although you can use symbolism tools on individual symbol instances, they are most effective when used on symbol sets. When working with individual symbol instances, most of these tasks are easily accomplished using the tools and commands you use on regular objects.

—From Illustrator Help

Working with Creative Cloud Libraries

Creative Cloud Libraries are an easy way to create and share stored content such as images, colors, text styles, Adobe Stock assets, Creative Cloud Market assets, and more between Adobe Photoshop CC, Adobe Illustrator CC, Adobe InDesign CC, and certain Adobe mobile apps.

● **Note:** In order to use Creative Cloud Libraries, you will need to be signed in with your Adobe ID and have an Internet connection.

Creative Cloud Libraries connects to your Creative Profile, putting the creative assets you care about at your fingertips. When you create vector artwork in Illustrator and save it to a Library, that asset is available to use in all of your Illustrator files. Those assets are automatically synced and can be shared with anyone with a Creative Cloud account. As your creative team works across Adobe desktop and mobile apps, your shared library assets are always up to date and ready to use anywhere.

In this section, you'll explore CC Libraries and use them in your project.

Adding assets to CC Libraries

The first thing you'll learn about is how to work with the Libraries panel (Window > Libraries) in Illustrator and add assets to it. You'll open an existing document in Illustrator to capture assets from.

1　Choose File > Open. If a panel appears, click Open in the panel. You could also choose File > Open again. In the Open dialog box, navigate to the Lessons > Lesson13 folder and select the Sample.ai file on your hard disk. Click Open to open the file.

● **Note:** The Missing Fonts dialog box may appear. You need an Internet connection to sync the fonts. The syncing process may take a few minutes. Click Sync Fonts to sync all of the missing fonts to your computer. After they are synced and you see the message stating that there are no more missing fonts, click Close. If you have an issue syncing, you can go to Help (Help > Illustrator Help) and search for "Find missing fonts."

2　Choose View > Fit Artboard In Window.

Using this document, you will capture artwork, colors, and type formatting to be used in the TShirt.ai document.

3　Choose Window > Libraries to open the Libraries panel.

By default, you have one library to work with called "My Library." You can add your design assets to the default library, or you can create an unlimited number of Libraries—maybe to save assets according to clients or projects.

4　Choose Select > Deselect.

5 Select the Selection tool (↖), and click the type area that contains the text "The Guitar Company." In the Libraries panel, click the Add Paragraph Style button to capture the text formatting and save it in the Library.

The paragraph style will be added to the currently selected library. In this case, it is adding it to my default library called "My Library."

Note: If a paragraph style does not have the font associated with it on the local computer, a warning icon is displayed at the bottom-right corner of the Paragraph Style thumbnail in the Libraries panel.

6 Hover the pointer over the new asset in the Libraries panel, and you'll see a tooltip that shows the captured formatting. Double-click the name, and change it to **Guitar**. Press Enter or Return to accept the name change.

The paragraph and character formatting has now been saved in a paragraph style called "Guitar" in the Libraries panel. If you later apply this formatting to text, a Guitar paragraph style will be added to that document in the Paragraph Styles panel.

7 Click to select the brown guitar shape in the document.

8 In the Libraries panel, click the Add Fill Color button to save the color.

If artwork has a fill and/or stroke, the options at the bottom of the Libraries panel will change. For instance, if selected artwork has no stroke, then the Add Stroke Color button will not appear.

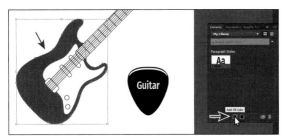

As you save assets in the Libraries panel, notice how it is organized by asset type. You can change the appearance of the items (icons or list) by clicking the buttons in the upper-right corner of the Libraries panel.

► **Tip:** You can double-click the name of an asset in the Libraries panel to edit it.

9 Drag across the black shape in the lower-right corner with the text "Guitar" on it to select all of the artwork. Drag the selected artwork into the Libraries panel. When a plus sign (+) and a name (such as "Artwork 1") appears, release the mouse button to add the graphic.

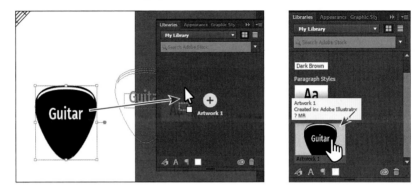

You can also select artwork and click the Add Graphic button (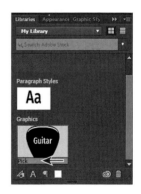) at the bottom of the Libraries panel. The assets you store as a graphic in a Creative Cloud Library retain their vector form. When you reuse a graphic from a Creative Cloud Library in another Illustrator document, it is in vector form.

10 Position the pointer over the new guitar asset, most likely named "Artwork 1" in the Libraries panel. Double-click the name, and change it to **Pick**. Press Enter or Return to accept the name change.

11 Choose File > Close to close the Sample.ai file and return to the TShirt.ai file. Don't save the file if asked.

Notice that the Libraries panel still shows the assets in the default library named "My Library." The Libraries and their assets are available no matter which document is open in Illustrator.

► **Tip:** You can share your Library with others by choosing the Library you want to share in the Libraries panel and then choosing Share Link from the panel menu.

Using Library assets

Now that you have some assets in the Libraries panel, once synced those assets will be available to other applications and apps that support Libraries, as long as you are signed in with the same Creative Cloud account. Next, you will use those assets in the TShirt.ai file.

1 While still on the 2 T-Shirt artboard, choose View > Fit Artboard In Window.

2 Select the Type tool, and click in a blank area of the artboard. Type **Rock On**.

3 Select the Selection tool (➤) and, with the type object still selected, click the Guitar paragraph style thumbnail in the Libraries panel to apply the text formatting.

4 Choose Window > Type > Paragraph Styles. If a warning dialog appears, click OK.

In the Paragraph Styles panel, notice the new style named "Guitar."

5 With the type area selected, change the Fill color to white in the Control panel. Change Font Size to **40 pt**.

6 Drag the type area onto the black T-shirt below the guitars, like you see in the figure.

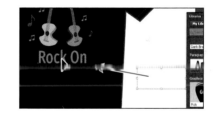

7 Drag the Pick asset from the Libraries panel onto an empty area of the artboard.

▶ **Tip:** As you'll learn in the next section, graphics you drag from the Libraries panel are linked. If you Option-drag (Mac OS) or Alt-drag (Windows) the artwork from the Libraries panel into a document, it will be embedded by default.

8 Choose File > Save, and leave the artwork selected.

Later, when you add artwork to the perspective grid, you'll use the color you saved in the Libraries panel to see how that works.

Updating a Library asset

When you drag a graphic from your library to an Illustrator project, it is automatically placed as a linked asset. If you make a change to a library asset, the linked instances will update in your projects. Next, you'll see how to update the asset.

1   With the Pick asset still selected on the artboard, look in the upper-left corner of the Control panel. Click the words "Linked File" to open the Links panel.

In the Links panel that appears, you will see the name of the Pick asset, as well as a cloud icon to the right of the name. The cloud icon indicates that the artwork is a linked Library asset.

● **Note:** You'll learn more about the Links panel in Lesson 14, "Using Illustrator CC with Other Adobe Applications."

2   Back in the Libraries panel, double-click the Pick asset thumbnail.

The artwork will appear in a new, temporary document.

3   With the Selection tool, click to select the black shape. Change the Fill color to a gray with the tooltip "C=0 M=0 Y=0 K=70" in the Control panel.

4   Choose File > Save, and then choose File > Close.

In the Libraries panel, the graphic thumbnail should update to reflect the appearance change you made.

5 Back in the TShirt.ai document, the pick graphic on the artboard should have updated. If it hasn't, with the pick artwork still selected on the artboard, click the Linked File link in the Control panel. In the Links panel, with the Pick row selected, click the Update Link button (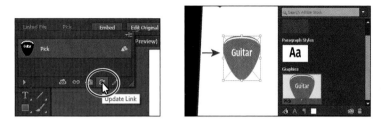) at the bottom of the panel.

6 With the artwork still selected, click the Embed button in the Control panel.

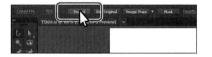

The artwork is no longer linked to the original Library item and will not update if the Pick library item is updated. That also means it is not directly editable in the document. Just know that Libraries panel artwork that is embedded after it has been placed will typically have a clipping mask applied.

7 With the Selection tool, Shift-drag the corner of the pick artwork to make it smaller. Drag the artwork between the guitars.

You may need to drag the guitars to position the artwork like you see in the following figure.

8 Choose Select > Deselect, and then choose File > Save.

9 Choose Window > Workspace > Reset Essentials.

10 In the Layers panel (Window > Layers) collapse all layers and click the main layer named "Content" to select it.

Working with the perspective grid

In Illustrator, using the Perspective Grid tool (▦) and the Perspective Selection tool (▶▦), you can easily draw or render artwork in perspective. You can define the perspective grid in one-point, two-point, or three-point perspective; define a scale move the grid planes; and draw objects directly in perspective. You can even attach flat art onto the grid planes by dragging with the Perspective Selection tool.

In this section, you will create perspective artwork for the T-shirt.

1 Choose 1 Perspective from the Artboard menu in the lower-left corner of the Document window.

2 Choose View > Fit Artboard In Window. Choose View > Zoom Out once.

3 Select the Perspective Grid tool (▦) in the Tools panel.

The default two-point perspective grid (which is nonprinting) appears on the artboard and can be used to draw and snap content in perspective. The two-point grid (for short) is composed of several *planes* or surfaces, by default—left (blue), right (orange), and a ground plane (green).

The following figure shows the default perspective grid by itself, with all of its options showing (you won't see the ruler, for instance, by default). It may be helpful to refer to this figure as you progress through the lesson.

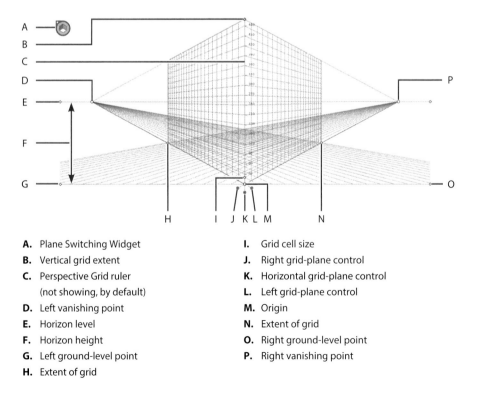

A. Plane Switching Widget	**I.** Grid cell size
B. Vertical grid extent	**J.** Right grid-plane control
C. Perspective Grid ruler (not showing, by default)	**K.** Horizontal grid-plane control
D. Left vanishing point	**L.** Left grid-plane control
E. Horizon level	**M.** Origin
F. Horizon height	**N.** Extent of grid
G. Left ground-level point	**O.** Right ground-level point
H. Extent of grid	**P.** Right vanishing point

Using a preset grid

To begin this part of the lesson, you'll work with the perspective grid, starting with an Illustrator preset. The perspective grid, by default, is set up as a two-point perspective. You can easily change the grid to a one-point, two-point, or three-point grid using presets, which is what you'll do next.

1 Choose View > Perspective Grid > Three Point Perspective > [3P-Normal View]. Notice that the grid changes to a three-point perspective.

   In addition to showing vanishing points for each wall, there is now a point showing those walls receding into the ground or high in space.

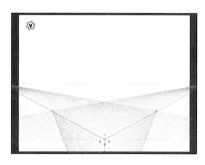

Note: A one-point perspective can be very useful for roads, railway tracks, or buildings viewed so that the front is directly facing the viewer. Two-point perspective is useful for drawing a cube, such as a building, or for two roads going off into the distance, and it typically has two vanishing points. Three-point perspective is usually used for buildings seen from above or below.

2 Choose View > Perspective Grid > Two Point Perspective > [2P-Normal View]. Notice that the grid changes back to the default two-point perspective.

Adjusting the perspective grid

To create artwork in the perspective you want, you can adjust the grid using the Perspective Grid tool (⊞) or using the View > Perspective Grid > Define Grid command. If you have content on the grid, you can make changes to it, although it will be easier to establish what your grid looks like before you add content.

In this section, you'll make a few adjustments to the grid.

1 Make sure that the Smart Guides are on (View > Smart Guides).

2 With the Perspective Grid tool (⊞) selected, position the pointer over the left ground-level point (circled in the figure). When the pointer changes (▶✥), drag it up to move the whole perspective grid. Match the position in the figure as closely as you can, but it does not have to match exactly.

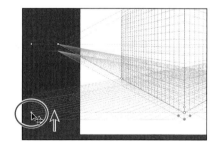

Note: You may need to zoom out to see the ground-level point.

   The left and right ground-level points allow you to drag the perspective grid to a different position on the artboard or to a different artboard altogether. In this example, you didn't really need to move the grid since you are creating perspective artwork that will become a part of the existing artwork on the 2 T-Shirt artboard, but it's important to understand how to achieve this.

3 Press Command+− (Mac OS) or Ctrl+− (Windows), to zoom out.

4 Position the pointer over the right end of the horizon line, and the pointer shows a vertical arrow (↕). Click and drag down a bit until you see approximately 230 pt in the gray measurement label next to the pointer.

The closer you are zoomed into the grid, the finer the increments that you can adjust it with.

Next, you will adjust the planes so that you can draw a cube that shows one side more than the other. This requires that you move a vanishing point.

5 Choose View > Perspective Grid > Lock Station Point.

This locks the left and right vanishing points so that they move together.

▶ **Tip:** If you had artwork on the grid, it would move with the grid.

6 With the Perspective Grid tool, position the pointer over the right vanishing point (circled in the figure). When the pointer includes a horizontal arrow (↔), drag to the right until the measurement label shows an X value of approximately 11 in.

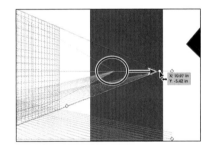

This changes both planes on the grid, and the perspective artwork you create will have a more visible right face.

Setting the grid up for your drawing is an important step in creating the artwork with the perspective you desire. Next, you will access some of the perspective grid options you have already adjusted, and more, using the Define Perspective Grid dialog box.

7 Choose View > Fit Artboard In Window.

8 Choose View > Perspective Grid > Define Grid.

9 In the Define Perspective Grid dialog box, change the following options:

- Units: **Inches**
- Gridline Every: **0.3 in**

Changing the Gridline Every option adjusts the grid cell size and can help you be more precise when drawing and editing on the grid, since content snaps to the lines of the grid by default. Notice that you can also change the Scale of the grid, which you might want to do if real-world measurements are involved. You can also edit settings, like Horizon Height and Viewing Angle, on the artboard, using the Perspective Grid tool. Leave the Grid Color & Opacity settings at their defaults.

▶ **Tip:** After setting the Define Perspective Grid settings, you can save them as a preset to access later. In the Define Perspective Grid dialog box, change the settings, and then click the Save Preset button (⬛).

Note: If the rest of the values in the Define Perspective Grid dialog box don't match the figure, that's okay. Don't attempt to match the values since it can change your grid in unexpected ways.

When you have finished making changes, click OK. The grid will change in appearance slightly. The grid should now look pretty close to this (but doesn't have to match *exactly*):

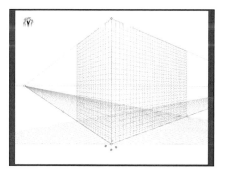

Note: To learn more about the options in the Define Perspective Grid dialog box, search for "Perspective drawing" in Illustrator Help (Help > Illustrator Help).

10 Choose View > Perspective Grid > Lock Grid.

This command restricts the grid movement and other grid-editing features of the Perspective Grid tool. You can only change the visibility and the grid plane position, which you will work with later in this lesson.

11 Choose File > Save.

Note: When you select a tool other than the Perspective Grid tool (⬛), you cannot edit the perspective grid. Also, if the perspective grid is locked, you cannot edit most of the grid settings with the Perspective Grid tool. You can edit a locked grid by choosing View > Perspective Grid > Define Grid.

Drawing artwork in perspective

To draw objects in perspective, you can use the line tools or the shape tools (except for the Flare tool) while the grid is visible. Before you begin drawing using any of these tools, you need to select a grid plane to attach the content to, using the Plane Switching Widget or keyboard shortcuts.

When the perspective grid is showing, a Plane Switching Widget appears in the upper-left corner of the Document window by default. The grid plane that is selected in the Plane Switching Widget is the active grid plane of the perspective grid to which you'll add content. In the widget, you can select the planes, as well as see their keyboard shortcut when you hover over each part of the widget.

1 Select the Rectangle tool (▣) in the Tools panel.

2 Select Left Grid(1), in the Plane Switching Widget (if it's not already selected).

► Tip: When drawing in perspective, you will find that you can still use the usual keyboard shortcuts for drawing objects, such as Shift-drag to constrain.

► Tip: You can turn off grid snapping by choosing View > Perspective Grid > Snap To Grid. Snapping is enabled by default.

3 Position the pointer at the origin of the perspective grid (where you see the red X in the figure). Notice that the cursor has an arrow pointing to the left (◄), indicating that you are about to draw on the left grid plane. Drag up and to the left, until the gray measurement label shows an approximate width of 1.2 in and a height of approximately 3.3 in. As you drag, the shape should be snapping to the gridlines.

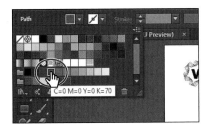

Zooming in brings more gridlines into view that are closer to the vanishing point. That's why, depending on the zoom level, your grid may not match the figures exactly, and that's okay.

4 With the rectangle selected, change the Fill color to the dark gray swatch with the named "C=0 M=0 Y=0 K=70" in the Control panel. Press the Escape key to hide the Swatches panel.

5 Change the Stroke color to None (▨), if necessary, in the Control panel.

There are many ways to add content to the perspective grid. Next, you'll create another rectangle a different way.

6   With the Rectangle tool still selected, click Right Grid(3) in the Plane Switching Widget to draw in perspective on the right grid plane.

7   Position the pointer over the upper-right corner of the rectangle you just drew. When the word "anchor" appears, click. In the Rectangle dialog box, the width and height of the last rectangle you drew are showing. Click OK.

Notice that the pointer now has an arrow pointing to the right (➡), indicating that content you create will appear on the right grid plane.

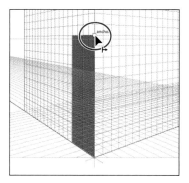
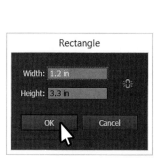
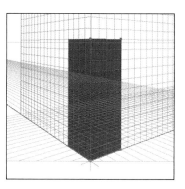

8   With the rectangle selected, change the Fill color in the Control panel to the light gray swatch with the named "C=0 M=0 Y=0 K=5." Press the Escape key to hide the Swatches panel.

9   Change the Stroke color to None (☑), if necessary, in the Control panel.

In this example, you don't need to create a top or bottom to the cube since the top is above the horizon line. If you needed to draw a top to the cube you are creating, you would select the perspective Horizontal Grid(2) in the Plane Switching Widget to draw in perspective on the ground (horizontal) plane.

10 Choose View > Perspective Grid > Hide Grid to hide the perspective grid and to see your artwork.

11 Choose Select > Deselect, and then choose File > Save.

▶ **Tip:** You can also show and hide the perspective grid by pressing Shift+Command+I (Mac OS) or Shift+Ctrl+I (Windows) to toggle back and forth.

Selecting and transforming objects in perspective

You can select objects in perspective using selection tools, such as the Selection tool (▶) and the Perspective Selection tool (▶). The Perspective Selection tool uses the active plane settings to select the objects. If you use the Selection tool to drag an object that was drawn in perspective, it maintains its original perspective, but it doesn't change to match the perspective grid.

Next, you will resize the last rectangle you drew.

Note: If the grid doesn't appear, you can choose View > Perspective Grid > Show Grid.

1 Position the pointer over the Perspective Grid tool (⊞), click and hold down the mouse button, and then select the Perspective Selection tool (▶). Notice that the perspective grid appears again.

2 Click the rectangle with the light gray fill on the right grid plane to select it.

Tip: Zooming into the grid may make it easier when resizing content.

3 With the Perspective Selection tool selected, drag the middle-right point of the rectangle to the right. When the measurement label shows a width of about 3 in, release the mouse button. Make sure that the rectangle is snapping to the gridlines.

Dragging a shape or resizing it will do so in perspective with the Perspective Selection tool.

Note: Depending on the resolution of your screen, you may see the Transform options in the Control panel.

4 With the Perspective Selection tool, click to select the first rectangle you created (on the left plane). Click the word "Transform" in the Control panel, and then click the right-middle point of the reference point locator (⊞) in the Control panel. With the Constrain Width And Height Proportions option deselected (🔲), change Width to **1.5 in**, if necessary.

Tip: Selecting artwork with the Perspective Selection tool selects the grid plane that it is on (in the Plane Switching Widget).

Aside from scaling artwork and performing other transformations, you can also drag artwork in perspective with the Perspective Selection tool. For example, dragging artwork on the horizontal grid up or down with the Perspective Selection tool makes it smaller and larger. Dragging it up moves the artwork "farther away" in perspective, and dragging it down moves it "closer" in perspective.

5 Choose Select > Deselect, and then choose File > Save.

Moving planes and objects together

As you saw in the beginning of this section, it's usually best to adjust the grid before there is artwork on it. But Illustrator allows you to move objects by moving the grid planes. This can be good for precise perpendicular movement.

Next, you will move a grid plane and artwork together.

1   Select the Zoom tool (🔍), and click the bottom of the perspective grid twice, slowly, to zoom into the grid.

2   Select the Perspective Selection tool (▶🔲). Position the pointer over the left grid plane control (circled in the following figure), and double-click. In the Left Vanishing Plane dialog box, change Location to **-0.15 in**, select Move All Objects, and click OK.

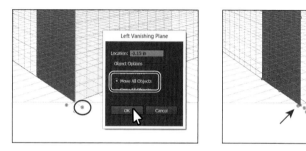

► Tip: If you move a plane using the grid plane control, you can also choose Edit > Undo Perspective Grid Edit to put the plane back to its original location.

In the Left Vanishing Plane dialog box, the Do Not Move option allows you to move the grid plane and not the objects on it. The Copy All Objects option allows you to move the grid plane and to bring a copy of the objects on the grid plane with it. The Location option in the Left Vanishing Plane dialog box starts at the station point, which is 0. The station point is indicated by the very small green diamond on the perspective grid, above the horizontal grid control. You can also drag grid plane controls with the Perspective Selection tool to adjust them. By default, dragging a grid plane control moves the grid plane but not the artwork.

► Tip: You can hold down Option (Mac OS) or Alt (Windows) and drag a grid plane control to move the grid plane and copy the content. Dragging a grid plane control while pressing the Shift key moves the objects with the grid plane without copying them.

3   With the Perspective Selection tool selected, drag the right-middle point of the dark gray rectangle to the left to make it narrower. Stop dragging when the point snaps to a gridline and the gray measurement label shows a width of approximately 1.39 in.

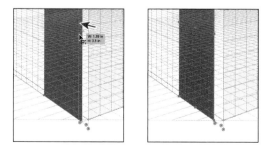

► Tip: If you select an object or objects on the grid plane first and then drag the grid plane control while holding down the Shift key, only the selected objects move with the grid plane.

Drawing artwork with no active grid

There will be times when you need to draw or add content that is not meant to be in perspective. In a case like that, you can select No Active Grid in the Plane Switching Widget to draw without regard to the grid. Next, you'll draw a rectangle that will become a flat corner on the cube.

1 Choose View > Fit Artboard In Window.

2 Select the Rectangle tool (▦) in the Tools panel.

3 Select No Active Grid(4), in the Plane Switching Widget.

4 Position the pointer on the upper-right corner point of the dark gray rectangle on the left plane. When the word "anchor" appears, click and drag down and to the right. Snap to the lower-left corner of the light gray rectangle on the right plane. Release the mouse button when the word "anchor" appears.

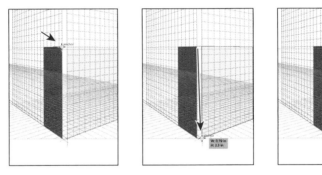

5 With the rectangle selected, change the Fill color in the Control panel to the light gray swatch with the named "C=0 M=0 Y=0 K=20." Press the Escape key to hide the Swatches panel.

6 Choose Select > Deselect, and then choose File > Save.

Adding and editing text in perspective

You cannot add text directly to a perspective plane; however, you can bring text into perspective after creating it off of the perspective grid. Next, you will add some text and then edit it in perspective.

1 Select the Type tool (T) in the Tools panel. Click in a blank area on the artboard, and type **AMP**.

2 Select the text with the Type tool, change Font to Myriad Pro (or another font if you don't have that one), ensure that Font Style is Regular, and change Font Size to **16 pt** in the Control panel.

3 Select the Perspective Selection tool (➤🔳) in the Tools panel. Press the number 3 key on the keyboard to select the Right Grid(3) plane in the Plane Switching Widget. Drag the text into the upper-right corner of the larger box.

4 Select the Zoom tool and zoom in.

5 With the Perspective Selection tool selected, double-click the text object to enter Isolation mode. The Type tool is selected automatically.

6 Insert the cursor before the word "AMP," and type **Guitar** with a spacebar space after it. You may need to zoom in so you can more easily see it (I did).

7 Select the Perspective Selection tool (➤🔳), and double-click the artboard to exit Isolation mode.

8 Drag the "Guitar AMP" text so it fits in the corner of the light gray box, if necessary.

▶ **Tip:** You can also enter Isolation mode to edit text by clicking the Edit Text button (🔳) in the Control panel. To exit Isolation mode, you can also click twice on the gray arrow that appears below the document tab at the top of the Document window.

Moving objects in a perpendicular direction

Now you're going to add several circles to the grid and copy one in a direction perpendicular to the current location. This technique is useful when creating parallel objects, such as the legs of a chair.

1 Click and hold down on the Rectangle tool in the Tools panel. Select the Ellipse tool.

You may want to zoom out a bit for the next steps.

2 Making sure that the right plane is selected in the Plane Switching Widget, Shift-drag to create a small circle that has a width and height of roughly 2 in. Release the mouse button and then the key.

3 Press the D key to apply the default fill and stroke to the circle.

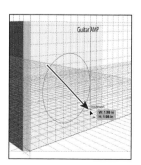

▶ **Tip:** To move objects from one plane to another, begin dragging artwork on the grid with the Perspective Selection tool, without releasing the mouse button yet. Press the number 1, 2, or 3 key (depending on which grid you intend to attach the objects to) to switch to the grid plane of your choice. These keyboard commands work only from the main keyboard and not from the extended numeric keypad.

4 With the circle selected, change the Fill color in the Control panel to None (⬜), make sure that the Stroke color is black, and change the Stroke weight to **10 pt** in the Control panel.

5 Select the Perspective Selection tool (▶⬛) in the Tools panel, and drag the circle roughly into the center of the light gray rectangle.

6 With the circle still selected, choose Edit > Copy and then Edit > Paste In Front.

● **Note:** Depending on your screen resolution, the Transform options (like Width) may appear in your Control panel.

7 With the new circle selected, click the word "Transform" in the Control panel and, making sure that the Constrain Width And Height Proportions option (⬛) is selected and the right-middle point of the Reference Point is selected (⬛), change Width to **1.3 in**.

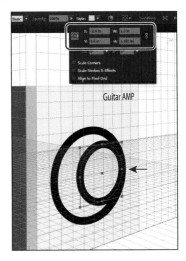

8 Ensure that the smaller circle is positioned roughly like you see in the figure at right.

● **Note:** The keyboard shortcut 5, which is for perpendicular movement (and the keyboard shortcuts 1, 2, 3, and 4 for plane switching) while drawing or moving objects, works only from the main keyboard and not from the extended numeric keypad.

9 With the Perspective Selection tool selected, hold down the number 5 key and drag the smaller circle, by its stroke, to the left a bit. When the circle looks something like the first part of the following figure, release the mouse, and then release the 5 key.

10 Choose Object > Arrange > Bring To Front to bring the smaller circle to the front, if necessary.

▶ **Tip:** While pressing the number 5 key and dragging, you could press Option (Mac OS) or Alt (Windows) to copy the object that you are dragging.

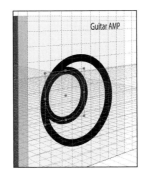

This action moves the object parallel to its current location and scales it in perspective.

11 Choose Select > Deselect, and then choose File > Save.

Moving a plane to match an object

When you want to draw or bring objects in perspective at the same depth or height as an existing object, such as the smaller circle, you can bring the corresponding grid to the desired height or depth. Next, you will move the right grid plane to the same depth as the smaller circle and add a logo to it.

1   With the Perspective Selection tool () selected, click to select the small circle again.

2   Choose Object > Perspective > Move Plane To Match Object.

    Now anything you add to the right grid plane will be at the same depth as the smaller circle.

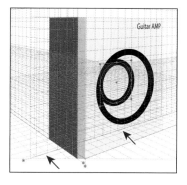

Bringing content into perspective

If you have already created content that is not in perspective, Illustrator provides an option to bring objects into perspective on an active plane in the perspective grid. You will now add a logo, which happens to be a symbol, to the perspective grid.

1   With the Perspective Selection tool (►a) selected, make sure that the Right Grid(3) is selected in the Plane Switching Widget.

2   Choose View > Fit Artboard In Window.

    In the upper-left corner of the artboard, you'll see artwork for a logo that is a symbol instance. Next, you'll drag the symbol instance into perspective.

3   With the Perspective Selection tool, drag the logo symbol instance in the upper-left corner of the artboard into the center of the smaller circle to attach it to the right grid plane.

    Notice that the logo is behind the other artwork on the artboard. Content on the perspective grid has the same stacking order as content you draw off of the perspective grid.

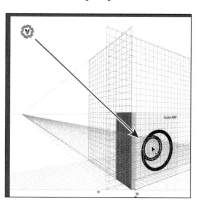

Note: Symbols that you wish to bring into perspective cannot contain such things as raster images, envelopes, or gradient meshes.

▶ **Tip:** Instead of dragging an object onto the plane using the Perspective Selection tool, you can also select the object with the Perspective Selection tool, choose the plane using the Plane Switching Widget, and then choose Object > Perspective > Attach To Active Plane. This adds the content to the active plane, but it doesn't change its appearance.

4 Choose Object > Arrange > Bring To Front to bring the logo on top of the other artwork.

5 Choose Select > Deselect.

6 In the Symbols panel (Window > Symbols), drag out the symbol named "Button."

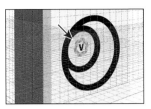

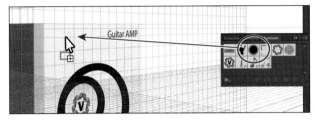

You may want to zoom in a bit to the artwork for the next step.

7 With the Perspective Selection tool, make sure that the Right Grid(3) is selected in the Plane Switching Widget, and drag the button onto the light gray rectangle. See the first part of the following figure for placement.

8 Drag the symbol instance to the right. As you drag, press Option+Shift (Mac OS) or Alt+Shift (Windows) and continue dragging to create a copy. Release the mouse button and then the modifier keys.

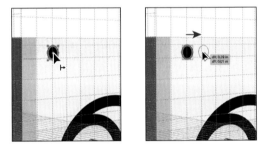

Editing symbols in perspective

After bringing symbols into perspective, you may need to edit them. Just know that functionalities, such as replacing a symbol or breaking a link to a symbol instance, do not work on symbols in perspective. Next, you'll make a change to the logo.

1 Select the Zoom tool (🔍) in the Tools panel, and zoom into the logo.

● **Note:** You could also double-click the symbol with the Perspective Selection tool to edit it.

2 Select the Selection tool (▶) in the Tools panel, and double-click the logo you just dragged into perspective. Click OK in the warning dialog that appears. Click to select the "V" artwork.

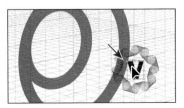

This enters Symbol Editing mode and hides the rest of the artwork on the artboard.

3   Change the Fill color in the Control panel to the red swatch with the name "CMYK Red." Press the Escape key to hide the Swatches panel.

4   Double-click away from the symbol content to exit Symbol Editing mode so that you can edit the rest of the content.

5   Choose Select > Deselect, if necessary.

Finishing Up

There are a few small things yet to do on the perspective artwork, and in this section, you'll finish up.

1   Choose View > Fit Artboard In Window.

2   Select the Perspective Selection tool (▶⬚) in the Tools panel. Click to select the light gray rectangle on the right grid plane. Choose Object > Perspective > Move Plane To Match Object.

The right grid plane is now back to where it was earlier in the lesson.

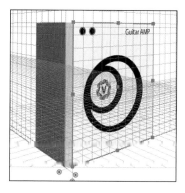

3   With the light gray rectangle still selected, choose Edit > Copy and then choose Edit > Paste In Front.

4   With the copy selected, change the Fill color in the Control panel to Black. Press the Escape key to hide the Swatches panel.

5   Press the Shift key and drag the top-middle point down to make the rectangle a bit smaller. Use the first part of the following figure as a guide.

6   Choose Object > Arrange > Bring To Front.

7   Change Opacity to **95%** in the Control panel.

▶ **Tip:** Pressing the Shift key with the pointer over the grid will hide all planes in the perspective grid except for the active one.

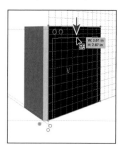
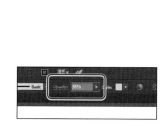
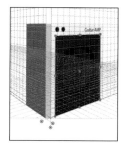

8 Choose Select > All On Active Artboard. Choose Edit > Copy.

9 Choose 2 T-Shirt from the Artboard menu in the lower-left corner of the Document window.

10 Choose Edit > Paste.

11 Choose Object > Perspective > Release With Perspective.

12 Choose Object > Group.

13 Choose Object > Arrange > Send To Back.

14 Select the Selection tool (▶) in the Tools panel, and Shift-drag a corner of the selected artwork to make it smaller. When you the gray measurement label shows an approximate width of 1.6, release the mouse button and then the Shift key.

15 Arrange all the artwork like you see in the following figure. I wound up moving some of the musical notes symbol instances as well to make it look a bit better.

16 Choose Select > Deselect.

17 Choose File > Save, and then choose File > Close.

Review questions

1 What are three benefits of using symbols?

2 How do you update an existing symbol?

3 What is a dynamic symbol?

4 In Illustrator, what type of content can you save in a Library?

5 Explain how to embed a linked library graphic asset.

6 Before drawing content on a grid plane, what must be done to ensure that the object is on the correct grid plane?

Review answers

1 Three benefits of using symbols are as follows:

- You can edit one symbol, and all instances are updated.

- You can map artwork to 3D objects (not discussed in the lesson).

- Using symbols reduces file size.

2 To update an existing symbol, double-click the symbol icon in the Symbols panel, double-click an instance of the symbol on the artboard, or select the instance on the artboard and then click the Edit Symbol button in the Control panel. Then you can make edits in Isolation mode.

3 When a symbol is saved as Dynamic, you can change certain appearance properties of instances using the Direct Selection tool (⬚) without editing the original symbol.

4 In Illustrator, you can save colors (fill and stroke), graphic assets, and type formatting.

5 By default in Illustrator, when a graphic asset is dragged from the Libraries panel into a document, a link is created to the original Library asset. In order to embed a graphic asset, select the asset in the document, and click Embed in the Control panel. Once embedded, the graphic will no longer update if the original library asset is edited.

6 The correct grid plane must be selected by choosing it in the Plane Switching Widget. You can select it by using the following keyboard commands: Left Grid(1), Horizontal Grid(2), Right Grid(3), or No Active Grid(4); or by selecting content on the grid you want to choose with the Perspective Selection tool (⬚).

14 USING ILLUSTRATOR CC WITH OTHER ADOBE APPLICATIONS

Lesson overview

In this lesson, you'll learn how to do the following:

- Place linked and embedded graphics in an Illustrator file.
- Place multiple images at once.
- Apply color edits to images.
- Create and edit clipping masks.
- Use text to mask an image.
- Make and edit an opacity mask.
- Sample color in a placed image.
- Work with the Links panel.
- Embed and unembed images.
- Replace a placed image with another and update the document.
- Package a document.

 This lesson takes approximately 60 minutes to complete.

Download the project files for this lesson from the Lesson & Update Files tab on your Account page at www.peachpit.com and store them on your computer in a convenient location, as described in the "Getting Started" section of this book.

Your Account page is also where you'll find any updates to the chapters or to the lesson files. Look on the Lesson & Update Files tab to access the most current content.

You can easily add an image created in an image-editing program to an Adobe Illustrator file. This is an effective method for incorporating images into your vector artwork or for trying Illustrator special effects on bitmap images.

Getting started

Before you begin, you'll need to restore the default preferences for Adobe Illustrator CC. Then you'll open the finished art file for this lesson to see what you'll create.

Note: If you have not already downloaded the project files for this lesson to your computer from your Account page, make sure to do so now. See the "Getting Started" section at the beginning of this book.

1   To ensure that the tools and panels function exactly as described in this lesson, delete or deactivate (by renaming) the Adobe Illustrator CC preferences file. See "Restoring default preferences" in the "Getting Started" section at the beginning of the book.

2   Start Adobe Illustrator CC.

3   Choose File > Open. Locate the file named L14_end.ai in the Lessons > Lesson14 folder that you copied onto your hard disk.

This is a small poster for a vacation destination, and you will add and edit graphics in this lesson.

4   Choose View > Fit Artboard In Window and leave it open for reference, or choose File > Close.

Note: The fonts in the L14_end.ai file have been converted to outlines (Type > Create Outlines) to avoid having missing fonts.

5   Choose File > Open. If a panel appears, click Open in the panel. You could also choose File > Open again. In the Open dialog box, navigate to the Lessons > Lesson14 folder and select the L14_start.ai file on your hard disk. Click Open to open the file. This is a small poster for a travel company, and you will add and edit graphics in this lesson.

Note: You need an Internet connection to sync the fonts. The syncing process may take a few minutes.

6   The Missing Fonts dialog box may appear. Click Sync Fonts to sync all the missing fonts to your computer. After they are synced and you see the message stating that there are no more missing fonts, click Close.

If you can't get the fonts to sync (a "Syncing Typekit fonts..." message doesn't go away), you can go to the Creative Cloud desktop application and choose Assets > Fonts to see what the issue may be (refer to the section "Changing font family and font style" in Lesson 8, "Adding Type to a Poster," for more information on how to resolve it). You can also just click Close in the Missing Fonts dialog box and ignore the missing fonts as you proceed. A third method is to click the Find Fonts button in the Missing Fonts dialog box and replace the fonts with a local font on your machine.

Note: You can also go to Help (Help > Illustrator Help) and search for "Find missing fonts.

7   Choose File > Save As. In the Save As dialog box, navigate to the Lesson14 folder, and open it. Name the file **GreenIsle.ai**. Leave the Format option set to Adobe Illustrator (ai) (Mac OS) or the Save As Type option set to Adobe Illustrator (*.AI) (Windows), and then click Save. In the Illustrator Options dialog box, leave the Illustrator options at their default settings. Click OK.

8   Choose View > Fit Artboard In Window.

9   Choose Window > Workspace > Reset Essentials to reset the Essentials workspace.

Working with Adobe Bridge

Adobe Bridge CC is an application available with your Adobe Creative Cloud subscription. Bridge provides you with centralized access to all the media assets you need for your creative projects.

Bridge simplifies your workflow and keeps you organized. You can batch edit with ease, add watermarks, and even set centralized color preferences. You can access Adobe Bridge from within Illustrator by choosing File > Browse In Bridge.

Combining artwork

You can combine Illustrator artwork with images from other graphics applications in a variety of ways for a wide range of creative results. Sharing artwork among applications lets you combine continuous-tone paintings and photographs with vector art. Illustrator lets you create certain types of raster images, and Adobe Photoshop excels at many additional image-editing tasks. The images edited or created in Photoshop can then be inserted into Illustrator.

Note: To learn more about working with vector and raster images, see the "Introducing Adobe Illustrator" section in Lesson 1, "Getting to Know the Work Area."

This lesson steps you through the process of creating a composite image, including combining bitmap images with vector art and working between applications. You will add photographic images created in Photoshop to a small poster created in Illustrator. Then you'll adjust the color of an image, mask an image, and sample color from an image to use in the Illustrator artwork. You'll update a placed image and then package the file.

Placing image files

You can bring raster artwork from Photoshop or other applications into Illustrator using the Open command, the Place command, the Paste command, drag-and-drop operations, and the Library panel. Illustrator supports most Adobe Photoshop data, including layer comps, layers, editable text, and paths. This means that you can transfer files between Photoshop and Illustrator without losing the ability to edit the artwork.

● **Note:** Illustrator includes support for DeviceN rasters. For instance, if you create a Duotone image in Photoshop and place it in Illustrator, it separates properly and prints the spot colors.

When placing files using the File > Place command, no matter what type of image file it is (JPG, GIF, PSD, etc.), it can be either embedded or linked. *Embedding* files stores a copy of the image in the Illustrator file, and the Illustrator file size increases to reflect the addition of the placed file. *Linked* files remain separate external files, and a link to the external file is placed in the Illustrator file. A linked file does not add significantly to the size of the Illustrator file. Linking to files can be a great way to ensure that image updates are reflected in the Illustrator file. The linked file must always accompany the Illustrator file, or the link will break and the placed file will not appear in the Illustrator artwork.

Placing an image

First, you will place a JPEG (.jpg) image into your document.

1   Click the Layers panel icon (⬛) to open the
    Layers panel. In the Layers panel, select the
    layer named "Pictures."

    When you place an image, it is added to the
    selected layer. The layer already includes
    several shapes you see off the left edge of
    the artboard.

2   Choose File > Place.

3   Navigate to the Lessons >
    Lesson14 > images folder, and select
    the Kayak.jpg file. Make sure that
    Link is selected in the Place dialog
    box. Click Place.

    The pointer should now show the
    loaded graphics cursor. You can see
    "1/1" next to the pointer, indicating
    how many images are being placed
    (1 of 1), and a thumbnail so you can
    see what image you are placing.

4 Position the loaded graphics cursor near the upper-left corner of the artboard, and click to place the image. Leave the image selected.

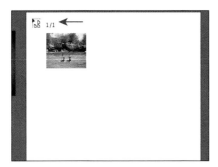

▶ **Tip:** The X on a selected image indicates that the image is linked (with edges showing, View > Show Edges).

Position the loaded graphics cursor.

Click to place the image.

The image appears on the artboard, with the upper-left corner of the image placed where you clicked. The image is 100% of its original size. You could also have dragged with the loaded graphics cursor to size the image as you placed it. Notice in the Control panel that, with the image selected, you see the words "Linked File," indicating that the image is linked to its source file, together with other information about the image. By default, placed image files are linked to their source file. So, if the source file is edited (outside of Illustrator), the placed image in Illustrator is updated. Deselecting the Link option while placing embeds the image file in the Illustrator file.

Scaling a placed image

You can duplicate and transform placed images just as you do other objects in an Illustrator file. Unlike vector artwork, you need to consider the resolution of the raster image content in your document since raster images without enough resolution may look pixelated when printed. Working in Illustrator, if you make an image smaller, the resolution of the image increases. If you make an image larger, the resolution decreases. Next, you will move, resize, and rotate the Kayak.jpg image.

● **Note:** Transformations performed on a linked image in Illustrator, and any resulting resolution changes, do not change the original image. The changes apply only to the image within Illustrator.

1 Holding down the Shift key, use the Selection tool (▶) to drag the lower-right bounding point toward the center of the image until the measurement label shows a width of approximately 5 in. Release the mouse button, and then release the key.

▶ **Tip:** To transform a placed image, you can also open the Transform panel (Window > Transform) and change settings there.

After resizing the image, notice that the PPI (Pixels Per Inch) value in the Control panel is approximately 150. PPI refers to the resolution of the image. Other transformations like rotation can also be applied to images using the various methods you learned in Lesson 5, "Transforming Artwork."

▶ **Tip:** Much like other artwork, you can also Option+Shift-drag (Mac OS) or Alt+Shift-drag (Windows) a bounding point around an image to resize from the center, while maintaining the image proportions.

2 Click the Linked File text link on the left end of the Control panel to see the Links panel. With the Kayak.jpg file selected in the Links panel, click the Show Link Info arrow in the lower left corner of the panel to see information about the image.

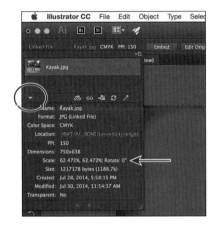

You can see the scale percentage as well as rotation information, size, and much more.

3 Choose Select > Deselect, and then choose File > Save.

Placing a Photoshop image with Show Import Options

When you place image files in Illustrator, you have the ability to change image options when the file is imported (when available). For instance, if you place a Photoshop file (.psd), you can choose to flatten the image or even to preserve the original Photoshop layers in the file. Next, you'll place a Photoshop file, set import options, and embed it in the Illustrator file.

1 In the Layers panel, click the eye icon (◉) for the Pictures layer to hide the contents, and then select the Background layer.

2 Choose File > Place.

● **Note:** You may not see a preview for the Photoshop file, even though the figure shows one, and that's okay.

3 In the Place dialog box, navigate to the Lessons > Lesson14 > images folder, and select the Lilypads.psd file. In the Place dialog box, set the following options:

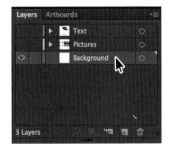

- Link: **Deselected** (Deselecting the Link option embeds an image file in the Illustrator file. Embedding the Photoshop file allows for more options when it is placed, as you'll see.)

- Show Import Options: **Selected** (Selecting this option will open an import options dialog box where you can set import options before placing.)

4 Click Place.

The Photoshop Import Options dialog box appears because you selected Show Import Options in the Place dialog box.

● **Note:** Even though you select Show Import Options in the Place dialog box, the Import Options dialog box will not appear if the image doesn't have multiple layers.

5 In the Photoshop Import Options dialog box, set the following options:

- Layer Comp: **All**
  (A layer comp is a snapshot of a state of the Layers panel that you create in Photoshop. In Photoshop, you can create, manage, and view multiple versions of a layout in a single Photoshop file. Any comments associated with the layer comp in Photoshop will appear in the Comments area.)

▶ **Tip:** To learn more about layer comps, see "Importing artwork from Photoshop" in Illustrator Help (Help > Illustrator Help).

- Show Preview: **Selected**
  (Preview displays a preview of the selected layer comp.)

- Convert Layers To Objects: **Selected** (This option and the next one are available only because you deselected the Link option and chose to embed the Photoshop image.)

- Import Hidden Layers: **Selected** (to import layers hidden in Photoshop)

6 Click OK.

● **Note:** A color mode warning may appear in the Photoshop Import Options dialog box. This indicates that the image you are placing may not be the same color mode as the Illustrator document. For this image (and going forward), if a color warning dialog box appears, click OK to dismiss it.

7 Position the loaded graphics cursor in the upper-left corner of the artboard, and click to place the image.

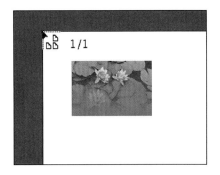

Rather than flatten the file, you have converted the Lilypads.psd Photoshop layers to layers that you can show and hide in Illustrator. When placing a Photoshop file in particular, if you had left the Link option selected (to link to the original PSD file), the only option in the Options section of the Photoshop Import Options dialog box would have been to flatten the content.

8 In the Layers panel, click the Locate Object button (⊙) to reveal the image content in the Layers panel. You may want to drag the left edge of the Layers panel to see more of the layer names.

Notice the sublayers of Lilypads.psd. These sublayers were Photoshop layers in Photoshop and appear in the Layers panel in Illustrator because you chose not to flatten the image when you placed it. Also notice that, with the image still selected on the page, the Control panel shows the word "Group" on the left side and includes an underlined link to "Multiple Images." When you place a Photoshop file with layers and you choose to convert the layers to objects in the Photoshop Import Options dialog box, Illustrator treats the layers as separate sublayers in a group. This particular image had a layer mask in Photoshop applied to Layer 0, which is why the image appears to fade.

9 Click the eye icon (⊙) to the left of the Color Fill 1 sublayer to hide it.

10 Choose Select > Deselect, and then choose File > Save.

Placing multiple images

In Illustrator you can also place multiple files in a single action. Next, you'll place two images at once and then position them.

1 In the Layers panel, click the disclosure triangle (▼) to the left of the Background layer to collapse the layer contents. Click the visibility column of the layers named "Pictures" and "Text" to show the contents for each, and then ensure that the Background layer is selected.

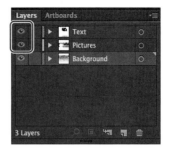

2 Choose File > Place.

3 In the Place dialog box, select the Water.jpg file in the Lessons > Lesson14 > images folder. Command-click (Mac OS) or Ctrl-click (Windows) the image named Text.psd to select both image files. Deselect the Show Import Options option and make sure that the Link option is *not* selected. Click Place.

▶ **Tip:** You could also select a range of files in the Place dialog box by pressing the Shift key.

● **Note:** The Place dialog box you see in Illustrator may show the images in a different view, like a List view, and that's okay.

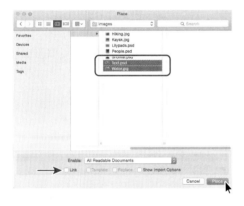

4 Position the loaded graphics cursor on the left side of the artboard. Press the Right or Left Arrow key (or Up and Down Arrow keys) a few times to see that you can cycle between the image thumbnails. Make sure that you see the water image thumbnail, and click the left edge of the artboard, about halfway down, to place the image.

Whichever thumbnail is showing in the loaded graphics cursor when you click in the Document window is placed.

● **Note:** The figure shows after clicking to place the Water.jpg image.

▶ **Tip:** To discard an asset that is loaded and ready to be placed, use the arrow keys to navigate to the asset, and then press the Escape key.

5 Press and hold the spacebar and drag to the left so that you see the area off the right side of the artboard.

6 Position the loaded graphics cursor off the right side of the artboard. Click and drag down and to the right, stopping when the image is roughly as big as you see in the figure. Leave the image selected.

You can either click to place an image at 100% or click and drag to place an image and size it as you place it in the Document window. By dragging when you place an image, you are resizing the image. Resizing an image in Illustrator will most likely result in a different resolution than the original. Once again, you can look at the PPI (Pixels Per Inch) value in the Control panel to see the resolution of the image. The original PPI of the Text.psd image was 150 PPI.

7 With the Text.psd image (the image of the green leaf) still selected, drag the selected art indicator (the colored box) in the Layers panel up to the Text layer to move the image to the Text layer.

8 Choose View > Fit Artboard In Window.

Applying color edits to an image

In Illustrator, you can convert images to a different color mode (such as RGB, CMYK, or grayscale) or adjust individual color values. You can also saturate (darken) or desaturate (lighten) colors or invert colors (create a color negative).

In order to edit colors in the image, the image needs to be embedded in the Illustrator file. If the file is linked, you can edit the color of the image in a program like Photoshop and then update it in Illustrator.

1 In the Layers panel, click the eye icons (👁) in the visibility column for the Pictures and Text layers to hide their contents.

2 With the Selection tool (↖), click to select the Lilypads.psd image at the top of the artboard.

3 Choose Edit > Edit Colors > Adjust Color Balance.

4 In the Adjust Colors dialog box, drag the sliders or enter values for the CMYK percentages to change the colors in the image. You can press Tab to move between the text fields. I used the following values:

- C= **5**
- M= **−25**
- Y= **10**
- K= **0**

Feel free to experiment a little. Select Preview so that you can see the color changes. Click OK.

Note: To see the results, you may need to select and deselect Preview as you change options in the Adjust Colors dialog box.

Note: If you later decide to adjust the colors of the same image by choosing Edit > Edit Colors > Adjust Color Balance, the color values will be set to 0 (zero).

5 Choose Select > Deselect, and then choose File > Save.

6 In the Layers panel, click the visibility column for the Pictures and Text layers to show their contents. Click the eye icon (◉) in the visibility column for the Background layer to hide its contents.

Masking images

Note: You will hear people use the phrases "clipping mask," "clipping path," and "mask." The way most of us refer to them, they mean the same thing.

To achieve certain design effects, you can apply a *clipping mask (clipping path)*, or an object whose shape masks other artwork so that only areas that lie within the shape are visible. In the first part of the figure at right is an image with a white circle on top. In the second part of the figure, the white circle was used to mask the image.

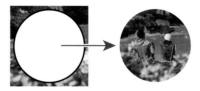

Image with a white circle on top.

The circle masking part of the image.

Only vector objects can be clipping paths; however, any artwork can be masked. You can also import masks created in Photoshop files. The clipping path and the masked object are referred to as the *clipping set*.

Applying a simple mask to an image

In this short section, you'll see how to let Illustrator create a simple mask for you on the Kayak.jpg image so that you can hide part of the image.

Tip: You can also apply a clipping mask by choosing Object > Clipping Mask > Make.

1   With the Selection tool (➤) selected, click the Kayak.jpg image to select it (the first image you placed). Click the Mask button in the Control panel.

Clicking the Mask button applies a clipping mask to the image in the shape and size of the image. In this case, the image itself does not look any different.

Note: You may need to drag the left edge of the Layers panel to the left to see more of the names, like I did for the figure.

2   In the Layers panel, click the Locate Object button (🔍) at the bottom of the panel.

Notice the <Clipping Path> and <Linked File> sublayers that are contained within the <Clip Group> sublayer. The <Clipping Path> object is the clipping path (mask) that was created, and the <Clip Group> is a set that contains the mask and the object that is masked (the linked image).

Editing a clipping path (mask)

In order to edit a clipping path, you need to be able to select it. Illustrator offers several ways to do this. Next, you will edit the mask you just created.

1 With the kayak image still selected on the artboard, click the Edit Contents button (⬛) in the Control panel and, in the Layers panel, notice that the <Linked File> sublayer (in the <Clip Group>) is showing the selected-art indicator (small color box) to the far right of the sublayer name.

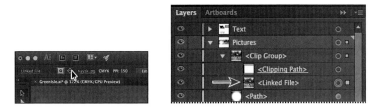

2 Click the Edit Clipping Path button (⬛) in the Control panel, and notice that the <Clipping Path> is now selected (it's showing the selected-art indicator in the Layers panel).

When an object is masked, you can edit the mask, the object that is masked, or both. Use these two buttons to select which to edit. When you first click to select an object that is masked, you will edit both the mask and the masked object.

3 With the Edit Clipping Path button (⬛) selected in the Control panel, choose View > Outline.

4 Use the Selection tool (▶) to drag the top-middle bounding point of the selected mask down until the measurement label shows a height of approximately 3.25 in.

5 Choose View > GPU Preview (or Preview On CPU if that is all that is available).

6 Click Transform (or X, Y, W, or H) in the Control panel (or open the Transform panel [Window > Transform]), and ensure that the center of the Reference Point is selected (⬛). Make sure that the Constrain Width And Height Proportions is off (⬛), and change Width to **3.5 in**. If you see that Height is not 3.25 in, go ahead and make it so.

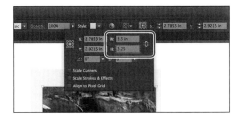

Tip: You can also double-click a clip group (object masked with a clipping path) to enter Isolation mode. You can then either click the masked object (the image in this case) to select it or click the edge of the clipping path to select the clipping path. After you are finished editing, you can then exit Isolation mode using a variety of methods as discussed in previous lessons (like pressing the Escape key).

Tip: You can also edit a clipping path with transformation options, like rotate, skew, etc., or by using the Direct Selection tool (▶).

7 In the Control panel, click the Edit Contents button () to edit the Kayak.jpg image, *not* the mask.

▶ **Tip:** You can also press the arrow keys on the keyboard to reposition the image.

8 With the Selection tool (➤), be careful to drag from within the bounds of the mask, down a little bit, and release the mouse button. Notice that you are moving the image and not the mask.

With the Edit Contents button () selected, you can apply many transformations to the image, including scaling, moving, rotating, and more.

9 Choose Select > Deselect, and then click the image again to select the entire clip group. Drag the image onto the light gray rectangle, and position it like you see in the figure.

10 Choose Select > Deselect, and then choose File > Save.

Masking an object with text

In this section, you'll use text as a mask for an image you placed. In order to create a mask from text, the text needs to be on top of the image, as you'll see.

1 With the Selection tool (➤) selected, drag the green leaf image (Text.psd) from off the right side of the artboard on top of the "ISLE" text.

2 Choose Object > Arrange > Send To Back. You should see the "ISLE" text now. Make sure that the image is positioned roughly like you see in the figure.

● **Note:** If the Text. psd image is not as wide as the "ISLE" text, make sure you resize the image, holding down the Shift key to constrain the proportions. Don't worry if it's larger than you see in the figure.

3 With the image still selected, Shift-click the "ISLE" text to select them both. Right-click over the selected content, and choose Make Clipping Mask from the context menu.

You can edit the Text.psd image and the clipping mask separately, just as you did previously with the masked Kayak.jpg image.

▶ **Tip:** You can also choose Object > Clipping Mask > Make.

4 With the text still selected, open the Graphic Styles panel (Window > Graphic Styles) and select the Text Shadow graphic style to apply a drop shadow.

5 Choose Select > Deselect, and then choose File > Save.

Masking an object with multiple shapes

You can easily create a mask from either a single shape or multiple shapes. In order to create a clipping mask with multiple shapes, the shapes first need to be converted to a compound path. This can be done by selecting the shapes that will be used as the mask and choosing Object > Compound Path > Make. Ensure that the compound path is on top of the content to be masked, and then choose Object > Clipping Mask > Make.

Creating an opacity mask

An *opacity mask* is different from a *clipping mask* because it allows you to mask an object and alter the transparency of artwork. You can make and edit an opacity mask using the Transparency panel. In this section, you'll create an opacity mask for the Water.jpg image so that it fades into the blue color of the background shape.

1 In the Layers panel, click the disclosure triangles for all layers (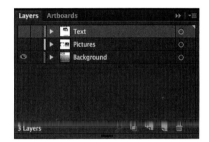) to collapse the contents, if necessary. Click the visibility column to the left of the Background layer to see its contents. Click the eye icon ( ) to the left of the Pictures and Text layers to hide their contents.

2 With the Selection tool selected, click the water image on the artboard.
Choose Align To Artboard from the Align To menu, if necessary, in the Control panel. Click the Horizontal Align Center button ( ) and then the Vertical Align Center button ( ) in the Control panel to align the image to the artboard.

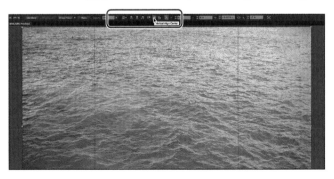

3 Select the Rectangle tool () in the Tools panel, and click in the approximate center of the artboard. In the Rectangle dialog box, change Width to **9 in** and Height to **8 in**. Click OK. This will become the mask.

4 Press the D key to set the default stroke (black, 1pt) and fill (white) for the new rectangle.

5 Select the Selection tool (▶), and with the rectangle selected, click the Horizontal Align Center button (▣) and then the Vertical Align Bottom button (▣) in the Control panel to align the rectangle to the bottom center of the artboard.

Note: The object that is to become the opacity mask (the masking object) needs to be the top selected object on the artboard. If it is a single object, like a rectangle, it does not need to be a compound path. If the opacity mask is to be made from multiple objects, they need to be grouped.

Note: If you wanted to create a mask that was the same dimensions as the image, instead of drawing a shape, you could have simply clicked the Make Mask button in the Transparency panel.

6 Press the Shift key, and click the Water.jpg image to select it as well.

7 Choose Window > Transparency to open the Transparency panel. Click the Make Mask button, and leave the artwork selected.

After clicking the Make Mask button, the button now shows as "Release." If you were to click the button again, the image would no longer be masked.

Click the Make Mask button.

Notice the result.

Editing an opacity mask

Next, you'll adjust the opacity mask that you just created.

1. In the Transparency panel, Shift-click the mask thumbnail (as indicated by the white rectangle on the black background) to disable the mask.

   Notice that a red X appears on the mask in the Transparency panel and that the entire Water.jpg image reappears in the Document window.

Tip: To disable and enable an opacity mask, you can also choose Disable Opacity Mask or Enable Opacity Mask from the Transparency panel menu.

2. In the Transparency panel, Shift-click the mask thumbnail to enable the mask again.

3. Click to select the mask thumbnail on the right side of the Transparency panel. If the mask isn't selected on the artboard, click to select it with the Selection tool (⬆).

   Clicking the opacity mask in the Transparency panel selects the mask (the rectangle path) on the artboard. With the mask selected, you can't edit other artwork on the artboard. Also, notice that the document tab shows (<Opacity Mask>/Opacity Mask), indicating that you are now editing the mask.

Tip: To show the mask by itself (in grayscale if the original mask had color in it) on the artboard, you can also Option-click (Mac OS) or Alt-click (Windows) the mask thumbnail in the Transparency panel.

4. Click the Layers panel icon (⬛) on the right side of the workspace to reveal the Layers panel.

   In the Layers panel, notice that the layer <Opacity Mask> appears, indicating that the mask—rather than the artwork that is being masked—is selected.

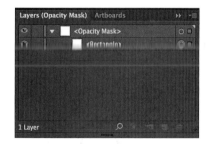

5. With the mask selected in the Transparency panel and on the artboard, click the Fill color in the Control panel, and select a white-to-black linear gradient, called White, Black.

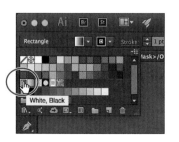

You will now see that where there is white in the mask, the Water.jpg image is showing, and where there is black, it is hidden. The gradient mask gradually reveals the image.

6 Make sure that the Fill box (toward the bottom of the Tools panel or in the Swatches panel) is selected.

7 Select the Gradient tool () in the Tools panel. Holding down the Shift key, position the pointer close to the bottom of the Water.jpg image. Click and drag up to just below the top of the mask shape, as shown in the figure. Release the mouse button, and then release the Shift key.

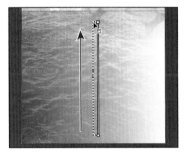
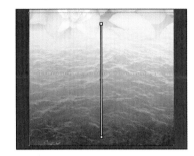

Drag to edit the opacity mask.   Notice the result.

8 Click the Transparency panel icon (), and notice how the mask has changed appearance in the Transparency panel.

Next, you'll move the image but not the opacity mask. With the image thumbnail selected in the Transparency panel, both the image and the mask are linked together by default so that if you move the image, the mask moves as well.

● **Note:** You have access to the link icon only when the image thumbnail, not the mask thumbnail, is selected in the Transparency panel.

9 In the Transparency panel, click the image thumbnail so that you are no longer editing the mask. Click the link icon (⧉) between the image thumbnail and the mask thumbnail. This allows you to move just the image or the mask, but not both.

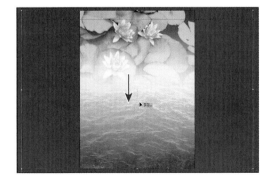

● **Note:** The position of Water.jpg does not have to match the figure exactly.

10 With the Selection tool, begin dragging the Water.jpg image down. As you drag, press and hold the Shift key to constrain the movement vertically. After you drag a little, release the mouse button, and then release the Shift key to see where it is positioned.

11 In the Transparency panel, click the broken link icon () between the image thumbnail and the mask thumbnail to link the two together again.

12 Choose Object > Arrange > Send To Back to send the Water.jpg image behind the Lilypads.psd image. It won't look like anything has changed on the artboard, but later you will attempt to select the Lilypads.psd image, and it will need to be on top of the Water.jpg image.

13 Choose Select > Deselect, and then choose File > Save.

Sampling colors in placed images

You can *sample*, or *copy*, the colors in placed images to apply the colors to artwork. Sampling colors enables you to easily make colors consistent in a file that combines images and Illustrator artwork.

1 In the Layers panel, make sure that all of the layers are collapsed, and then click the visibility column to the left of the Text and Pictures layers to show the layer contents on the artboard.

2 With the Selection tool (➤) selected, click the text "green."

3 Make sure that the Fill box (toward the bottom of the Tools panel) is selected.

4 Select the Eyedropper tool (✎) in the Tools panel, and Shift-click a green area in one of the lily pads to sample and apply a green color to the text. You can try sampling the color of different images and content, if you want. The color you sample is applied to the selected text.

Note: Using the Shift key with the Eyedropper tool allows you to apply only the sampled color to the selected object. If you don't use the Shift key, you apply all appearance attributes to the selected object.

5 Choose Select > Deselect.

Working with image links

When you place images in Illustrator and either link to them or embed them, you can see a listing of these images in the Links panel. You use the Links panel to see and manage all linked or embedded artwork. The Links panel displays a small thumbnail of the artwork and uses icons to indicate the artwork's status. From the Links panel, you can view the images that have been linked to and embedded, replace a placed image, update a linked image that has been edited outside of Illustrator, or edit a linked image in the original application, such as Photoshop.

Finding link information

When you place an image, it can be helpful to see where the original image is located, what transformations have been applied to the image (such as rotation and scale), and more information. Next, you will explore the Links panel to discover image information.

1   Choose Window > Workspace > Reset Essentials.

2   Choose Window > Links to open the Links panel.

    Looking in the Links panel, you will see a listing of all the images you've placed. Images with a name to the right of the image thumbnail are linked, and those images without a name are embedded. You can also tell whether an image has been embedded by the embedded icon (◫).

▶ **Tip:** You can also double-click the image in the Layers panel list to see the image information.

3   Scroll in the panel, if necessary, and select the Kayak.jpg image (which shows the name to the right of the thumbnail). Click the toggle arrow in the lower-left corner of the Layers panel to reveal the link information at the bottom of the panel.

    You will see information, such as the name, original location of the image, file format, resolution, modification and creation dates, transformation information, and more.

4   Click the Go To Link button (⬚) below the list of images. The Kayak.jpg image will be selected and centered in the Document window. The words "Linked File" will appear in the Selection Indicator of the Control panel (on the left end).

5   In the Control panel, click the link "Kayak.jpg" to reveal a menu of options.

    The menu of options that appears mirrors those options found in the Links panel. If you were to select an embedded image, you would instead see the link named Embedded in the Control panel. Clicking that orange link (default color) would show the same menu options, but some of them would be inaccessible.

6   Press the Escape key to hide the menu and leave the Kayak.jpg image selected.

Embedding and unembedding images

As was mentioned previously, if you choose not to link to an image when placing it, the image is embedded in the Illustrator file. That means that the image data is stored within the Illustrator document. You can choose to embed an image later, after placing and linking to it, if you choose. Also, you might want to use embedded images outside of Illustrator or to edit them in an image-editing application like Photoshop. Illustrator allows you to unembed images, which saves the embedded artwork to your file system as a PSD or TIFF file (you can choose) and automatically links it to the Illustrator file. Next, you will embed an image in the document.

● **Note:** Neither 1-bit images nor images that are either locked or hidden can be unembedded.

1 With the Kayak.jpg image still selected, click the Embed button in the Control panel to embed the image.

The link to the original image file is removed, and the image data is embedded in the Illustrator document. Visually, you can tell the image is embedded because it no longer has the X going through the middle of it (with the image selected and edges showing [View > Show Edges]) and an embed icon () appears in the Links panel to the far right of the name.

● **Note:** Certain file formats, like PSD, show an Import Options dialog box when you embed the image, allowing you to select placement options.

With an image embedded, you may realize that you need to make an edit to that image in a program like Adobe Photoshop. You can just as easily unembed an image, which is what you'll do next to the Kayak.jpg image.

2 With the Kayak.jpg image still selected on the artboard, click the Unembed button in the Control panel. You can also choose Unembed from the Links panel menu (▼▤).

3 In the Unembed dialog box, navigate to the Lessons > Lesson14 > images folder (if you are not already there). Choose TIFF (*.TIF) from the File Format menu (Mac OS) or from the Save As Type (Windows) menu, and click Save.

● **Note:** The embedded Kayak.jpg image data is unembedded from the file and saved as a TIFF file in the images folder. The kayak image on the artboard is now linked to the TIFF file.

Replacing a linked image

You can easily replace a linked or embedded image with another image to update the artwork. The replacement image is positioned exactly where the original image was, so no adjustment should be necessary if the new image is of the same dimensions. If you scaled the image that you are replacing, you may need to resize the replacement image to match the original. Next, you will replace several images.

1 With the Selection tool (↖) selected, drag the gradient-filled rectangle off the left edge of the artboard on top of the Kayak.tif image, centering it on the image using the Smart Guides.

2 Choose Object > Arrange > Bring To Front to bring the gradient-filled rectangle on top of the image.

3 In the Layers panel, click the edit column to the left of the Background layer to lock the layer content on the artboard.

4 Drag across the Kayak.tif image, the gradient-filled rectangle, and the light gray rectangle beneath it to select the artwork.

5 Choose Object > Group.

6 Drag the new group up so that its top aligns with the top of the artboard.

7 Choose View > Smart Guides to turn them off.

8 Option-drag (Mac OS) or Alt-drag (Windows) the group down to create a copy. Use the figure as a guide for where to position the copy.

9 Repeat this two more times so that you have four image groups on the artboard and they are positioned roughly like you see in the following figure.

In the Links panel, you will see a series of Kayak.tif images listed in the panel.

Next, you will replace the images and then rotate the pictures.

10 Click the second group from the top on the artboard. In the Links panel, with one of the Kayak.tif images selected, click the Relink button () below the list of images.

11 In the Place dialog box, navigate to the Lessons > Lesson14 > images folder and select People.psd. *Make sure that the Link option is selected.* Click Place to replace the kayak image with the People.psd image.

When you replace an image, any color adjustments made to the original image are not applied to the replacement. However, masks applied to the original image are preserved. Any layer modes and transparency adjustments that you've made to other layers also may affect the image's appearance.

> **Tip:** The new image is masked in the same shape. If you need to edit either the image or the clipping path, you could click the Edit Contents button (▣) or the Edit Clipping Path button (▣) in the Control panel.

12 Click the third group from the top on the artboard. In the Links panel, with the Kayak.tif image selected, click the Relink button (⬚) below the list of images.

13 In the Place dialog box, navigate to the Lessons > Lesson14 > images folder and select Hiking.jpg. *Make sure that the Link option is selected.* Click Place to replace the kayak image with the new image.

14 Click the bottom group. In the Links panel, with one of the Kayak.tif images selected, click the Relink button (⬚) below the list of images.

15 In the Place dialog box, navigate to the Lessons > Lesson14 > images folder and select Snorkel.psd. Make sure that the Link option is selected. Click Place to replace the kayak image with the Snorkel.psd image.

16 Choose View > Smart Guides to turn them on.

17 Choose Select > Deselect. Click the top image group with the Kayak.tif image. Position the pointer just off the upper-right corner, and when you see the rotate arrows (↱), click and drag to the left until you see approximately 10° in the measurement label.

18 Click the group with the People.psd image just below the top group and rotate the group to the right, until you see approximately −5° in the measurement label. Rotate the Hiking.jpg group to the left until you see approximately 10° in the measurement label. Rotate the Snorkel.psd image group to the right until you see approximately −10° in the measurement label.

19 Choose File > Save.

Packaging a file

When you *package* a file, you create a folder that contains a copy of the Illustrator document, any necessary fonts, copies of the linked graphics, and a report that contains information about the packaged files. This is an easy way to hand off all necessary files for an Illustrator project. Next, you will package the poster files.

1 Choose File > Package. In the Package dialog box, set the following options:

- Click the folder icon (⬛), and navigate to the Lesson14 folder, if you are not already there. Click Choose (Mac OS) or Select Folder (Windows) to return to the Package dialog box.
- Folder name: **GreenIsle** (remove "_Folder" from the name)
- Options: Leave at default settings.

2 Click Package.

The Copy Links option *copies* all the linked files to the new folder it creates. The Collect Links In Separate Folder option creates a folder called Links and copies the links into there. The Relink Linked Files To Document option updates the links within the Illustrator document to link to the new copies.

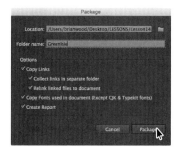

3 In the next dialog box that discusses font-licensing restrictions, click OK. Clicking Back would allow you to deselect Copy Fonts Used In Document (Except CJK & Typekit fonts).

4 In the final dialog box to appear, click Show Package to see the package folder.

In the package folder should be a folder called Links that contains all the linked images. The GreenIsle Report (.txt file) contains information about the document contents.

5 Return to Illustrator, and choose File > Close.

Review questions

1 Describe the difference between *linking* and *embedding* in Illustrator.

2 What kinds of objects can be used as masks?

3 How do you create an opacity mask for a placed image?

4 What color modifications can you apply to a selected object using effects?

5 Describe how to replace a placed image with another image in a document.

6 Describe what *packaging* does.

Review answers

1 A *linked file* is a separate, external file connected to the Illustrator file by a link. A linked file does not add significantly to the size of the Illustrator file. The linked file must accompany the Illustrator file to preserve the link and to ensure that the placed file appears when you open the Illustrator file. An *embedded file* is included in the Illustrator file. The Illustrator file size reflects the addition of the embedded file. Because the embedded file is part of the Illustrator file, no link can be broken. You can update linked and embedded files using the Relink button (▣) in the Links panel.

2 A mask can be a simple or compound path and masks (such as an opacity mask) may be imported with placed Photoshop files. You can also create layer clipping masks with any shape that is the topmost object of a group or layer.

3 You create an opacity mask by placing the object to be used as a mask on top of the object to be masked. Then you select the mask and the object(s) to be masked, and either click the Make Mask button in the Transparency panel or choose Make Opacity Mask from the Transparency panel menu.

4 You can use effects to change the color mode (RGB, CMYK, or grayscale) or to adjust individual colors in a selected object. You can also saturate or desaturate colors or invert colors in a selected object. You can apply color modifications to placed images, as well as to artwork created in Illustrator.

5 To replace a placed image with a different image, select the image in the Links panel. Then click the Relink button (▣), and locate and select the replacement image. Click Place.

6 *Packaging* is used to gather all of the necessary pieces for an Illustrator document. Packaging creates a copy of the Illustrator file, the linked images, and the necessary fonts (if desired), and it gathers the copies into a folder.

15 PREPARING CONTENT FOR THE WEB

Lesson overview

In this lesson, you'll learn how to do the following:

- Align content to the pixel grid.

- Work with the Slice and Slice Selection tools.

- Use the Save For Web command.

- Generate, export, and copy/paste CSS (Cascading Style Sheets) code.

- Save artwork as SVG.

 This lesson takes approximately 30 minutes to complete.

Download the project files for this lesson from the Lesson & Update Files tab on your Account page at www.peachpit.com and store them on your computer in a convenient location, as described in the "Getting Started" section of this book.

Your Account page is also where you'll find any updates to the chapters or to the lesson files. Look on the Lesson & Update Files tab to access the most current content.

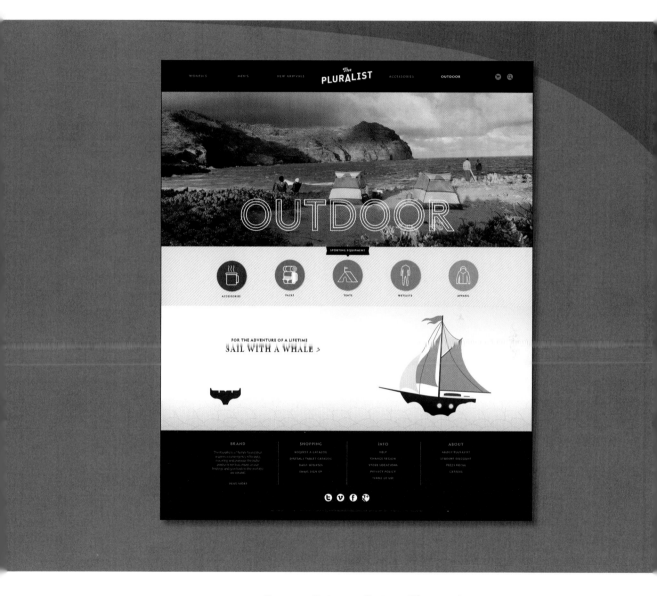

You can optimize your Illustrator CC content for use on the web and in screen presentations using various methods. For example, you can slice artwork and save it for the web, export CSS and image files, and generate SVG (Scalable Vector Graphics) in the form of an SVG file or SVG code.

Getting started

Before you begin, restore the default preferences for Adobe Illustrator CC.

● **Note:** If you have not already downloaded the project files for this lesson to your computer from your Account page, make sure to do so now. See the "Getting Started" section at the beginning of this book.

1 To ensure that the tools and panels function exactly as described in this lesson, delete or deactivate (by renaming) the Adobe Illustrator CC preferences file. See "Restoring default preferences" in the "Getting Started" section at the beginning of the book.

2 Start Adobe Illustrator CC.

3 Choose File > Open. In the Open dialog box, navigate to the Lessons > Lesson15 folder. Select the L15_start.ai file, and click Open. This lesson contains a fictitious business name, address, and website address for the purposes of the project.

4 The Missing Fonts dialog box will most likely appear. Click Sync Fonts to sync all the missing fonts to your computer (your list may not match the figure). After they are synced and you see the message stating that there are no more missing fonts, click Close.

If you can't get the fonts to sync (a "Syncing Typekit fonts…" message doesn't go away), you can go to the Creative Cloud desktop application and choose Assets > Fonts to see what the issue may be (refer to the section "Changing font family and font style" in Lesson 8, "Adding Type to a Poster," for more information on how to resolve it).

You can also just click Close in the Missing Fonts dialog box and ignore the missing fonts as you proceed. A third method is to click the Find Fonts button in the Missing Fonts dialog box and replace the fonts with a local font on your machine.

● **Note:** If you don't see Reset Essentials in the Workspace menu, choose Window > Workspace > Essentials before choosing Window > Workspace > Reset Essentials.

5 Choose Window > Workspace > Reset Essentials to ensure that the workspace is set to the default settings.

6 Choose View > Fit Artboard In Window.

● **Note:** If you see a warning dialog box referring to spot colors, just click Continue.

7 Choose File > Save As. In the Save As dialog box, navigate to the Lessons > Lesson15 folder, and name the file **WebDesign.ai**. Leave the Format option set to Adobe Illustrator (ai) (Mac OS) or the Save As Type option set to Adobe Illustrator (*.AI) (Windows), and then click Save. In the Illustrator Options dialog box, leave the Illustrator options at their default settings, and then click OK.

8 Choose Select > Deselect, if necessary.

Saving content for the web

Using Illustrator CC, you can save your artwork for the web using a variety of methods and formats. If you need web images for use in a website or an onscreen presentation, you can use the File > Save For Web command. Images can be saved in several file formats, such as GIF, JPEG, and PNG. These three formats are optimized for use on the web and are compatible with most browsers, yet each has different capabilities.

Tip: To learn more about working with web graphics, search for "File formats for exporting artwork" in Illustrator Help (Help > Illustrator Help).

If you are building a website or want to hand off content to a developer, you can transform the visual designs in Illustrator to CSS styles using the CSS Properties panel (Window > CSS Properties) or File > Export command. Illustrator allows you to easily export CSS or copy and paste CSS from Illustrator into your HTML editor. You can also export Scalable Vector Graphics (SVG) using a variety of methods.

In the first part of the section on creating web content, you will focus on the pixel grid and on slicing content for export using the Save For Web command. Then you will translate your design into CSS for use in a website.

Aligning content to the pixel grid

Before you save content for the web, it's important to understand the pixel grid in Illustrator. It's critical that raster images look sharp, especially standard web graphics at 72 pixels per inch (PPI) resolution. To enable web designers to create pixel-accurate designs, you can align artwork to the pixel grid. The *pixel grid* is a grid of 72 squares per inch, vertically and horizontally, that is viewable when you zoom to 600% or higher with Pixel Preview mode enabled (View > Pixel Preview).

Tip: To learn about working with text and anti-aliasing, see the PDF named "TextAntiAliasing.pdf" in the Lessons > Lesson_extras folder.

When the pixel-aligned property is enabled for an object, all the horizontal and vertical segments in the object get aligned to the pixel grid, which makes strokes appear especially crisp. When you create a new document, you can set the Align New Objects To Pixel Grid option at the document level. This makes all artwork that can be aligned to the pixel grid (this does not include Live Shapes such as rectangles) align to it automatically. You can also align content to the pixel grid after the content has been created, as you will do in this section.

1   Choose File > New. In the New Document dialog box, choose Web from the Profile menu. Click the triangle to the left of the word "Advanced," toward the lower-left corner of the dialog box.

In the Advanced settings, you can see that Color Mode is RGB for all artwork you create, Raster Effects is Screen (72 ppi), and Align New Objects To Pixel Grid is selected.

2   Click Cancel.

3 In the WebDesign.ai file, choose File > Document Color Mode, and you will see that RGB Color is selected.

After you create a document, you can change the document color mode. This sets the default color mode for all new colors you create and the existing swatches. RGB is the correct color mode to use when creating content for the web or for onscreen presentations.

4 Select the Zoom tool (🔍), and zoom in to the cup icon with the word "Accessories" beneath it, roughly in the middle of the artboard, to zoom in closely.

5 Choose View > Pixel Preview to preview a rasterized version of the design.

Preview mode   Pixel Preview mode

▶ **Tip:** You can turn off the pixel grid by choosing Illustrator CC > Preferences > Guides & Grid (Mac OS) or Edit > Preferences > Guides & Grid (Windows) and deselecting Show Pixel Grid (Above 600% Zoom).

6 Choose 600% from the View menu in the lower-left corner of the Document window (in the Status bar), and make sure you can still see the cup icon above the "Accessories" text.

By zooming in to at least 600%, and with Pixel Preview turned on, you can see a pixel grid appear, as in the figure. The pixel grid divides the artboard into 1 pt. (1/72-inch) increments. For the next steps, you need to see the pixel grid (zoom level of 600% or greater).

7 Select the Selection tool (▶), and click to select the larger white shape that is part of the cup. Notice that the straight edges of the shape look a little "fuzzy."

8 Click the word "Transform" (or X, Y, W, or H) in the Control panel, and select Align To Pixel Grid at the bottom of the Transform panel.

▶ **Tip:** You can choose Select > Object > Not Aligned To Pixel Grid to select all artwork in the document that is eligible to be, but is not currently, aligned to the pixel grid. You can then select Align To Pixel Grid in the Transform panel. Be careful! If you align text that has been converted to outlines, the text can change appearance in ways you didn't intend.

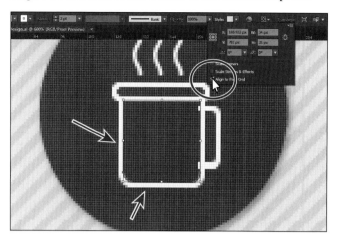

Objects that are pixel-aligned but do not have any straight vertical or horizontal segments, are not modified to align to the pixel grid. For example, because a rotated rectangle does not have straight vertical or horizontal segments, it is not nudged to produce crisp paths when the pixel-aligned property is set for it.

9 Choose View > Fit Artboard In Window.

Notice that the entire artboard is not fit in the window. This is because Pixel Preview is on and you are viewing the artwork at 100%.

10 Click the word "Transform" (or X, Y, W, or H) in the Control panel, and then click the Transform panel menu icon ( ).

Notice that Align New Objects To Pixel Grid is selected. This option sets all new artwork to be aligned to the pixel grid automatically. If this document were created using a Print profile, it would not be selected, but you could turn it on here. Bringing nonaligned objects into documents with the Align New Objects To Pixel Grid option enabled does not automatically pixel-align those objects. To make such objects pixel-aligned, select the object, and then select the Align To Pixel Grid option from the Transform panel. You cannot pixel-align objects such as Live Shapes, rasters, raster effects, and text objects because such objects do not have real paths.

11 Press the Escape key to hide the Transform panel.

12 Choose Select > Deselect (if available), and then choose File > Save.

Slicing content

If you create artwork on an artboard and choose File > Save For Web, Illustrator creates a single image file the size of the artboard. One way around that would be to create multiple artboards for artwork, each containing a piece of the web page like a button, and save each artboard as a separate image file.

Note: To learn more about creating slices, search for "Create slices" in Adobe Illustrator Help (Help > Illustrator Help).

You can also design your artwork on an artboard and slice the content. In Illustrator, you can create *slices* to define the boundaries of different web elements in your artwork. For example, if you design an entire web page on an artboard and you want to save a particular vector shape as a button for your website, that artwork can be optimized in GIF or PNG format, while the rest of the image is optimized as a JPEG file. You can isolate the button image by creating a slice. When you save the artwork as a web page using the Save For Web command, you can choose to save each slice as an independent file with its own format and settings.

Next, you will create a new layer that will contain the slices, and then you will create slices for different parts of the artwork.

Note: To learn more about creating layers, see the section "Creating layers and sublayers" in Lesson 9, "Organizing Your Artwork with Layers."

1 Click the Layers panel icon () to open the Layers panel. Option-click (Mac OS) or Alt-click (Windows) the Create New Layer button (🔲) at the bottom of the Layers panel. In the Layer Options dialog box that appears, change the name of the layer to **Slices**, and click OK. Make sure that the new Slices layer is selected and is at the top of the layer stack.

When you create slices, they are treated as objects and are listed in the Layers panel and can be selected, deleted, resized, and more. It helps to keep them on their own layer so that you can more easily manage them, but this isn't necessary.

2 Press Command+– (Mac OS) or Ctrl+– (Windows) to zoom out.

3 Select the Zoom tool (🔍), and drag a marquee around the Pluralist logo at the top of the artboard.

4 Select the Slice tool (✂) in the Tools panel. Click and drag a slice around the logo. See the figure for help. Don't worry about it fitting perfectly right now; you will edit it later.

When you create a slice, Illustrator divides the surrounding artwork into automatic slices to maintain the layout of the page. Auto slices account for the areas of your artwork that you did not define as a slice. Illustrator regenerates auto slices every time you add or edit your own slices. Also, notice the number in the upper-left corner of the slice you created. Illustrator numbers slices from left to right and from top to bottom, beginning in the upper-left corner of the artwork.

5 Choose View > Fit Artboard In Window.

6 With the Selection tool ( ) selected, click the sailing ship in the middle of the artboard.

7 In the Layers panel, select the Slices layer to ensure that the new slice is on it.

8 Choose Object > Slice > Create From Selection.

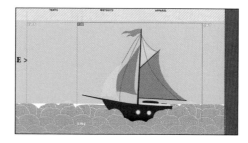

This is another way to make a slice from existing content. Take a look at the Object > Slice menu because there are a lot of great commands in there.

9 Choose Select > Deselect.

Selecting and editing slices

Editing user-created slices is necessary, for instance, when sliced content changes or when what is included in the slice needs to change.

1 Press Command+− (Mac OS) or Ctrl+− (Windows) to zoom out. Select the Zoom tool ( ), and zoom in to the Pluralist logo at the top of the artboard.

2 Select the Slice Selection tool ( ) from the Slice tool group in the Tools panel by clicking and holding down the Slice tool ( ).

3 Click in the center of the slice over the Pluralist logo. The selected slice is highlighted, and four corner bounding points appear.

The Slice Selection tool allows you to edit slices you've created using different methods. You can also select a user slice with the Selection ( ) or Direct Selection ( ) tools by clicking the stroke (edge) of the slice or from within the Layers panel.

4 Position the pointer over the lower-right corner of the selected slice. When a double arrow appears, click and drag toward the center of the logo until it fits tighter around the logo content. Make sure to include all of the logo content within the slice area.

5 Position the pointer over the left side of the selected slice. When a double arrow appears, click and drag right a bit closer to the edge of the logo.

When adjusting slices manually, you should include all appearance attributes, such as drop shadows, in the slice area. This can be difficult if the shadow is blurry. Using the Object > Slice > Create From Selection command creates a slice that surrounds all appearance properties, such as effects, if those effects are applied directly to the artwork and not to the layer the artwork is on (with multiple objects on the same layer). Using the Slice Selection tool, you can click and drag a slice, copy and paste it, delete it, and much more.

6 Try adjusting the other sides of the slice so that they are closer to the logo.

You want to ensure that the artwork and effects such as drop shadows are contained within slices so they will not appear to be cut off when the image is later optimized.

7 Choose Select > Deselect.

8 Choose View > Lock Slices so that you cannot select them.

Using the Save For Web command

After slicing your artwork, if necessary, you can then optimize that artwork for use on the web. You can use the File > Save For Web command to select optimization options and to preview optimized artwork. The key to the effective use of images on a website is finding the balance of resolution, size, and color to achieve optimal quality.

1 Choose View > Hide Slices.

While working on your artwork, you don't have to have the slices showing. This allows you to concentrate on selecting artwork without selecting slices. You can also hide the layer that the slices are on if you created a layer for them in the Layers panel.

2 Select the Selection tool ( ), and click the dark blue bar behind the logo.

3 Choose Object > Hide > Selection.

The logo will look like it has disappeared, but that's because it's white. When you save sliced content using the Save For Web command, all content that is showing in a slice will be flattened into a raster image. If you want to have transparency in the selected artwork (part of the image will be see-through), you need to first hide what you don't want to save. The areas where you see the artboard in a slice can be transparent, depending on the type of image you choose.

4 Choose View > Show Slices.

5 Choose File > Save For Web.

6 In the Save For Web dialog box, click the 2-Up tab at the top of the dialog box to select that display option, if it's not already selected.

Note: To resize the slices, you need to make sure they are unlocked. Choose View > Lock Slices. (If a checkmark appears to the left of the menu item, they are locked.)

This shows a split window with the original artwork on the left and the optimized artwork on the right (usually). You can tell which is the original artwork because it shows "Original: 'WebDesign.ai'" along with a file size below one of the preview areas. The optimized preview shows a file type such as PNG-24 and a file size below the preview area.

7 With the Slice Select tool ( ) selected (by default), click in the optimized area on the right. Click to select the slice that covers the Pluralist logo at the top of the artboard, if it isn't selected already. A red arrow is pointing to it in the figure.

Note: You may need to choose Fit On Screen from the View menu in the lower-left corner of the dialog box to see all of the artwork.

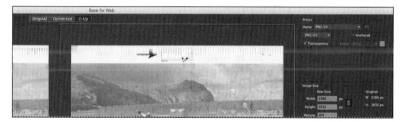

You can tell when a slice is selected because the artwork isn't dimmed and it has a light brown border around it.

8 In the Preset area on the right side of the dialog box, choose PNG-24 from the Optimized File Format menu (below Name), if it isn't already selected. Make sure the Transparency option is selected (below the Optimized File Format menu).

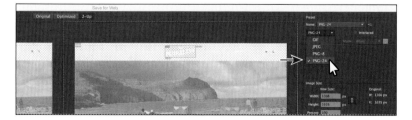

You can choose from four file formats, including GIF, JPEG, PNG-8, and PNG-24, as well as set the options for each in the Preset area. The available options change depending on the file format you select. If your image contains multiple slices that you are going to save, be sure to select each separately in the preview area and optimize all the slices.

9 Choose Selected Slices from the Export menu, if necessary.

Any slices that you select in the Save For Web dialog box will be exported. You can select multiple slices, after you've assigned optimization settings to them, by Shift-clicking the desired slices. By choosing All User Slices from the Export menu, all slices that you created will be exported.

10 Click the Preview button in the lower-left corner of the dialog box to launch the default web browser on your computer and to preview the sliced content. After previewing the content, close the browser, and return to Illustrator.

● **Note:** If nothing happens after clicking the Preview button, try clicking again. You may also need to click the Select Browser Menu button (⬛) to the right of the Preview button and choose Edit List to add a new browser.

▶ **Tip:** In the Save For Web dialog box, the Done button will save the optimization settings with the file, without actually generating any images. The Cancel button will not save the settings or generate images.

11 In the Save For Web dialog box, click Save. In the Save Optimized As dialog box, navigate to the Lessons > Lesson15 folder, and open it. Change the name to **Logo.png**, and click Save.

In your Lesson15 folder is a new images folder that Illustrator created. In that folder, you can see the single image that is labeled according to the name entered in the Save Optimized As dialog box, with the slice number appended to the end.

12 Choose View > Hide Slices.

13 Choose Object > Show All.

14 Choose Select > Deselect, and then choose File > Save.

Creating CSS code

As mentioned earlier, you can transform the visual designs in Illustrator to CSS styles using the CSS Properties panel (Window > CSS Properties) or the File > Export command. This is a great way to move the styling from your web design in Illustrator straight to your HTML editor or to hand it off to a web developer.

● **Note:** Exporting or copying CSS from Illustrator CC does not create HTML for a web page. It is intended to create CSS that is applied to HTML you create elsewhere, such as in Adobe Dreamweaver®.

Cascading Style Sheets are a collection of formatting rules, much like paragraph and character styles in Illustrator, that control the appearance of content in a web page. Unlike paragraph and character styles in Illustrator, CSS can control not only the look and feel of text but also the formatting and positioning of page elements found in HTML.

● **Note:** To learn more about CSS, visit the "Understanding Cascading Style Sheets" section of Adobe Dreamweaver Help (https://helpx.adobe.com/dreamweaver/using/cascading-style-sheets.html).

An example of CSS code

The great thing about generating CSS from your Illustrator artwork is that it allows for flexible web workflows. You can export all of the styling from a document, or you can just copy the styling code for a single object or a series of objects and paste it into an external web editor, like Adobe Dreamweaver. But creating CSS styling and using it effectively requires a bit of setup in your Illustrator CC document, and that's what you'll learn about first.

Setting up your design for generating CSS

If you intend to export or copy and paste CSS from Illustrator CC, slicing is not a necessary part of that process, but setting up the Illustrator CC file properly before creating CSS allows you to name the CSS styles that are generated. In this section, you'll look at the CSS Properties panel and see how you can set up the content for style export using *named* or *unnamed* content.

1 Choose View > Fit Artboard In Window, and then press Command+– (Mac OS) or Ctrl+– (Windows) to zoom out.

2 Choose Window > Workspace > Reset Essentials.

3   Choose Window > CSS Properties to open the CSS Properties panel.

Using the CSS Properties panel, you can do the following:

- Preview CSS code for selected objects.

- Copy CSS code for selected objects.

- Export generated styling for selected objects to a CSS file (along with any images used).

- Change options for the CSS code exported.

- Export the CSS for all objects to a CSS file.

4   With the Selection tool (⬆) selected, click to select the blue rectangle behind the navigation and logo at the top of the artboard (see the following figure).

Take a look in the CSS Properties panel, and you will see that a message appears in the preview area. Instead of CSS code (which is what the preview area typically shows), the message states that the object needs to be named in the Layers panel or you need to allow Illustrator to create styling from "unnamed objects."

5   Open the Layers panel, and click the Locate Object button (🔍) at the bottom of the panel to easily find the selected object in the panel.

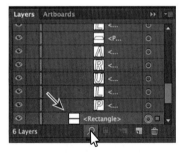

6   Double-click the name of the selected <Rectangle> object in the Layers panel, and change the name to **navbar** (lowercase). Press Enter or Return to make the change.

7   Look in the CSS Properties panel again, and you should see a style named .navbar.

When content is unnamed in the Layers panel, a CSS style is not created for it by default. If you name the object in the Layers panel, the CSS is generated, and the name of the style created matches the object name in the Layers panel. Illustrator creates styles called *classes* for most content.

For objects in the design (not including text objects, as you will see), the name you give them in the Layers panel should match the class name in the HTML that is created in a separate HTML editor, like Dreamweaver. But, you can also forgo naming the objects in the Layers panel and simply create generic styles that you can then export or paste into an HTML editor and name there. You will see how to do that next.

8   With the Selection tool, click to select the brown circle behind the cup you aligned to the pixel grid earlier. In the CSS Properties panel, a style will not appear since the object is unnamed in the Layers panel (it just has the generic <Path> name).

9   Click the Export Options button ( ) at the bottom of the CSS Properties panel.

The CSS Export Options dialog box that appears contains export options that you can set, such as which units to use, which properties to include in the styles, and other options, such as which Vendor prefixes to include.

10 Select Generate CSS For Unnamed Objects, and click OK.

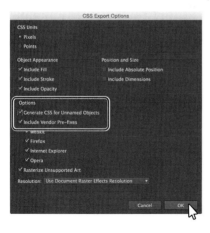

11 Look in the CSS Properties panel again. With the brown circle still selected, a style called .st0 appears in the preview area of the CSS Properties panel.

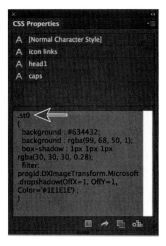

.st0 is short for "style 0" and is a generic name for the formatting that is generated. Every object that you don't name in the Layers panel will now be named .st1, .st2, and so on, after turning on Generate CSS For Unnamed Objects. This type of style naming can be useful if, for instance, you are creating the web page yourself and you are going to paste or export the CSS from Illustrator and name it in your HTML editor or if you simply needed some of the CSS formatting for a style you already have in your HTML editor.

12 Choose Select > Deselect, and then choose File > Save.

Working with character styles and CSS code

Note: Currently, paragraph styles are not taken into account when naming styles in the CSS code that is generated.

Illustrator will create CSS styles based on text formatting, as well. Formatting, such as font family, font size, leading (called *line-height* in CSS), color, kerning and tracking (collectively called *letter-spacing* in CSS), and more, can be captured in the CSS code. Any character styles that are applied to text in your design are listed in the CSS Properties panel as a CSS style and have the same name as the character style. Text that has formatting applied, without a character style applied, will have a generic CSS style name when Illustrator generates the style.

Next, you will create and then apply a character style to text.

1 In the CSS Properties panel, notice the style named [Normal Character Style], toward the top of the panel.

In the CSS Properties panel, only character styles that are applied to text appear. The Normal Character Style is applied to text by default, so it appears in the panel. If you create character styles but don't apply them to text, they will not appear in the CSS Properties panel.

2 Choose Window > Type > Character Styles to open the Character Styles panel.

3 Select the Zoom tool and zoom into the text on the left end of the footer. Specifically the text with the heading "BRAND."

4 Select the Type tool (**T**) in the Tools panel. Select the entire paragraph that begins with "The Pluralist is a lifestyle brand..."

5 Option-click (Mac OS) or Alt-click (Windows) the style named "p" in the Character Styles panel to apply it to the selected text.

6 Select the Selection tool (▶), and with the text object still selected, you will see the character style named "p" in the CSS Properties panel list. This indicates that it is applied to text in the design. You will also see CSS code in the preview area of the panel.

▶ **Tip:** You can also use the character styles listed in the CSS Properties panel as a way to apply the styles to text.

Selecting a text object will show all the generated CSS code for the styling used in the entire text area. With just the text selected, the CSS is not shown in the CSS Properties panel.

7 With the Selection tool, click the type object in the footer that contains the "Shopping" heading. Look in the CSS Properties panel, and you will see a series of CSS styles listed. These are the styles applied to all the text in the type area.

Selecting a type area gives you the ability to see all the CSS code generated from the styling. It is also a great way to be able to copy or export all the text formatting from a selected type area.

Working with graphic styles and CSS code

CSS code can also be copied or exported for any graphic styles that are applied to content. Next, you'll apply a graphic style and see the CSS code for it.

1 Scroll back up the artboard so that you can see the Ship and the "SAIL WITH A WHALE" text above the footer. With the Selection tool ($\blacktriangle$), click to select the blue rectangle behind the ship. You may want to zoom out a bit.

Tip: Like selecting a character style in the CSS Properties panel to apply the formatting, you can also select content and select an Object style listed in the CSS Properties panel to apply it.

2 Open the Graphic Styles panel (Window > Graphic Styles). Click the graphic style named "GradientBox."

Looking in the CSS Properties panel, you will see the object style named "GradientBox" listed, because it is applied to content in your document.

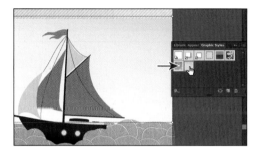

You will also see CSS code for a style. Mine is named ".content_3_," but yours may be different. The CSS code is the same as for the GradientBox graphic style you just saw since that graphic style is applied. But it's not naming the style with the "GradientBox" name, since the graphic style is just a way to apply formatting and the CSS code is being generated for that particular object. Remember, this is an unnamed style because you didn't rename the rectangle object in the Layers panel.

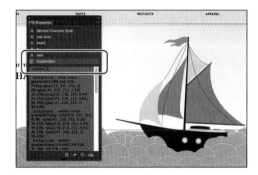

3 Leave the rectangle selected, and then choose File > Save.

Copying CSS

At times, you may need to capture only a bit of CSS code from part of your design to paste into your HTML editor or to send to a web developer. Illustrator lets you copy and paste CSS code easily. Next, you will copy the CSS for a few objects and learn about how grouping can change the way CSS code is generated.

1   With the rectangle still selected, click the Copy Selected Style button () at the bottom of the CSS Properties panel. This copies the CSS code currently showing in the panel.

   ● **Note:** You may see a yield sign icon (⚠) at the bottom of the panel when certain content is selected. It indicates that not all of the Illustrator appearance attributes (such as the multiple strokes applied to the shape) can be written in the CSS code for the selected content.

   Next, you will select multiple objects and copy the generated CSS code at the same time.

2   With the Selection tool (▶) selected and the rectangle still selected, Shift-click the brown circle to select both objects. Once again, you may need to zoom out a bit.

   In the CSS Properties panel, you will not see any CSS code since you need to have Illustrator generate the code for more than one selected object.

3   Click the Generate CSS button () at the bottom of the panel.

   The code for two CSS styles, .st0 and .content_3_ (yours may be different), now appears in the bottom half of the CSS Properties panel. Your style names may be different, and that's okay. To see both styles, you may need to scroll down in the panel. Yours may also be in a different order, and that's okay.

   > **Tip:** When CSS code appears in the CSS Properties panel for selected content, you can also select part of the code and right-click the selected code and then choose Copy to copy just that selection.

   With both styles showing in the CSS Properties panel, you could copy the styles and paste them into your HTML editor code or paste them into an email to send to a web developer, for instance.

4 With the Selection tool, click to select the ship.

In the CSS Properties panel, you will see CSS code for an .image style. That code contains a background-image property. When Illustrator encounters artwork (or raster images) that it can't make CSS code from or a group of objects, it rasterizes the exported content (*not* the

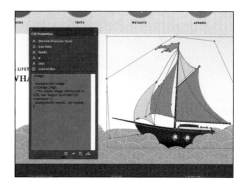

artwork on the artboard) when you export the CSS code. The CSS code that is generated can be applied to an HTML object, like a div, and the PNG image will be applied as a background image in the HTML object.

5 Select the Zoom tool, and zoom into the cup and brown circle. Drag a marquee selection across the brown circle and cup shapes to select all of them.

6 Click the Generate CSS button (🖼) at the bottom of the CSS Properties panel to generate the CSS code for the selected artwork.

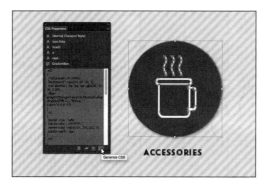

You will see the CSS code for all the selected objects in the panel. If you were to copy the CSS code now, the images would not be created, only the code referring to them. To generate the images, you need to export the code, which you will do in the next section.

7 Choose Object > Group to group the objects together. Leave the group selected for the next section.

Notice that, in the CSS Properties panel, a single CSS style is now showing (.image). Grouping content tells Illustrator to create a single image (in this case) from the grouped content. Having a single web image would most likely be better if you intend on placing it on a web page.

Exporting CSS

You can also export part or all of the CSS code for your page design. Exporting CSS code has the distinct advantages of creating a CSS file (.css) and exporting PNG files for content that is considered unsupported. In this section, you will see both methods.

1   With the group still selected, click the Export Selected CSS button (⬛) at the bottom of the CSS Properties panel.

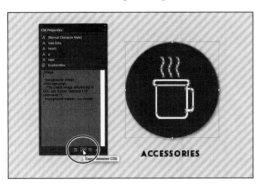

2   In the Export CSS dialog box, make sure that the filename is WebDesign. Navigate to the Lessons > Lesson15 > ForCSSExport folder, and click Save to save a CSS file named WebDesign.css and a PNG image file.

3   In the CSS Export Options dialog box, leave all settings at default, and click OK.

▶ **Tip:** You can choose a resolution for rasterized artwork in the CSS Export Options dialog box. By default, it uses the Document Raster Effects resolution (Effect > Document Raster Effects Settings).

4   Go to the Lessons > Lesson15 > ForCSSExport folder on your hard drive. In that folder, you should now see the WebDesign.css file and an image named image.png.

As stated earlier, the CSS code that was generated assumes that you are going to apply the CSS styling to an object in your HTML editor and that the image will become a background image for the object. With the image generated, you can use it for other parts of your web page as well. Next, you will export all the CSS from the design, after setting a few CSS options.

5   Back in Illustrator, choose File > Export. In the Export dialog box, set the Format option to CSS (css) (Mac OS) or the Save As Type option to CSS (*.CSS) (Windows). Change the filename to **WebDesign_all**, and make sure that you navigate to the Lessons > Lesson15 > ForCSSExport folder. Click Export.

● **Note:** You can also export all of the CSS from your design by choosing Export All from the CSS Properties panel. If you want to change the export options first, you can set them by clicking the Export Options button (▣) at the bottom of the CSS Properties dialog box.

6 In the CSS Export Options dialog box, leave all the options at their default settings, and click OK. You most likely will see a dialog box telling you that images will be overwritten. Click OK.

Position and size properties are not added to the CSS code by default. In certain situations, you will need to export CSS with those options selected. The Include Vendor Pre-fixes options are selected by default. *Vendor prefixes* are a way for certain browser makers (each is listed in the dialog box) to add support for new CSS features. You can choose to exclude these prefixes by deselecting them.

● **Note:** Your file sorting and icons may look different in the ForCSSExport folder, and that's okay.

7 Go to the Lessons > Lesson15 > ForCSSExport folder, and you will see the new CSS file named WebDesign_all.css and a series of images created because the Rasterize Unsupported Art option was selected in the CSS Export Options dialog box.

8 Return to Illustrator, and choose Select > Deselect.

9 Close the CSS Properties panel, and choose Window > Workspace > Reset Essentials.

10 Choose File > Save (if necessary).

Saving artwork as SVG

SVG (Scalable Vector Graphics) are used to define vector-based graphics for the web that won't lose quality if they are zoomed or resized, such as a logo. They are a vector format that describes images as shapes, paths, text, and filter effects. The resulting files are compact and provide high-quality graphics on the web, in print, and even on resource-constrained, handheld devices. Most major modern web browsers—such as Mozilla Firefox, Internet Explorer 9+, Google Chrome, Opera, and Safari—have at least some support for viewing SVG.

Illustrator allows you to select vector artwork, choose Edit > Copy, and then simply paste the SVG code that it generates into HTML in an HTML editor, or you can export or save as an SVG (.svg) file. In this section, you'll export as SVG (.svg) and explore the SVG export options using the File > Export command.

Note: There are two methods in Illustrator for generating SVG. You can choose either File > Save As or File > Export. The Export option is what is covered in this section. If you choose File > Save As and choose SVG in the Save As dialog box, you will see in the SVG Options dialog box a message and a link indicating a more modern SVG export. Clicking the Try button will take you to another SVG Options dialog box found when you choose File > Export.

1   Choose View > Pixel Preview to turn off Pixel Preview.

2   Choose View > Fit Artboard In Window.

3   With the Selection tool (▶) selected, click the tent icon on the green circle in the center of the artboard. This selects a group of shapes.

4   Option-drag (Mac OS) or Alt-drag (Windows) a copy of the tent icon off the left edge of the artboard (outside of the artboard area).

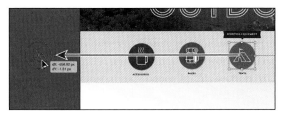

5   Choose Object > Artboards > Fit To Selected Art.

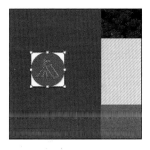

When saving artwork as SVG, the artboard size is important. Notice that the artboard is cropped very closely to the edges of the tent icon now. The artboard size will determine the dimensions of the SVG file just like it would in PNG or JPG. Since the Fit To Selected Art command simply resized and moved the one artboard in the document, you will need to undo this later or make a new artboard for the web design content.

6   Choose File > Export. In the Export dialog box, set the following options:

   •   Choose SVG (svg) from the Format menu (Mac OS) or SVG (*.SVG) from the Save As Type menu (Windows).

   •   Name the file **tent-icon.svg**.

   •   Navigate to the Lessons > Lesson15 folder (if necessary).

- Select Use Artboards and leave All selected. (There is only one artboard currently in the document, the size of the tent icon, so there is no need to select which artboard in the Export dialog box. If there were more than one artboard, you would need to select Range and type in the correct artboard number for your icon, in this case.)

7 Click Export.

In the Export dialog box, when you choose to export as SVG, by default the Use Artboards option is not selected. This means that all artwork (even if it's outside of an artboard on the canvas), regardless of how many artboards in the document, will be saved in one SVG file. If you select Use Artboards and click Export without choosing which artboards, each artboard will be exported as a separate SVG file. By setting a range in the Export dialog box, you can determine which artboards are saved as separate SVG files. If you wanted to save a series of icons as SVG, for instance, you could create artboards for each and select Use Artboards to create a series of SVG files—one for each artboard.

▶ **Tip:** If you didn't select the Use Artboards option in the Export dialog box, you could click the world icon at the bottom of the SVG Options dialog box to launch your default browser and view the SVG file. Similarly, if you wanted to see the actual SVG code that is created, you could click the Show Code button in the SVG Options dialog box to open the SVG content in an editor.

8 The SVG Options dialog box will open. There are several options for creating the SVG, but the default settings work well most of the time.

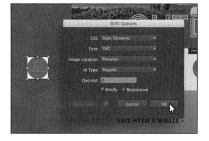

The SVG Options range from how styling for elements should be written in the code to how any fonts should be handled. To learn more about the SVG Options, search for "SVG" in Illustrator Help (Help > Illustrator Help).

9 Click OK in the SVG Options dialog box.

If you were to look in the Lessons > Lesson15 folder, you should see tent-icon-01.svg.

10 Choose Edit > Undo Fit Artboard To Selected Art to put the artboard back behind the main page design. You may need to undo several times.

11 Choose File > Close to close the WebDesign.ai file without saving.

Copy and paste from Illustrator

You can also select and copy artwork in Illustrator and then paste it into your favorite text editor (like Brackets) and SVG code will be generated and pasted. Instead of generating an SVG file, the code is pasted inline.

This can be useful if you want to edit the code yourself or even manipulate the contents with CSS or JavaScript.

SVG and fonts

When it comes to fonts in artwork exported as SVG, you need to be careful. Not all browsers fully support all fonts used in your SVG file. It's best to use a web-safe font or convert the fonts to outlines. Since converting fonts to outlines can increase file size greatly, best practice is to outline fonts only when you have a few words in the artwork, for instance. If you feel comfortable working with the generated SVG code and CSS, you can also create a reference to a hosted font, for instance, but that is beyond the scope of this section.

When you export as SVG (File > Export), in the SVG Options dialog box, there are two options for fonts: SVG and Convert To Outlines.

SVG is the default option and is the format defined by the W3C (World Wide Web Consortium). The SVG option offers maximum support by SVG viewers, but the text may not be very refined. The second option, Convert To Outlines, can be useful if you want to convert your text content into SVG paths and ensure that the text looks like it did in Illustrator. This can be used, for instance, for an icon with a few characters in a word like "Home." If you use more complex fonts, such as script fonts, the file size of your SVG file can increase greatly if you choose Convert To Outlines. Converting fonts to outline in SVG can also make the SVG file less accessible.

Review questions

1 Why do you align content to the pixel grid?

2 Name the three image file types that can be chosen in the Save For Web dialog box.

3 Describe the difference between *named* and *unnamed* content when it comes to generating CSS.

4 What is SVG, and why is it useful?

Review answers

1 Aligning content to the pixel grid is useful for providing a crisp appearance to the edges of artwork. When Align To Pixel Grid is enabled for supported artwork, all the horizontal and vertical segments in the object are aligned to the pixel grid.

2 The three image file types that can be chosen in the Save For Web dialog box are JPEG, GIF, and PNG. PNG has two versions: PNG-8 and PNG-24.

3 Named content is content whose layer name in the Layers panel has been changed. When content is unnamed in the Layers panel (the default layer name is used), a CSS style is not created for the content by default. If you name the object in the Layers panel, the CSS is generated, and the name of the style created matches the object name in the Layers panel. To generate CSS styles for unnamed content, you need to enable this in the CSS Export Options dialog box by clicking the Export Options button (▦) in the CSS Properties panel.

4 SVG, or Scalable Vector Graphics (SVG), is a file format that is used to define vector-based graphics for the web that won't lose quality if they are zoomed or resized, such as a logo. The resulting files are compact and provide high-quality graphics on the web, in print, and even on resource-constrained, handheld devices.

INDEX

NUMBERS

3D effects, 352–353. *See also* rotating objects

A

AATCs (Adobe Authorized Training Centers), 5

Adobe Bridge CC, 403

Adobe CC applications
combining artwork, 403
placing image files, 404–411

Adobe Color website, 203

Adobe Illustrator
finding resources for, 55
installation, 2
starting, 32–33

Adobe PDF, creating, 148

Adobe resources, 5

Adobe Stock, enhancements, 9

.ai extension, appearance of, 106

Align options, 25

aligning
anchor points, 68
to artboard, 69
content to pixel grid, 429–431
to key objects, 67–68
paragraphs, 234

alignment, stopping, 68

alignment guides, using with Selection tool, 61

Alt key. *See* keyboard shortcuts

Anchor Point tool, using with coffee cup, 177

anchor points
aligning, 68
closing, 169
deleting and adding for coffee cup, 175
joining, 108
in paths, 158

preferences, 63
seeing, 62
selecting, 64
smooth vs. corner, 157
undoing, 165

appearance attributes. *See also* attribute rows
applying to layers, 268–269, 345
copying for colors, 200
editing, 339–340
removing from layers, 360
reordering, 344–345
unhiding, 340

Appearance panel
adding strokes and fills, 341–343
options in, 338
shortening, 340

Application bar, 34

area type
adding, 220
converting between point type, 222
in port and out port, 224

arranging objects, 72–74

arrowheads, adding to paths, 179

Art brushes. *See also* brushes
applying, 315–316
creating using raster images, 316–317
editing, 318

Artboard Options button, 129

Artboard tool, 35

artboards
adding to documents, 127–128
aligning to, 69
Constrain Width and Height Proportions icon, 129
creating, 128
deleting, 128
editing, 128–129
fitting in Document window, 47

navigating, 51–53

renaming, 53, 129–130

reordering, 130–131

resizing, 129

switching from global rulers, 132

artwork. *See also* objects

aligning, 25

assigning colors to, 209–211

combining Adobe CC applications, 403

drawing without active grid, 392

editing colors in, 207–208

moving between layers, 258–259

positioning using Smart Guides, 136

positioning with Transform panel, 135–136

saving as SVG (Scalable Vector Graphics), 445–446

selecting and copying, 449

selecting with Magic Wand tool, 64–65

selecting with Perspective Selection tool, 390

transforming, 19

view commands, 46–47, 50

viewing transformation of, 141

zooming into, 46–48

aspect ratio, 288

assets. *See* CC Libraries

attribute rows, deleting, 347. *See also* appearance attributes

Auto Sizing, using with type, 221

B

Bezier curve, 157

bitmap images, 32

bleed area, identifying, 79

Blend tool, 35

blended objects. *See also* objects

creating, 294–296

editing, 295

expanding, 297

modifying, 296–297

releasing, 296

reshaping spines of, 296–297

types of, 294

blends, creating, 18–19

Blob Brush tool

drawing with, 328–329

merging paths with, 330

resizing, 329

bounding boxes

resetting, 142

turning off, 90

using with Selection tool, 61

brightness, adjusting for user-interface, 46

Bristle brushes

changing options for, 319

and graphic tablets, 322

painting with, 320–322

brush strokes, removing, 314

brushes

Blob Brush tool, 328–332

Bristle, 319–322

Calligraphic, 309–314

editing, 313–314

Pattern type, 322–327

previewing changes to, 313

removing from objects, 309, 314, 327

types of, 309

using, 26–27

Bullseye Coffee example, 151

Buzz Soda poster, 217

C

Calligraphic brushes. *See also* Paintbrush tool

choosing, 309–310

Paintbrush tool, 310–311

Caps Lock key, using with Knife tool, 100

case of text, changing, 233

CC Libraries

adding assets to, 378–380

editing assets, 380

enhancements, 6

fonts, 378–379

Links panel, 382

sharing, 380

updating assets, 382–383

using assets, 381

Change Screen Mode icon in Tools panel, 35

character formatting, changing, 232–233. *See also* fonts

character styles

creating and applying, 241

editing, 242

using with CSS code, 440–441

verifying, 246

characters, nudging, 238

circles, creating and editing, 87–88

Clear Appearance button, using with graphic styles, 359–360

clipping masks
creating, 29, 270–272
explained, 412

closed paths, creating type on, 246–247

closing, panels, 42

closing paths, 174

Cmd key. *See* keyboard shortcuts

CMYK (cyan, magenta, yellow, black) color mode, 189, 192

coffee bean, finishing, 183

coffee cup
Anchor Point tool, 177
deleting and adding anchor points, 175
drawing, 166–169
smooth points and corner points, 176

CoffeeShop.ai file, naming, 165

collapsing, panels, 41

color edits, applying to images, 410–411

color groups. *See also* groups
creating, 201
editing, 204–206
reapplying colors in, 210

Color Guide panel, 202–203

Color icon in Tools panel, 35

color modes, 189

Color panel, creating custom colors, 191–192

Color Picker, creating color with, 196–197

color ramp, deleting colors from, 284

color spectrum, changing in Color Picker, 196–197

color swatches
creating copies of, 193–194
editing, 194–196
libraries, 197
making global, 196
saving, 192–193

Color Themes panel, 203

color variations, choosing, 202

coloring. *See also* Live Paint
with Bristle brushes, 320–322
explained, 190
with patterns, 300–304
with precision, 315

colors. *See also* font color; smooth color blend; tint of color
adjusting, 200
applying, 14, 190–191
assigning to artwork, 209–211
copying appearance attributes, 200
editing, 14, 207–208
and layers, 256
naming, 192
sampling in placed images, 419

Column Graph tool, 35

columns
switching between, 37
of text, 236–237

combining shapes, 96–97
compound paths, 117–118
with Pathfinder panel, 115–117
with Shape Builder tool, 113–114

Command key. *See* keyboard shortcuts

compound paths, creating, 117–118

content. *See also* transforming content
aligning to pixel grid, 429–431
bringing into perspective, 395–396
flipping in place, 139
named and unnamed, 437–440
slicing, 432–433

content drawn inside, editing, 100

Control panel, 34, 38–39
docking, 37
dragging, 37
opening panels in, 90

copying
appearance attributes for colors, 200
colors in placed images, 419
CSS (Cascading Style Sheets), 443–444
objects while dragging, 394
and pasting from Illustrator, 449
symbol instances, 368

corner points, 154
converting between smooth points, 176
converting smooth points to, 161–162
rounding, 173
vs. smooth points, 157

corner types, accessing, 84

corner widget
accessing, 82
dragging, 83

CSS (Cascading Style Sheets)
. (period) before styles, 438
copying, 443–444
explained, 437
exporting, 445–446
letter-spacing, 440
line-height, 440
setting up design for, 437–440
styles as classes, 438
CSS code
using character styles with, 440–441
using graphic styles with, 442
CSS Properties panel, 429, 437
Export Options button, 439
.st0, 440
Ctrl key. *See* keyboard shortcuts
Curvature tool, 35, 170–171
curved paths, 157–158. *See also* paths
curves
combining with straight lines, 163–164
drawing series of, 160
drawing with Pen tool, 159
editing, 172–177
cutting
with Knife tool, 109–110
with Scissors tool, 107–108

D

dashed lines, creating, 178. *See also* lines
data recovery, 8, 56
Default Fill and Stroke, 35
default preferences, restoring, 3
deleting. *See also* removing
anchor points for coffee cup, 175
artboards, 128
attribute rows, 347
layers, 254
preferences file, 3–4
saved workspaces, 44
deselecting. *See also* selecting
objects, 61, 159
paths, 155, 169
shapes, 97
DeviceN rasters, support for, 404
"diadem," using with pattern swatches, 300
Direct Selection tool, 35, 62
direction points, 158, 162
Discover Green Isle example, 401

Display Color Bars button, 208
distributing objects, 68–69
docking
Control panel, 37
panels, 44
Tools panel, 37
document grid, 82
document profiles, choosing, 79
document setup options, editing, 131
Document window, 34
documents
adding artboards to, 127–128
arranging, 53–55
changing units for, 133
creating, 12, 78–79
cycling between, 54
returning to, 55
scrolling through, 49
tiling, 54–55
downloading project files, 32
dragging
corner widget, 83
grid plane controls, 391
with Selection tool, 63
shapes, 88
symbol thumbnails, 372
Draw Behind mode, 35, 98–99
Draw Inside mode, 35, 99
Draw Normal icon in Tools panel, 35
drawing
artwork without active grid, 392
with Blob Brush tool, 328–329
coffee cup, 166–169
with Curvature tool, 170–171
curves with Pen tool, 159
editing content drawn inside, 100
freeform paths with Pencil tool, 180–181
lines, 91–92
objects in perspective, 388–389
with Paintbrush tool, 310–311
with Pencil tool, 16
series of curves with Pen tool, 160
with Shaper tool, 19–20
shapes, 13, 94–95
straight lines with Pencil tool, 181–183
Drawing modes, toggling between, 99
duplicating
layer content, 261–262
symbols, 373–374

dX and dY measurements, 62

dynamic symbols, 7, 370–371.
See also symbols

E

Edit Colors dialog box, editing color groups
in, 204–206

editing

appearance attributes, 339–340

Art brushes, 318

artboards, 128–129

blended objects, 295

brushes, 313–314

character styles, 242

circles, 87–88

color swatches, 194–196

colors, 14, 207–208

colors in radial gradients, 285–287

content drawn inside, 100

curves, 172–177

document setup options, 131

effects, 347

ellipses, 86–87

with Eraser tool, 331–332

gradients, 278, 283–284

paragraph styles, 240

paths and points for coffee cup, 173–174

paths and shapes, 107–112

paths with Paintbrush tool, 312–313

paths with Pencil tool, 181

Pattern brushes, 326–327

patterns, 304

polygons, 88–89

rectangles, 80–81

shapes in compound shapes, 116

shapes with Shaper tool, 95–96

slices, 433–434

strokes, 15

symbols, 369

symbols in perspective, 396–397

text in perspective, 392–393

triangles, 88–89

educators, resources for, 5

effects

3D, 352–353

applying, 346

distorting objects with, 139–141

editing, 347

Illustrator (vector), 345

Offset Path, 349–350

Photoshop (raster), 345

scaling, 362

Warp, 348–349

working with, 29

ellipses, creating and editing, 86–87

enhancements

Adobe Stock, 9

CC (Creative Cloud) Libraries, 6

data recovery, 8

Dynamic symbols, 7

Live Shapes, 8

Safe Mode, 9

Shaper tool, 6–7

Smart Guides, 8

SVG export, 7

zoom, pan, and scroll, 8

envelope warp, reshaping text with,
243–245

Eraser tool, 35

editing with, 331–332

using, 111–112

exporting CSS (Cascading Style Sheets),
445–446

Eyedropper tool, 35

sampling formatting with, 21

sampling text formatting, 242

F

FESTIVAL text, applying raster effect to,
350–353

files

opening, 32–33

packaging, 424

Fill box, 35

fills. *See also* gradient fills

adding with Appearance panel, 341–343

applying linear gradients to, 277

changing for paths, 166

Filter Gallery dialog box, using with raster
effects, 350–351

flipping content, 139

floating tool panels, collapsing, 36

font color, changing, 231. *See also* colors

font family and style, changing, 226–229

font size, changing, 230

fonts, 2. *See also* character formatting; type
  and SVG (Scalable Vector Graphics), 450
  syncing Typekit fonts, 226–228
formatting, sampling with Eyedropper tool, 21
Free Transform tool, 35, 145–147. *See also*
  Transform panel
freeform paths, drawing with Pencil tool,
  180–181. *See also* paths
Fritz, Danielle, 21

G

Get Colors From Selected Art button, 208
global color, creating, 194–196
global rulers, switching from artboards, 132
glyphs, working with, 233
GPU (Graphics Processing Unit), 48
gradient annotator, hiding, 280
gradient fills, explained, 277. *See also* fills
Gradient icon in Tools panel, 35
Gradient panel, 277
gradient rotation, entering, 282
Gradient tool, 35
gradients. *See also* linear gradients; radial
  gradients
  adding transparency to, 291–293
  applying to objects, 290
  applying to strokes, 283
  creating, 22–23
  editing, 22–23, 278
  saving, 279
gradients on strokes, editing, 283–284
graphic styles
  applying, 354–357, 361
  applying to layers, 360–361
  applying to text, 358
  Clear Appearance button, 359–360
  creating, 355–357
  Fill attribute rows, 356
  options for, 354
  updating, 358–360
  using with CSS code, 442
grid plane, moving with artwork, 391
grid snapping, turning off, 388
gridlines, specifying spacing between, 82
Group Selection tool, 72
grouping items, 70
groups. *See also* color groups
  Isolation mode, 70–71
  merging, 264

nesting, 71
ungrouping, 72
guides and rulers, 132–134
Guitar symbol instance, 369

H

Hand tool, 35
handles, constraining, 167, 174
Help feature, accessing, 55
hidden objects, selecting, 73–74
Horizontal Distribute Center button, 68
horizontal guide, creating, 133
HTML5 markup, using, 439
hue-forward sorting, 209
hyphenating paragraphs, 234

I

Illustrator
  finding resources for, 55
  installation, 2
  starting, 32–33
  vector effects, 345
image links, 419–424
Image Trace, 22, 101–102
images. *See also* Photoshop images;
  placed images
  applying color edits to, 410–411
  embedding and unembedding, 421
  masking, 412–419
  placing, 21, 404–405, 409–410
  resizing, 406
importing plain-text files, 223–224
indenting paragraphs, 234
inks, process and spot, 197
installing Illustrator, 2
Isolation mode
  entering to edit text, 393
  exiting, 271, 322
  seeing shapes in, 100
  selecting shapes in, 100
  using with groups, 70–71

J

JAZZ text, offsetting stroke for, 349–350
Join tool, 183–184
JPEG image, placing, 404–405

K

key objects, aligning to, 67–68

keyboard shortcuts

    artwork, 46

    closing paths, 174

    combining shapes, 113

    constraining handles, 167

    copying objects while dragging, 394

    corner widget, 82

    deselecting paths, 169

    drawing shapes, 80

    drawing stars, 92–93

    duplicating layer content, 261

    horizontal guide, 133

    joining ends of paths, 184

    perpendicular movement, 394

    perspective grid, 389

    plane switching, 394

    rotating objects, 142

    selecting nonsequential layers, 262

    selecting text, 234

    tools, 35–36

    vertical guide, 133

    zooming in, 302

Knife tool, cutting with, 109–110

L

Lasso tool, 35

layer content

    duplicating, 261–262

    moving between layers, 258–260

    showing, 261

Layer Options dialog box, opening, 254

layers, 257–258. *See also* sublayers; symbol layers

    applying appearance attributes to, 268–269, 345

    applying graphic styles to, 360–361

    and color, 256

    creating, 254–255

    creating for slices, 432–433

    deleting, 254

    explained, 252

    hiding and showing, 268

    locating, 257–258

    merging, 262–264

    pasting, 264–266

    removing appearance attributes, 360

    renaming, 262

    reordering, 260, 266

    selecting, 219, 262

    viewing, 267–268

    working with, 15–16

Layers panel

    features, 253

    Missing Fonts dialog box, 253

    navigating content in, 259

    opening, 252

letters. *See* characters

line segments, selecting, 35, 155

linear gradients. *See also* gradients

    applying to fills, 277, 280–282

    applying to strokes, 282

    explained, 277

lines, drawing, 91–92. *See also* dashed lines; straight lines

link information, finding, 420

linked images, replacing, 421–424

Links panel, using with CC Libraries, 382

Live Paint. *See also* painting

    Bucket tool, 213

    groups, 212

    modifying groups, 214

Live Shapes, enhancements, 8

logo sample, 32

lowercase text, creating, 233

M

Magic Wand tool, 35, 64–65

marquees

    creating selections with, 63–64

    using with shapes, 113

masking images, 412–419

Measurement Labels, deselecting, 136

Mediterranean Cruise poster, 307

merging

    groups, 264

    layers, 262–264

    paths with Blob Brush tool, 330

Mesh tool, 35

Microsoft Word documents, placing, 224

Missing Fonts dialog box, 253

modes, switching between, 50

N

naming
    colors, 192
    selections, 65
Navigator panel, 51
nesting groups, 71

O

objects. *See also* artwork; blended objects;
    selecting objects
    aligning, 67–69
    applying gradients to, 290
    arranging, 72–74
    deselecting, 61, 159
    distorting with effects, 139–141
    distributing, 68–69
    drawing in perspective, 388–389
    hiding and locking, 74
    matching planes to, 395
    moving between planes, 393–394
    moving in perpendicular direction,
        393–394
    moving planes with, 391
    positioning precisely, 135–136
    reflecting, 138–139
    rotating, 141–142
    scaling, 137–138
    selecting, 65
    selecting in perspective, 390, 395
    shearing, 143–144
    transforming in perspective, 390
    ungrouping, 72
    unlocking, 74
Offset Path effect, applying, 349–350
Option key. *See* keyboard shortcuts
Outline and Preview modes, toggling
    between, 50
Outline mode
    effect of, 88
    selecting in, 66
Outline Stroke option, 121
outlining text, 248

P

Package command, using with Typekit
    fonts, 230
package report, creating, 424
packaging files, 424

Paintbrush tool, 35. *See also* Calligraphic
    brushes
    drawing with, 310–311
    editing paths with, 312–313
painting. *See also* Live Paint
    with Bristle brushes, 320–322
    explained, 190
    with patterns, 300–304
    with precision, 315
panel groups, 42–44
panel menus, 45
panels, 34, 40–41
    closing, 42
    collapsing, 41
    docking, 44
    opening in Control panel, 90
    resetting, 40
    resizing, 43
    returning to full-size view, 42
    showing and hiding, 42
    unhiding, 40
panning with Navigator panel, 51
PANTONE MATCHING SYSTEM (PMS),
    198–199
paragraph formatting, changing, 234–235
paragraph styles
    creating and applying, 239–240
    editing, 240
pasting layers, 264–266
Pathfinder panel, 115–117
paths. *See also* curved paths; freeform paths
    adding arrowheads to, 179
    anchor points, 158
    changing fills for, 166
    closing, 174
    combining with Shaper tool, 118
    deselecting, 155, 169
    direction lines, 158
    direction points, 158, 162
    editing, 107–112
    editing with Paintbrush tool, 312–313
    editing with Pencil tool, 181
    joining, 108–109
    joining ends of, 184
    merging with Blob Brush tool, 330
    segments, 158
    selecting with Pen tool, 154–156
paths and points, editing for coffee cup,
    173–174

Pattern brushes
    applying, 326
    changing tiles in, 327
    creating, 324–325
    editing, 326–327
    tiles in, 322
    using, 322–323
Pattern Editing mode, 302
Pattern Objects, finding, 324
Pattern Options panel, 302–303
pattern swatches, sorting, 300
patterns
    applying, 300–301, 303
    creating, 301–303
    editing, 304
    scaling with shapes, 304
PDF (Portable Document Format),
    creating, 148
Pen tool, 35
    combining curves and straight lines,
        163–164
    curved paths, 157–158
    deselecting objects, 159
    drawing coffee cup, 166–169
    drawing curves, 159–160
    selecting paths, 154–156
    setting anchor points for paths, 166
    smooth points to corner points, 161–162
    straight lines, 156–157
    toggling preview, 153
    Undo Cut option, 155
    using, 153–154
Pencil tool
    drawing freeform paths with, 180–181
    drawing straight lines with, 181–183
    drawing with, 16
    editing paths with, 181
perspective
    adding text in, 392–393
    drawing objects in, 388–389
    editing text in, 392–393
    selecting objects in, 390
    transforming objects in, 390
perspective grid
    adjusting, 385–387
    default, 384
    defining, 387
    hiding planes in, 397

one-point perspective, 385
    showing and hiding, 389
    tool, 35
    turning off grid snapping, 388
    using presets, 385
Perspective Selection tool, 390, 395
Photoshop (raster) effects
    applying, 350–353
    explained, 345
    Filter Gallery dialog box, 350–351
    Texturizer settings, 351
Photoshop images, placing, 406–408.
    See also images
pixel grid
    aligning content to, 429–431
    turning off, 430
Place dialog box, 409
placed images. See also images
    sampling colors in, 419
    scaling, 405–406
plain-text files, importing, 223–224
planes
    hiding in perspective grid, 397
    moving to match objects, 395
    moving with objects, 391
PMS (PANTONE MATCHING SYSTEM),
    198–199
point type
    converting between area type, 222
    entering text as, 219
points and paths, editing for coffee cup,
    173–174
polygons, creating and editing, 88–89
poster files, packaging, 424
preferences, resetting, 3, 32
Preview and Outline modes, toggling
    between, 50
print, choosing document profile for, 79
process inks, using, 197
project files
    accessing, 2–3
    downloading, 32

R

radial gradients. See also gradients
    adjusting, 288–289
    applying to artwork, 285
    aspect ratio, 288

editing colors in, 285–287

explained, 277

repositioning centers of, 289

raster effects

applying, 350–353

explained, 345

Filter Gallery dialog box, 350–351

Texturizer settings, 351

raster images, 32

creating Art brushes from, 316–317

recommended PPI (pixels per inch), 429

Recolor Artwork dialog box, accessing, 207, 209

recovering data, 56

rectangles

creating and editing, 80–81

rounding, 83–85

rounding corners, 82–83

Scale Corners option, 83

selecting and moving, 85

tool, 35

Transform options, 81

reflecting

objects, 138–139

spoon shape, 172

removing. *See also* deleting

appearance attributes from layers, 360

brush strokes, 314

brushes from objects, 309, 314, 327

shapes, 95

renaming

artboards, 129–130

layers, 262

Reset Essentials option, 33, 126

resetting

bounding boxes, 142

panels, 40

preferences, 32

workspaces, 44

resizing

artboards, 129

Blob Brush tool, 329

fonts, 230

images, 406

slices, 435

type objects, 235–238

ResortCompany.com example, 31

resources, finding for Illustrator, 55.
See also websites

restoring default preferences, 3

RGB (red, green, blue) color mode, 189

Rock On T-shirt example, 365

Rotate dialog box, accessing, 140

Rotate tool, 35

rotating objects, 141–142. *See also* 3D effects

rounding

corner points, 173

corners of shapes, 13, 82–83

rectangles, 83–85

rulers and guides, 132–134

S

Safe Mode, enhancements, 9

Sail with a Whale example, 275

sampling. *See* copying

Save for Web command, 432, 434–436

saved versions, reverting to, 61

saving

artwork as SVG (Scalable Vector Graphics), 445–446

color swatches, 192–193

content for web, 429–436

gradients, 279

preferences file, 3–4

tint of color, 199–200

workspaces, 44

Scale Corners option, 83

scaling

objects, 137–138

placed images, 405–406

strokes and effects, 362

tool, 35

Scissors tool, cutting with, 107–108

scrolling through documents, 49

selecting. *See also* deselecting

artwork with Magic Wand tool, 64–65

and copying artwork, 449

hidden objects, 73

layers, 219

line segments, 155

objects in perspective, 390

in Outline mode, 66

paths with Pen tool, 154–156

shapes in Isolation mode, 100

similar objects, 65

slices, 433–434

text, 234

using Group Selection tool, 72

selecting objects. *See also* objects
    behind, 73–74
    Direct Selection tool, 62
    reverting to saved versions, 61
    without fills, 61
selection preferences, displaying, 63
Selection tool, 35
    alignment guides, 61
    bounding box, 61
    dragging with, 63
    Smart Guides, 61
selections
    creating with marquees, 63–64
    naming, 65
Shape Builder tool, 17, 35, 113–115
shape modes in Pathfinder panel, 115–117
Shaper tool, 35
    combining paths with, 118
    combining shapes, 96–97
    drawing shapes, 94–95
    drawing with, 19–20
    editing shapes with, 95–96
    enhancements, 6–7
shapes
    Bring To Front option, 117
    circles, 87–88
    combining, 113–118
    deselecting, 97
    drawing, 13
    editing, 107–112
    ellipses, 86
    erasing parts of, 112
    moving, 116
    polygons, 88–89
    rectangles, 80–84
    removing, 95
    rounding corners of, 13
    selecting, 116
    selecting and dragging, 88
    selecting and moving, 85
    separating, 100
    stars, 92–94
    triangles, 88–89
sharing CC Libraries, 380
shearing objects, 143–144
Shift key. *See* keyboard shortcuts
Shirt example, 251
Shoreline Park example, 187

shortcuts. *See* keyboard shortcuts
similar objects, selecting, 65
Slice tool, 35
slices
    hiding, 434
    resizing, 435
slicing content, 432–434
Smart Guides
    changing colors of, 85
    enhancements, 8
    positioning artwork with, 136
    using with Selection tool, 61
smooth color blend, creating and editing,
    298–299. *See also* colors
smooth points
    vs. corner points, 157
    converting between corner points,
        161–162, 176
    creating, 168–169
spaces, adding for paragraphs, 234
spoon
    editing paths and points, 173–174
    reflecting, 172
    rounding corner points, 173
spot inks, using, 197
stars, creating, 92–94
starting Illustrator, 32–33
Status bar, 34
Stiles, Dan, 106
straight lines. *See also* lines
    combining with curves, 163–164
    drawing with Pen tool, 156–157
    drawing with Pencil tool, 181–183
Stroke box, 35
Stroke panel, opening, 90
strokes
    adding with Appearance panel, 341–343
    applying linear gradients to, 282
    changing width and alignment, 90–91
    editing, 15
    outlining, 121
    scaling, 362
sublayers, creating, 256. *See also* layers
SVG (Scalable Vector Graphics)
    export enhancements, 7
    and fonts, 450
    saving artwork as, 445–446
Swap Fill and Stroke tool, 35

swatch libraries, 197

Swatches panel vs. PANTONE swatches, 199

symbol instances, copying, 368

symbol layers, 376. *See also* layers

symbol libraries, using, 367–369

symbol names, displaying, 368

Symbol Options dialog box, 371

symbol sets, 377

Symbol Sprayer tool, 35, 377

symbol thumbnails, dragging, 372

symbolism tools, 377

symbols. *See also* dynamic symbols

    breaking links to, 376–377

    creating, 372–373

    duplicating, 373–374

    editing, 369, 396–397

    replacing, 374–375

    using, 27–28

Symbols panel, 367

T

text. *See also* type

    adding at points, 219

    adding in perspective, 392–393

    applying graphic styles to, 358

    applying Typekit fonts to, 228–229

    changing case of, 233

    editing in perspective, 392–393

    modifying with Touch Type tool,
        237–238

    reshaping with preset envelope warp,
        243–245

    selecting, 234

    styling with Warp effects, 348–349

    threading, 224–225

    warping, 243–245

    wrapping, 242–243

text columns, creating, 236–237

text fields, moving between, 278

text formatting, sampling, 242

text outlines, creating, 248

text styles, creating and applying, 239–242

threading text, 224–225

tiling documents, 54–55

tint of color, creating and saving, 199–200.
    See also colors

Tools panel, 33–38

tooltips, turning on and off, 36

Touch Type tool, modifying text with,
    237–238

Touch workspace, 49. *See also* workspaces

touch-enabled features, Free Transform
    tool, 147

tracing images, 101–102

tracking, changing for characters, 233

Transform panel, positioning artwork with,
    135–136. *See also* Free Transform tool

Transform tool, using, 19

transformed artwork, viewing, 141

transforming content. *See also* content

    distorting objects with effects, 139–140

    entering values for, 137

    Free Transform tool, 145–147

    positioning objects, 135–136

    reflecting objects, 138–139

    rotating objects, 141–142

    rulers and guides, 132–134

    scaling objects, 137–138

    shearing objects, 143–144

transforming placed images, 405

transparency, adding to gradients, 291–293

triangles, creating and editing, 88–89

T-shirt example, 365

type. *See also* fonts; text

    area type, 220

    auto sizing, 221

    creating on closed paths, 246–247

type objects, resizing and reshaping,
    235–238

type on paths, creating, 245–246

Type tool, 23–25, 35

Typekit fonts

    applying to text, 228–229

    Package command, 230

    syncing, 226–228

U

Unite button vs. Shape Builder tool, 115

units for documents, changing, 133

unlocking objects, 74

uppercase text, creating, 233

V

vector effects, explained, 345

vector graphics, 32, 212–214

Vertical Distribute Center button, 68

vertical guide, creating, 133
video, choosing document profile for, 79
view commands, using with artwork, 46–47
viewing artwork, 50

W

Warp effects, styling text with, 348–349
warping text, 243–245
web
    aligning content to pixel grid, 429–431
    choosing document profile for, 79
    saving content for, 434–436
    selecting and editing slices, 433–434
    slicing content, 432–433
websites. *See also* resources
    AATCs (Adobe Authorized Training Centers), 5
    Adobe Color, 203
    fonts and installation, 2
    Fritz, Danielle, 21
    Illustrator resources, 4–5
    installing Illustrator, 2
    resources for educators, 5
    Typekit fonts, 226

Width tool, 35
    outlining strokes, 121
    using, 119–121
Word documents, placing, 224
workspaces. *See also* Touch workspace
    Application bar, 34
    Control panel, 38–39
    deleting, 44
    Document window, 34
    panels, 40–45
    resetting and saving, 44
    Status bar, 34
    Tools panel, 33–38
wrapping text, 242–243

Z

zoom, pan, and scroll, enhancements, 8
zooming in, 35, 47–48
    to artwork, 46
    and panning with Navigator panel, 51
    to patterns, 302

Contributors

 Brian Wood   Brian Wood is a web developer and the author of eleven training books (Adobe Illustrator, Adobe InDesign, Adobe Muse, and Adobe DPS), as well as numerous training videos on Dreamweaver & CSS, InDesign, Illustrator, Acrobat, Adobe Muse and others.

In addition to training many clients large and small, Brian speaks regularly at national conferences, such as Adobe MAX and the HOW conference, as well as events hosted by AIGA and other industry organizations. To learn more, check out www.youtube.com/askbrianwood or visit www.brianwoodtraining.com.

Production Notes

The *Adobe Illustrator CC Classroom in a Book (2015 release)* was created electronically using Adobe InDesign CC 2015. Art was produced using Adobe InDesign, Adobe Illustrator, and Adobe Photoshop.

References to company names, websites, or addresses in the lessons are for demonstration purposes only and are not intended to refer to any actual organization or person.

Images

Photographic images and illustrations are intended for use with the tutorials.

Typefaces used

Adobe Myriad Pro and Adobe Warnock Pro are used throughout this book. For more information about OpenType and Adobe fonts, visit www.adobe.com/type/opentype/.

Team credits

The following individuals contributed to the development of this edition of the *Adobe Illustrator CC Classroom in a Book (2015 release)*:

Writer/Design: Brian Wood
Project Editor: Victor Gavenda
Production Editor: Danielle Foster
Technical Editor: Chad Chelius
Copyeditor: Kim Wimpsett
Keystroking: Megan Ahearn
Compositor: Brian Wood
Proofreader: Patricia Pane
Indexer: Valerie Perry
Cover design: Eddie Yuen
Interior design: Mimi Heft

Lesson project credits

The following individuals contributed artwork for the lesson files for this edition of the *Adobe Illustrator CC Classroom in a Book (2015 release)*:

A Quick Tour of Adobe Illustrator CC (2015 release): The hand lettering for this project was created by Danielle Fritz (www.behance.net/danielle_fritz).

Lesson 4: The artwork for this project was created by Dan Stiles (www.danstiles.com).

The fastest, easiest, most comprehensive way to learn

Adobe Creative Cloud

Classroom in a Book®, the best-selling series of hands-on software training books, helps you learn the features of Adobe software quickly and easily.

The **Classroom in a Book** series offers what no other book or training program does—an official training series from Adobe Systems, developed with the support of Adobe product experts.

To see a complete list of our Classroom in a Book titles covering the 2015 release of Adobe Creative Cloud go to:

www.adobepress.com/cc2015

Adobe Photoshop CC Classroom in a Book (2015 release)
ISBN: 9780134308135

Adobe Illustrator CC Classroom in a Book (2015 release)
ISBN: 9780134308111

Adobe InDesign CC Classroom in a Book (2015 release)
ISBN: 978013431000

Adobe Dreamweaver CC Classroom in a Book (2015 release)
ISBN: 9780134309996

Adobe Premiere Pro CC Classroom in a Book (2015 release)
ISBN: 9780134309989

Adobe After Effects CC Classroom in a Book (2015 release)
ISBN: 9780134308128

Adobe Photoshop Lightroom CC (2015 release) / Lightroom 6 Classroom in a Book
ISBN: 978013392482

Adobe Lightroom and Photoshop CC for Photographers Classroom in a Book (2015 release)
ISBN: 9780134288611

Adobe Acrobat DC Classroom in a Book
ISBN: 9780134171838

Adobe**Press**